Cisco® IP Routing Handbook

Cisco® IP Routing Handbook

Paul Cernick
Mark H. Degner
Keith Kruepke

M&T Books

An imprint of IDG Books Worldwide, Inc.

Foster City, CA ■ Chicago, IL ■ Indianapolis, IN ■ New York, NY

Cisco® IP Routing Handbook

Published by
M&T Books
An Imprint of IDG Books Worldwide, Inc.
919 E. Hillsdale Blvd., Suite 400
Foster City, CA 94404
www.idgbooks.com (IDG Books Worldwide
Web site)

ISBN: 0-7645-4695-3

Printed in the United States of America

10 9 8 7 6 5 4 3 2 1

1O/SV/QY/QQ/FC

Distributed in the United States by IDG Books Worldwide, Inc.

Distributed by CDG Books Canada Inc. for Canada; by Transworld Publishers Limited in the United Kingdom; by IDG Norge Books for Norway; by IDG Sweden Books for Sweden; by IDG Books Australia Publishing Corporation Pty. Ltd. for Australia and New Zealand; by TransQuest Publishers Pte Ltd. for Singapore, Malaysia, Thailand, Indonesia, and Hong Kong; by Gotop Information Inc. for Taiwan; by ICG Muse, Inc. for Japan; by Intersoft for South Africa; by Eyrolles for France; by International Thomson Publishing for Germany, Austria, and Switzerland; by Distribuidora Cuspide for Argentina; by LR International for Brazil; by Galileo Libros for Chile; by Ediciones ZETA S.C.R. Ltda. for Peru; by WS Computer Publishing Corporation, Inc., for the Philippines; by Contemporanea de Ediciones for Venezuela; by Express Computer Distributors for the Caribbean and West Indies; by Micronesia Media Distributor, Inc. for Micronesia; by Chips Computadoras S.A. de C.V. for Mexico; by Editorial Norma de Panama S.A. for Panama; by American Bookshops for Finland.

For general information on IDG Books Worldwide's books in the U.S., please call our Consumer Customer Service department at 800-762-2974. For reseller information, including discounts and premium sales, please call our Reseller Customer Service department at 800-434-3422.

For information on where to purchase IDG Books Worldwide's books outside the U.S., please contact our International Sales department at 317-572-3993 or fax 317-572-4002.

For consumer information on foreign language translations, please contact our Customer Service department at 800-434-3422, fax 317-572-4002, or e-mail rights@idgbooks.com.

For information on licensing foreign or domestic rights, please phone +1-650-653-7098.

For sales inquiries and special prices for bulk quantities, please contact our Order Services department at 800-434-3422 or write to the address above.

For information on using IDG Books Worldwide's books in the classroom or for ordering examination copies, please contact our Educational Sales department at 800-434-2086 or fax 317-572-4005.

For press review copies, author interviews, or other publicity information, please contact our Public Relations department at 650-653-7000 or fax 650-653-7500.

For authorization to photocopy items for corporate, personal, or educational use, please contact Copyright Clearance Center, 222 Rosewood Drive, Danvers, MA 01923, or fax 978-750-4470.

Library of Congress Cataloging-in-Publication Data

Degner, Mark H.
    Cisco IP routing handbook / Mark H. Degner, Keith Kruepke, Paul Cernick.
        p.   cm.
    ISBN 0-7645-4695-3 (alk. paper)
    1. Routers (Computer networks)--Handbooks, manuals, etc. I. Kruepke, Keith. II. Cernick, Paul. III. Title.
    TK5105.543 .D44   2000
    004.6'2--dc21   00-058198

 is a registered trademark or trademark under exclusive license to IDG Books Worldwide, Inc. from International Data Group, Inc. in the United States and/or other countries.

 is a trademark of IDG Books Worldwide, Inc.

ABOUT IDG BOOKS WORLDWIDE

Welcome to the world of IDG Books Worldwide.

IDG Books Worldwide, Inc., is a subsidiary of International Data Group, the world's largest publisher of computer-related information and the leading global provider of information services on information technology. IDG was founded more than 30 years ago by Patrick J. McGovern and now employs more than 9,000 people worldwide. IDG publishes more than 290 computer publications in over 75 countries. More than 90 million people read one or more IDG publications each month.

Launched in 1990, IDG Books Worldwide is today the #1 publisher of best-selling computer books in the United States. We are proud to have received eight awards from the Computer Press Association in recognition of editorial excellence and three from Computer Currents' First Annual Readers' Choice Awards. Our best-selling ...For Dummies® series has more than 50 million copies in print with translations in 31 languages. IDG Books Worldwide, through a joint venture with IDG's Hi-Tech Beijing, became the first U.S. publisher to publish a computer book in the People's Republic of China. In record time, IDG Books Worldwide has become the first choice for millions of readers around the world who want to learn how to better manage their businesses.

Our mission is simple: Every one of our books is designed to bring extra value and skill-building instructions to the reader. Our books are written by experts who understand and care about our readers. The knowledge base of our editorial staff comes from years of experience in publishing, education, and journalism — experience we use to produce books to carry us into the new millennium. In short, we care about books, so we attract the best people. We devote special attention to details such as audience, interior design, use of icons, and illustrations. And because we use an efficient process of authoring, editing, and desktop publishing our books electronically, we can spend more time ensuring superior content and less time on the technicalities of making books.

You can count on our commitment to deliver high-quality books at competitive prices on topics you want to read about. At IDG Books Worldwide, we continue in the IDG tradition of delivering quality for more than 30 years. You'll find no better book on a subject than one from IDG Books Worldwide.

John Kilcullen
Chairman and CEO
IDG Books Worldwide, Inc.

Eighth Annual
Computer Press
Awards ≥1992

WINNER
Ninth Annual
Computer Press
Awards ≥1993

WINNER

WINNER
Tenth Annual
Computer Press
Awards ≥1994

WINNER
Eleventh Annual
Computer Press
Awards ≥1995

IDG is the world's leading IT media, research and exposition company. Founded in 1964, IDG had 1997 revenues of $2.05 billion and has more than 9,000 employees worldwide. IDG offers the widest range of media options that reach IT buyers in 75 countries representing 95% of worldwide IT spending. IDG's diverse product and services portfolio spans six key areas including print publishing, online publishing, expositions and conferences, market research, education and training, and global marketing services. More than 90 million people read one or more of IDG's 290 magazines and newspapers, including IDG's leading global brands — Computerworld, PC World, Network World, Macworld and the Channel World family of publications. IDG Books Worldwide is one of the fastest-growing computer book publishers in the world, with more than 700 titles in 36 languages. The "...For Dummies®" series alone has more than 50 million copies in print. IDG offers online users the largest network of technology-specific Web sites around the world through IDG.net (http://www.idg.net), which comprises more than 225 targeted Web sites in 55 countries worldwide. International Data Corporation (IDC) is the world's largest provider of information technology data, analysis and consulting, with research centers in over 41 countries and more than 400 research analysts worldwide. IDG World Expo is a leading producer of more than 168 globally branded conferences and expositions in 35 countries including E3 (Electronic Entertainment Expo), Macworld Expo, ComNet, Windows World Expo, ICE (Internet Commerce Expo), Agenda, DEMO, and Spotlight. IDG's training subsidiary, ExecuTrain, is the world's largest computer training company, with more than 230 locations worldwide and 785 training courses. IDG Marketing Services helps industry-leading IT companies build international brand recognition by developing global integrated marketing programs via IDG's print, online and exposition products worldwide. Further information about the company can be found at www.idg.com.   1/26/00

Credits

Acquisitions Editors
Judy Brief
Jim Sumser

Project Editors
Luann Rouff
Sharon Eames
Kurt Stephan

Technical Editor
Lou Gilman

Copy Editors
Lane Barnholtz
KC Hogue
Nancy Rapoport

Proof Editor
Patsy Owens

Project Coordinators
Marcos Vergara
Danette Nurse

Graphics and Production Specialists
Bob Bihlmayer
Jan Contestable
Michael Lewis

Quality Control Technician
Dina F Quan

Book Designer
Jim Donohue

Illustrators
Mary Jo Weis
Rashell Smith
Karl Brandt

Proofreading and Indexing
York Production Services

Cover Image
© Noma/Images.com

About the Authors

Paul Cernick, Mark Degner, and Keith Kruepke all work for N2N Solutions, Inc. N2N is a Cisco Gold Partner in the Chicago area.

Paul Cernick, CCIE #5383, manages the internal engineer training program, as well as consults on network design, security, and troubleshooting. His internetworking experience includes roles ranging from project manager to network analyst. Additionally, he has taught Cisco curriculum as a Certified Cisco Systems Instructor (CCSI) for N2N. He has authored several design documents and proposals, along with articles published in industry trade magazines.

Mark Degner is a consulting engineer in the security practice at N2N. There he develops and implements network security and internetworking solutions for customers. He has written for a leading trade publication, and his accreditations include the Cisco Certified Network Professional (CCNP) and Cisco Certified Design Professional (CCDP).

Keith Kruepke is a consulting engineer in the infrastructure practice at N2N. He plans, designs, and implements networks for many different environments. He holds a Bachelor of Computer Science degree from Marquette University and several professional certifications from Microsoft and Cisco, including the CCNP and CCDP.

To my new bride Lisa.
Her loving support and encouragement
through many nights spent apart to allow me
time to work on the text was truly amazing.
Thank you Lisa for being you. Love you the most.
-Paul

To my parents, Herbert and Christel Degner,
whose positive guidance over the years gave me the
confidence and ability to take on a project as daunting as
a book. Their unconditional love and constant support
will be sorely missed by all those who knew them.
-Mark

To my family,
in appreciation for everything I've learned
from them. And to Maribel, in thanks for
everything I've learned from her.
-Keith

Preface

Why do you need this book? Simply put, there isn't another book out there like it. We have worked in the networking industry for many years, and during that time we have read dozens of books on computers and routing. While all of these books have something to offer, we felt that none of them were complete. It was our intention to write a book about IP routing that connects technical detail to practical examples and live configurations. With the exception of Chapter 1, which covers some basics of Cisco routers and IP routing, you will not find any low-level review chapters. Instead, you will find chapter after chapter of readable technical detail relating to all facets of Cisco IP routing.

Is This Book for You?

As the authors of this book, we assume that you already have a solid understanding of IP addressing and subnetting. This is required before you can develop an understanding of IP routing. Additionally, the writing style demands that you know the Open System Interconnection (OSI) networking model and the layer interactions within the model itself. Every effort has been made to describe the IP routing topics in a structured manner. Additionally, as each topic is discussed and explained, look for accompanying router configurations that illustrate what the text is discussing.

Through its content, design, and style, this book is a reference tool that enables you to get IP routing running on your network. It provides just the right amount of detail to help you fix the problem at hand without drowning you in lengthy discussions that do not pertain to your current situation. Because of the examples included throughout the text, you will not find cursory overviews of concepts that leave you wondering, "OK, but *how* do I do *that* with my routers?"

How This Book Is Organized

This book is organized into nine chapters and four appendixes. The chapters of the book explain important concepts about IP routing, including the IP routing protocols themselves. The appendixes cover smaller topics that are helpful in many IP routing environments. Depending on the structure of their networks, some readers will find the appendixes more useful than others.

Chapters

Each chapter in this book covers the following information to provide you with the most thorough understanding of its topic:

- Basics — Explains the concepts of the routing protocol
- Configuring — Line-by-line descriptions of how the routing protocol is used in the Cisco environment
- Troubleshooting — Steps and procedures for tackling real world routing problems

Chapter 1, "Introduction to IP Routing," explains the necessary details of accessing and configuring Cisco routers, and it introduces the concept of routing.

Chapter 2, "Routing Information Protocol," covers the first important IP routing protocol. The characteristics of RIP are the foundation for most routing protocols today. Because of its widespread support in networking equipment, many internetworks still run RIP in some places. Therefore, this chapter will be useful for many network administrators.

Chapter 3, "Interior Gateway Routing Protocol and Enhanced Interior Gateway Routing Protocol," looks at two routing protocols available from Cisco. It explains both and focuses on their unique characteristics, such as their metrics and unequal-cost load balancing.

Chapter 4, "Open Shortest Path First," covers one of the most widely used routing protocols today. Because of the many configuration options available for OSPF, it is important to understand this protocol thoroughly when planning your topology.

Chapter 5, "Integrated System to Integrated System," explains another important routing protocol in use today. Originally designed to route Connectionless-mode Network Service (CLNS), IS-IS was adapted to route IP, as well. It shares many characteristics with OSPF and is simpler in many ways.

Chapter 6, "Border Gateway Protocol Version 4," covers the external gateway protocol in use on the Internet today. It focuses on preparing for and implementing a BGP environment. If you plan on establishing multiple links to the Internet, you need to know the information in this chapter.

Chapter 7, "Static and Default Routing," cuts through years of misconceptions about these two concepts with a thorough explanation of each. It emphasizes the importance of understanding and configuring static and default routing properly, especially in conjunction with the particular routing protocol in use. No matter what routing protocol(s) you may be using, it is unlikely that you will be able to avoid the use of static and default routes.

Chapter 8, "Redistributing Routes," is particularly important in multiprotocol environments, which tend to be very common. Whether you are migrating your network from one routing protocol to another, or merging networks that utilize different protocols, this chapter contains vital information that you should know when planning how the routing protocols should interact.

Chapter 9, "Dial-on-Demand Routing," discusses the alternative to dedicated connections between sites. This chapter will be particularly useful to organizations that cannot afford dedicated connections or those that are looking to implement low-cost backup for their WAN links. Several DDR solutions are presented in this chapter.

Appendixes

In addition to the material that makes up the core of IP routing with Cisco, this book covers several topics that are useful in many IP internetworks. This material has been arranged in the four appendixes, which are described here.

Appendix A, "Configuring Access Lists," discusses the construction and application of IP access lists on Cisco routers. It demonstrates several uses of access lists and provides configuration examples.

Appendix B, "Virtual Local Area Network Routing," explains Virtual Local Area Networks (VLANs) and several methods for routing information between them. This appendix will be of particular interest to users of Cisco's Catalyst switches, especially the multilayer LAN switches, such as the Catalyst 5000 and 6000 families.

Appendix C, "Network Address Translation," covers the configuration of NAT on Cisco routers. NAT is commonly used between internal networks and the Internet. It enables administrators to use internal addressing that can be adapted to a particular environment, while preserving registered address space on the Internet. In addition, NAT offers some low-level security by disguising the source of Internet traffic.

Appendix D, "Using Cisco's Hot Standby Router Protocol," explains this redundancy feature available from Cisco. It is particularly useful on LANs that support hosts that cannot discover their gateway automatically. The appendix also provides configuration examples.

Acknowledgments

We would like to thank all of our family and friends, who have been patient with us throughout the process of writing this book. Your support was a great help.

We would also like to thank Allen Schmidt and Andy Fox, two of our colleagues and friends that have helped us with material for this book. And thanks to all those who have helped us learn, be it in the classroom, in the workplace, or elsewhere.

Our thanks also go to the following authors, whose work was of tremendous help: Jeff Doyle, Bassam Halabi, Andrew Bruce Caslow, Ivan Pepelnjak, and Thomas M. Thomas. We are sure many will recognize these names from their books. Finally, thanks to the authors of other materials we have consulted, including the RFCs and the Cisco documentation.

Contents at a Glance

Contents

Chapter 1

Introduction to IP Routing

To gain the most value from this book you must have a solid understanding of Cisco router configuration fundamentals and interneworking concepts. This chapter, therefore, is broken into two sections. The first section covers the necessary commands needed to effectively configure IP routing protocols in a Cisco router environment. Included also is a discussion of the context-sensitive help available from the Cisco operation system. The second part of this chapter is devoted to refreshing your understanding of internetworking topics most pertinent to the chapters that come later in the book. Foremost on this list is the differences between Distance Vector and Link State routing protocols, and their accompanying strengths and weaknesses.

Interacting with Cisco Routers

This section covers the necessary details of accessing and configuring Cisco routers. It assumes that you have used routers of some flavor before, and only need a brief introduction to get comfortable with moving around inside the Cisco router environment.

Cisco routers run an operating system called the *Cisco Internetworking Operating System*, or *Cisco IOS*. It is built around a Unix kernel, and those of you familiar with moving around inside Unix will find the transition to IOS very easy, because many commands and syntax structures are very similar. The IOS comes in many flavors and versions, each offering different

functions. Because this book focuses on Cisco IP routing protocols, the
screenshots shown in the book reflect mostly Cisco IOS release 11.2(15)
enterprise, which includes the full bevy of IP routing options.

Tip

For a full explanation of Cisco IOS version and coding information, see Cisco's Web site.

Accessing the Cisco Router

Cisco routers can be configured from several sources, but access through
the console port and the virtual terminal lines are the most important, and
the most relevant for our discussion: *Data-Communications Equipment*
(DCE) interface, often an RJ-45 connection located on the back of the
physical router. You'll need a console cable and DB-9 connector hooked up
between the router and the machine being used to configure the router.
Most any terminal emulation software will work, including HyperTermi-
nal, which is included with Windows operating systems.

The virtual terminals, commonly referred to as *Telnet Ports,* are another
popular way of accessing a Cisco router. Using this method, a person
accesses the router IOS through a configured router interface and logs
invia the network interfaces of the router. This method of accessing the
router relies on several factors: First, that the router is running a usable
IOS. Second, that the router has been configured, at least minimally, for IP,
which is the underlying protocol that the Telnet programs uses. And
finally, that the machine being used to access the router has network access
to the router.

Now that two of the many different methods of accessing the router
IOS have been discussed, the remainder of this book deals with configuring the router from the console port. This level and type of access
allows a connection to the router that is generally unaffected by routing
and software configuration errors; that's good, because configuring routing, specifically IP routing, is what we are setting out to do!

Accessing the Cisco IOS

Assuming your cabling and terminal settings are good, pressing Enter a few times will display text similar to what is shown here:

```
Access tty17 is now available
```

```
Press RETURN to get started.
```

The Cisco IOS works similarly to Unix in that it offers a command-line interpreter. This interpreter, called *EXEC,* runs at two levels: *user EXEC* and *privileged EXEC,* and each has accompanying passwords. These modes are akin to user access and root access from the Unix world. The line passwords are typically applied to the virtual terminals and console port connections. The user is required to enter an initial password to access user EXEC mode when attempting to enter the router via Telnet or the console port. After the initial login, , the router enters user EXEC mode, which is indicated by the router name and an angle bracket (>). To enter privileged EXEC mode, type enable from the command line as shown here:

```
User Access Verification

Password:
access>enable
Password:
access#
```

After entering the correct "enable" password, which may be different from the initial user password, the prompt changes to router name#. This indicates that the command-line interpreter is now running in privileged EXEC mode, called *Privileged mode* or *enable mode*, which provides access to many more features and configuration options than are available in user mode.

Unlike some operating systems, which offer varying levels of access to the system, the Cisco IOS is basically all or nothing, save for some advanced security options that give you a limited degree of access granularity. In user mode, what you can see, and what you can do is very limited, whereas privileged mode gives you unfettered access.

Using Context-Sensitive Help

One of the endearing qualities of the Cisco IOS is its availability to context-sensitive help. By simply typing a question mark '?' at the command line and pressing Enter, a list of command options are displayed as shown:

```
access>?
Exec commands:
    connect         Open a terminal connection
    disable         Turn off privileged commands
    disconnect      Disconnect an existing network connection
    enable          Turn on privileged commands
    exit            Exit from the EXEC
    help            Description of the interactive help system
    lock            Lock the terminal
    login           Log in as a particular user
    logout          Exit from the EXEC
    name-connection Name an existing network connection
    pad             Open a X.29 PAD connection
    ping            Send echo messages
    ppp             Start IETF Point-to-Point Protocol (PPP)
    resume          Resume an active network connection
    rlogin          Open an rlogin connection
    show            Show running system information
    slip            Start Serial-line IP (SLIP)
    systat          Display information about terminal lines
```

```
telnet          Open a telnet connection

terminal        Set terminal line parameters

traceroute      Trace route to destination
--More--
```

Obviously, using the **?** in privileged EXEC mode yields many more command options than entering the same command in user mode, because privileged mode has a higher level of access to the router. However, the question mark (?) is useful beyond being able to display a laundry list of all available commands. Many commands in the Cisco IOS are long, and often contain multiple words; typing a question mark next to a partially completed command will display all the commands beginning with those letters as shown here:

```
access#con?
configure  connect


access#con
```

Additionally, by separating a command and a question mark with a space, the router will display the next keyword or argument expected, as in the following example:

```
access#clock ?
  set  Set the time and date


access#clock
```

Finally, as you become more skilled at moving around inside the Cisco IOS, it becomes cumbersome to type commands in their entirety. To help save time, the IOS allows and understands commands that are not grammatically complete, but are unique abbreviations, as shown below:

```
access#clo s
```

This command will be correctly interpreted as **clock set**. By using the question mark after the "s," the next required argument may be discerned. Using abbreviated commands will become second nature after using the IOS *command line interface* (CLI) for a while, and will also greatly reduce the amount typing necessary in the long run. Note that the router maintains a record of commands entered. By manipulating the up and down arrows on the keyboard, commands that have been used can be quickly recalled without the need to retyping them.

Tip

Pressing Tab after an abbreviated command will automatically complete the command word.

Configuring the Router

Up to this point, our discussion has centered on moving within the Cisco IOS. However, the real action happens when you begin configuring the router. Although it was pointed out that a Cisco router could be configured from many sources, the majority of time, configuring a router is performed either from a Telnet session or from the console port. That said, we want the router to take input commands from the Telnet session or terminal program being used to manipulate the router. To enable this, type 'configure terminal, or config t from privileged EXEC mode as follows:

```
access#config t
Enter configuration commands, one per line. End with CNTL/Z.
access(config)#
```

This command leaves the IOS in global configuration mode. From here, commands can be issued that affect the router as a whole. For example, the name of the router and the enable password are set in this mode. However, oftentimes you will use commands that apply only to certain parts of the router, such as adding an IP address to an interface, for example.

To handle the task of applying specific details to specific parts of he router, the IOS separates the different configuration tasks into *subconfiguration modes*. The modes, which are laid out similarly to an upside-down tree, start with global configuration mode, as shown next. Typing an additional command from global configuration mode accesses the submodes.

```
Global Configuration Mode          Access(config)#

Interface Mode                     Access(config-if)#

Subinterface Mode                  Access(config-subif)#

Line Mode                          Access(config-line)#

Router Mode                        Access(config-router)#
```

For example, to enter commands that specifically address the RIP routing protocol, enter `router rip` from global configuration mode, as seen in the following example. That will take the IOS to a subconfiguration mode, as shown by the prompt. At that point, all subsequent commands entered will apply to the RIP routing process.

```
access(config)#router rip
access(config-router)#
```

The command-line prompt always reflects the current configuration mode that the IOS is operating in. To exit any given subconfiguration mode, simply type `exit` at the prompt. It is a common mistake to enter commands that are not appropriate for the given configuration mode. Always be sure to verify the current mode by noting the command-line prompt.

One configuration skill that will be invaluable as our discussion of IP routing continues is the construction of what are called *access control lists*, or *ACLs*. An ACL is basically a filter that lets you shape and mold the way traffic, both user data and routing data, flows in your network. ACLs are used extensively in almost all of the routing protocols we will visit, and for this reason a solid understanding of their construction and use is paramount. Appendix A offers an introduction to understanding, constructing, and using ACLs in a variety of situations.

Viewing Router Configurations

Obtaining information about the status of the Cisco router is of vital importance. As configurations grow more complex and changes are made to the configuration files, being able to discern their effects will become paramount. In the Cisco IOS, the task of examining router statistics is accomplished through the use of detailed `show` commands. `show` commands are often issued from privileged EXEC mode and can display to the screen information ranging from IP routing tables to the status of a serial interface. A partial listing of the show commands is as follows:

```
access#show ?
  access-expression  List access expression
  access-lists       List access lists
  aliases            Display alias commands
  appletalk          AppleTalk information
  arap               Show Appletalk Remote Access statistics
  arp                ARP table
  async              Information on terminal lines used as router interfaces
  bridge             Bridge Forwarding/Filtering Database [verbose]
  buffers            Buffer pool statistics
  cdp                CDP information
  clock              Display the system clock
  cmns               Connection-Mode networking services (CMNS) information
  compress           Show compression statistics.
  configuration      Contents of Non-Volatile memory
  controllers        Interface controller status
  debugging          State of each debugging option
  decnet             DECnet information
  dhcp               Dynamic Host Configuration Protocol status
  dialer             Dialer parameters and statistics
  dnsix              Shows Dnsix/DMDP information
  dxi                atm-dxi information
  entry              Queued terminal entries
  flash              System Flash information
  flh-log            Flash Load Helper log buffer
  frame-relay        Frame-Relay information
  history            Display the session command history
  hosts              IP domain-name, lookup style, nameservers, and host
  interfaces         Interface status and configuration
  ip                 IP information
  ipx                Novell IPX information
  line               TTY line information
  llc2               IBM LLC2 circuit information
```

```
logging          Show the contents of logging buffers

memory           Memory statistics

ntp              Network time protocol

printers         Show LPD printer information

privilege        Show current privilege level

processes        Active process statistics

protocols        Active network routing protocols

queue            Show queue contents

queueing         Show queueing configuration

registry         Function registration information

reload           Scheduled reload information

rhosts           Remote-host+user equivalences

rif              RIF cache entries
```

To display, or show the current configuration file running on the router simply type show running-config from privileged EXEC mode. This command is perhaps the most useful and most used show command of the Cisco IOS, because it displays very succinctly all the commands in effect on the given router. Many people adept at Cisco IOS troubleshooting will go straight to the show run command to get an overview of what the router is doing at the current time. From there you can drill down to more detailed and specific show commands to suit the situation.

All commands entered into a router through the console port or a Telnet session, regardless of the configuration mode, are immediately put into effect. This is because the commands are entered and executed from a file called *running-configuration*, which is held in RAM. When a router initially boots up, assuming a normal boot, a file called *startup-configuration* is read from an area of the router called Nonvolatile RAM (NVRAM). This file is moved from NVRAM into RAM where it becomes the running-configuration file. NVRAM preserves the configuration of the router and serves as a backup in the event of a power cycle or power loss. It must be mentioned, however, that a backup of the running-config to the startup-config is not automatic. If changes are made to the running-config from the terminal, the file must be manually copied into NVRAM with the following command:

```
access#copy running-config startup-config
Building configuration...
```

```
[OK]
access#
```

In so far as showcommands pertain to IP routing, show ip route is the most helpful. This command outputs the IP routing table that the router is currently using to make forwarding decisions, as shown here:

```
access#sh ip route
Codes: C - connected, S - static, I - IGRP, R - RIP, M - mobile, B - BGP
       D - EIGRP, EX - EIGRP external, O - OSPF, IA - OSPF inter area
       N1 - OSPF NSSA external type 1, N2 - OSPF NSSA external type 2
       E1 - OSPF external type 1, E2 - OSPF external type 2, E - EGP
       i - IS-IS, L1 - IS-IS level-1, L2 - IS-IS level-2, * - candidate default
       U - per-user static route, o - ODR


Gateway of last resort is not set

     172.16.0.0/24 is subnetted, 8 subnets
I       172.16.55.0 [100/8726] via 172.16.35.5, 00:01:09, Serial1
C       172.16.34.0 is directly connected, Serial0.4
C       172.16.35.0 is directly connected, Serial1
O       172.16.24.0 [110/128] via 172.16.34.4, 18:36:27, Serial0.4
O IA    172.16.22.0 [110/134] via 172.16.34.4, 18:35:57, Serial0.4
C       172.16.23.0 is directly connected, Serial0.2
I       172.16.5.0 [100/8976] via 172.16.35.5, 00:01:09, Serial1
C       172.16.3.0 is directly connected, Loopback0
access#
```

The specifics of what is contained in the IP routing table are described in detail in upcoming sections. Other helpful commands to use when configuring IP routing include show IP protocols and show router <routing protocol name>, for example, show router OSPF. These commands will give more detailed descriptions of the configuration specifics of the routing protocols in use on the router. You'll learn more about the details these commands provide later on in the book, in the chapters where specific IP routing protocols are covered.

Understanding Debug Commands

Debugging commands on a Cisco router are powerful tools that can be used to output a bevy of real-time information about router statistics. The volume of information displayed to the screen by the debug commands can often be overwhelming. However, with time and practice, debugging can become an invaluable tool for diagnosing routing and configuration errors. To enable debugging on the router, from privileged EXEC mode, type debug <argument(s)>. For example, to start debugging of IP Routing Information Protocol (RIP) events, use the following command:

```
access#debug ip rip
RIP protocol debugging is on
access#
```

At this point, any information in the way of RIP routing updates and events will be displayed to the screen as seen in the following output. From here, you can discover potential routing problems by watching the live interaction of the RIP routing process. These commands often have use far beyond that of simple show commands. Debugging commands are credited with displaying *what* a router is doing step by step versus *how* a router is configured, which is displayed through show commands.

```
r5#debug ip rip
RIP protocol debugging is on
r5#
RIP: received update from 172.16.35.3 on Serial1
     172.16.34.0 in 1 hops
     172.16.23.0 in 1 hops
     172.16.3.0 in 1 hops
RIP: sending update to 255.255.255.255 via Loopback0 (172.16.5.5)
     subnet 172.16.55.0, metric 1
     subnet 172.16.34.0, metric 2
     subnet 172.16.35.0, metric 1
     subnet 172.16.23.0, metric 2
     subnet 172.16.3.0, metric 2
```

```
RIP: sending update to 255.255.255.255 via Serial1 (172.16.35.5)

    subnet 172.16.55.0, metric 1

    subnet 172.16.5.0, metric 1

RIP: sending update to 255.255.255.255 via TokenRing0 (172.16.55.5)

    subnet 172.16.34.0, metric 2

    subnet 172.16.35.0, metric 1

    subnet 172.16.23.0, metric 2

    subnet 172.16.5.0, metric 1

    subnet 172.16.3.0, metric 2

RIP: received update from 172.16.35.3 on Serial1

    172.16.34.0 in 1 hops

    172.16.23.0 in 1 hops

    172.16.3.0 in 1 hops

r5#
```

Tip

Debugging information is output to the console port terminal by default. If you are logged into a router via a Telnet session, entering the `Terminal Monitor` command will redirect the debug information to your Telnet display.

Note that debugging commands have an extreme effect on a router's performance. A small Cisco router can be brought to its knees if too many debugging sessions are running at once. Debugging should not be a permanent solution in any routing environment. Once information has been extracted from the debugging process, it should be disabled by issuing the following command:

```
access#no debug all
All possible debugging has been turned off
access#
```

Routing Warm-Up

The way routing happens is the essence of this book. Understanding what exactly is out there in terms of routing options can be a daunting task, to be sure. While specific characteristics and methods for individual protocols are forthcoming, a brief overview of the world of routing will help to put everything in perspective.

Understanding Routing versus Routed

Understanding the difference between routed and routing protocols is key to the remainder of the discussions in this book. Routed protocols—for example, IP, IPX, and AppleTalk—are the workhorses of the network. They contain an addressing format that provides for both network and host information. A routed protocol packet is analogous to a postal mail letter containing both a street name and an individual house number. The letter itself is the entity that carries information or payload from one location to another

Beyond the letter with its addressing, there must also be some system or process in place to make sure letter distribution happens efficiently and in a timely manner. In the computer world this is the job of the routing protocol. Routing protocols such as RIP, Interior Gateway Routing Protocol (IGRP), Open Shortest Path First (OSPF), and Enhanced Interior Gateway Routing Protocol (EIGRP) are the languages spoken between routers; these protocols enable the routers to learn about networks they do not physically connect to. If a piece of routed information arrives in a router for a network that does not physically connect to the router, the router will know where to forward the information, because of the routing protocol, in order to get that information to its destination. This concept is no different in the postal mail system. To send a letter from Dallas to Chicago, the Dallas post office will first note that the letter is destined for a remote street, and then forward it to a Chicago post office that has better knowledge of the letter's final destination. Similarly, routers pass information from location to location until some router is directly connected to the destination network.

Describing Types of Routing

The way routing happens is a complex process, even when localized to routing a specific routed protocol, such as IP. Routing, as we now know, is the process of getting information from one location to another. This may not always pertain to computer data; we have seen, for example, that postal mail is routed, as are phone calls. However, this is a book about IP routing, so we had better start talking about routing as it relates specifically to networks and IP data. A network route is a path from a sending machine to a destination machine. Routers learn about these non-connected routes through one of three methods:

- Default routes — manually entered commands that enable a route of last resort
- Static routes — manually entered commands that explicitly state a given path to a destination
- Dynamic routes — dynamically learned routes sent from other participating routers

These three types of routing methods pertain to all protocols, but from here on out our discussions will focus solely on IP routing. While all three methods are integral to forming a complete understanding of the routing process, static and default routes share many similarities and thus are discussed in their entirety later on, in Chapter 7.

All dynamic routing protocols fall into a hierarchical categorization, as shown in Figure 1-1:

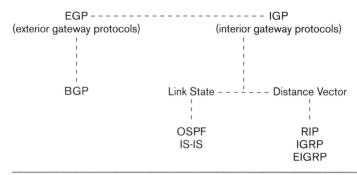

Figure 1-1 *Hierarchical categorization of IP routing protocols*

At the highest level, routing protocols fall into one of two broad categories, Exterior Gateway Protocols (EGPs) or Interior Gateway Protocols (IGPs). Generally, an IGP runs within an Autonomous System (AS), and an EGP runs between ASs. An Autonomous System can be thought of as a set of network devices under a common administration. The best example of this interaction is the Internet, which connects thousands of companies; each runs its own IGP, each has its own AS, and all are connected together by means of an EGP.

Technically, there are a few different types of EGPs, but the one predominately in use today is Border Gateway Protocol (BGP) version 4. BGP, covered in Chapter 6, is perhaps the most complex of all routing protocols. On the IGP side of the hierarchy there is one further categorization, that of Distance Vector (DV) and Link State (LS). All IGP routing protocols fall into one of these two types. The distinction and differences between DV and LS are discussed later in this chapter. For now, understand that Figure 1-1 addresses only IP routing protocols. Other routed protocols, such as IPX and AppleTalk, have their own routing protocols, which also fall into the preceding categories but are not covered here.

Routing Considerations

The process of routing, and consequently, the routing protocol, encompasses several essential functions that the routing algorithms must be able to perform in order to be effective. The routing protocol must have a method to send and receive information about connected and non-local networks. The protocol must have some way to compute a best path to non-local networks. And finally, the protocol must have a facility for adapting to topology changes in the network. Each of these requirements is discussed in reference to its specific IP routing protocol in later chapters.

The magic of routing protocols can be seen by examining the routing table of a given router. The routing table contains a real-time view of all the networks, connected and remote, that a router is currently routing packets to. As our discussion continues into specific protocols, it will be important to understand how this table is maintained and updated. While many examples of routing tables are discussed throughout the book in regard to a specific protocol, a quick rundown of the key components in a table entry is appropriate now. Consider the following excerpt from an IP routing table:

```
R   172.16.3.0  [120/2] via 172.16.4.1, 00:00:10, Ethernet 0
```

The letter in the far-left column represents the routing protocol used to learn about the route, in this case, "R" for RIP. The first IP address is the actual IP network the router is routing to. The number in brackets is a combination of administrative distance and metric, both of which are described next. The address after the word "via" is the IP address of the next hop router. In lay terms, we think of this address as the *next hop logical* address, or the router to which the payload is sent in order to reach the given network. The timer represents the amount of time elapsed since the router last heard of the route from the via address router. And finally, "Ethernet 0" represents the outbound interface from which the route was learned and subsequently the interface through which packets are routed out for the given route.

Administrative Distance

Administrative distance (AD) has nothing to do with distance; rather, it is a measure of the "believability" for a given routing information source. A router will often learn information about a specific network from multiple sources. For instance, a router may learn of network 192.168.10.0/24 from RIP as well as from OSPF. These different sources are advising the router to take different paths depending upon the routing protocol. A routing table can only contain routing information to a network from one source. This being the case, the router must choose the routing source that is most trustworthy. To accomplish this, an integer value from 0 to 255 is assigned to each type of routing source. See Figure 1-2 for a comparison of ADs.

Route Source	Administrative Distance
Directly Connected Interfaces	0
Static Route	1
External BGP	20
Internal EIGRP	90
IGRP	100
OSPF	110
IS-IS	115
RIP	120
External EIGRP	170
Internal BGP	200
Unknown	255

Figure 1-2 *The administrative distance of several IP routing protocols*

Figuring out which is best using the default table works in the same way as golf scoring: the lower score wins. Thus, the lower the integer value assigned, the more believable a routing source. You may notice that a static route, a route that is manually entered, has an AD of 1. Care should be taken when entering static routes, because—right or wrong—the router will believe what is manually entered over all other routing sources.

Finally, it is important to note that in a multiple routing protocol environment, just because a routing protocol on a given router has a high AD, this does not prevent the router from sending and receiving network updates for that protocol. The router will continue to process the protocol. However, as long as another routing protocol with a better (smaller) AD is available and sends information about the same networks, the less trusted protocol will not make the final cut and consequently will not be used in the routing table. For example, if a router is receiving routing updates about network 192.168.10.0/24 from both RIP and IGRP, the IGRP route will be installed in the routing table. This will happen because IGRP has a lower AD than RIP, 100 versus 120, respectively.

Metrics

Each routing protocol must have some way of calculating the best path to take to get to a given non-local network. The determination of "best" is usually calculated using metrics that are computed in an algorithm, which assigns a number, or cost, to the path. This ability is necessary because a router will often have multiple paths to the same network. The router must determine which of those multiple paths is best and should be entered into the routing table, or if both paths are equally good and thus should be load-balanced. The metric variables that go into computing a cost can be as simple as counting the number of routers it takes to reach a given network, as is the case with RIP. Or, the metric computation can take into account many variables, including load, reliability, maximum transmission unit (MTU), delay, and bandwidth, as is the case with IGRP, for example. Most metrics are passed between routers so that a metric value can be cumulative as routing updates propagate the network. This is evident in the preceding routing table entry, which uses a hop count metric of 2. That is to say, network 172.16.3.0 is two hops away from the router. The specific metric variables in use for a given protocol are discussed in detail in their respective chapters.

Convergence

Convergence is a term used to describe the process by which routers in a given system have a consistent view of the networking topology. That is to say, all routers know about all networks. You can imagine that in a large network, knowledge of a network failure on one side of the network can potentially take a long time to travel across to the other side. The length of time needed to again bring all the routers to a consistent view with best-path information is known as the convergence time. You will see in later chapters that the ability to converge quickly is tied to the ability to recognize the existence of, or lack of, neighbors. Neighbors are two or more routers that share a common link. If a neighbor disappears, or a new neighbor is enabled, being able to quickly recognize and disseminate that information directly affects the convergence time of the system. You will learn that different routing protocols have different methods for accomplishing this task.

Understanding Dynamic Routing

The different categories of routing were discussed above broad strokes. Now it's time to drill down a bit and look at the nuts and bolts of dynamic routing.

Distance vector routing

Distance vector, or DV, routing relies on an algorithm called the Bellman-Ford algorithm, aptly named for its developers. The algorithm works by having routers periodically broadcast entire copies of their own routing table to all directly connected neighbors. Contained in this update are the networks the router knows about, and the distance — measured as a hop count, for example — for each of those networks. The information contained in these updates is then compared against the current routing table, and from this meshing a new routing table is generated. This process happens between all routers running a given DV protocol and in this manner, the algorithm can compute a cumulative distance for any given network. The concept of relying on your neighbors for their routing tables, which were built using knowledge from other neighbors, leads to DV routing being called *routing by rumor*. As a packet is routed through a DV network, the packet follows the shortest, and thus best, path to its destination. This results in the packet hopping from next hop logical to next hop logical, and thus following a route with a shorter and shorter hop count metric until it finally arrives at a router that is directly connected to the destination network.

Topology change with distance vector routing As mentioned before, routing information is disseminated through the network by means of broadcast updates of routing tables to directly connected neighbors. Because the update contains the hop count for a given network, the receiving router increments the hop count by one and enters the new information into its table. In this manner, should a router hear about a route to a network with a lower hop count than it already has, it would replace its current route with the better information it learned from its neighbor. Then, on the next periodic update cycle, this new information would be pushed to the other neighbors by broadcasting the updated routing information. However, this process of pushing new or changed information on a periodic cycle via broadcasts can often take several minutes in a medium-to large-scale network. That delay in convergence can have potentially disastrous effects on the routing system, as you'll see in the next section. This process of cumulative hop counting is shown in Figure 1-3:

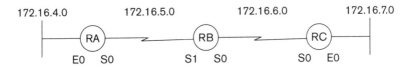

| 172.16.4.0 | | 172.16.5.0 | | 172.16.6.0 | | 172.16.7.0 |

| RA | RB | RC |
| E0   S0 | S1   S0 | S0   E0 |

RTA			RTB			RTC		
Network	INT	Hop	Network	INT	Hop	Network	INT	Hop
172.16.4.0	E0	0	172.16.5.0	S1	0	172.16.6.0	S0	0
172.16.5.0	S0	0	172.16.6.0	S0	0	172.16.7.0	E0	0
172.16.6.0	S0	1	172.16.4.0	S1	1	172.16.5.0	S0	1
172.16.7.0	S0	2	172.16.7.0	S0	1	172.16.4.0	S0	2

Figure 1-3 *A simple network with hop count as the routing protocol metric*

Problems and solutions with distance vector routing DV routing is not without its problems. One major problem with DV routing is the potential for *routing loops* to form. Figure 1-4 shows the classic example of how a routing loop can happen:

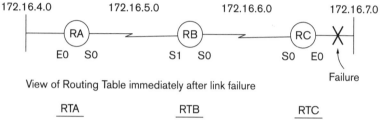

172.16.4.0   172.16.5.0   172.16.6.0   172.16.7.0

RA   RB   RC   ✗

EO   SO   S1   SO   SO   EO   Failure

View of Routing Table immediately after link failure

RTA			RTB			RTC		
Network	INT	Hop	Network	INT	Hop	Network	INT	Hop
172.16.4.0	E0	0	172.16.5.0	S1	0	172.16.6.0	S0	0
172.16.5.0	S0	0	172.16.6.0	S0	0	*172.16.7.0	S0	Down*
172.16.6.0	S0	1	172.16.4.0	S1	1	172.16.5.0	S0	1
172.16.7.0	S0	2	172.16.7.0	S0	1	172.16.4.0	S0	2

View of Routing Table after routing update was sent from RB to RC causing the formation of the routing loop

RTA			RTB			RTC		
Network	INT	Hop	Network	INT	Hop	Network	INT	Hop
172.16.4.0	E0	0	172.16.5.0	S1	0	172.16.6.0	S0	0
172.16.5.0	S0	0	172.16.6.0	S0	0	*172.16.7.0	E0	2*
172.16.6.0	S0	1	172.16.4.0	S1	1	172.16.5.0	S0	1
172.16.7.0	S0	2	*172.16.7.0	S0	1*	172.16.4.0	S0	2

Figure 1-4 *A simple network after a failure has happened, and the subsequent routing loop that is formed between routers B and C*

When Network 172.16.7.0 fails, router C marks the failure in its table and stops routing packets out E0. Before router C can tell the rest of its neighbors, it receives an update from router B with a route to network 172.16.7.0 and a hop count of 1. Router C compares this information with its table, sees that its route to 172.16.7.0 is down, and enters a new route to 172.16.7.0 with a hop count of 2 out its S0 interface. Now when a packet arrives in router B for network 172.16.7.0, it gets forwarded to Router C, which checks its routing table and forwards the packet back to Router B; the cycle then repeats itself, thus creating a routing loop.

To stop this problem of routing loops, several solutions were incorporated to tackle the problem in tandem. *Split horizons with poison reverse* works to combat potential routing loops by marking routes that were learned in on an interface as unreachable when subsequently sending a updates out the said interface. Using Figure 1-4, RB would advertise networks 172.16.6.0/24 and 172.16.7.0/24 to RC with a the hop count set to infinity. This behavior would stop the routing loop described in the preceding paragraph; Router C would not install a route to network 172.16.7.0/24 towards Router B, because that the hop count was set to infinity. As an added safeguard to prevent loops, *holddown timers* are employed. If a routing update that increases the metric of a given network is learned, that information is accepted; however, the route is put in 'holddown,' which precludes the router from listening to any further updates about that particular network for the duration of the holddown. The rationale is that if a route is unable to change states again after a recent state change, this will give the networking system a chance to settle down and stabilize. Holddown timers limit the impact of links that are flapping up and down repeatedly, thus causing the network to be in a constant state of flux. This solution does come with a cost, however. As a result of holddown timers, a network cannot converge any faster than the length of the timer, which is typically three times the update cycle of the routing protocol plus 10 seconds. The benefit of holddown timers is that bad or suboptimal routing information is less likely to make it into the routing tables. Finally, triggered or flash updates are used to speed the transfer of topology change to other routers. Should a route fail, instead of waiting for the periodic update to pass knowledge of the failed route to the neighboring routers, an immediate routing update will be sent containing just the changed information will be sent to all connected neighbors. At that point, depending on the routing protocol in use, either the information will continue to be flashed through the network, or the information will be spread by the normal cycle of periodic updates.

Link-state routing

Link-state, or LS, routing protocols operate by using an algorithm commonly called the Shortest Path First (SPF) algorithm, which was developed by E. W. Dijkstra. LS is generally considered to be a more complex method of routing than DV. Instead of relying on rumored information from directly connected neighbors, each router in an LS system maintains a complete topology of the network. This topology map and the resulting routing table are formed using the following process: Initially, all the routers establish adjacencies with each of their directly connected neighbors. Next, they share information about the links and networks that they are connected to through what are called Link State Advertisements (LSAs). This information is gathered and flooded further through the network to more distant neighbors until all routers in the system have an identical database of all the LSAs in the system. Once a complete topological database is formed, the SPF algorithm is run by each router to derive a unique routing table from the computing router's perspective. It is important to remember that as a result of SPF, each router will have a different routing table, but all will have identical databases.

Topology change with LS routing LS routing handles network changes and failures quite differently than DV routing. As you may recall, DV periodically broadcasts the entire routing table regardless of whether the state of the network has changed or not. With LS, by contrast, when a route fails or a new route is added, the router directly connected sends out an LSA, which is flooded throughout the network. This in turn causes the routers in the system to recalculate their routing table by means of the SPF algorithm. Initially, this may not seem any better, but the key is that generally, unless there is a network-state change, the routers are not sending LSAs or recompiling routing tables. This characteristic leads to a protocol that is very efficient in stable environments. However, it should be noted that despite being bandwidth friendly, for example, not sending entire copies of routing tables, the SPF algorithm does take a fair amount of processing power every time it is run.

Link state routing problems and solutions LS routing protocols, despite being a cut above DV protocols, are not without their own problems. Recall that in the event of a network failure or change, an LSA is flooded out, which triggers other routers to recalculate their routing tables. In some redundant networking topologies, LSAs may have multiple paths with which to reach distance routers. Depending on the speed of those links, some LSAs may arrive before others. This may not seem to be a problem until we consider the case of a failed link coming back up immediately after the failure. What will happen is a distant router will receive multiple LSAs—some with link failure, some with link restoration. Which LSA should the router believe to be correct, and thus use to recalculate the routing table? The answer to this problem is quite simple. Because the same router is generating the LSAs, a time stamp or sequence number is applied to each LSA, enabling the receiving router to simply choose the latest information.

Another problem that can manifest in LS routing systems is a situation in which your topology database grows too large because of too many links. Remember that in a given system all the routers have knowledge of all the links, and any time a failure or addition of a link happens, every router in the system must recalculate the routing table. This characteristic can become to great a burden in terms of memory requirements and processing power. To make LS routing more scalable, and to address the above problem, the concept of *areas* was introduced. Each link or network is assigned to an area; each area in a system maintains a separate topology database. Special border routers are configured to handle the passage of networking information between areas on a controlled level. The effect of this separation is that individual failures in a given area only affect routers in that area, leaving border areas free from having to recalculate the routing table. Figure 1-5 illustrates this concept:

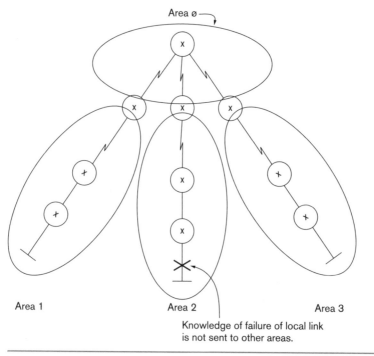

Area ø

Area 1

Area 2

Area 3

Knowledge of failure of local link
is not sent to other areas.

Figure 1-5 *A network utilizing areas as a way of localizing network failure*

Link State versus Distance Vector

LS routing protocols, as you can see, are more complex and require more configuration than DV routing protocols. And as a result, a well-planned and configured LS environment can scale effectively to thousands of routers. This does not mean, however, that LS is the right choice over DV in all situations. In a smaller network, where bandwidth is plentiful, using DV may absolutely be the best choice for its ease of configuration and troubleshooting. And irrespective of LS or DV, we mustn't overlook static and default routing as acceptable and often preferred methods of routing. Each of these routing types — LS, DV, and static/default — is addressed in detail in the following chapters.

Wrap-Up

As this chapter concludes, evaluate your skills to verify that you are comfortable moving on into the more meaty routing protocol configuration chapters. You should be confident moving around within the Cisco IOS and using the help features such as context-help and command completion. Also, the major differences between DV and LS should be clear. Finally, confirm you are confident in your understanding of how packets flow through routers and use the routing tables on the way to their final destinations. The upcoming chapters give you the skills necessary to configure the leading IP routing protocols in use today in a multitude of environments.

Chapter 2

Routing Information Protocol

Perhaps the best-known routing protocol of all time, due in part to its longevity, Routing Information Protocol (RIP) for IP first surfaced in force sometime in the early 1970s. Despite RIP's notoriety in the industry, it is often looked upon as an antiquated and unsophisticated protocol. While this is partly true, it is just this unsophisticated nature that has sustained, and will continue to sustain, RIP into the twenty-first century. RIP survives today in two flavors. RIPv1 is the original, described in RFC 1058; RIPv2 is described in RFC 1723. RIPv2 is not a new protocol by any means, but rather an attempt to refine RIPv1 and address some of its shortcomings. This chapter deals predominately with RIPv1, the version in widespread use today. The new bells and whistles added to RIPv2 are described later in the "Advanced Configuration" section. That being said, make no mistake, RIP will never win any awards for style. Due to its configuration simplicity and widespread installation base, though, RIP continues to flourish today.

Explaining RIP Characteristics

RIP, like every routing protocol, has certain characteristics that define the way it behaves. Understanding these behaviors is paramount in order to effectively manage and troubleshoot RIP. This section begins with a description of the metrics used by RIP and then discusses the timers involved. It finishes with a discussion of classful routing as it pertains to RIP.

Metrics and Administrative Distance

RIP is a classful, distance vector routing protocol. Most notably, as is the case with all classful routing protocols, there are no means for RIP to send a subnet mask in the routing updates. This limitation is explored in detail later in the chapter; for now, remember that when an update is sent or received, *no* mask information will be included. The default administrative distance (AD) of RIP is 120. For AD, the lower the number, the more believable the routing source, making RIP not very believable in comparison to other routing protocols. To alter the default AD, use the following command:

```
RA(config)#router rip

RA(config-router)#distance n <where n is from 1 to 255>
```

The metric used by RIP is the infamous hop count, which, as you will recall, does *not* take into account bandwidth, delay, or other variables. Hop count is calculated by simply adding up the number of routers between a given router and the remote network. RIP always chooses the path with the lowest hop count as "best," sometimes resulting in sub optimal routing decisions, as shown in Figure 2-1.

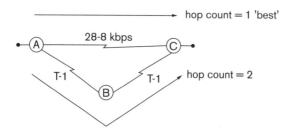

Figure 2-1 *A simple network showing the limitations of the hop count metric used by RIP*

RIP is a distance vector routing protocol, and as such employs all the tactics described in Chapter 1 to protect against routing loops. Additionally, defining a maximum hop count of 15, with 16 being "infinity," meaning unreachable, provides a means for the protocol to identify and battle a routing loop, but this definition also limits the legitimate size for a given network. Remember, when RIP was being developed, no one anticipated a network 15 hops wide; in fact, you would have had a hard time convincing people that there would ever be a need for 15 routers.

RIP can load balance across multiple *equal* cost paths. By default, RIP is configured for load balancing on four equal cost paths, and a range from one (no load balancing) to six is configurable. To change the default, use the following command:

```
R1(config)#router rip
R1(config-router)#maximum-paths n <where n is from 1 to 6>
```

Once again, the metric employed by RIP is hop count only, so the term "equal" is subject to the constraints of hop count. As you can see in Figure 2-2, trying to load balance between a 64-kbps ISDN line and a 45-Mbps T-3 line may not be what you want to do.

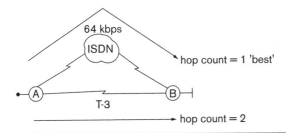

Figure 2-2 *Another example of sub optimal routing problems caused by using the hop count metric only*

Timers

RIP uses several timers to create and manage the routing table. The following output shows the timers in use:

```
R1#sh ip protocol
Routing Protocol is "rip"
  Sending updates every 30 seconds, next due in 8 seconds
  Invalid after 180 seconds, hold down 180, flushed after 240
  Outgoing update filter list for all interfaces is
  Incoming update filter list for all interfaces is
  Redistributing: rip
  Default version control: send version 1, receive any version
    Interface      Send  Recv   Key-chain
    Ethernet1       1    1 2
```

```
    Loopback0        1     1 2
    Serial3          1     1 2
Routing for Networks:
    172.16.0.0
    192.168.61.0
Routing Information Sources:
    Gateway          Distance      Last Update
    192.168.61.1        120        00:00:06
    172.16.14.4         120        00:00:15
Distance: (default is 120)
```

RIP sends out broadcast routing table updates every 30 seconds to all directly connected neighbors, using UDP port 520. Technically, the update timer is a randomly computed value between approximately 25 to 30 seconds, with the variation used to combat table synchronization. Table synchronization arises when multiple routers, sharing the same broadcast domain, begin sending their broadcast updates simultaneously, which can in effect overwhelm the medium being used. The invalid timer is used as an aging mechanism. This timer establishes the period for which a route can remain in the routing table without being refreshed by a routingtable update. If an established route is not refreshed for a period of six update intervals (180 seconds), the route is marked unreachable and possibly down, but it is still left in the table. The holddown and flush timers are then triggered and used as the length of time a route can remain in the table before being removed completely. The holddown timer and flush timer run concurrently, and the flush timer expires 60 seconds after the holddown timer expires.

The holddown timer can also be set when an update is received for a route already established in the table. This happens when an update is received about a network with a hop count of 16, which is considered inaccessible. It is important to note that even though the route is marked as possibly down, packets destined for that network will still be routed as normal.

While the network route is in holddown, no further updates about that route will be considered. After the holddown timer expires, the route will still be listed in the routing table as possibly down, however, any updates it receives for the network will be used. If no update is received, and the flush timer expires, then the route will finally be removed from the table.

As you can now see, the loss of routing updates about established networks can take a painfully long time to expire out of the routing table completely because the invalid, holddown, and flush timers all have to run to zero. And even if a router is told of a failed route, as learned from a network update with a hop count of 16, the holddown and flush timers must run to zero. This slow convergence can cause black holes to form in your internetwork, a condition where routes that are no longer available are still maintained in a routing table.

The timers described above can be altered using the following command. It is important to note that when changing these timers, it is crucial to change the timers for *all* the routers in a given RIP routing domain.

```
R1(config-router)#timers basic update invalid holddown flush
```

Classful Routing

As stated earlier, the distinguishing characteristic of a classful routing protocol, in this case RIP, is that subnet masks are not sent in the routing updates for destination networks. When making a routing table lookup decision, if the gateway of last resort or the default route is not set, the protocol uses the following process:

The protocol examines the destination network portion of a packet and consults the routing table to see if a match exists for the major classful network. If it does not find a match, the protocol drops the packet and returns an Internet Control Message Protocol (ICMP) message to the sender. If it finds the major network, it further examines the routing table in order to determine if a subnet of the major network exists for the given destination network. Again, if the protocol does not find a major network, it drops the packet and returns an ICMP message. If it finds the subnet, or the major network is found with no accompanying subnets, it forwards the packet to the next hop IP address, as specified after the word "via" in the routing table.

The following routing-table output shows an example of each of these conditions. Network 128.30.0.0/16 is a RIP route for which there are no known subnets, and 172.16.0.0/16 shows an example of a major network with accompanying subnets.

```
R1#sh ip route

Gateway of last resort is not set

C     192.168.61.0/24 is directly connected, Ethernet1
R     128.30.0.0/16 [120/1] via 192.168.61.1, 00:00:16, Ethernet1
      172.16.0.0/24 is subnetted, 8 subnets
R        172.16.55.0 [120/5] via 172.16.14.4, 00:00:02, Serial3
R        172.16.34.0 [120/1] via 172.16.14.4, 00:00:02, Serial3
R        172.16.35.0 [120/5] via 172.16.14.4, 00:00:02, Serial3
C        172.16.14.0 is directly connected, Serial3
R        172.16.4.0 [120/1] via 172.16.14.4, 00:00:02, Serial3
R        172.16.5.0 [120/5] via 172.16.14.4, 00:00:02, Serial3
C        172.16.1.0 is directly connected, Loopback0
R        172.16.3.0 [120/5] via 172.16.14.4, 00:00:03, Serial3
      10.0.0.0/24 is subnetted, 1 subnets
C        10.1.1.0 is directly connected, Ethernet0
R1#
```

The major effect of masking information not being sent in the routing updates is that the sending router has no positive way to determine how many network bits are being used in other parts of the network. To solve this problem, the router has to make certain assumptions, and these RIP assumptions can also lead to problems. The only absolutes the router knows for sure are the classful boundaries of major networks, and the subnet masking of major networks for which it has directly connected interfaces. Consider Figure 2-3.

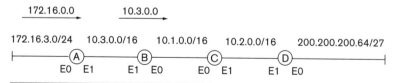

172.16.0.0   10.3.0.0

172.16.3.0/24   10.3.0.0/16   10.1.0.0/16   10.2.0.0/16   200.200.200.64/27

  (A)   (B)   (C)   (D)

EO   E1   E1   EO   EO   E1   E1   EO

Figure 2-3 *A network configuration using RIP that will result in auto-summarized networks*

In this example, when Router A prepares to send a routing update to Router B for network 172.16.3.0/24 out interface E1, which is part of network 10.3.0.0/16, a major network boundary is being passed. Because Router A can't know for sure what mask is potentially used by other routers in the direction of Router B, it has to fall back to the known assumptions, in this case the major network 172.16.0.0 with a 16-bit mask. As a result, when Router A sends the update to Router B, network 172.16.0.0/16 will be sent instead of the more granular (specific) network 172.16.3.0/24. Conversely, when Router B prepares to send a routing table update to Router C for network 10.3.0.0/16 out interface E0, which is part of network 10.1.0.0/16, no major network boundary is passed because both have the same length mask, 16 bits. As a result, the granularity is preserved and network 10.3.0.0/16 will be sent. It is important to note that RIP will not function properly if two different subnet masks are configured for the same major network. In the case of Router B, if interface E1 had a 16-bit mask and E0 had a 24-bit mask, no updates about network 10.0.0.0/8 or any 10.0.0.0 subnet would be sent.

These summarization features of RIP along major network boundaries is a process sometimes called *subnet hiding*. You will learn in the "Troubleshooting RIP" section how the auto-summarization features that RIP employs can cause some strange routing tendencies to arise.

Configuring RIP

Configuring RIP is not a complicated process. However, the protocol's shortcomings in terms of complexity can lead to some unique troubleshooting scenarios. In this section, we start with a basic configuration and then move forward to examine some complicated and tricky scenarios.

Basic RIP Configuration

Despite all of RIP's shortcomings as a routing protocol, it does offer ease of configuration. There just are not many configuration options, which in part lends to its popularity and continued widespread use in the face of fancier, more complicated protocols. Figure 2-4 illustrates a straightforward network configured for RIP.

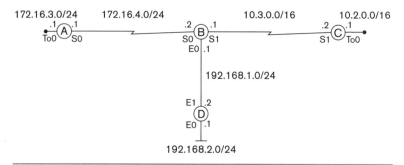

Figure 2-4 *A basic network configured using RIP*

To start the RIP routing process on any router, enter the following text from global config mode:

```
RD(config)#router rip
RD(config-router)#
```

The command prompt leaves you in the sub configuration mode for RIP. Once in this mode, all subsequent commands entered here will pertain to the RIP process you just created. To leave this mode, simply type **exit**, and to reenter type **router rip**. The next task is to get RIP running on your interfaces. Unlike what you may expect, never enable RIP by configuring the interfaces themselves. Instead, use the *network* command:

```
RD(config)#router rip
RD(config-router)#network 192.168.1.0
RD(config-router)#network 192.168.2.0
```

Referencing Figure 2-4, these commands will start RIP on interfaces E0 and E1 because those interfaces have IP addresses that are on the networks you configured for RIP. It is important to realize that nowhere did you specifically tell RIP to start on E0 or E1. Rather, an association is made between the configured IP addresses and the configured network statements. Also note that in addition to no masking information being configured, you are forced to use classful network statements. That is, had the network you were starting RIP on been part of a subnetted address — 192.168.1.64/27, for example — our network statement would still remain the same as shown in the previous example. This is evident by the configuration for router B, shown here:

```
RB(config)#router rip
RB(config-router)#network 192.168.1.0
RB(config-router)#network 172.16.0.0
RB(config-router)#network 10.0.0.0
```

Even though router B has directly connected interfaces on subnetted major networks, 172.16.4.0/24 and 10.3.0.0/16, the statements are still input using their classful representations. That being the case, routers A and C only need one network statement each to start RIP on both interfaces, respectively.

```
RA(config)#router rip
RA(config-router)#network 172.16.0.0


RC(config)#router rip
RC(config-router)#network 10.0.0.0
```

These commands are all that is necessary to start RIP running and exchanging updates.

As a review of the concepts covered in the first part of this chapter, please examine the following routing table from router D:

```
RD#sh ip route

Gateway of last resort is not set

R    172.16.0.0/16 [120/1] via 192.168.1.1, 00:00:28, Ethernet0
R    10.0.0.0/8 [120/1] via 192.168.1.1, 00:00:28, Ethernet0
C    192.168.1.0/24 is directly connected, Ethernet0
C    192.168.2.0/24 is directly connected, Ethernet1
RD#
```

Notice that router D has knowledge of four routes, two directly connected routes and two RIP routes. The two numbers in brackets display the AD and hop count; in this case, 120 and 1, respectively. If more than one equal-cost route existed to a given network, this would be displayed by the existence of two "via" lines for one destination network route. Using Figure 2-4 as a reference, you can discern that the RIP routes are summarizations coming as a result of crossing a major network boundary. Router D, for example, does not have granular knowledge of router A's To0 network 172.16.3.0/24; instead, a summarized route to 172.16.0.0/16 has been installed with a next hop via address of 192.168.1.1 toward router B.

To further strengthen the concepts discussed, also review the following routing table from router A:

```
RA#sh ip route


Gateway of last resort is not set


R    10.0.0.0/8 [120/1] via 172.16.4.2, 00:00:20, Serial0

R    192.168.1.0/24 [120/1] via 172.16.4.2, 00:00:20, Serial0

R    192.168.2.0/24 [120/2] via 172.16.4.2, 00:00:20, Serial0

     172.16.0.0/24 is subnetted, 2 subnets

C       172.16.4.0 is directly connected, Serial0

C       172.16.3.0 is directly connected, TokenRing0

RA#
```

Notice that router A has knowledge of five routes, two directly connected routes and three RIP routes. Router A, unlike router D, has granular knowledge of the 172.16.0.0/16 major network because its S0 and To0 interfaces are part of the major network. However, router A still only sees a summarization of network 10.0.0.0/8 because 10.0.0.0 had to pass through a boundary router to get to router A.

Using Passive-Interfaces

The **passive-interface** command is not an RIP-specific command; however, it is often applied to RIP configurations because of the classful nature of the protocol. Recall from Figure 2-4 that router C's RIP configuration only contained one *network* command, which in effect started the RIP process on both the S1 and To0 interfaces. Imagine now that hanging off that token ring of router C were some RIP-enabled Unix machine that you did not have control over. Despite your not having control over the machine, it is still your responsibility to make sure it does not receive routing updates from router C. The answer to this problem is simple: do not send the updates at all. This is accomplished with the following configuration on router C:

```
RC(config)#router rip
RC(config-router)#network 10.0.0.0
RC(config-router)#passive-interface to0
```

This configuration has the effect of stopping routing updates from propagating onto the token ring. Due to the classful nature of the RIP network statement, you had no way of saying "start RIP on network 10.3.0.0/16, but not 10.2.0.0/16. Instead, use the `passive-interface` command. It is important to note that while the `passive-interface` command stops routing updates from being sent on a given interface, it does not stop a routing update from being received on the same interface. To stop updates from being received, a more specific set of tools is employed, usually through the use of route filtering, which is described in Chapter 8.

Advanced Configuration

With a solid understanding of RIP and its basic configurations under your belt, we will now show you some of the more advanced configurations available with RIP. These options are not necessarily needed in every network running RIP, and they certainly should not be implemented without proper planning and justification.

Configuring unicast updates

One of the chief complaints often voiced about RIP is that the broadcast nature of the routing updates causes too much overhead, which unduly burdens non-RIP speaking devices that are located on a shared medium. Additionally, some transport mediums — Frame-Relay, for example — do not allow network broadcasts. However, it still may be necessary to support a routing protocol, such as RIP, in this environment.

To overcome these limitations, RIP uses the "neighbor" command. Again, referencing Figure 2-4, imagine the serial link between router A and router B is Frame-Relay, and you wish to limit the broadcast load on the Ethernet link between router B and router D. The following configuration of router B shows how to satisfy these conditions:

```
RB(config)#router rip
RB(config-router)#network 172.16.0.0
RB(config-router)#network 10.0.0.0
RB(config-router)#network 192.168.1.0
RB(config-router)#neighbor 192.168.1.2
RB(config-router)#neighbor 172.16.4.1
```

With the addition of the neighbor commands to the configuration, now instead of updates being broadcast out S0 and E0, the updates are unicast to the configured neighbor addresses. This enables routing connectivity on the frame-relay link and reduces broadcast traffic on the Ethernet link.

Changing RIP metrics

Sometimes it is necessary to alter the hop-count metric of RIP for certain routes, often when a backup link has been deployed. (see Figure 2-5).

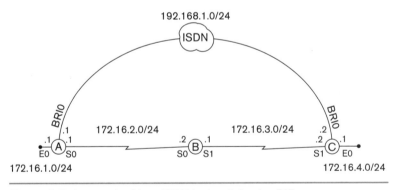

Figure 2-5 *A network with an ISDN backup link using RIP*

Router A's connection to 172.16.4.0/24 on router C should normally be through router B. The ISDN link to router C should only be used if the serial links between the routers failed. The problem arises in the hop-count metric. From router A's perspective, the ISDN link is the "best" path because network 172.16.4.0/24 is only one hop away, versus the path through router B, which takes two hops. To solve this issue, an offset list is used. Examine the following configuration from router A:

```
RA(config)#access-list 10 permit 172.16.4.0 0.0.0.0
RA(config)#router rip
RA(config-router)#network 172.16.0.0
RA(config-router)#offset-list 10 in 2 BRI0
```

The last line of the configuration list above can be read as follows: For RIP updates that come in interface BRI0 that meet the criteria of access list 10 — in this case, if the update is network 172.16.4.0/24 only — add two to the metric.

The result of this configuration is that the path to 172.16.4.0/24 through the ISDN link is now seen as being three hops away and, thus, less favorable than the serial link through router B. The configuration of router C would be similar to router A's configuration, except the access list would permit network 172.16.1.0/24.

Note that although in the preceding configuration you altered the route as it came *into* the interface, you could have altered the routed as it went *out of* the interface, as well. Additionally, remember that when you implement an offset list, you are essentially raising the metric for a given route. If you do this on a live router, the routes you alter will be put in holddown and marked unreachable until the holddown timer expires. The significance is that when you look at the routing table, you will see a bunch of routes marked as possibly down, when that is not in fact the case. Routing continues but the situation may cause some heartburn if you aren't looking out for it.

RIPv2 overview

RIPv2 is an extension of RIPv1, and it addresses key shortcomings of RIPv1. Of all the benefits of RIPv2, the highlights include the following:

- Subnet mask in the routing updates
- Authentication of routing updates
- Multicast route updates

RIPv2 offers other benefits, but this section is not meant to be an exhaustive discussion of RIPv2, but rather an introduction that will empower you to configure and use some of RIPv2's key new features. The fact that the route updates now carry a subnet mask enables RIPv2 to be called a *classless routing protocol*. This means that different size subnet masks can be present in the routing domain for the same major network. Additionally, with the introduction of a subnet mask in the update, RIPv2 can take advantage of route summarization along classless boundaries, which helps greatly to reduce the size of the routing tables, making the routers more efficient. Multicast route updates are sent to address 224.0.0.9, enabling more efficient use of bandwidth. Because the update is now multicast, only configured routers that belong to the multicast group 224.0.0.9 — in this case, RIPv2-enabled routers — have to process the updates. Variable-Length Subnet Masking (VLSM), multicast updates and route summarization are discussed in further detail in upcoming chapters as they pertain to OSPF and BGP. The fact of the matter is, even though RIPv2 has the capacity for these advanced features, it still only allows a hop-count limit of 15, which is far too limiting for many of today's networks. For that reason, many networks will not deploy RIPv2; instead, they migrate to an advanced protocol, such as OSPF or EIGRP, which have virtually no size limitations.

Defining the RIP version By default, a router configured for RIP will send only RIPv1, but will listen and accept RIPv1 and RIPv2. To configure the router to *only* send and accept RIPv2, use the following command:

```
RA(config)#router rip
RA(config-router)#version 2
```

Likewise, to configure a router to send and receive *only* RIPv1 use the following command:

```
RA(config)#router rip
RA(config-router)#version 1
```

There may be times when simply running purely RIPv1 or purely RIPv2 is not sufficient. Look at Figure 2-6. From the diagram, you can ascertain that there is a mix of RIPv1 and RIPv2 routers, and a RIP-enabled Unix host, running in the same network, on the same segment. To address this issue, you can configure the type of RIP updates to be sent and received on an interface-by-interface basis. Look at the following configuration for router B to see how this is accomplished.

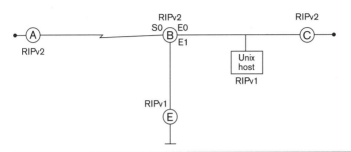

Figure 2-6 *A network with routers and computers running both RIPv1 and RIPv2*

```
RB(config)#router rip

RB(config-router)#version 2

**text omitted***

RB(config)#interface e1

RB(config-if)#ip rip send version 1

RB(config-if)#ip rip receive version 1

RB(config)#interface e0

RB(config-if)#ip rip send version 1 2
```

From the preceding configuration, and from referencing Figure 2-6, you can see that because RIPv2 is running by default on router B, the S0 link to router A can be left as is, natively RIPv2. However, the E1 link to router E has been altered on the interface to *only* send and receive RIPv1. In contrast, the E0 link is configured to send *both* RIPv1 and RIPv2. The sending of both RIPv1 and RIPv2 is necessary so that the Unix host will receive RIP updates. Router B does not need to be configured to receive RIPv1 updates because the Unix host will not be sending any routing updates, only listening. Because RIPv2 is natively running on router B, it will be able to receive version 2 updates from router C without further configuration.

Configuring authentication The last configuration topic to be covered with RIPv2 deals with authentication. RIPv2 enables you to configure routers to authenticate route updates from neighbor peers using clear text passwords or MD5 authentication. To enable the authentication, you must first define a *key chain,* and at least one key to be used as the password on each router. The key chain name can be different on each router; however, the routers must use an identical key. Once you have defined the keys, you must enable their use on the desired interfaces. Figure 2-7 shows a simple network that you will configure to authenticate routing updates.

RIPv2 Authentication

Figure 2-7 *A simple network with 2 routers that will be configured to authenticate routing updates*

Look at the following configuration of router A:

```
RA(config)#key chain cisco
RA(config-keychain)#key 1
RA(config-keychain-key)#key-string systems
***text omitted***
RA(config)#interface S0
RA(config-if)#ip rip authentication key-chain systems
RA(config-if)#ip rip authentication mode md5
```

In the preceding configuration, a key chain of "cisco" has been configured with the key name "systems." The key is being used for MD5 route-update authentication on S0, which is the link to router B. A similar configuration would exist on router B. Remember, when configuring route-update authentication between two routers, always make sure that the key string and the authentication mode match. The command debug ip rip events can be used to troubleshoot and diagnose such configuration errors.

Troubleshooting RIP

Now that you have a solid understanding of RIP and the configuration options available, you can examine the options available to you if things don't go as planned. As with any skill, troubleshooting is more about experience than anything else. The tools described in this section give you a framework to begin troubleshooting, but only over time, as you examine many different scenarios, will your skills be honed.

Debugging RIP

Debugging RIP is usually straightforward due to the simplicity of the protocol. Following are three extremely useful commands in terms of troubleshooting RIP:

- debug ip rip
- clear ip route *
- show ip route

Starting from the bottom and working up, the show ip route command gives the current view of the routing table at any given moment. It is important to note that the show ip route command does not automatically update changes to the screen. The command should be entered several times in an environment that is in a state of flux to make sure you are seeing the most current view of the network.

In addition to the show ip route command by itself, an individual routing table entry can be listed, as shown here:

```
R1#sh ip route 172.16.34.0
Routing entry for 172.16.34.0/24
  Known via "rip", distance 120, metric 4294967295 (inaccessible)
  Redistributing via rip
  Advertised by rip (self originated)
  Last update from 172.16.14.4 on Serial3, 00:00:23 ago

  Hold down timer expires in 164 secs
```

Using a specific route after the show ip route commands gives much of the same information as the plain command, but also shows the amount of time left on the holddown timer, should one exist as it does in the preceding example. This can be extremely helpful when trying to troubleshoot convergence issues. If you are impatient or need to see changes take effect immediately, use the clear ip route * command to flush the entire routing table. Take care when using this command as it can place a large strain on the network and the routers in terms of CPU processing and bandwidth use. Experience has shown that flushing the table completely is sometimes necessary in order for a change to take effect, even though you probably wouldn't expect this at should not have to be the case. It is a trick of the trade that no one likes to admit, but nonetheless, is effective.

The first command, debug ip rip, is invaluable for showing what the router is sending and receiving in terms of RIP updates. Please review the following output from debug:

```
R1#debug ip rip

RIP protocol debugging is on

R1#

11:14:38: RIP: sending v1 update to 255.255.255.255 via Ethernet1 (192.168.61.2)

11:14:38:      network 172.16.0.0, metric 1

11:14:38: RIP: sending v1 update to 255.255.255.255 via Loopback0 (172.16.1.1)

11:14:38:      subnet  172.16.34.0, metric 2

11:14:38:      subnet  172.16.14.0, metric 1

11:14:38:      subnet  172.16.4.0, metric 2

11:14:38:      network 192.168.61.0, metric 1

11:14:38:      network 192.168.76.0, metric 2

11:14:38: RIP: sending v1 update to 255.255.255.255 via Serial3 (172.16.14.1)

11:14:38:      subnet  172.16.1.0, metric 1

11:14:38:      network 192.168.61.0, metric 1

11:14:38:      network 192.168.76.0, metric 2

11:14:38: RIP: sending v1 update to 192.168.61.6 via Ethernet1 (192.168.61.2)

11:14:38:      network 192.168.76.0, metric 2

11:14:38:      network 172.16.0.0, metric 1

11:14:50: RIP: received v1 update from 172.16.14.4 on Serial3

11:14:50:      172.16.34.0 in 1 hops

11:14:50:      172.16.4.0 in 1 hops

11:14:52: RIP: received v1 update from 192.168.61.1 on Ethernet1

11:14:52:      192.168.76.0 in 1 hops

11:15:06: RIP: sending v1 update to 255.255.255.255 via Ethernet1 (192.168.61.2)

11:15:06:      network 172.16.0.0, metric 1
```

The preceding output shows exactly what networks are being sent and have received on particular interfaces. The bold portion of the output shows that a neighbor command has been configured and that the router is now sending unicast routing updates out E1. The debug output enables you to see where and what summarization is taking place. Again, using the bold portion, can see that the unicast updates being sent out E1 include the summarized 172.16.0.0/16 network, which is a result of crossing a major network boundary. Should a route be absent on a router where you expect one to appear, you can use the debug command to verify the announcement of the route on each router until the offending router is isolated.

Most routing problems as they relate to RIP revolve around a problem known as *discontinuous subnets*. Figure 2-8 shows a common configuration error that can lead to some hard-to-interpret results, if you have not seen them before. Notice that the token ring interfaces of routers A and C both have subnets configured for the major network 10.0.0.0/8. Additionally, they share connections to router B on the major network 172.16.0.0/16. The problem in this scenario is that router A and router C now become boundary routers. As a result, they will summarize the major network 10.0.0.0/8 toward router B, which causes router B to believe there are two equal cost paths to network 10.0.0.0/8, as shown in the routing table for router B. This phenomenon leads to network 10.0.0.0/8 becoming discontiguous.

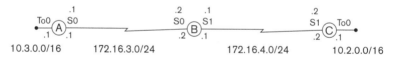

Figure 2-8 *A RIP network configured so that major network 10.0.0.0 is discontiguous*

```
RB#show ip route


Gateway of last resort is not set


R    10.0.0.0 [120/1] via 172.16.3.1, 00:00:23, Serial0

             [120/1] via 172.16.4.2, 00:00:23, Serial1

     172.16.0.0 255.255.255.0 is subnetted, 2 subnets

C       172.16.4.0 is directly connected, Serial1

C       172.16.3.0 is directly connected, Serial0

RB#
```

With this configuration, as shown in the output following this paragraph, an attempt by router B to ping the token ring interface of router A results in router B round-robin load sharing the pings between its two paths and, thus, a 40–60 percent success rate, depending on which way the first ping packet goes — a strange result indeed.

```
RB#ping 10.3.0.1

Type escape sequence to abort.

Sending 5, 100-byte ICMP Echos to 10.3.0.1, timeout is 2 seconds:

!.!.!

Success rate is 60 percent (3/5), round-trip min/avg/max = 28/29/32 ms

RB#
```

There are two possible solutions to the preceding problem. First, you could change the addressing between routers A and B, and B and C to be subnets of the major network 10.0.0.0/8, like the token ring interfaces. However, in the real world, just deciding to "change" an addressing scheme that is already in place may not be readily acceptable. That being the case, the second option is to use secondary IP addresses. Instead of changing the current addressing scheme and causing network interruption, you could overlay a second IP address on the existing structure between router A and B, and B and C. The trick is to add secondary addresses that are part of the 10.0.0.8/ major network, as described earlier in the discussion. The major network 10.0.0.0/8 is then unified across the network, and it will no longer be summarized at the border routers because, in effect, there are no longer any border routers. configuration for router A and B that accomplishes the secondary addressing. Please note that only the additional commands necessary are shown:

```
RA(config)#interface s0

RA(config-if)#ip address 10.4.0.1 255.255.0.0 secondary


RB(config)#interface s0

RB(config-if)#ip address 10.4.0.2 255.255.0.0 secondary


RB(config)#interface s1

RB(config-if)#ip address 10.5.0.1 255.255.0.0 secondary
```

```
RC(config)#interface s1
RC(config-if)#ip address 10.5.0.2 255.255.0.0 secondary
```

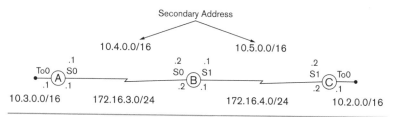

Figure 2-9 *The same network as Figure 2-8 with secondary IP addressing added to make network 10.0.0.0/8 no longer discontiguous*

While this "secondary" addressing solves the configuration and connectivity problems, note that the router views this new addressing as separate data, creating additional bandwidth usage as a result of routing updates being propagated onto this "new" link. Hopefully, this configuration will rarely be necessary, but it can be used as a workaround until a unified addressing scheme is implemented. Take a look at the new routing table for router B, following this paragraph. It shows that router B does have specific routes to 10.3.0.0/16 and 10.2.0.0/16, which now enables you to successfully ping either token ring interface.

```
RB#show ip route

Gateway of last resort is not set

10.0.0.0 255.255.0.0 is subnetted, 3 subnets
R       10.2.0.0 [120/1] via 10.5.0.2, 00:00:00, Serial1
R       10.3.0.0 [120/1] via 10.4.0.1, 00:00:00, Serial0
C       10.4.0.0 is directly connected, Serial0
C       10.5.0.0 is directly connected, Serial1
    172.16.0.0 255.255.255.0 is subnetted, 2 subnets
C       172.16.4.0 is directly connected, Serial1
C       172.16.3.0 is directly connected, Serial0
RB#
```

Watching Out for Gotchas

Thus far in this chapter, the RIP configuring and troubleshooting has been fairly straightforward, but you need to be aware of a potential stumbling block. Because RIP is a simplistic routing protocol, there are no means to configure and use route-update authentication. Most other routing protocols, as you will see, have some method for validating the routing-update source of neighbors. Unfortunately, this is not an option with RIP, and therefore, any router configured to run RIP accepts routing updates from *any* source. Initially, this may not sound like a problem if you have control over all your routers. However, many new devices, as well as legacy devices, that run a type of RIP program, typically *gated* or *routed*, are out there, potentially lurking in your environment. The true problems surface when these machines, potentially out of your control, send incorrect or inconsistent routing updates towardstoward RIP-enabled routers. With no way of authenticating these updates, the RIP routers accept and propagate the potentially damaging information throughout the routing domain.

The work around for this problem is to configure some sort of access control list to block the updates from the known offenders or to convert your routing domain to use a more advanced routing protocol, such as RIPv2, which does have provisions for authenticating routing update sources. Otherwise, you'll have to hunt down the administrators of the offending boxes and tell them they *can't* do something, and we all know how well administrators like it when you start restricting what they can and can't do.

Wrap-Up

No one will ever try to argue that RIP is the best or most flashy routing protocol around. At least they won't win the argument. However, no one will ever deny RIP's widespread use and ease of configuration. RIP has become a little bit like COBOL is in the programming world. It will almost surely never go away completely. For that reason, along with it being an excellent protocol to begin to learn routing on, it always behooves you to know a little something about it.

The configurations in this chapter are not complex in comparison to other protocols, such as BGP and OSPF. But that lack of complexity was out of design. RIP was designed and widely implemented during a time when networks were much simpler and the demands put upon them were far less than today. Currently, Today RIP has mostly been relegated to the fringes of the network, where it is needed to support a few legacy hosts that need the protocol in order to run. But as long as it is present in our networks, people who can configure and support RIP will be needed. In its day, RIP did the job that nothing prior to it could, providing connectivity from a routing standpoint and paving the way for all the other protocols in use today.

Chapter 3

Interior Gateway Routing Protocol and Enhanced Interior Gateway Routing Protocol

Interior Gateway Routing Protocol (IGRP) was developed by Cisco as a replacement for Routing Information Protocol (RIP). It is a distance vector routing protocol and, therefore, works in much the same was as RIP. However, Interior Gateway Routing Protocol (IGRP) overcomes some of the more severe limitations of RIP. IGRP uses link characteristics in assigning route metrics, as opposed to hop count. Therefore, IGRP responds better to actual network topology than does RIP. In addition, IGRP is more efficient than RIP because it sends periodic traffic less often and uses more efficient update packets. The primary sacrifice made for these advantages is that it is a Cisco-proprietary protocol and, as such, cannot be used with other vendors' equipment.

Enhanced IGRP (EIGRP) was also developed by Cisco to be an efficient, responsive, and loop-free routing protocol. It is a unique routing protocol that exhibits behavior similar to both distance vector and link state protocols. Although EIGRP is a distance vector protocol in the information it shares and the way it chooses routes, it overcomes some of the limitations of both RIP and IGRP by incorporating some of the features of link state protocols. EIGRP uses the same information as IGRP to calculate route metrics, but it eliminates the need for periodic updates. Like IGRP, EIGRP is a Cisco-proprietary protocol.

Although IGRP and EIGRP have similar names, they are very different protocols at heart. From the way they share information to the way they process it, their behavior differs greatly. However, there is one strong similarity between IGRP and EIGRP—they are both designed to choose routes in the same way, using metrics based on link characteristics. In fact, these two protocols are designed to work together seamlessly despite their differences. Although each of these protocols could easily have a chapter of its own, this chapter looks at them together to take advantage of their similarities.

Understanding IGRP

Although it was developed by Cisco to overcome limitations of RIP, IGRP is a classic distance vector routing protocol. As such, it shares many characteristics with RIP, including the following:

- Routers send periodic broadcasts of their full routing tables to exchange routing information.

- Conceptually, the cost of a route is calculated by adding the cost advertised by a neighbor to the local cost to reach that neighbor.

- IGRP uses split horizon, reverse poisoning, holddown timers, and hop count to prevent routing loops.

However, the following characteristics of IGRP differentiate it significantly from RIP and result in a unique protocol:

- The default timers used by IGRP are much longer than those used by RIP—usually three times longer.

- IGRP imposes a maximum diameter of 100 hops on a network (and can be configured to allow up to 255 hops). RIP only allows networks of 15 hops.

- IGRP uses a metric based on route characteristics to choose routes, rather than the hop count. By default, the metric incorporates bandwidth and delay, but it can be configured to include reliability and load as well.

- When broadcasting its routing table, IGRP can send up to 104 routes in one update packet. The maximum for RIP is 25 routes per packet.

- IGRP is a Cisco-proprietary routing protocol, so it cannot be used with equipment from other vendors.

IGRP is a very simple protocol to understand and configure. It is similar to RIP in most behaviors, but the enhancements provide some significant improvements to the routing decisions and efficiency on the network.

IGRP Basics

IGRP routers exchange routing information with neighboring routers by broadcasting their entire routing tables periodically. Each router uses the information in the routing table broadcasts from its neighbors to determine its best routes to every destination network.

IGRP is a classful routing protocol, so it does not communicate network mask information in the routing updates. Thus, one limitation of RIP persists in IGRP—it cannot be used on a network in which a major (aka, classful) network has been broken up into discontiguous subnets. At boundaries between major networks, IGRP automatically summarizes the routes to their classful boundary.

IGRP routers belong to a particular Autonomous System (AS). The AS is comprised of all routers that share routing information. The AS is identified by number, which can be in the range of 1 through 65,535. All routers in the same AS share routing information with each other; routers ignore routing information from other ASes. The AS number of a router is assigned when entering the `router igrp` configuration command.

IGRP allows networks to have wider diameters than RIP. RIP networks are limited to 15 hops, but IGRP networks are limited to 100 hops by default. In addition, IGRP uses link characteristics to calculate route metrics rather than the hop count. Therefore, IGRP tends to do a better job of choosing the best route in networks with multiple paths. The following sections describe the particulars of IGRP in more detail.

Routing Table Updates

IGRP routers use an *update interval* of 90 seconds by default, which is three times the update interval used by RIP. In addition, IGRP conserves network bandwidth by using more efficient update packets. IGRP does not use a User Datagram Protocol (UDP) port to communicate, as does RIP; instead, IGRP is assigned a protocol identifier (9, for those of you who are keeping track) for the IP header. Because no UDP header is required, more of the packet can be used by IGRP itself. IGRP also uses a more efficient message format than RIP, so there are no unused fields in the routing updates. Finally, an IGRP packet has a higher maximum size than a RIP packet. All of these factors mean that each IGRP update packet can contain up to 104 routing entries, as opposed to the 25-route limit in a RIP packet.

IGRP uses a randomization factor of 20 percent to stagger the update packets, so the update interval actually varies between 72 and 90 seconds. The default *invalid timer* for IGRP is 270 seconds (three times the update interval). This is the length of time that the router considers a route valid without hearing another update about it. If this timer is exceeded, the route is declared unreachable and is advertised as such.

An IGRP router uses the *flush timer* to determine how long it should keep a route in the routing table after the route becomes inaccessible. By default, the flush timer is 630 seconds (seven times the update interval). While the flush timer is running, the route remains in the routing table and is replaced by any updates received about that destination from any neighbor. When the flush timer expires, the route is completely removed from the routing table.

The *holddown timer* is 280 seconds (three times the update interval, plus ten seconds). When a route becomes invalid, the advertising router marks the destination as unreachable in its routing updates. This causes receiving routers to put the route into holddown. While the route is in holddown, the router ignores any routing updates about that destination. Note that it continues to use that route during this time. This prevents routing loops when a route goes down.

These four timers are used in the same way as their RIP counterparts. In addition, IGRP makes use of triggered updates, so topology changes will not go unnoticed by a neighbor for 90 seconds. One behavioral difference from RIP is that IGRP allows a *sleeptime* to be configured. When a triggered update is received, the router delays sending a periodic update for the amount of the sleeptime.

All of these timers can be changed by using the `timers basic` configuration command. In addition, the use of the holddown timer can be disabled, but this should only be done on loop-free internetworks. Eliminating holddown speeds up reconvergence, but remember that it exists to prevent routing loops when there is a topology change. Also, make sure that all changes to the timers or holddown are configured on every router in the internetwork. Otherwise, you may end up with unexpected results.

Caution

Change IGRP timers only when there is a valid reason to do so on your internetwork. Changing these timers can significantly impact network performance. Decreasing them generates more network traffic in the form of periodic updates; increasing them slows convergence after topology changes. These impacts must be considered carefully when changing timers.

Metrics

One of the biggest advantages of IGRP over RIP is that it does not use the hop count as the routing metric. In some networks, due to bandwidth or other considerations, the path with the fewest hops is not necessarily the best path. IGRP tracks the hop count for each route to prevent routing loops, but this value is not included in the calculation of the route metric. The maximum hop count is 100 by default (it can be changed to any value 1 through 255), and any route with a hop count higher than the maximum is considered unreachable.

IGRP uses two metrics for each route — a *vector metric* and a *composite metric*. The vector metric consists of several individual values, based on the characteristics of the route: the bandwidth, delay, reliability, load, hop count, and MTU. The composite metric is a single value calculated from some of the values in the vector metric. The composite metric is used in making routing decisions, but it is not included in route updates between neighbors. Route updates contain only the vector metric. By default, IGRP uses only the bandwidth and delay when calculating the composite metric of a route. It can be configured to include reliability and/or load in the metric calculation as well.

Every interface has a recognized bandwidth, which is used by IGRP to calculate vector metrics. The default bandwidth for most interfaces, such as Ethernet and Token Ring, is accurate and should not be changed. However, Serial interfaces default to a bandwidth of 1.544 Mbps regardless of the actual speed of the link. When the default bandwidth is not the most accurate value, use the bandwidth configuration command to manually set the recognized bandwidth of an interface. Note that the recognized bandwidth has no impact whatsoever on the actual speed of traffic on the interface; it only affects the information used by the routing protocols.

The bandwidth, *BW*, of a route is the lowest bandwidth of any individual link in the route. After receiving a route update from a neighbor, the router chooses the lower of these two values: the bandwidth in the routing update and the bandwidth of the link to the neighbor. *BW* is in units of Kbps, which are the same units as the value displayed by the show interfaces command and the value accepted by the bandwidth configuration command. After determining *BW*, the router performs the following calculation to determine the value of *B*, which is used to calculate the composite metric:

$$B = 10^7 \div BW$$

The *delay* of a link is a rough measure of the amount of time it takes for traffic to traverse it. Each type of router interface has a default delay, and the delay of a particular interface can be changed with the delay configuration command.

The delay of a route, *D*, is the sum of all delay values for all of the links in the route. The receiving router simply adds the delay of the network on which it received the update to the delay in the route advertisement. *D* is in units of tens of microseconds, as is the value accepted by the delay interface configuration command. On the other hand, the delay value displayed by the show interfaces command is in microseconds.

Reliability is used to indicate how prone a link is to failure. It is based on a fraction of 255, so a reliability of 255 indicates that the link is considered 100 percent reliable. If the reliability is 128, the link is about 50 percent reliable. Reliability is measured dynamically and is based on a five-minute average, weighted to minimize the impact of sudden changes. It is displayed by the show interfaces command.

The reliability of a route, *R*, is the lowest reliability of any link in the route. The router calculating the metric chooses either the reliability advertised by its neighbor or the reliability of the link to the neighbor, whichever is lower.

Load is a measurement of the amount of traffic on a link, as a fraction of the bandwidth available. Like reliability, load is based on a fraction of 255, so a 100 percent loaded link has a load of 255. Load is based on a five-minute average, also weighted in such a way as to minimize the effect of sudden changes in the load of the link. It is also displayed by the show interfaces command.

The load, *L*, of a route is the highest load of any individual link in the route. Each router compares the load advertised by its neighbor with the load of the network on which the update was received, and it chooses the higher value.

Using these variables, IGRP calculates the composite metric with the following equation:

$$metric = \left(K1 \times B + \frac{K2 \times B}{256 - L} + K3 \times D \right) \times \frac{K5}{R + K4}$$

Caution

There is one exception to the use of this equation in IGRP metric calculation. When the constant *K5* is set to zero, the final fraction is not used in the computation at all. (If this were not so, the equation would yield a metric of zero whenever *K5* equals zero.)

All of the constants, *K1–K5*, can be configured using the metric weights configuration command. By default, *K1* and *K3* equal one, and the others equal zero. Therefore, the equation above can be reduced to the following when no changes are made to the default constants:

metric = B + D

Setting the K-constant values determines how much influence each component of the vector metric has on the composite metric. Be sure you know what you are doing when changing these values, as they have a significant impact on the routing on your internetwork. Keep in mind that they must be configured identically on all IGRP routers in order for routing to be reliable.

Load Balancing and Variance

By default, IGRP load balances across four paths. Using the maximum-paths configuration command, IGRP can load balance across any number of paths from one to six.

A unique feature of IGRP (and EIGRP) is that it can load balance across unequal-cost paths as well. When doing unequal-cost load balancing, the router must still determine which routes are acceptable and which are not. To do this, it uses a factor called *variance*. The variance is a multiplier that is used to calculate the maximum acceptable metric for an unequal-cost route to be included in the routing table.

After calculating the composite metrics for all of its routes, a router always enters the lowest-cost route(s) to each destination in the routing table. The metric for that lowest-cost route is also multiplied by the variance to find the acceptable metric limit for that destination. Any other routes to the same destination that have a metric less than or equal to the acceptable metric limit are also entered into the routing table. Therefore, if the variance is two, the router includes any additional routes to the same destination that have a cost up to twice that of the lowest-cost route. By default, the variance is one, limiting load balancing to only equal-cost routes.

When load balancing across unequal-cost paths, the router load balances proportionately to the metric of each route. Therefore, if two routes to the same destination are included in the routing table, and one has a metric that is three times that of the other, the router sends three packets along the lower-cost route for each packet it sends along the other route.

Tip

When troubleshooting intermittent connectivity problems, remember the load balancing behavior of IGRP. For example, if one out of every three ping packets fails, there is a good chance that unequal-cost load balancing is sending the failing packets across a different route.

Redistributing with EIGRP

Normally an administrator must manually configure a router to redistribute between two routing protocols, but one important exception exists. When IGRP and EIGRP share the same AS number, a router running both routing processes automatically redistributes routes in both directions. If this behavior is not desired, be sure to choose two different AS numbers.

Cross-Reference

You can still get IGRP and EIGRP to redistribute with different AS numbers by using the configuration commands covered in Chapter 8.

IGRP in the Routing Table

When IGRP is finished calculating route metrics and choosing routes, it inserts its routes into the IP routing table. The following routing table contains IGRP routes:

```
C    192.168.12.0/24 is directly connected, Serial0

C    192.168.13.0/24 is directly connected, Serial1

C    192.168.1.0/24 is directly connected, TokenRing0

I    192.168.2.0/24 [100/41312] via 192.168.12.2, 00:00:10, Serial0

I    192.168.3.0/24 [100/41312] via 192.168.13.3, 00:00:59, Serial1

I    192.168.23.0/24 [100/43062] via 192.168.13.3, 00:00:59, Serial1
                     [100/43062] via 192.168.12.2, 00:00:10, Serial0
```

From this routing table, you can see that each IGRP route is tagged with an "I" at the start of the line. After the destination network address, the administrative distance for IGRP (100 by default) is displayed, followed by the composite metric. The rest of the information is common to all IP routing table entries, and it includes the next hop, age, and outbound interface of the route.

Understanding EIGRP

EIGRP was developed by Cisco to overcome the limitations of distance vector routing protocols without requiring the overhead of link state routing protocols. Although it shares part of its name with IGRP, the two protocols have only a couple of similarities:

- EIGRP and IGRP are both Cisco-proprietary routing protocols.
- Like IGRP, EIGRP uses a metric that includes the bandwidth and delay of a route by default. It can also be configured to include reliability and load. The EIGRP metric is the same as the IGRP metric multiplied by a factor of 256.

In addition to these few similarities with IGRP, EIGRP has some important differences that make it completely unique:

- EIGRP does not use a periodic interval to exchange routing updates. Routers send incremental updates only when topology changes occur.
- EIGRP uses Hello packets to identify neighbors and establish adjacencies.
- EIGRP keeps information about neighbors' routes in a topology database. This information is used for quick recovery from route failure.

Some of these characteristics that differentiate EIGRP from IGRP are similar to link state protocols — for example, the use of Hellos, incremental updates, and the topology database. However, EIGRP does not maintain a whole network map in its topology database, and the metrics are calculated based on route information from neighbors, which is a distance vector behavior. Because of the similarities to both types of routing protocols, EIGRP is sometimes considered a hybrid protocol.

Because of its hybrid nature, EIGRP is usually a very fast-converging protocol. Despite the efficiency of EIGRP traffic, routing information gets propagated very quickly throughout the network. This can make EIGRP an excellent routing protocol for use in Cisco-only environments.

EIGRP Basics

EIGRP achieves a high degree of efficiency by incorporating the best features of both distance vector and link state protocols. By performing route calculations as a distance vector protocol, EIGRP routers do not need to save topology information about the entire internetwork. However, it does not broadcast its full routing table periodically to its neighbors. Instead, like link state protocols, EIGRP establishes adjacencies with its neighbors by sending Hello packets. Routing updates are sent between neighbors only when there is a topology change.

In addition to the efficiency that EIGRP gains from using Hellos rather than full routing table broadcasts, it reacts quickly to topology changes by using the information it stores in its topology database. Although it does not save information about the entire internetwork, EIGRP maintains a database of the routes that each of its neighbors has in its routing table.

When there is a topology change that makes the active route invalid, EIGRP checks the routing tables of its neighbors (which it stores in its topology database) and determines if any neighbors have another route to that destination. This way, the routing process has the capability to choose a new route immediately, without waiting for information from other routers.

Like IGRP, EIGRP routers belong to an AS. All routers in the AS share routing information, but they do not share information with routers in other ASes. The AS is identified by number, which can be in the range of 1 through 65,535. The AS number is assigned to the router when you enter the router eigrp configuration command.

The strongest likeness between IGRP and EIGRP is their metric. EIGRP calculates metrics in the same way as IGRP, except that it multiplies the metric by a factor of 256. This allows for easy conversion of metrics between the two protocols. The following sections describe EIGRP in more detail.

Adjacencies and Hello Packets

Like link state routing protocols, EIGRP uses Hello packets to establish adjacencies between neighboring routers. This saves bandwidth because the small Hello packets replace large broadcast packets that contain full routing table information. The Hellos allow EIGRP routers to learn of their neighbors as they become available, and they can check their neighbors' configurations to determine whether an adjacency is in order. After establishing a new adjacency, a router exchanges all of its pertinent routing information with the neighbor. Using those established adjacencies, EIGRP determines which neighbors are affected by topology changes and sends updates only to the affected neighbors.

Rather than broadcasting information to its neighbors, EIGRP multicasts Hellos using a well-known destination address. This saves processing cycles on other network devices that do not speak EIGRP. When any device receives a broadcast, it must process the packet to determine whether or not it needs the information. On the other hand, multicast packets can be filtered by the Network Interface Card (NIC) hardware, which prevents the device from needlessly processing the packet.

EIGRP Hellos contain the following information:

- The EIGRP version number
- The AS number

- The values of the K-constants, *K1–K5*
- The hold time

At this time, the EIGRP version is always 1. The AS number is assigned by the administrator when configuring EIGRP. The K-constants are used to calculate the metric of each EIGRP route. The hold time indicates how long the receiving router should wait before removing the sending router from the neighbor table, unless another Hello is received.

An EIGRP router establishes an adjacency with a neighbor only if both are using the same AS number and the same values of the K-constants. This way, administrators can separate routers into multiple EIGRP ASes, and routers do not establish an adjacency if they are using different information to make their routing decisions.

Establishing an adjacency is not a two-way process, as in OSPF. In EIGRP, when a router receives a valid Hello from a neighbor, it immediately establishes an adjacency and enters the neighbor into its neighbor table. This may all take place before the neighbor has received a Hello from this router, which makes the adjacency one-way. However, unlike OSPF, there is no way for EIGRP to determine whether its neighbor has recognized it as a neighbor. If this router attempts to send routing information to its new neighbor while the adjacency is still one-way, the neighbor will ignore the updates until it has first received a Hello from this router.

Routing Updates

The use of Hello packets to establish and maintain adjacencies provides EIGRP with the flexibility to use incremental routing updates. In addition, the routing updates are *bounded*, meaning they are sent only to the neighbors that are affected.

The key to EIGRP routing updates is the use of its *Reliable Transport Protocol (RTP)*. EIGRP RTP uses a mix of multicast and unicast packets to achieve a maximum of reliability with a minimum of bandwidth use. Acknowledgements (ACKs) and replies are always sent as unicast packets to particular neighbors. Hellos, queries, and updates are sent as multicast packets whenever possible (EIGRP uses the multicast IP address 224.0.0.10.). They may be sent as unicast packets to each neighbors over any transmission medium that does not allow the use of multicasts. In addition, whenever a router needs to retransmit a multicast packet to a neighbor that has not acknowledged the packet, it retransmits that packet as a unicast.

Hello packets and ACKs are unreliable in nature and need not be acknowledged. Updates, queries, and replies are reliable and require acknowledgement. Every reliable packet sent by a router has a sequence number, which is incremented for every packet sent from the router. The sequence number is global to all EIGRP packets sent from the router, independent of the destination, so reliable unicast and multicast packets use the same pool of sequence numbers. Therefore, a router receives a non-contiguous series of sequence numbers from each of its neighbors. Because sequence numbers are noncontiguous, all neighbors must acknowledge each reliable packet individually. The sending router queues outgoing packets destined for a neighbor until the currently outstanding packet to that neighbor is acknowledged. Although this slows down delivery of packets, it assures reliability and keeps bandwidth use to a minimum.

All reliable packets can be acknowledged by an ACK packet, but the acknowledgement can also be contained in another unicast packet destined for that neighbor. Whenever possible, a *piggyback ACK* is used. Every EIGRP packet contains a sequence number field and a separate ACK field. The sequence number field in an ACK packet is always zero, and the ACK field in most other EIGRP packets is zero. However, if the outgoing packet is unicast, the ACK field can contain the sequence number of a packet to be acknowledged, yielding a piggyback ACK.

To determine an appropriate retransmission interval for unacknowl-edged packets, EIGRP routers measure the round trip time (RTT) of each packet that is sent to and acknowledged by a neighbor. Using the packet RTTs for each neighbor, the router calculates a smoothed round trip time (SRTT) and stores it in the neighbor table. It also calculates the mean SRTT for all routers on each interface and stores that as a property of the interface.

The initial retransmission timeout (RTO) for each packet sent to a neighbor is calculated as a function of the SRTT and the pacing interval. (See "EIGRP Pacing" for an explanation of the pacing interval.) For each retransmission of the packet, the RTO is increased by 50 percent, until the maximum number of retries is reached. RTP retransmits a packet 16 times before declaring a neighbor dead. Note that the neighbor is declared dead regardless of the remaining hold time.

Metrics

EIGRP metrics are calculated in a similar way to IGRP metrics. They are both calculated based on the same characteristics — bandwidth, delay, reliability, and load — and those affect the metric in the same way. In fact, the two metrics are almost the same — the EIGRP metric is simply a factor greater than the IGRP metric.

Because EIGRP and IGRP use such a similar metric, please read the "Metrics" section under "Understanding IGRP" earlier in this chapter before continuing with this section. Most of the information in that section is also true for EIGRP, so it will not be repeated here. There are a few differences, however, which are explained next.

Tip

The use of load and reliability in metric calculation is discouraged with EIGRP. The incremental updates used by EIGRP make these two values of limited use. With IGRP, the router recalculates those values with each periodic update, but with EIGRP, the values reflect the properties of the link at the time of the most recent incremental update. Therefore, that information is unlikely to be current and would not be meaningful.

The following equation is used by EIGRP to calculate the composite metric:

$$metric = 256 \times \left(K1 \times B + \frac{K2 \times B}{256 - L} + K3 \times D \right) \times \frac{K5}{R + K4}$$

Note that the only difference with the IGRP metric equation is the inclusion of the first multiplication term (256). As with IGRP, the last (rightmost) fraction in the equation is only used if $K5$ is not equal to zero. The terms B, D, L, and R all have the same meaning as in the IGRP equation.

The K-constants are also the same as those in IGRP, and they default to the same values ($K1 = K3 = 1$, and $K2 = K4 = K5 = 0$.) Therefore, with those values unchanged, the EIGRP metric equation can be reduced to the following:

$metric = 256 \times (B + D)$

The K-constants need to be the same across all EIGRP routers in order for routing to function correctly. In fact, EIGRP routers include the values of the K-constants in their Hello packets. If two neighbors have different values for their K-constants, they cannot become adjacent.

Load Balancing and Variance

Load balancing works exactly the same for EIGRP as it does for IGRP. Please refer to the section "Load Balancing and Variance" within the section "Understanding IGRP" for the detailed explanation.

EIGRP Pacing

In order to prevent routing updates from consuming too much bandwidth on lower-speed links, EIGRP uses a unique mechanism known as *pacing*. With pacing, EIGRP limits its traffic to a fraction of the recognized bandwidth of an interface (the default or that configured with the `bandwidth` configuration command). The limited traffic includes anything generated by EIGRP, including Hellos, updates, queries, replies, and ACKs.

By default, EIGRP limits itself to 50 percent of the bandwidth of an interface. To change the percentage of bandwidth used by EIGRP, use the `ip bandwidth-percent eigrp` interface configuration command.

Feasible Successors

The reason that EIGRP converges so quickly has a lot to do with the use of *feasible successors*. An understanding of feasible successors is integral to understanding EIGRP as a whole. Feasible successors (or the lack thereof) significantly impact the convergence time during topology changes.

Feasible successors are a fairly simple concept — they resemble backup routes. Using the example network shown in Figure 3-1, this section explains the procedure that is followed by R1 when it calculates its route(s) to 192.168.5.0/24. Assume that R1 has received all routing updates from its neighbors and that the internetwork is currently stable.

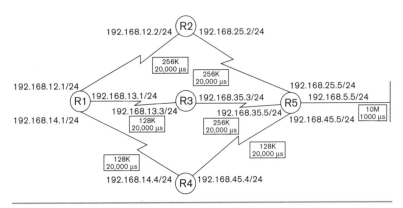

Figure 3-1 *A small EIGRP network with several redundant paths. The bandwidth and delay of each link are indicated.*

The routing information that R1 receives from its neighbors (R2, R3, and R4) includes each neighbor's vector metric to 192.168.5.0/24. With this information, R1 calculates its own vector metric to 192.168.5.0/24 through each neighbor. Then it calculates its own composite metric for each route, along with each neighbor's composite metric to the same destination. The values computed by R1 are as follows:

Neighbor Metric	Local Bandwidth	Local Delay	Local Comp. Metric	Neighbor Bandwidth	Neighbor Delay	Neighbor Comp. Metric
R2	256	4100	11,049,472	256	2100	10,537,472
R3	128	4100	21,049,600	256	2100	10,537,472
R4	128	4100	21,049,600	128	2100	20,537,600

Tip

It is important to note here that the delay values in the table are a tenth of those that you get by adding the values in the diagram. Remember that the composite metric calculation uses delay in units of tens of microseconds, rather than microseconds.

The path with the lowest local composite metric is chosen as the active route. In this case, R1 chooses to route through R2 to reach 192.168.5.0/24 because the local metric for the path through R2 is the lowest. Because R2 is the downstream neighbor (or next hop) for the active route, it is called the *successor* for 192.168.5.0/24.

The metric that R1 advertises to its neighbors is 11,049,472—the metric of the active route. This metric is also R1's feasible distance to 192.168.5.0/24.

After choosing the successor and determining the feasible distance, R1 looks for any feasible successors to reach 192.168.5.0/24. For that destination, it compares the composite metric of each neighbor with its feasible distance. Any neighbor with a metric lower than R1's feasible distance becomes a feasible successor. Because R3's metric (10,537,472) is lower than the feasible distance and R4's metric (20,537,600) is greater, R3 is a feasible successor to 192.168.5.0/24, but R4 is not.

When using variance to do unequal-cost load balancing, only feasible successors are included, even though the route through other neighbors may be valid based on the variance. As a rule, a router never considers a neighbor that is not a feasible successor to a destination to be a valid route to that destination.

The reasoning behind the selection of feasible successors is as follows: If a neighbor has a lower metric to a destination than the local router, then it cannot be routing through the local router. If R3 were routing to 192.168.5.0/24 through R1, by definition, R3's metric to 192.168.5.0/24 would have to be greater than the feasible distance of R1. Because this is not the case, R3 must be downstream from R1 toward the destination.

This brings up an important aspect of feasible successors: Not all possible downstream routers are necessarily selected as feasible successors. In the example, R4 is still downstream from R1 (it is not routing through R1 to reach 192.168.5.0/24), but it is not chosen as a feasible successor because R1 does not know the route selected by R4; the metric is the only information it can use to guess. Because R4 has a higher metric to reach 192.168.5.0/24 than R1, there is a chance that R4 could be routing through R1. R1 cannot take the chance of creating a routing loop, so it must assume the worst and not include R4 as a feasible successor.

The drawback to this method is that in some cases, potential downstream neighbors are not chosen as feasible successors. This means that the network may not converge as quickly in some cases after a topology change. However, this method prevents routing loops from forming while the network is converging. For more information on convergence, please read the following section on Diffusing Update Algorithm (DUAL).

Diffusing Update Algorithm

The *Diffusing Update Algorithm* (*DUAL*) is the heart of EIGRP. It provides a convergence method for EIGRP that avoids routing loops throughout the convergence process. Like Dijkstra's algorithm (used in link state routing protocols such as OSPF and IS-IS), DUAL is very complex, and a thorough explanation is well beyond the scope of this text. However, a basic understanding of DUAL is required to understand routing with EIGRP. With this understanding, you should be able to follow the events that take place when your network converges.

When a router receives an update from the successor for a particular destination that indicates an increase in the metric, it tries to find a better route to the destination. To find a better route, it first looks for a feasible successor to that destination. If a feasible successor is found with a better metric, then the router immediately chooses that neighbor as the new successor. It also notifies its neighbors of the increase in its own metric to the destination. In this case, the route remains passive.

When a router cannot make a decision on its own in response to a topology change, it starts a diffusing computation. There are three reasons that a router may need to start a diffusing computation:

- No alternate route exists.
- The new best route still goes through the successor that is advertising the increased metric.
- The new best route does not go through a feasible successor.

The diffusing computation requires the router to query its neighbors for information regarding the destination in question. It starts by marking the particular route active in the topology table. Then it creates a table of neighbor responses so that it can track whether or not it has received responses from all neighbors. It also starts an active timer for the route, which is three minutes by default.

Then the router sends a query to each neighbor. First, each receiving router uses the information in the query to eliminate previously learned information from the sending router about that route. Then it processes the query in the following way:

- If the router has no information about the destination in question, it immediately replies with an infinite metric.

- If the route is already active, the router sends information about its current best route and stops processing this query.

- If the query is not from the successor, the router replies with its current best route, and the route remains passive.

- If the query is received from the only successor and there are no other EIGRP neighbors (this is a stub router), it replies with an infinite metric.

- If the router has other routes toward the destination, it selects the new best route and reports the new route to the query sender.

- If no alternate route exists, the new best route is through the router that sent the query, or the new best route is not through a feasible successor, the router propagates the query to is neighbors. Its neighbors go through this same process upon receiving the propagated query.

A querying router stores all responses in its topology table. After all of the neighbors have responded to a query, the router does one of two things. If it propagated the query from another router, it formulates its response to that router based on the new topology information. If it is the router that originated the query, it selects a new best route from the updated topology table, if a route exists. When a new route is chosen, the router sends an update to its neighbors.

If any router waits so long for a reply that the active timer for that route expires, the route is declared stuck-in-active (SIA). The unresponsive neighbor is declared dead and removed from the routing table. In addition, all routes from that neighbor are removed from the topology database. The default active timer is three minutes, and it can be changed in the EIGRP configuration. SIAs usually indicate a problem in the internetwork, and they should generally not happen.

As you can see from the layout of these basic rules, a diffusing computation can be complicated. This is especially true when a router is responding to multiple events at one time, such as when a link outage affects routes to many destinations. However, the well-defined rules that DUAL follows can help an administrator understand the events during a diffusing computation.

Redistributing with IGRP

Normally an administrator must manually configure a router to redistribute between two routing protocols, but one important exception exists. When IGRP and EIGRP share the same AS number, a router running both routing processes automatically redistributes routes in both directions. If this behavior is not desired, be sure to choose two different AS numbers.

Cross-Reference

You can still get IGRP and EIGRP to redistribute with different AS numbers by using the configuration commands covered in Chapter 8.

EIGRP in the Routing Table

After calculating the metrics for the routes and determining the load balancing for each destination, EIGRP installs its routes into the IP routing table. The following routing table contains EIGRP routes:

```
C    192.168.12.0/24 is directly connected, Serial0

C    192.168.13.0/24 is directly connected, Serial1

C    192.168.1.0/24 is directly connected, TokenRing0

D    192.168.2.0/24 [90/10575872] via 192.168.12.2, 22:26:00, Serial0

D    192.168.3.0/24 [90/10575872] via 192.168.13.3, 22:26:00, Serial1

D    192.168.23.0/24 [90/11023872] via 192.168.13.3, 22:26:00, Serial1
                     [90/11023872] via 192.168.12.2, 22:26:00, Serial0
```

From this routing table, you can see that EIGRP routes are tagged with a "D" at the start of each line. If there is no other tag before the destination IP network address, the route was internally generated by the EIGRP routing process. However, any routes that are redistributed from another routing protocol or static routes are tagged with "EX" (for external).

After the destination IP network address, you can see the administrative distance and composite metric in brackets. The administrative distance for internal EIGRP routes is 90 by default. External EIGRP routes have a default administrative distance of 170. Therefore, even though EIGRP is a highly preferred routing protocol, EIGRP external routes are less preferred and can be replaced by routes from other routing protocols. This helps prevent routing loops associated with redistribution.

EIGRP Authentication

EIGRP has the capability to authenticate routing updates using an MD5 cryptographic checksum. Unlike some of the other routing protocols that support authentication, there is no option in EIGRP to use plain-text passwords. Although this may seem odd, you should not use plain-text passwords with other protocols unless absolutely necessary. Because Cisco controls all implementations of EIGRP, and because they included MD5 authentication from the start, there will never be a case when an EIGRP router does not support MD5.

The authentication information is carried in all EIGRP packets. An authentication example is included with the EIGRP configuration examples later in this chapter.

Configuring IGRP

Configuring IGRP is very similar to configuring RIP. Both are very simple to configure, and they usually only require additional modification if there is some special need on the particular network. Although you can tweak the behavior with fine detail by changing timers and interface parameters, it is advised that you do so only for some very specific reason on your network.

Basic IGRP Configuration

The network shown in Figure 3-2 is a small, three-site network that is fully meshed, and each site has only one LAN. This network is sufficient to demonstrate most configuration options for IGRP.

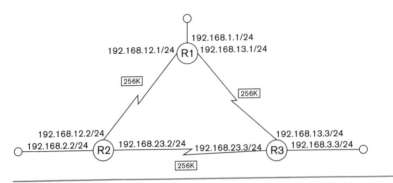

Figure 3-2 *A simple internetwork with three sites, each with one LAN. The bandwidth of each link is indicated.*

Getting a router to communicate with other routers running IGRP is very simple. Simply enable the IGRP routing process on the router and then configure the networks on which IGRP will run. Remember that all routers must share the same IGRP AS number, or they will ignore each other's routing updates. The configuration of R1 is as follows:

```
interface Serial0
 ip address 192.168.12.1 255.255.255.0
 bandwidth 256
!
interface Serial1
 ip address 192.168.13.1 255.255.255.0
 bandwidth 256
!
interface TokenRing0
 ip address 192.168.1.1 255.255.255.0
!
router igrp 1
 network 192.168.12.0
 network 192.168.13.0
 network 192.168.1.0
```

R2 and R3 are configured in the same way, with the exception of the interface IP addresses and IGRP network statements. With all three routers configured as such, waiting long enough for the routing updates to be sent (at most 90 seconds) reveals IGRP routes in R1:

```
R1#show ip route
Codes: C - connected, S - static, I - IGRP, R - RIP, M - mobile, B - BGP
       D - EIGRP, EX - EIGRP external, O - OSPF, IA - OSPF inter area
       N1 - OSPF NSSA external type 1, N2 - OSPF NSSA external type 2
       E1 - OSPF external type 1, E2 - OSPF external type 2, E - EGP
       i - IS-IS, L1 - IS-IS level-1, L2 - IS-IS level-2, * - candidate default
       U - per-user static route, o - ODR


Gateway of last resort is not set


C    192.168.12.0/24 is directly connected, Serial0
C    192.168.13.0/24 is directly connected, Serial1
C    192.168.1.0/24 is directly connected, TokenRing0
I    192.168.2.0/24 [100/41312] via 192.168.12.2, 00:00:10, Serial0
I    192.168.3.0/24 [100/41312] via 192.168.13.3, 00:00:59, Serial1
I    192.168.23.0/24 [100/43062] via 192.168.13.3, 00:00:59, Serial1
                     [100/43062] via 192.168.12.2, 00:00:10, Serial0
```

Notice that not only are the routes to 192.168.2.0/24 and 192.168.3.0/24 present, but the route to the serial link 192.168.23.0/24 is present, and it is being load balanced across two equal-cost paths through R2 and R3.

Modifying Load Balancing Behavior

With the current configuration of the example network, you can see that R1 is load balancing across two equal-cost paths to the destination 192.168.23.0/24. By default, IGRP load balances across a maximum of four equal-cost paths. However, it can be configured to load balance across any number of paths from one to six. To change this behavior, use the max-imum-paths command in IGRP configuration mode:

```
R1(config-router)#maximum-paths 6
```

Note that the `maximum-paths` statement has the same effect on unequal-cost load balancing (when enabled) as it does on equal-cost load balancing. Only the specified number of routes are accepted into the routing table for load balancing of either type.

You can enable unequal-cost load balancing in IGRP with the `variance` command. The `variance` command accepts an integer value in the range of 1 through 128. The default value is 1, which means that no unequal-cost load balancing will take place. For a thorough explanation of how variance works, please read "Load Balancing and Variance" in the section "Understanding IGRP."

The network in Figure 3-3 has the same layout of that in Figure 3-2. However, the link between R1 and R3 is 128 Kbps, rather than 256 Kbps.

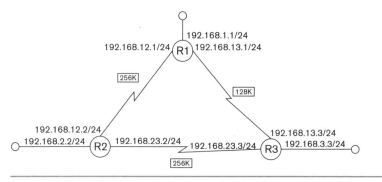

Figure 3-3 *A very simple, small network with unequal bandwidth links. The bandwidth of each link is indicated.*

In this network, R2 is the preferred route to 192.168.3.0/24 and 192.168.23.0/24 from R1 because of the bandwidth difference. Therefore, R2 is selected as the next hop for that destination in the routing table of R1, as shown here:

```
R1#sh ip route

Codes: C - connected, S - static, I - IGRP, R - RIP, M - mobile, B - BGP

       D - EIGRP, EX - EIGRP external, O - OSPF, IA - OSPF inter area

       N1 - OSPF NSSA external type 1, N2 - OSPF NSSA external type 2

       E1 - OSPF external type 1, E2 - OSPF external type 2, E - EGP

       i - IS-IS, L1 - IS-IS level-1, L2 - IS-IS level-2, * - candidate default
```

```
        U - per-user static route, o - ODR

Gateway of last resort is not set

C    192.168.12.0/24 is directly connected, Serial0

C    192.168.13.0/24 is directly connected, Serial1

C    192.168.1.0/24 is directly connected, TokenRing0

I    192.168.2.0/24 [100/41312] via 192.168.12.2, 00:00:37, Serial0

I    192.168.3.0/24 [100/43312] via 192.168.12.2, 00:00:37, Serial0

I    192.168.23.0/24 [100/43062] via 192.168.12.2, 00:00:37, Serial0
```

Note that networks 192.168.3.0/24 and 192.168.23.0/24 each have only one route in the routing table. To change the variance of R1 to two, use the following IGRP configuration command:

```
R1(config-router)#variance 2
```

With the updated variance, the routing table of R1 looks like this:

```
R1#sh ip route

Codes: C - connected, S - static, I - IGRP, R - RIP, M - mobile, B - BGP

       D - EIGRP, EX - EIGRP external, O - OSPF, IA - OSPF inter area

       N1 - OSPF NSSA external type 1, N2 - OSPF NSSA external type 2

       E1 - OSPF external type 1, E2 - OSPF external type 2, E - EGP

       i - IS-IS, L1 - IS-IS level-1, L2 - IS-IS level-2, * - candidate default

       U - per-user static route, o - ODR

Gateway of last resort is not set

C    192.168.12.0/24 is directly connected, Serial0

C    192.168.13.0/24 is directly connected, Serial1

C    192.168.1.0/24 is directly connected, TokenRing0

I    192.168.2.0/24 [100/41312] via 192.168.12.2, 00:00:37, Serial0

I    192.168.3.0/24 [100/43312] via 192.168.12.2, 00:00:37, Serial0

                    [100/80375] via 192.168.13.3, 00:00:44, Serial1

I    192.168.23.0/24 [100/43062] via 192.168.12.2, 00:00:37, Serial0

                     [100/82125] via 192.168.13.3, 00:00:44, Serial1
```

Notice that the routes to both 192.168.3.0/24 and 192.168.23.0/24 are being load balanced across unequal-cost paths. The metrics of the paths through R3 are just under twice those of the paths through R2, which meets the requirement of a variance of two.

When doing unequal-cost load balancing, there is an implicit `traffic-share balanced` command as part of the configuration. This means that load balancing is done in such a way that each path receives an amount of traffic inversely proportional to its metric. In the preceding example, R2 receives twice as much traffic destined for 192.168.3.0/24 as R3 because the metric through R3 is about twice that of the metric through R2. You can see this by looking at the details of the routing table entry:

```
R1#show ip route 192.168.3.0

Routing entry for 192.168.3.0/24

  Known via "igrp 1", distance 100, metric 43312

  Redistributing via igrp 1

  Advertised by igrp 1 (self originated)

  Last update from 192.168.12.2 on Serial0, 00:00:03 ago

  Routing Descriptor Blocks:

  * 192.168.12.2, from 192.168.12.2, 00:00:03 ago, via Serial0

    Route metric is 43312, traffic share count is 2

    Total delay is 42500 microseconds, minimum bandwidth is 256 Kbit

    Reliability 255/255, minimum MTU 1500 bytes

    Loading 1/255, Hops 1

  192.168.13.3, from 192.168.13.3, 00:00:23 ago, via Serial1

    Route metric is 80375, traffic share count is 1

    Total delay is 22500 microseconds, minimum bandwidth is 128 Kbit

    Reliability 255/255, minimum MTU 1500 bytes

    Loading 1/255, Hops 0
```

Notice that the route through R2 has a traffic share count of 2, whereas the route through R3 has a traffic share count of 1. This is the ratio in which the two routes receive traffic to that destination.

However, it is also possible to have IGRP install unequal-cost paths into the routing table but route only over the lowest-cost path(s). This can aid reconvergence time, and it may help with troubleshooting to have more paths appear in the routing table, even if you do not want to route across them.

In order to have the router retain multiple paths but route over only those with the lowest cost, you must start by configuring the variance as shown above, so the additional routes appear in the routing table. Then add the following command to the IGRP configuration:

```
R1(config-router)#traffic-share min
```

Now the traffic is only routed across the lowest-cost path(s), but other paths that meet the variance requirement also appear in the routing table. No change can be seen in the full routing table, but a look at the details of the specific destination reveals the following:

```
R1#show ip route 192.168.3.0

Routing entry for 192.168.3.0/24

  Known via "igrp 1", distance 100, metric 43312

  Redistributing via igrp 1

  Advertised by igrp 1 (self originated)

  Last update from 192.168.12.2 on Serial0, 00:00:46 ago

  Routing Descriptor Blocks:

  * 192.168.12.2, from 192.168.12.2, 00:00:46 ago, via Serial0

      Route metric is 43312, traffic share count is 1

      Total delay is 42500 microseconds, minimum bandwidth is 256 Kbit

      Reliability 255/255, minimum MTU 1500 bytes

      Loading 1/255, Hops 1

    192.168.13.3, from 192.168.13.3, 00:01:10 ago, via Serial1

      Route metric is 80375, traffic share count is 0

      Total delay is 22500 microseconds, minimum bandwidth is 128 Kbit

      Reliability 255/255, minimum MTU 1500 bytes

      Loading 1/255, Hops 0
```

Now the traffic share count through R2 is 1, and the traffic share count through R3 is zero (0). Therefore, as long as the route through R2 is valid, R3 will not receive any traffic from R1 bound for 192.168.3.0/24.

Controlling Route Selection

To change the calculation done to select routes, you can use the `metric weights` command to change the values of the K-constants used in the IGRP metric equation. By default, $K1 = K3 = 1$, and $K2 = K4 = K5 = 0$. This means that only bandwidth and delay are used in the metric calculations by default. To change any or all of these values, enter the following command in IGRP configuration mode:

```
R1(config-router)#metric weights 0 K1 K2 K3 K4 K5
```

Note that the $K1 - K5$ variables must be replaced with integers in the range of 0 through 4,294,967,295. The zero in the preceding example is the type of service (ToS) metric, and it is not currently supported. It is recommended that the K-constants be changed only if you fully understand their impact. Some of the most common configurations include the following:

- To configure IGRP to use bandwidth, delay, load, and reliability as intended by the designers of the protocol, set all K-constants to 1:

  ```
  metric weights 0 1 1 1 1 1
  ```

- To configure IGRP to use only delay in metric calculations, set the following:

  ```
  metric weights 0 0 0 1 0 0
  ```

  This can be used to make IGRP disregard bandwidth. Note that if the delay of each interface is configured to be the same value, IGRP will effectively route based on hop count.

- To configure IGRP to use only the bandwidth in metric calculations, set the following:

  ```
  metric weights 0 1 0 0 0 0
  ```

  This will result in the path with the lowest end-to-end bandwidth always being chosen above all other possible routes.

Any other configurations are not recommended, unless the administrator is confident of the outcome. It is especially dangerous to change the constants to values other than 1 or 0, as that can severely impact the composite metric. Make sure to configure all IGRP routers with the same K-constants.

To make IGRP more or less preferred to other routing protocols, you can use the `distance` command. The default administrative distance of IGRP is 100, but it can be changed locally. For example, to make IGRP the most preferred source of routes after connected and static routes, enter the following configuration command:

```
R1(config-router)#distance 10
```

The configured administrative distance is only locally significant, and it appears in the IGRP routing table entries.

To make a particular route less appealing to a router, an offset list can be used to increase its metric. Offset lists can also be used in RIP, and they work the same way. They provide finer control over the routes chosen to certain destinations.

Refer to the same example network shown in Figure 3-3 again, and assume that R1 is not configured for unequal-cost load balancing. Traffic from R1 destined for192.168.3.0/24 is routed through R2, as shown in this routing table:

```
R1#show ip route
Codes: C - connected, S - static, I - IGRP, R - RIP, M - mobile, B - BGP
       D - EIGRP, EX - EIGRP external, O - OSPF, IA - OSPF inter area
       N1 - OSPF NSSA external type 1, N2 - OSPF NSSA external type 2
       E1 - OSPF external type 1, E2 - OSPF external type 2, E - EGP
       i - IS-IS, L1 - IS-IS level-1, L2 - IS-IS level-2, * - candidate default
       U - per-user static route, o - ODR


Gateway of last resort is not set


C    192.168.12.0/24 is directly connected, Serial0
C    192.168.13.0/24 is directly connected, Serial1
C    192.168.1.0/24 is directly connected, TokenRing0
I    192.168.2.0/24 [100/41312] via 192.168.12.2, 00:01:02, Serial0
I    192.168.3.0/24 [100/43312] via 192.168.12.2, 00:01:02, Serial0
I    192.168.23.0/24 [100/43062] via 192.168.12.2, 00:01:02, Serial0
```

If we would rather have traffic to 192.168.3.0/24 routed through R3 but do not want to change the bandwidth and/or delay of any interfaces (this would affect all routes), we can use the following configuration commands:

```
R1(config)#access-list 20 permit 192.168.3.0 0.0.0.0
R1(config)#router igrp 1
R1(config-router)#offset-list 20 in 50000 Serial 0
```

This adds 50,000 to any inbound routes received on Serial0 that match access list 20. Access list 20 matches only 192.168.3.0. Because of the increased metric, the route through R2 goes into holddown on R1, but after the holddown timer expires, the metric of that route is 93,315, which is greater than the metric through R3. Therefore, R3 is chosen as the next hop, as shown here:

```
R1#show ip route
Codes: C - connected, S - static, I - IGRP, R - RIP, M - mobile, B - BGP
       D - EIGRP, EX - EIGRP external, O - OSPF, IA - OSPF inter area
       N1 - OSPF NSSA external type 1, N2 - OSPF NSSA external type 2
       E1 - OSPF external type 1, E2 - OSPF external type 2, E - EGP
       i - IS-IS, L1 - IS-IS level-1, L2 - IS-IS level-2, * - candidate default
       U - per-user static route, o - ODR


Gateway of last resort is not set

C    192.168.12.0/24 is directly connected, Serial0
C    192.168.13.0/24 is directly connected, Serial1
C    192.168.1.0/24 is directly connected, TokenRing0
I    192.168.2.0/24 [100/41312] via 192.168.12.2, 00:00:38, Serial0
I    192.168.3.0/24 [100/80375] via 192.168.13.3, 00:00:13, Serial1
I    192.168.23.0/24 [100/43062] via 192.168.12.2, 00:00:38, Serial0
```

An offset list can be applied to either inbound or outbound route updates, depending on the desired result.

Caution

Using the `offset-list` command changes the metrics of routes that are advertised or received. If the metric of an active route is increased locally or on a neighbor, the route may go into holddown and be advertised as unreachable until the holddown timer expires.

Changing IGRP Timers

Another means of modifying the behavior of IGRP to better suit a particular network is to change its timers. Like other IGRP behaviors, the timers should only be changed when necessary and after careful evaluation of the consequences. It is also important to make sure that all routers are configured with the same timers, or the IGRP routing process will fail to function correctly.

The following configuration command changes the IGRP timers:

```
R1(config-router)#timers basic update invalid holddown flush [sleep]
```

Each of the timer values must be an integer with a maximum of 4,294,967,295. The minimum value for the update and holddown timers is 0, and the minimum value for the others is 1. The sleep timer is not required when entering this command. For a detailed explanation of each of these timers, please read "Routing Table Updates" in the section "Understanding IGRP."

To disable holddown, use the following command in IGRP configuration mode:

```
R1(config-router)#no metric holddown
```

This prevents routes from entering holddown when they become inaccessible. This has the advantage of speedier reconvergence, but disabling holddown also makes routing loops more likely. Disable holddown only on internetworks that are built without loops.

Modifying Other IGRP Behavior

IGRP includes the hop count in the vector metric to detect routing loops. The maximum hop count of an IGRP network is 100, and it can be configured to be as high as 255 hops. This offers a significant increase in flexibility over RIP, which has a maximum hop count of 15. To set the maximum hop count, use the following command in IGRP configuration mode:

```
R1(config-router)#metric maximum-hops 20
```

The parameter accepted by the command is the number of hops, in the range of 1 through 255. If IGRP encounters a route with a hop count greater than the maximum, it considers that route unreachable. An excessively high maximum hop count makes it harder to detect routing loops, but a low maximum hop count results in valid routes being discarded as unreachable. Choose a maximum hop count carefully, and make sure that all routers on the network are configured with the same value.

If the network attached to a particular interface should be included in routing updates, it must be listed in a classful network command in the IGRP configuration. However, this also configures the router to send IGRP routing updates from that interface. To disable this behavior but still advertise that network, use the passive-interface configuration command. For example, to disable the sending of IGRP updates to the 192.168.1.0/24 LAN, issue the following IGRP configuration command on R1:

```
R1(config-router)#passive-interface TokenRing 0
```

Please note that making TokenRing0 a passive interface only suppresses outbound routing updates. Any updates received on a passive interface are processed as any other routing update. To configure a router to ignore routing updates on an interface, apply an access list to inbound traffic on that interface.

By default, IGRP uses broadcast routing updates to send its routing table to all hosts on a network. However, some media, including Frame Relay networks, do not allow the use of broadcasts. To use IGRP when broadcasts are not allowed, explicitly configure IGRP with the addresses of all neighbors on the network in question. The neighbor command simply takes an IP address, as shown here:

```
R10(config-router)#neighbor 192.168.10.1
```

When configured with this command, R10 sends unicast routing table advertisements to 192.168.10.1.

Split horizon is enabled for IGRP by default, but it can be disabled on individual interfaces. Split horizon is a critical feature of distance vector protocols, and disabling it is discouraged in most cases. The most common reason to disable split horizon is that it prevents hub routers on nonbroadcast multi-access (NBMA) networks (such as Frame Relay or X.25) from advertising routes learned from spoke routers to other spoke routers. In this case, disabling split horizon allows the hub router to advertise routes learned from the NBMA network back to the routers on the NBMA network. To disable split horizon, enter the following configuration command in interface configuration mode:

```
R1(config-if)#no ip split-horizon
```

Configuring EIGRP

Getting a network to run EIGRP is a very simple task. As with IGRP, the only required steps are enabling the EIGRP routing process and defining the networks on which EIGRP should run. However, EIGRP does offer additional options for advanced configuration, over and above those offered by IGRP.

Basic EIGRP Configuration

In this example, we configure the small three-site network shown in Figure 3-2 to run EIGRP. The configuration of R1 as shown here is almost identical to its configuration when running IGRP:

```
interface Serial0
 ip address 192.168.12.1 255.255.255.0
 bandwidth 256
!
interface Serial1
 ip address 192.168.13.1 255.255.255.0
 bandwidth 256
!
```

```
interface TokenRing0
 ip address 192.168.1.1 255.255.255.0
!
router eigrp 1
 network 192.168.12.0
 network 192.168.13.0
 network 192.168.1.0
```

The configurations of R2 and R3 are different only in regard to IP host and network addressing. In addition, the routing table with the EIGRP routes looks much like it did earlier for IGRP:

```
R1#show ip route
Codes: C - connected, S - static, I - IGRP, R - RIP, M - mobile, B - BGP
       D - EIGRP, EX - EIGRP external, O - OSPF, IA - OSPF inter area
       N1 - OSPF NSSA external type 1, N2 - OSPF NSSA external type 2
       E1 - OSPF external type 1, E2 - OSPF external type 2, E - EGP
       i - IS-IS, L1 - IS-IS level-1, L2 - IS-IS level-2, * - candidate default
       U - per-user static route, o - ODR


Gateway of last resort is not set


C    192.168.12.0/24 is directly connected, Serial0
C    192.168.13.0/24 is directly connected, Serial1
C    192.168.1.0/24 is directly connected, TokenRing0
D    192.168.2.0/24 [90/10575872] via 192.168.12.2, 20:43:03, Serial0
D    192.168.3.0/24 [90/10575872] via 192.168.13.3, 20:43:03, Serial1
D    192.168.23.0/24 [90/11023872] via 192.168.13.3, 20:43:03, Serial1
                     [90/11023872] via 192.168.12.2, 20:43:03, Serial0
```

This similarity is really not limited to IGRP and EIGRP. Most routing protocols, if configured correctly on this network, should end up with a routing table similar to this one. However, the differences here are of particular importance. First, the EIGRP metrics are 256 times higher than those from IGRP. Second, the age of the routes is much higher than would ever be seen in IGRP (over 20 hours in this case) because EIGRP uses incremental updates, whereas IGRP uses periodic updates. An EIGRP route does not have an age limit, so it continues to age until it becomes unavailable or a better route is found. Not only is an IGRP route refreshed every 90 seconds, but it also has a flush timer that prevents routes from getting more than 630 seconds old before being removed from the routing table. It is important to remember that the age of each route in the routing table reflects the behavior of its source routing protocol.

Disabling Auto-Summarization

Unlike IGRP, EIGRP is a classless routing protocol. Therefore, it includes subnet mask information with the routing updates that it sends. This allows routes to subnets to be preserved across the entire internetwork, regardless of classful network boundaries. However, by default, EIGRP has auto-summarization enabled. The auto-summarization feature causes subnets to be summarized as the major network when crossing boundaries between major networks. This mimics the behavior of classful routing protocols such as RIP and IGRP, and it helps EIGRP work better with those protocols.

Auto-summarization can be a useful feature when working on a network that has no discontiguous subnets in a major network. Note that auto-summarization does not change the ability of EIGRP to handle VLSM — the masks within a major network are always retained. However, those masks do not traverse major network boundaries.

If this behavior is not desired, you can disable it with the following command:

```
R1(config-router)#no auto-summary
```

With auto-summarization disabled, subnets from all major networks are propagated in routing updates throughout the internetwork. Make sure to configure this setting on all routers in the EIGRP AS.

Modifying Load Balancing Behavior

The following options available to modify EIGRP load balancing are the same as those available for IGRP:

- The `maximum-paths` command specifies the maximum number of paths across which the router should do load balancing. The default is four, and valid values are 1 through 6.

- The `variance` configuration command enables unequal-cost load balancing on a router. The variance parameter entered on the command line is a multiplier. The cost to the destination using the lowest cost path is multiplied by the variance to determine what the highest allowed metric to the destination should be. Note that only feasible successors are included for unequal-cost load balancing.

- The `traffic-share min` command allows the administrator to configure the router to install unequal-cost paths in the routing table (based on the variance) but to route only across the lowest cost path(s).

All three of these commands are explained in "Modifying Load Balancing Behavior" in the section "Configuring IGRP." Their effects are exactly the same for EIGRP as for IGRP, so please see that section for more detailed information.

Controlling Route Selection

As in IGRP, you can use the `metric weights` command to change the values of the K-constants used in the EIGRP metric equation. This will change the calculation used to determine metrics. Also like IGRP, the default values for the constants are $K1 = K3 = 1$ and $K2 = K4 = K5 = 0$. This means that only bandwidth and delay are used in the metric calculations by default. Unlike IGRP, however, it is not recommended that you change $K2$, $K4$, or $K5$. These values control the use of load and reliability, which are more or less meaningless without periodic updates. Therefore, unless you have good reason, only change the values of $K1$ and $K3$ to modify the behavior of EIGRP.

To change the values of the K-constants, enter the following command in EIGRP configuration mode:

```
R1(config-router)#metric weights 0 K1 K2 K3 K4 K5
```

The $K1-K5$ variables above must be replaced with integers in the range of 0 through 4,294,967,295. The zero in the preceding example is the type of service (ToS) metric, and it is currently not supported.

The values of the K-constants need to be the same across all routers in the same EIGRP AS. EIGRP routers include the K-constants in their Hello packets — neighbors with different values cannot establish an adjacency.

To make EIGRP more or less preferred to other routing protocols, you can use the `distance eigrp` command. The default administrative distance of EIGRP is 90 for internal routes and 170 for external routes (routes redistributed from other routing processes). To treat EIGRP external routes the same as internal routes, enter the following configuration command:

```
R1(config-router)#distance eigrp 90 90
```

The configured administrative distance is only locally significant, and it appears in the EIGRP entries in the routing table.

You can use the `offset-list` command to increase the metric of particular EIGRP routes. Offset lists work the same way in EIGRP as they do in IGRP. With the basic EIGRP configuration for the example network in Figure 3-2, traffic destined from R1 to 192.168.3.0/24 is routed through R3, as shown in this topology table entry:

```
R1#show ip eigrp topology 192.168.3.0
IP-EIGRP topology entry for 192.168.3.0/24
  State is Passive, Query origin flag is 1, 1 Successor(s), FD is 10575872
  Routing Descriptor Blocks:
  192.168.13.3 (Serial1), from 192.168.13.3, Send flag is 0x0
      Composite metric is (10575872/704000), Route is Internal
      Vector metric:
        Minimum bandwidth is 256 Kbit
        Total delay is 22500 microseconds
        Reliability is 255/255
        Load is 1/255
        Minimum MTU is 1500
        Hop count is 1
  192.168.12.2 (Serial0), from 192.168.12.2, Send flag is 0x0
      Composite metric is (11087872/10575872), Route is Internal
      Vector metric:
        Minimum bandwidth is 256 Kbit
        Total delay is 42500 microseconds
        Reliability is 255/255
        Load is 1/255
        Minimum MTU is 1500
        Hop count is 2
```

If, for any reason, we would rather have traffic to 192.168.3.0/24 routed through R2 but do not want to change the bandwidth and/or delay of any interfaces (because this affects all routes), we can use the following configuration commands:

```
R1(config)#access-list 30 permit 192.168.3.0 0.0.0.0
R1(config)#router eigrp 1
R1(config-router)#offset-list 30 in 10000000 Serial 1
```

Now the router adds 10,000,000 to any inbound routes received on Serial1 that match access list 30, which matches 192.168.3.0/24. It is necessary to clear the neighbor relationship with R3 in order to receive an update that can then be modified by R1. After issuing the `clear ip eigrp neighbors serial 1` command, the topology table is updated:

```
R1#show ip eigrp topology 192.168.3.0
IP-EIGRP topology entry for 192.168.3.0/24
  State is Passive, Query origin flag is 1, 1 Successor(s), FD is 11087872
  Routing Descriptor Blocks:
  192.168.12.2 (Serial0), from 192.168.12.2, Send flag is 0x0
      Composite metric is (11087872/10575872), Route is Internal
      Vector metric:
        Minimum bandwidth is 256 Kbit
        Total delay is 42500 microseconds
        Reliability is 255/255
        Load is 1/255
        Minimum MTU is 1500
        Hop count is 2
  192.168.13.3 (Serial1), from 192.168.13.3, Send flag is 0x0
      Composite metric is (20575872/10704000), Route is Internal
      Vector metric:
        Minimum bandwidth is 256 Kbit
        Total delay is 413125 microseconds
        Reliability is 255/255
        Load is 1/255
        Minimum MTU is 1500
        Hop count is 1
```

Note that the offset is added to both the local metric and the calculated value for the neighbor's metric. Offset lists can be applied to either inbound or outbound routes, depending on the desired result.

Configuring EIGRP Pacing

EIGRP pacing prevents the routing protocol from over-utilizing slow links. Based on the recognized bandwidth of an interface, a router uses only a certain percent of the bandwidth for routing protocol traffic. By default, EIGRP uses only 50 percent of the bandwidth of a link. Because modifying the configured bandwidth of a link has other effects on the network (such as changing the routing metric), the preferred method of regulating EIGRP traffic is to change the bandwidth percentage. You can do this by entering the following command in interface configuration mode:

```
R1(config-if)#ip bandwidth-percent eigrp 1 25
```

This command sets the pacing percentage to 25 percent. The integer following the keyword eigrp is the AS number of the EIGRP routing process. Note that you can set the percentage to be greater than 100 percent, which can be useful when the bandwidth of the interface has been set artificially low.

Changing EIGRP Timers

The interval at which EIGRP sends Hello packets can be changed on a per-interface basis. By default, most interfaces send Hellos every five seconds. The one exception is NBMA networks, which default to a 60-second Hello interval. To change the default Hello interval for a particular interface, enter the following command in interface configuration mode:

```
R1(config-if)#ip hello-interval eigrp 1 30
```

After the keyword eigrp on the command line is the AS number of the EIGRP routing process. It is followed by the number of seconds to wait between sending Hellos from the interface.

Within its Hello packets, an EIGRP router advertises a hold time, which is the amount of time that the neighboring router should wait for another Hello. If no Hello is received before the hold time expires, the sending router is considered dead. The default hold time is 15 seconds for all networks, with the exception of NBMA networks, which default to 180 seconds. You should change the hold time on any interface on which you change the Hello interval from the default. (Usually, a hold time of three times the Hello interval is recommended.) To change the default hold time, enter the following command in interface configuration mode:

```
R1(config-if)#ip hold-time eigrp 1 90
```

As when changing the Hello interval, you must specify the EIGRP AS number (1 in this case). The final integer entered in the command is the number of seconds to be advertised as the hold time for this interface.

The final timer that EIGRP uses is the active timer, which is used to determine when a route is SIA. When a router sends or forwards a query, it starts an active timer for the active route. If the active timer expires, any unresponsive neighbors are presumed dead and removed from the neighbor table, along with their routes from the topology database. The default active timer is three minutes, and entering the following command in EIGRP configuration mode can change it:

```
R1(config-router)#timers active-time 5
```

The integer entered on the command line is the number of minutes to use for the active timer. Increasing this value can prevent routes from being declared SIA unnecessarily. Because an SIA entry results in the router and all of its routes being removed from the topology table, changing the timer can be a problem if done in error. But it is also important to realize that this also increases the time it takes the router to recover if a neighbor is truly incapable of replying. Changing the active timer is only recommended if necessary due to the specific needs of a particular internetwork. Normally, a functioning network will not cause any routes to be SIA, so the value of the active timer should not be important.

The active timer can also be completely disabled. This is definitely *not* recommended and should only be done if the administrator is confident that it is necessary. If this is done, the routing table may never converge during diffusing computation. To disable the active timer, enter the following configuration command:

```
R1(config-router)#timers active-time disabled
```

Configuring Authentication

EIGRP has the capability of using MD5 cryptographic checksums to authenticate routing updates. It is available with IOS 11.3 or later. To configure EIGRP to perform authentication, you have to start by configuring the router with a key chain. A *key chain* is a protocol-independent feature of the Cisco IOS for configuring and managing cryptographic keys. Key chain management is not covered in depth here, but the following configuration commands are sufficient to create a usable key chain:

```
R1(config)#key chain Test
R1(config-keychain)#key 1
R1(config-keychain-key)#key-string TestKey1
```

The key chain command creates a key chain with the name Test. It also puts you into key chain configuration mode. The key command specifies which key to configure, key 1 in this case, and it puts you into key configuration mode. Finally, the key-string command configures the string to use for that particular key in the key chain.

The key chain management commands accept-lifetime and send-lifetime (entered in key configuration mode) provide finer control over the keys in use on the network. In addition, they supply an easy method of periodically changing keys on the network, which enhances security. The use of these commands is encouraged, and you can find out more about them by checking Cisco's documentation.

Once a key chain is configured, it can be applied to an interface running EIGRP. This requires two interface configuration commands, as shown here:

```
R1(config)#interface TokenRing 0
R1(config-if)#ip authentication mode eigrp 1 md5
R1(config-if)#ip authentication key-chain eigrp 1 Test
```

With this configuration of TokenRing0, R1 attaches an MD5 cryptographic checksum to all outgoing EIGRP packets, using the first valid key in the key chain Test. In addition, any incoming packets are checked for a cryptographic checksum matching that which R1 would compute. If any packet is missing a checksum or has an invalid checksum, R1 ignores it. Any other router on the Token Ring network must use the same key string on that network to share information with R1.

Modifying Other EIGRP Behavior

Although EIGRP is a classless protocol, the `network` configuration command accepts only major network addresses. Therefore, in some cases, EIGRP may be running on more interfaces than is desired. In this case, the `passive-interface` configuration command can be used, shown here turning off EIGRP on TokenRing0:

```
R1(config-router)#passive-interface TokenRing 0
```

Note one significant difference between the behavior of passive interfaces in EIGRP and in IGRP. An IGRP passive interface does not advertise routing information, but it accepts routing information from other routers. On the other hand, making an interface passive in EIGRP prevents Hellos from being sent, thereby preventing any neighbor relationships on that interface. Because a neighbor relationship must be established before routing information can be exchanged, an EIGRP router never sends or receives any routing information on a passive interface. (Because no neighbor relationships can be formed on a passive interface, an EIGRP router ignores Hellos on passive interfaces.)

EIGRP tracks the hop count as part of the vector metric for all routes to help detect routing loops. Any routes with a hop count greater than the maximum are considered unreachable. The higher the hop count, the longer it may take to detect loops. The default maximum hop count for EIGRP is 100, but it can be changed using the following command:

```
R1(config-router)#metric maximum-hops 50
```

The parameter accepted by the command is the number of hops, in the range of 1 through 255. This value must be chosen carefully; if it is set too low, valid routes may be considered unreachable. In addition, make sure that all routers on the network are configured with the same maximum hop count.

Split horizon is enabled for EIGRP by default, but it can be disabled on an interface-by-interface basis. Split horizon is a crucial feature of distance vector protocols, and disabling it is discouraged in most cases. The most common reason to disable split horizon is that it prevents hub routers on NBMA networks (such as Frame Relay or X.25) from advertising routes learned from spoke routers to other spoke routers. In this case, disabling split horizon allows the hub router to advertise routes learned from the

NBMA network back to the routers on the NBMA network. To disable split horizon, enter the following configuration command in interface configuration mode:

```
R1(config-if)#no ip split-horizon eigrp 1
```

Note that using the `no ip split-horizon` command without the EIGRP identifier has no effect on the EIGRP routing process. It only affects RIP and IGRP.

Troubleshooting IGRP

Because IGRP is a standard distance vector routing protocol, it does not retain much extra information about the network topology. Most of the information available about IGRP can be found in the routing table. However, there are some ways of getting more detailed information about IGRP when troubleshooting a particular problem.

Caution

Before troubleshooting an IGRP problem, remember that IGRP is a classful protocol. As such, routes must be summarized at major network boundaries. Make sure that the problem you are troubleshooting is not simply the result of classful summarization.

Viewing IGRP Protocol Information

To see how IGRP is configured on a particular router, use the `show ip protocols` command. In addition to IGRP, this command displays information about all IP routing protocols running on the router. The following example output is from a router running only IGRP:

```
R1#show ip protocols
Routing Protocol is "igrp 1"
  Sending updates every 90 seconds, next due in 50 seconds
  Invalid after 270 seconds, hold down 280, flushed after 630
  Outgoing update filter list for all interfaces is not set
  Incoming update filter list for all interfaces is not set
  Incoming routes in Serial0 will have 50000 added to metric if on list 20
  Default networks flagged in outgoing updates
```

```
Default networks accepted from incoming updates

IGRP metric weight K1=1, K2=0, K3=1, K4=0, K5=0

IGRP maximum hopcount 100

IGRP maximum metric variance 1

Redistributing: igrp 1

Routing for Networks:

  192.168.12.0

  192.168.13.0

  192.168.1.0

Passive Interface(s):

  TokenRing0

Routing Information Sources:

  Gateway         Distance      Last Update

  192.168.13.3        100       00:00:25

  192.168.12.2        100       00:00:56

Distance: (default is 100)
```

The output of this command provides very detailed information about the IGRP routing process. First it displays the configured timers, including the remaining time until the current update timer expires. Then it displays filter lists and any offset lists. The router includes information about the way default networks are treated, and then it shows the current values of the K-constants, the maximum hop count, and the variance. The rest of the information is the same as would be printed for any other routing protocol: redistribution, networks IGRP is routing, passive interfaces, routing information sources, and administrative distance.

The show ip protocols command does an excellent job of showing exactly how the routing process is configured on a particular router. You can discover problems resulting from misconfiguration of a particular router by comparing the information in this output with similar output from other routers.

Viewing Interface Information

Most IGRP properties affect the system as a whole, rather than particular interfaces. However, four very important properties of an interface impact IGRP: the bandwidth, delay, load, and reliability. When trying to troubleshoot routing problems, it is important to check these values because they impact the metric of every route. The values are easily seen by using the show interfaces command:

```
R1#show interfaces Serial 0
Serial0 is up, line protocol is up
  Hardware is HD64570
  Internet address is 192.168.12.1/24
  MTU 1500 bytes, BW 256 Kbit, DLY 20000 usec, rely 255/255, load 1/255
  Encapsulation HDLC, loopback not set, keepalive set (10 sec)
  Last input 00:00:04, output 00:00:02, output hang never
  Last clearing of "show interface" counters never
  Input queue: 0/75/0 (size/max/drops); Total output drops: 0
  Queueing strategy: weighted fair
  Output queue: 0/64/0 (size/threshold/drops)
     Conversations  0/2 (active/max active)
     Reserved Conversations 0/0 (allocated/max allocated)
  5 minute input rate 0 bits/sec, 0 packets/sec
  5 minute output rate 0 bits/sec, 0 packets/sec
     96587 packets input, 6000788 bytes, 0 no buffer
     Received 35659 broadcasts, 0 runts, 0 giants
     623 input errors, 1 CRC, 0 frame, 0 overrun, 38 ignored, 1 abort
     97310 packets output, 6011155 bytes, 0 underruns
     0 output errors, 0 collisions, 242 interface resets
     0 output buffer failures, 0 output buffers swapped out
     481 carrier transitions
     DCD=up  DSR=up  DTR=up  RTS=up  CTS=up
```

The bold line holds the values of all four composite metric components, along with the MTU for that interface, which is also tracked by IGRP. Bandwidth is in units of Kbps, which is the same value accepted by the bandwidth configuration command and used in the IGRP composite metric equation. Delay is in units of microseconds, which is different from the value accepted by the delay configuration command. The delay command accepts a value that is in units of tens of microseconds, as is the value used in the composite metric equation. Reliability and load are fractions of 255, and the numerator shown is the value used in the calculation of the composite metric.

Viewing Detailed Route Information

When viewing the routing table as a whole, you can easily see exactly where packets destined for each network are routed. However, the routing table does not offer very detailed information about the routes that it has chosen. When using IGRP, you may wonder how the composite metric for a particular route was calculated. In this case, you can look at the routing information for one particular route by specifying the destination on the command line, as shown here:

```
R1#show ip route 192.168.3.0
Routing entry for 192.168.3.0/24
  Known via "igrp 1", distance 100, metric 80375
  Redistributing via igrp 1
  Advertised by igrp 1 (self originated)
  Last update from 192.168.13.3 on Serial1, 00:01:04 ago
  Routing Descriptor Blocks:
  * 192.168.13.3, from 192.168.13.3, 00:01:04 ago, via Serial1
      Route metric is 80375, traffic share count is 1
      Total delay is 22500 microseconds, minimum bandwidth is 128 Kbit
      Reliability 255/255, minimum MTU 1500 bytes
      Loading 1/255, Hops 0
```

This detailed display shows all relevant information about a particular route. In addition to the source routing protocol and router, the most useful information presented is the vector metric for the route—the delay, bandwidth, reliability, load, MTU, and hop count. Although it may be difficult to determine whether the composite metric is correct based on your understanding of the network, the presence of the vector metric in this output should break down the information into much more useful parts.

Monitoring Route Updates

Although detailed protocol and route information can be valuable when troubleshooting network problems, the lack of a route that should exist can still be puzzling. In this case, you may need to find out exactly what each router is advertising and receiving via IGRP. This is most easily accomplished by using two IGRP debug commands.

Debugging IGRP events causes messages to be displayed for each update sent or received by the router. To enable IGRP event debugging, enter the following command in privileged EXEC mode:

```
R1#debug ip igrp events
IGRP event debugging is on
```

When IGRP event debugging is enabled, you should see updates received from each neighbor at 90-second intervals, and you should also see updates sent from the local router every 90 seconds. Typical output looks like this:

```
IGRP: received update from 192.168.12.2 on Serial0
IGRP: Update contains 0 interior, 3 system, and 0 exterior routes.
IGRP: Total routes in update: 3
IGRP: received update from 192.168.13.3 on Serial1
IGRP: Update contains 0 interior, 3 system, and 0 exterior routes.
IGRP: Total routes in update: 3
IGRP: sending update to 255.255.255.255 via Serial0 (192.168.12.1)
IGRP: Update contains 0 interior, 3 system, and 0 exterior routes.
IGRP: Total routes in update: 3
IGRP: sending update to 255.255.255.255 via Serial1 (192.168.13.1)
IGRP: Update contains 0 interior, 3 system, and 0 exterior routes.
IGRP: Total routes in update: 3
IGRP: sending update to 255.255.255.255 via TokenRing0 (192.168.1.1)
IGRP: Update contains 0 interior, 5 system, and 0 exterior routes.
IGRP: Total routes in update: 5
```

The information printed includes the source or destination address and interface of the update, along with a summary of the routes contained in the update. Route information is summarized by the three types of routes: interior, system, and exterior. *Interior routes* are entries that are subnets of a directly connected major network (the same major network as on the sending or receiving interface). *System routes* are entries that are major networks, which means they may have already been summarized. Finally, *exterior routes* are entries that have been identified as default networks.

If the information provided by IGRP event debugging is not adequate to troubleshoot a particular problem, transaction debugging may fill the void. To enable transaction debugging, enter the following command in privileged EXEC mode:

```
R1#debug ip igrp transactions
IGRP protocol debugging is on
```

IGRP transaction debugging displays the entries that are included in each routing update, as shown by this example output:

```
IGRP: received update from 192.168.12.2 on Serial0
      network 192.168.2.0, metric 41312 (neighbor 2750)
      network 192.168.3.0, metric 43312 (neighbor 41312)
      network 192.168.23.0, metric 43062 (neighbor 41062)
IGRP: received update from 192.168.13.3 on Serial1
      network 192.168.2.0, metric 43312 (neighbor 41312)
      network 192.168.3.0, metric 41312 (neighbor 2750)
      network 192.168.23.0, metric 43062 (neighbor 41062)
IGRP: sending update to 255.255.255.255 via Serial0 (192.168.12.1)
      network 192.168.13.0, metric=41062
      network 192.168.1.0, metric=2750
      network 192.168.3.0, metric=41312
IGRP: sending update to 255.255.255.255 via Serial1 (192.168.13.1)
      network 192.168.12.0, metric=41062
      network 192.168.1.0, metric=2750
      network 192.168.2.0, metric=41312
IGRP: sending update to 255.255.255.255 via TokenRing0 (192.168.1.1)
      network 192.168.12.0, metric=41062
      network 192.168.13.0, metric=41062
      network 192.168.2.0, metric=41312
      network 192.168.3.0, metric=41312
      network 192.168.23.0, metric=43062
```

For each update sent and received, the router displays all of the networks contained in the update and their metrics (including the neighbor metric for inbound updates). Although the vector metric is not shown here, having the composite metric available should help determine why certain routes are not chosen. From there, it is up to you to investigate the reason for the composite metric, but that should be easily determined by visiting neighboring routers on the network.

Using both of these debugging commands together provides an easy-to-read list of updates, on which each list of networks is followed by a summary for that update, as shown for one update here:

```
IGRP: received update from 192.168.12.2 on Serial0

      network 192.168.2.0, metric 41312 (neighbor 2750)

      network 192.168.3.0, metric 43312 (neighbor 41312)

      network 192.168.23.0, metric 43062 (neighbor 41062)

IGRP: Update contains 0 interior, 3 system, and 0 exterior routes.

IGRP: Total routes in update: 3
```

Finally, these debug commands display useful information when a problem is detected. For example, if two routers on the same network are assigned addresses on different subnets, they should both detect the problem when receiving routing updates from each other. This message would be found on either router when debugging:

```
IGRP: received update from invalid source 192.168.3.3 on TokenRing0
```

Although a problem like this is easily found by just trying to ping the remote router, sometimes you may not remember to look for problems in the obvious places. In this case, the obvious errors that can be detected by a router are displayed while looking through debugging output.

Troubleshooting EIGRP

Unlike IGRP, EIGRP has many commands available to assist with troubleshooting the protocol. Of course, the cost of this advantage is increased complexity of the protocol, providing more places for problems to be introduced. However, when effectively using the available troubleshooting commands, most EIGRP configuration problems should be easily discovered.

Viewing EIGRP Protocol Information

The show ip protocols command provides a lot of useful information about the configuration of EIGRP on the local router. In addition to providing a place to find the configuration of EIGRP without needing to view the running-config, it also provides other information, such as routing information sources. An example of the output is shown here:

```
R1#show ip protocols
Routing Protocol is "eigrp 1"
  Outgoing update filter list for all interfaces is not set
  Incoming update filter list for all interfaces is not set
  Incoming routes in Serial1 will have 10000000 added to metric if on list 30
  Default networks flagged in outgoing updates
  Default networks accepted from incoming updates
  EIGRP metric weight K1=1, K2=0, K3=1, K4=0, K5=0
  EIGRP maximum hopcount 100
  EIGRP maximum metric variance 1
  Redistributing: eigrp 1
  Automatic network summarization is not in effect
  Routing for Networks:
    192.168.12.0
    192.168.13.0
    192.168.1.0
  Passive Interface(s):
    TokenRing0
  Routing Information Sources:
    Gateway         Distance      Last Update
    192.168.13.3          90      00:03:35
    192.168.12.2          90      00:03:36
  Distance: internal 90 external 170
```

The output of this command provides very detailed information about the EIGRP routing process. First it displays filter lists and any offset lists. Then the router includes information about the way default networks are treated, and it shows the current values of the K-constants, the maximum hop count, and the variance. Then it lists any routing protocols being redistributed, along with whether or not auto-summarization is enabled. Finally, it lists networks EIGRP is routing, passive interfaces, routing information sources, and the administrative distances for internal and external EIGRP routes.

Viewing Interface Information

The values used for the bandwidth, delay, reliability, and load of an interface can be viewed with the show interfaces EXEC command. These values are important to the operation of EIGRP and the calculation of metrics. Please see "Viewing Interface Information" in the section "Troubleshooting IGRP" for a detailed example.

The EIGRP properties of each interface can be viewed using the show ip eigrp interfaces EXEC command. It provides information about neighbors and traffic on each interface. An example of the output of this command follows:

```
R1#show ip eigrp interfaces
IP-EIGRP interfaces for process 1
```

Interface	Peers	Xmit Queue Un/Reliable	Mean SRTT	Pacing Time Un/Reliable	Multicast Flow Timer	Pending Routes
Se0	1	0/0	14	2/95	159	0
Se1	1	0/0	168	2/95	923	0

For each interface, the output lists the number of neighbors (labeled as Peers), the transmit queues, the mean SRTT, the pacing time, the multicast flow timer, and the pending routes. The transmit queues indicate the number of packets queued for transmission out the interface, and the pending routes column shows the number of routes in those packets. The pacing time is used to determine when packets should be sent out an interface, and the multicast flow timer indicates the maximum number of seconds in which the router will send multicast packets. For additional information, use the detail keyword, as shown here:

```
R1#show ip eigrp interfaces detail
IP-EIGRP interfaces for process 1
```

Interface	Peers	Xmit Queue Un/Reliable	Mean SRTT	Pacing Time Un/Reliable	Multicast Flow Timer	Pending Routes
Se0	1	0/0	15	2/95	159	0

Next xmit serial <none>

Un/reliable mcasts: 0/0 Un/reliable ucasts: 85/146

Mcast exceptions: 0 CR packets: 0 ACKs suppressed: 9

Retransmissions sent: 11 Out-of-sequence rcvd: 2

Se1	1	0/0	83	2/95	495	0

Next xmit serial <none>

Un/reliable mcasts: 0/0 Un/reliable ucasts: 93/152

Mcast exceptions: 0 CR packets: 0 ACKs suppressed: 0

Retransmissions sent: 38 Out-of-sequence rcvd: 8

To0	0	0/0	0	0/10	0	0

Next xmit serial <none>

Un/reliable mcasts: 0/0 Un/reliable ucasts: 0/0

Mcast exceptions: 0 CR packets: 0 ACKs suppressed: 0

Retransmissions sent: 0 Out-of-sequence rcvd: 0

In addition to the information shown earlier, this output also includes the following statistics for each interface: reliable and unreliable multicasts, reliable and unreliable unicasts, multicast exceptions, conditional receive packets, suppressed ACKs, retransmissions, and out-of-sequence packets received. A high or rapidly increasing number of retransmissions can indicate a problem with the link to the neighbor or with the neighbor itself. Suppressed ACKs are normal because the acknowledgements can be piggybacked on other EIGRP packets. When one neighbor on a multicast-capable interface falls behind the others with ACKs, a router uses multicast exceptions and conditional receive packets to maintain a separate state for that neighbor, so the up-to-date neighbors do not have to wait for more updates. These two counters usually indicate a problem with a neighbor on the interface.

Viewing Detailed Route Information

Using the show ip route command provides an accurate view of the way that a router is routing traffic to all known destinations. However, it does not provide detailed information about the routes. To view detailed infor-

mation about the routes, use the command and specify a particular route to
view, as shown here:

```
R1#show ip route 192.168.3.0

Routing entry for 192.168.3.0/24

  Known via "eigrp 1", distance 90, metric 10575872, type internal

  Redistributing via eigrp 1

  Last update from 192.168.13.3 on Serial1, 01:44:41 ago

  Routing Descriptor Blocks:

  * 192.168.13.3, from 192.168.13.3, 01:44:41 ago, via Serial1

     Route metric is 10575872, traffic share count is 1

     Total delay is 22500 microseconds, minimum bandwidth is 256 Kbit

     Reliability 255/255, minimum MTU 1500 bytes

     Loading 1/255, Hops 1
```

The additional information provided here is quite extensive. In addition
to the composite metric that can be viewed in the routing table, the vector
metric is also printed. This can help determine how a particular composite
metric was calculated. Make sure you verify the current values of the K-constants before trying to calculate the composite metric from the vector metric.

In addition to viewing detailed information about routes in the routing
table, the topology table maintained by EIGRP enables you to view information about all known routes to a destination, not just the best route.
Using the show ip eigrp topology command with various qualifiers
provides different information.

For example, entering the command without any additional qualifiers
prints the topology table as a list:

```
R1#show ip eigrp topology

IP-EIGRP Topology Table for process 1


Codes: P - Passive, A - Active, U - Update, Q - Query, R - Reply,

       r - Reply status


P 192.168.12.0/24, 1 successors, FD is 10511872

         via Connected, Serial0

P 192.168.13.0/24, 1 successors, FD is 10511872
```

```
        via Connected, Serial1
P 192.168.1.0/24, 1 successors, FD is 704000
        via Connected, TokenRing0
P 192.168.2.0/24, 1 successors, FD is 10575872
        via 192.168.12.2 (10575872/704000), Serial0
P 192.168.3.0/24, 1 successors, FD is 10575872
        via 192.168.13.3 (10575872/704000), Serial1
P 192.168.23.0/24, 2 successors, FD is 11023872
        via 192.168.12.2 (11023872/10511872), Serial0
        via 192.168.13.3 (11023872/10511872), Serial1
```

However, this default output only prints the successors and feasible successors for each destination. Using the all-links qualifier causes the entire topology table to be displayed:

```
R1#show ip eigrp topology all-links
IP-EIGRP Topology Table for process 1


Codes: P - Passive, A - Active, U - Update, Q - Query, R - Reply,
       r - Reply status


P 192.168.12.0/24, 1 successors, FD is 10511872, serno 1
        via Connected, Serial0
P 192.168.13.0/24, 1 successors, FD is 10511872, serno 7
        via Connected, Serial1
P 192.168.1.0/24, 1 successors, FD is 704000, serno 3
        via Connected, TokenRing0
P 192.168.2.0/24, 1 successors, FD is 10575872, serno 64
        via 192.168.12.2 (10575872/704000), Serial0
        via 192.168.13.3 (11087872/10575872), Serial1
P 192.168.3.0/24, 1 successors, FD is 10575872, serno 71
        via 192.168.13.3 (10575872/704000), Serial1
        via 192.168.12.2 (11087872/10575872), Serial0
P 192.168.23.0/24, 2 successors, FD is 11023872, serno 97
        via 192.168.12.2 (11023872/10511872), Serial0
        via 192.168.13.3 (11023872/10511872), Serial1
```

The two bold entries are routes that do not qualify as feasible succes-sors, so they were omitted from the previous output. For each route in the topology database, you can see the status (passive, active, and so on), the number of successors, the feasible distance (FD), and the serial number. Following that is one line for each routing information source for that des-tination. Each of these lines includes the local distance through that neigh-bor, along with the distance from the neighbor to the destination.

Two qualifiers filter the display to only certain routes. Using the `active` qualifier displays only active routes. Using the `pending` qualifier also dis-plays active routes, and it includes routes for which there are pending out-going updates (to be sent or to be acknowledged). In a router with many EIGRP routes, these two qualifiers make it easier to find routes of interest while troubleshooting.

To view the detailed topology information for any particular route, you can specify the destination address on the command line. This displays all sources for that route, along with more detailed information for each source. The output is shown here:

```
R1#show ip eigrp topology 192.168.3.0
IP-EIGRP topology entry for 192.168.3.0/24
  State is Passive, Query origin flag is 1, 1 Successor(s), FD is 10575872
  Routing Descriptor Blocks:
  192.168.13.3 (Serial1), from 192.168.13.3, Send flag is 0x0
      Composite metric is (10575872/704000), Route is Internal
      Vector metric:
        Minimum bandwidth is 256 Kbit
        Total delay is 22500 microseconds
        Reliability is 255/255
        Load is 1/255
        Minimum MTU is 1500
        Hop count is 1
  192.168.12.2 (Serial0), from 192.168.12.2, Send flag is 0x0
      Composite metric is (11087872/10575872), Route is Internal
      Vector metric:
        Minimum bandwidth is 256 Kbit
        Total delay is 42500 microseconds
        Reliability is 255/255
```

```
Load is 1/255

Minimum MTU is 1500

Hop count is 2
```

It is much easier to determine the reason that certain routes are chosen for the routing table by looking at this information. Having the vector metric available should help determine why certain routes are preferred over others.

There is one other special case that should be explained — zero-successor routes. When a route entry in EIGRP conflicts with an entry from another routing protocol, the protocol with the lower administrative distance is entered in the routing table. Because successors are a property of EIGRP, if an EIGRP route is not installed in the routing table, there is no successor for that route, resulting in a zero-successor route. Static routes are the most likely cause of zero-successor routes, but they can also appear if the administrative distance of another routing protocol has been configured to be less than that of EIGRP. Zero-successor routes are displayed with all other routes when viewing the entire topology table, but using the zero-successors qualifier results in only zero-successors being printed. In this example, the route to 192.168.3.0/24 is known by a static route:

```
R1#show ip eigrp topology zero-successors
IP-EIGRP Topology Table for process 1


Codes: P - Passive, A - Active, U - Update, Q - Query, R - Reply,
       r - Reply status


P 192.168.3.0/24, 0 successors, FD is Inaccessible
        via 192.168.13.3 (10575872/704000), Serial1
        via 192.168.12.2 (11087872/10575872), Serial0
```

EIGRP continues to store all topology information for zero-successor routes so that they can be used if the conflicting route becomes invalid.

Troubleshooting Neighbors

On some occasions, configuration changes do not seem to take effect immediately. A common cause of this is that the configuration change affects incoming updates from one or more neighbors. Because there are no periodic updates in EIGRP, a new incoming route may not have arrived since the configuration change. In this case, the simplest solution is to clear the neighbor relationship with one or more neighbors, using the following privileged EXEC command:

```
R1#clear ip eigrp neighbors
```

When this happens, the router removes all neighbors from its table and reestablishes its adjacencies after receiving Hellos from the neighbors again. Then it accepts routing information from the "new" neighbors and rebuilds its topology and routing tables.

Using an IP address of a particular neighbor or specifying an interface can mitigate the impact of the command. If a neighbor IP address is entered, only the adjacency with that neighbor is cleared. If an interface is specified, all neighbors through that interface are cleared. It is not a bad idea to get into the habit of using this command whenever you start troubleshooting a neighbor problem, but remember that this causes a short disruption in routing.

One of the first sources of information to check when experiencing problems with EIGRP is the neighbor table, which indicates which routers are recognized as neighbors. You can do this with the following command:

```
R1#show ip eigrp neighbors
IP-EIGRP neighbors for process 1
H   Address           Interface    Hold Uptime     SRTT   RTO  Q  Seq
                                   (sec)           (ms)        Cnt Num
0   192.168.13.3      Se1          11 10:18:47     15     570  0  91
1   192.168.12.2      Se0          10 18:09:05     15     570  0  80
```

This command displays one line of information for each EIGRP neighbor. You can also specify a particular interface on the command line, which results in output including only the neighbors through that interface.

The information displayed for each neighbor includes a locally assigned index (the H column — indicating the order in which the neighbors were discovered), the address, the interface, the remaining hold time, the amount of time the adjacency has been established, the SRTT, the RTO, the number of queued packets for that neighbor (the Q Cnt column), and the sequence number of the last packet received from the neighbor.

For a little more information about the neighbors, add the `detail` keyword to the command line, as shown here:

```
R1#show ip eigrp neighbors detail
IP-EIGRP neighbors for process 1
H    Address              Interface   Hold Uptime    SRTT   RTO  Q   Seq
                                      (sec)          (ms)        Cnt Num
0    192.168.13.3         Se1          11 10:18:47    15   570  0   91
     Version 11.2/1.0, Retrans: 1, Retries: 0
1    192.168.12.2         Se0          10 18:09:05    15   570  0   80
     Version 11.2/1.0, Retrans: 1, Retries: 0
```

The additional line for each neighbor shows the IOS version and EIGRP version of the neighbor. (The EIGRP version should always be 1.0 at this time.) Then it shows the number of retransmissions done, and the retry count for the packet currently being sent. The following output shows the information provided when there are pending packets for a neighbor.

```
R6#show ip eigrp neighbors detail
IP-EIGRP neighbors for process 1
H    Address              Interface   Hold Uptime    SRTT   RTO  Q   Seq
                                      (sec)          (ms)        Cnt Num
0    192.168.5.5          Et0          12 00:01:11     0  5000  1   0
     Last startup serial 14
     Version 11.3/1.0, Retrans: 15, Retries: 15, Waiting for Init, Waiting for Ini
t Ack
     UPDATE seq 49 ser 6-14 Sent 71796 Init Sequenced
```

This output indicates that there have been 15 retransmissions to the neighbor, and because the retries entry is 15, all of the retransmissions have been of the current packet. The current packet is an Init, which has not been acknowledged. After one more retransmission and timeout, the neighbor will be declared dead.

To monitor changes in neighbors as they happen, you can use the `debug eigrp neighbors` command, as shown here:

```
R1#debug eigrp neighbors
EIGRP Neighbors debugging is on
```

This causes the router to generate a message every time a neighbor is discovered or lost. For example, a newly discovered neighbor would be shown as follows:

```
EIGRP: New peer 192.168.13.3
```

When an interface goes down, the neighbor(s) on that interface are also considered down, and they are removed from the neighbor table. This sequence can be seen here:

```
%LINEPROTO-5-UPDOWN: Line protocol on Interface Serial1, changed state to down
%LINK-3-UPDOWN: Interface Serial1, changed state to down
EIGRP: Neighbor 192.168.13.3 went down on Serial1
```

If the neighbor dies but the interface stays up, the router does not know the neighbor is down until the hold time expires. When that happens, it immediately treats the neighbor as down:

```
EIGRP: Holdtime expired
EIGRP: Neighbor 192.168.13.3 went down on Serial1
```

Because EIGRP neighbor relationships are so crucial to the operation of the protocol, you can configure the router to log changes to neighbor adjacencies. Unlike most of the other troubleshooting commands, logging neighbor changes is a configuration option. This has the advantage of persisting even when the router restarts. In EIGRP configuration mode, enter the following command:

```
R1(config-router)#eigrp log-neighbor-changes
```

When using this command, make sure that you are logging messages to the internal buffer or to a syslog server. You should see the following log message when a new adjacency is formed:

```
%DUAL-5-NBRCHANGE: IP-EIGRP 1: Neighbor 192.168.5.5 (Ethernet0) is up: new adjac
ency
```

The following messages all indicate that the neighbor is down, but each one gives a different reason:

```
%DUAL-5-NBRCHANGE: IP-EIGRP 1: Neighbor 192.168.5.5 (Ethernet0) is down: holding
  time expired
```

```
%DUAL-5-NBRCHANGE: IP-EIGRP 1: Neighbor 192.168.5.5 (Ethernet0) is down: keychai

n changed

%DUAL-5-NBRCHANGE: IP-EIGRP 1: Neighbor 192.168.5.5 (Ethernet0) is down: retry 1

imit exceeded
```

The final command that helps troubleshoot problems with particular neighbors is the `debug ip eigrp neighbor` command. However, this command is unique in that it does not enable any debugging on its own. Instead, it modifies the scope of other debug commands. If the command is entered without any other EIGRP debugging enabled, the following error message is displayed:

```
R1#debug ip eigrp neighbor 1 192.168.13.3

First enable IP-EIGRP Route Events or EIGRP packet debug
```

One of the following two debug commands must be issued before `debug ip eigrp neighbor`:

- `debug ip eigrp` (IP EIGRP route events)
- `debug eigrp packet` (EIGRP packets)

When either of these two debug features is enabled, the `debug ip eigrp neighbor` command narrows the scope of the output to information only related to the neighbors listed. Both of these commands are explained in the following two sections.

Monitoring EIGRP Route Events

To see information about route events as they happen, you can debug EIGRP route events. To enable the display of route events, enter the following command in privileged EXEC mode:

```
R1#debug ip eigrp

IP-EIGRP Route Events debugging is on
```

Caution

Debugging EIGRP route events tends to display a lot of information. It is not recommended that you do this over a telnet connection.

Debugging EIGRP route events provides a look at the processing of routes as they are received by the router. Although this is a higher-level view than debugging EIGRP packets, small changes in the internetwork generate a great deal of output. This information may be hard to interpret while experiencing a problem, but it may be useful if saved for review later. This example output is from R1, after the link between R2 and R3 went down:

```
IP-EIGRP: Processing incoming QUERY packet

IP-EIGRP: Int 192.168.23.0/24 M 4294967295 - 0 4294967295 SM 4294967295 - 0 4294

967295

IP-EIGRP: Int 192.168.2.0/24 M 4294967295 - 9999872 4294967295 SM 4294967295 - 9

999872 4294967295

IP-EIGRP: 192.168.23.0/24, - do advertise out Serial1

IP-EIGRP: Int 192.168.23.0/24 metric 11023872 - 9999872 1024000

IP-EIGRP: 192.168.2.0/24, - do advertise out Serial1

IP-EIGRP: Int 192.168.2.0/24 metric 10575872 - 9999872 576000

IP-EIGRP: Int 192.168.23.0/24 metric 11023872 - 9999872 1024000

IP-EIGRP: 192.168.23.0/24, - do advertise out Serial1

IP-EIGRP: Int 192.168.23.0/24 metric 11023872 - 9999872 1024000

IP-EIGRP: Processing incoming UPDATE packet

IP-EIGRP: Int 192.168.2.0/24 M 4294967295 - 9999872 4294967295 SM 4294967295 - 9

999872 4294967295

IP-EIGRP: Processing incoming UPDATE packet

IP-EIGRP: Int 192.168.23.0/24 M 4294967295 - 9999872 4294967295 SM 4294967295 -

9999872 4294967295

IP-EIGRP: Processing incoming QUERY packet

IP-EIGRP: Int 192.168.23.0/24 M 4294967295 - 0 4294967295 SM 4294967295 - 0 4294

967295

IP-EIGRP: Int 192.168.3.0/24 M 4294967295 - 9999872 4294967295 SM 4294967295 - 9

999872 4294967295

IP-EIGRP: 192.168.23.0/24, - do advertise out Serial1

IP-EIGRP: Int 192.168.23.0/24 metric 4294967295 - 0 4294967295

IP-EIGRP: 192.168.3.0/24, - do advertise out Serial0

IP-EIGRP: Int 192.168.3.0/24 metric 10575872 - 9999872 576000

IP-EIGRP: Processing incoming REPLY packet
```

```
IP-EIGRP: Int 192.168.23.0/24 M 4294967295 - 9999872 4294967295 SM 4294967295 -

9999872 4294967295

IP-EIGRP: 192.168.23.0/24, - do advertise out Serial0

IP-EIGRP: Int 192.168.23.0/24 metric 4294967295 - 0 4294967295

IP-EIGRP: Processing incoming UPDATE packet

IP-EIGRP: Int 192.168.3.0/24 M 4294967295 - 9999872 4294967295 SM 4294967295 -

9999872 4294967295

IP-EIGRP: 192.168.23.0/24, - do advertise out Serial1

IP-EIGRP: Int 192.168.23.0/24 metric 4294967295 - 0 4294967295

IP-EIGRP: 192.168.23.0/24, - do advertise out Serial0

IP-EIGRP: Int 192.168.23.0/24 metric 4294967295 - 0 4294967295
```

This output shows each EIGRP packet that is received and all of the routes contained within those packets. In addition, it includes the metric information for each route as it arrives, along with the decisions about which interfaces should advertise the route. Because this information about each metric is retained in the topology database, this is probably not the most convenient source. However, if topology changes are happening rapidly, you can see their results in this debug output, even if the topology table is changing too quickly to monitor it using the show ip eigrp topology command.

Monitoring EIGRP Traffic

When troubleshooting brings you to the point of needing to know exactly what traffic is being sent and/or received, it is best to start with the simplest information. EIGRP tracks statistics for the various types of packets that it uses. You can view this information using the following command:

```
R1#show ip eigrp traffic
IP-EIGRP Traffic Statistics for process 1
  Hellos sent/received: 59652/73310
  Updates sent/received: 175/112
  Queries sent/received: 19/26
  Replies sent/received: 28/22
  Acks sent/received: 119/167
  Input queue high water mark 3, 0 drops
```

The output of this command is fairly self-explanatory. If the static information is of no help, it may be useful to wait for a short time and enter the command again. If a certain counter increases dramatically in a short time (with the exception of Hellos), then that may indicate a problem.

To view information about individual packets as the router sends or receives them, you can debug EIGRP packets. EIGRP packet debugging provides the useful option of displaying only the types of packets you are interested in seeing. For example, the context-sensitive help displays the following options:

```
R1#debug eigrp packets ?

  ack       EIGRP ack packets

  hello     EIGRP hello packets

  ipxsap    EIGRP ipxsap packets

  probe     EIGRP probe packets

  query     EIGRP query packets

  reply     EIGRP reply packets

  request   EIGRP request packets

  retry     EIGRP retransmissions

  terse     Display all EIGRP packets except Hellos

  update    EIGRP update packets

  verbose   Display all EIGRP packets

  <cr>
```

Caution

Debugging EIGRP packets tends to display a lot of information. It is not recommended that this be done over a telnet connection. Whenever possible, limit the debug to only one or two types of packets to reduce the amount of output.

With terse debugging enabled on R1, the following lines are about one-third of the those displayed when the link between R2 and R3 went down:

```
EIGRP: Received QUERY on Serial1 nbr 192.168.13.3

  AS 1, Flags 0x0, Seq 175/193 idbQ 0/0 iidbQ un/rely 0/0 peerQ un/rely 0/0

EIGRP: Enqueueing ACK on Serial1 nbr 192.168.13.3

  Ack seq 175 iidbQ un/rely 0/0 peerQ un/rely 1/0
```

```
EIGRP: Sending ACK on Serial1 nbr 192.168.13.3

  AS 1, Flags 0x0, Seq 0/175 idbQ 0/0 iidbQ un/rely 0/0 peerQ un/rely 1/0

EIGRP: Enqueueing REPLY on Serial1 nbr 192.168.13.3 iidbQ un/rely 0/1 peerQ un/r

ely 0/0 serno 204-205

EIGRP:  Requeued unicast on Serial1

EIGRP: Sending REPLY on Serial1 nbr 192.168.13.3

  AS 1, Flags 0x0, Seq 194/175 idbQ 0/0 iidbQ un/rely 0/0 peerQ un/rely 0/1 sern

o 204-205

EIGRP: Enqueueing UPDATE on Serial0 iidbQ un/rely 0/1 serno 206-206

EIGRP: Enqueueing UPDATE on Serial0 nbr 192.168.12.2 iidbQ un/rely 0/0 peerQ un/

rely 0/0 serno 206-206

EIGRP: Sending UPDATE on Serial0 nbr 192.168.12.2

  AS 1, Flags 0x0, Seq 195/161 idbQ 0/0 iidbQ un/rely 0/0 peerQ un/rely 0/1 sern

o 206-206

EIGRP: Received ACK on Serial1 nbr 192.168.13.3

  AS 1, Flags 0x0, Seq 0/194 idbQ 0/0 iidbQ un/rely 0/0 peerQ un/rely 0/1

EIGRP: Enqueueing UPDATE on Serial1 iidbQ un/rely 0/1 serno 206-206

EIGRP: Enqueueing UPDATE on Serial1 nbr 192.168.13.3 iidbQ un/rely 0/0 peerQ un/

rely 0/0 serno 206-206

EIGRP: Sending UPDATE on Serial1 nbr 192.168.13.3

  AS 1, Flags 0x0, Seq 196/175 idbQ 1/0 iidbQ un/rely 0/0 peerQ un/rely 0/1 sern

o 206-206

EIGRP: Received ACK on Serial0 nbr 192.168.12.2

  AS 1, Flags 0x0, Seq 0/195 idbQ 0/0 iidbQ un/rely 0/0 peerQ un/rely 0/1
```

As you can see, a lot of information is made available, and it happens very quickly. In addition to naming the neighbor and/or interface for which each packet is destined, the sequence and acknowledgement numbers are shown. Even though it is possible to follow what is going on from the output, in most cases the messages occur too quickly to make sense of them as they are shown. However, if you can save this information to a file, it can be used later to diagnose troubles.

When a router receives an update, the following traffic is typical of the sequence of events:

```
EIGRP: Received UPDATE on Serial1 nbr 192.168.13.3

  AS 1, Flags 0x0, Seq 179/202 idbQ 0/0 iidbQ un/rely 0/0 peerQ un/rely 0/0
```

```
EIGRP: Enqueueing ACK on Serial1 nbr 192.168.13.3
  Ack seq 179 iidbQ un/rely 0/0 peerQ un/rely 1/0
EIGRP: Sending ACK on Serial1 nbr 192.168.13.3
  AS 1, Flags 0x0, Seq 0/179 idbQ 0/0 iidbQ un/rely 0/0 peerQ un/rely 1/0
```

From this we can see that after receiving the update, the router queued and sent an acknowledgement. Similarly, the following activity occurs when a router needs to send an update:

```
EIGRP: Enqueueing UPDATE on Serial0 iidbQ un/rely 0/1 serno 212-212
EIGRP: Enqueueing UPDATE on Serial0 nbr 192.168.12.2 iidbQ un/rely 0/0 peerQ un/
rely 0/0 serno 212-212
EIGRP: Sending UPDATE on Serial0 nbr 192.168.12.2
  AS 1, Flags 0x0, Seq 204/165 idbQ 0/0 iidbQ un/rely 0/0 peerQ un/rely 0/1 sern
o 212-212
EIGRP: Received ACK on Serial0 nbr 192.168.12.2
  AS 1, Flags 0x0, Seq 0/204 idbQ 0/0 iidbQ un/rely 0/0 peerQ un/rely 0/1
```

In this output, there are two queuing messages, one for the interface and one for the neighbor. Then the packet is sent, followed by the receipt of the acknowledgement. Because of the large amount of information displayed by the debug eigrp packet command, it is wise to carefully consider which traffic needs to be monitored. If the occurrences of only one or two types of packets should provide enough information to aid in troubleshooting, then only those should be enabled. Otherwise, the amount of information shown will probably be too much to prove useful.

Diffusing Computations

Diffusing computations are probably the most complicated aspect of EIGRP, and they are difficult to troubleshoot. Of course, most problems should not require troubleshooting the diffusing computations themselves. Several of the troubleshooting commands previously explained can assist with interpreting the events surrounding a diffusing computation. For example, the show ip eigrp topology command conveniently labels the state of each route in the database. Any active routes are currently part of a diffusing computation. In addition, debugging EIGRP route events and traffic shows when queries and replies arrive and are sent.

There is one command that is intended specifically to help understand DUAL—the heart of the EIGRP routing process. It enables debugging messages regarding the DUAL finite state machine (FSM). Unfortunately, like a few of the other troubleshooting commands, topology changes tend to generate a lot of output. In fact, debugging the FSM provides the most detailed output about EIGRP. It can be enabled with the following privileged EXEC command:

```
R1#debug eigrp fsm
EIGRP FSM Events/Actions debugging is on
```

With FSM debugging enabled, the following output was captured on R1 when the link between R2 and R3 went down:

```
DUAL: dual_rcvquery():192.168.23.0/24 via 192.168.13.3 metric 4294967295/4294967
295, RD is 11023872
DUAL: Find FS for dest 192.168.23.0/24. FD is 11023872, RD is 11023872
DUAL:    192.168.12.2 metric 11023872/10511872
DUAL:    192.168.13.3 metric 4294967295/4294967295 found Dmin is 11023872
DUAL: Send reply about 192.168.23.0/24 to 192.168.13.3
DUAL: RT installed 192.168.23.0/24 via 192.168.12.2
DUAL: Send update about 192.168.23.0/24. Reason: lost if


<text omitted>


DUAL: dual_rcvupdate(): 192.168.3.0/24 via 192.168.12.2 metric 4294967295/429496
7295
DUAL: Find FS for dest 192.168.3.0/24. FD is 10575872, RD is 10575872
DUAL:    192.168.13.3 metric 10575872/704000
DUAL:    192.168.12.2 metric 4294967295/4294967295 found Dmin is 10575872
DUAL: Removing dest 192.168.3.0/24, nexthop 192.168.12.2
DUAL: RT installed 192.168.3.0/24 via 192.168.13.3
DUAL: Removing dest 192.168.23.0/24, nexthop 192.168.12.2
DUAL: No routes. Flushing dest 192.168.23.0/24
```

Over half of the output from that one event has been removed for read-ability. As you can see, the level of detail is very great and can help explain what is taking place in the route processing. With the increased level of detail also comes a greater number of messages that are difficult to inter-pret. However, an understanding of every single message is not needed to benefit from using this output in troubleshooting.

Tip

When debugging floods your console session with output, enter undebug all and press Enter. (The command can usually be abbreviated u all.) This should turn of all debugging. In some cases, the output will continue to scroll by on your console ses-sion until the session catches up with the output that has already been sent.

Wrap-Up

Both IGRP and EIGRP offer several advantages over other routing proto-cols. IGRP works in much the same way as RIP, but it consumes fewer network resources than RIP, and it uses a metric that more accurately reflects the properties of the routes. EIGRP cuts down on network resource consumption even further by eliminating periodic routing table updates. It also offers very fast convergence, reliable methods of propagat-ing routing information, and classless operation. Both protocols offer a high degree of customizability, providing the opportunity to make them work in the most efficient manner for each individual network.

Of course, the tradeoff for the advantages of these two protocols is that they can only be run on Cisco routers. In networks that meet this require-ment, however, there is good reason to choose IGRP or EIGRP. Even when a network includes equipment from other vendors in one or two areas, it is still possibile to redistribute between another routing protocol and IGRP or EIGRP. (See Chapter 8 for a thorough explanation of route redistribution.) Both of these protocols are strong choices for almost any network.

Chapter 4

Open Shortest Path First

Open Shortest Path First (OSPF) is one of the most popular and widely used routing protocols today. Two factors contribute to its popularity. First, OSPF is a link state protocol, and as such it overcomes many of the shortcomings of Routing Information Protocol (RIP) and other distance vector protocols. Second, OSPF is an open standard, so devices from multiple vendors can share information on the same internetwork. The Internet Engineering Task Force developed OSPF largely as a replacement for RIP, which was one of the few routing protocols available prior to the advent of OSPF. RIP continues to be a popular protocol due to its wide implementation base, but OSPF is growing fast as support for it becomes more common.

Several Requests for Comments (RFCs), all written by John Moy, define OSPF. OSPF Version 1 is defined in RFC 1131, but this version never evolved beyond the experimental stage. Version 2 is the version in use today and still the most recent version. The current specification is RFC 2328.

The advantages of OSPF include the following:

- Fast convergence
- Reduced risk of routing loops because all routers have full knowledge of the internetwork
- Route summarization, resulting in smaller routing tables
- Fully classless behavior, including support for Variable-Length Subnet Masks (VLSM) and supernets
- Reduced network bandwidth use because routers exchange routing information as needed, such as during a topology change
- Use of multicast packets, rather than broadcasts

Understanding OSPF

Because of the nature of link state routing protocols, OSPF can be somewhat complicated. Like all other routing protocols, OSPF should choose the routes with the lowest cost. However, the process by which OSPF makes its routing decision adds complexity. It is important to understand the behavior of OSPF to build effective OSPF networks and to troubleshoot any problems that occur. The characteristics that define OSPF are interrelated. This section explains them and their relationship.

OSPF Basics

Because OSPF is a link state protocol, OSPF routers create a routing table by building a link state database, which contains information regarding every router and network on the internetwork. The routers use that information to build a routing table. In order for this process to function reliably, all routers must have an identical copy of the link state database. Link state databases are built from link state advertisements (LSAs), which are generated by every router and flooded throughout the OSPF internetwork. LSAs come in several types, and a complete collection of LSAs gives the router an accurate map of the entire internetwork.

In OSPF, the metric used to determine the desirability of a path is called *cost*. A cost is assigned to every interface on a router. By default, the cost associated with an interface is inversely proportional to the bandwidth of the link to which the interface is connected. The cost of a path to a particular destination is the sum of the costs of all of the links between the router and the destination.

To create the routing table from the database of LSAs, the router runs Dijkstra's shortest path first algorithm to build a tree of least-cost routes, with itself as the root. A description of Dijkstra's algorithm is beyond the scope of this text, but it is sufficient to know that the algorithm enables a router to calculate the least-cost path(s) to each node on the internetwork. Each OSPF router run Dijkstra's algorithm from its own perspective, but the end result should be the same for all routers. The router enters the least-cost routes into its routing table, which may also include routes from other routing protocols.

Unlike RIP, OSPF does not regularly broadcast all of its routing information. Instead, routers use Hello packets to let their neighbors know that they are still up and running. If a router does not receive a Hello packet from one of its neighbors for a certain amount of time, it decides that the neighbor must no longer be running. OSPF routing updates are incremental, so usually routers only send updates when a topology change occurs.

OSPF can be a memory-intensive protocol because routers store all LSAs in their link state databases. On a large internetwork, memory requirements may make OSPF cost-prohibitive or may prevent organizations from running the protocol on existing hardware. To alleviate this problem, OSPF uses the concept of areas. An area is part of the OSPF Autonomous System (AS), in which all routers share a common link state database. Routers in different areas do not share the same link state database, but information is passed between areas within an AS through other types of LSAs.

Router IDs

When a router starts its OSPF routing process, it must determine its router ID (RID). The *RID* identifies the router throughout the OSPF internetwork and must be unique. All OSPF packets contain the RID, regardless of the sending interface. The router determines its RID by checking whether it has any loopback interfaces configured. If it does, the router chooses the numerically highest IP address of those on the loopback interfaces. If the router has no loopback interfaces, it chooses the numerically highest IP address of those on the physical interfaces. The interface from which the RID is chosen does not need to be running OSPF.

One benefit of loopback interfaces is that they are more stable than physical interfaces. If a router uses a physical-interface IP address as its RID, it has to choose a new RID if the interface experiences hardware failure, an administrative shutdown, or if its IP address is removed. In these cases, the router must prematurely age its old LSAs and send out new ones with the new RID. Two activities that do not have this effect are interface failure (other than hardware) or if the interface is deleted. As a result, removing a cable and other standard activities do not force the router to choose a new RID. Another significant benefit of using loopback interfaces is that they enable the administrator to assign the RIDs manually, making them easier to remember when working with the network.

OSPF Multicast Addresses

If OSPF used broadcast packets to exchange routing information, all nodes on the network would have to process the packets to determine whether or not the packets were meant for them. This would consume processing cycles of every node on the network. Instead, OSPF uses multicast IP and Media Access Control (MAC) addresses to exchange routing information. This allows other nodes on the network to operate uninterrupted, as their Network Interface Cards (NICs) are able to determine that the packets are not meant for those nodes. The destination IP address for all OSPF devices, known as *AllSPFRouters*, is 224.0.0.5, and the MAC address is 0100.5E00.0005. The destination IP address for designated routers (DRs) and backup designated routers (BDRs) is 224.0.0.6, known as *AllDRouters*, and the MAC address is 0100.5E00.0006.

OSPF Network Types

The type of network to which an interface is connected determines the default behavior for OSPF on that interface. The network type affects the formation of adjacencies and the way the router sets various timers associated with the interface. There are five network types in OSPF: broadcast networks, nonbroadcast multi-access (NBMA) networks, point-to-point networks, point-to-multipoint networks, and virtual links.

- *Broadcast networks* include Ethernet, Token Ring, and Fiber Distributed Data Interface (FDDI). These are multi-access networks that support the use of broadcasts and multicasts. On broadcast networks, OSPF routers use multicast packets to communicate, and they do not form adjacencies with all routers on the same network.

- *NBMA networks* include X.25, Frame Relay, and Asynchronous Transfer Mode (ATM). Although these are also multi-access networks, they do not support broadcasts. OSPF must use unicast packets to communicate between routers on NBMA networks. As on broadcast networks, adjacencies do not form between all routers on NBMA networks.

- *Point-to-point networks* include direct serial connections, such as leased lines. A point-to-point network has only two nodes, so an adjacency always forms between the two nodes. The routers use multicast OSPF packets (to 224.0.0.5) to exchange routing information on point-to-point networks.

- *Point-to-multipoint networks* are actually NBMA networks, but they are treated differently to avoid some of the problems associated with most NBMA networks. A point-to-multipoint network is treated as a collection of point-to-point networks. Therefore, the behavior of a point-to-multipoint network closely reflects that of a point-to-point network. Adjacencies are established between each pair of routers, and they communicate using multicast packets.

Unlike the other network types, *virtual links* are not associated with physical interfaces. Instead, they create links to the backbone area through nonbackbone areas. Virtual links must have area border routers (ABRs) as the endpoints and can only traverse areas with full routing information. They are treated as unnumbered point-to-point connections, and they use unicast packets to communicate because the packets need to be routed between neighbors.

Hello Packets and OSPF Timers

OSPF routers exchange *Hello packets* at certain intervals. In addition to functioning as keepalives between neighbors, Hello packets allow the discovery of OSPF neighbors, the establishment of neighbor relationships and adjacencies, and the election of designated routers. On broadcast, point-to-point, and point-to-multipoint networks, Hello packets are multicast. On NBMA networks and virtual links, Hello packets are unicast to the configured neighbors. OSPF uses three timers associated with Hello packets: HelloInterval, RouterDeadInterval, and PollInterval.

The *HelloInterval* determines how often a router will send Hello packets from each interface. The default HelloInterval depends on the network type. On broadcast and point-to-point networks, the default HelloInterval is 10 seconds, and on NBMA and point-to-multipoint networks, the default HelloInterval is 30 seconds. Routers must agree on the length of the HelloInterval for them to become neighbors. The HelloInterval is a property of the interface and can be changed with the command ip ospf hello-interval *seconds.*

The *RouterDeadInterval* is the amount of time a router will wait after the last Hello packet received from a neighbor until it decides the neighbor is down. The default RouterDeadInterval is four times the HelloInterval for all network types. Like the HelloInterval, the RouterDeadInterval is a property of the interface and must be the same for neighbor relationships to form. The RouterDeadInterval can be changed with the command `ip ospf dead-interval` *seconds*.

The *PollInterval* is used only on NBMA networks. When a neighbor is down, a Hello packet is sent to the neighbor every PollInterval. The default PollInterval is 60 seconds and can be changed on a per-neighbor basis with the command `neighbor` *address* `poll-interval` *seconds*.

Hello packets contain the following information: RID, area ID, network mask, authentication information, HelloInterval, RouterDeadInterval, router priority, RIDs of the DR and BDR, RIDs of all neighbors on that interface, and some options. OSPF routers check some of this information before they become neighbors.

Neighbors

OSPF neighbors are routers on the same network that agree on certain configuration parameters. If two routers on the same network do not agree on these required parameters, they cannot become neighbors. Routers must be neighbors before they can form an adjacency.

Routers form a neighbor relationship by analyzing the contents of each other's Hello packets to determine whether they agree on the required parameters. The following parameters must match for routers to become neighbors: area ID, network mask, authentication information, HelloInterval, RouterDeadInterval, and the options. If routers do not agree on these parameters, they cannot become neighbors. If they agree, each router puts the neighbor's RID into its own Hello packet. When a router receives a Hello with its own RID listed as a neighbor, it knows that the neighbor relationship has been formed. After forming a neighbor relationship, the routers must determine whether or not they will form an adjacency.

Adjacencies and Designated Routers

When two routers form an adjacency, they can exchange routing information. Whether or not two routers form an adjacency depends on the type of network connecting the routers. Point-to-point networks have only two routers, so those routers automatically form an adjacency. Because point-to-multipoint networks are regarded as a collection of several point-to-point networks, each pair of routers forms an adjacency. Virtual links are basically unnumbered point-to-point links, so the two routers on the ends of the virtual link also form an adjacency.

On broadcast and NBMA networks, neighbors do not necessarily form adjacencies. Unlike the other network types, several routers can be connected via the same multi-access network, rather than just two. If all n routers on a network were to establish adjacencies, each router would form *(n-1)* adjacencies, and there would be $n(n-1)/2$ adjacencies on that network. For a network with only four routers attached, the overhead is negligible, but for a large multi-access network, there would be significant overhead involved for each router to track so many adjacencies, and a large percent of the traffic on that network would consist of routing updates between every pair of adjacent routers.

To alleviate some of the potential overhead on multi-access networks, OSPF routers elect a *designated router* (*DR*) and *backup designated router* (*BDR*). The DR and BDR must form an adjacency with every neighbor on the network. However, the other routers only form adjacencies with the DR and BDR. The DR is responsible for distributing all LSAs to every OSPF router on that network, and it is also responsible for generating a separate LSA for the multi-access network. The BDR becomes the DR if the current DR goes down. The existence of the BDR allows the DR to be replaced almost immediately. After the BDR becomes the DR, a new BDR is elected.

Router Priority and DR Election

Every router interface has a priority, which influences the router's ability to become the DR or BDR on each network to which it is connected. The router priority is an 8-bit unsigned integer value, in the range 0 to 255. Higher priority values are preferred in the DR election process. The default priority on all Cisco router interfaces is 1, and the priority can be changed using the `ip ospf priority` `integer` command. A priority of 0 makes a router ineligible to become the DR or BDR. If all active routers on a network have a priority of 0, they cannot elect any DR or BDR, so no adjacencies can form. Note that priority only affects elections, so if a high-priority router becomes active on a network, it does not replace the current DR or BDR.

When a router starts running OSPF on an interface on a multi-access network, it sets a wait timer equal to the RouterDeadInterval. During that time, it attempts to learn the current DR and BDR from the Hellos of the other routers on that network. Until it recognizes a DR and BDR, the router will set the DR and BDR fields in its Hellos to 0.0.0.0. If it does not find a DR or BDR during the wait time, the router attempts to advertise itself as the DR.

The process of DR and BDR election follows these steps:

1. Make a list of all eligible routers (routers whose priority is greater than 0).

2. Remove all routers claiming to be the DR from the list.

3. If any routers claim to be the BDR, elect the one with the highest priority. If there is a tie, choose the numerically highest RID of the highest-priority routers.

4. If no routers claim to be the BDR, choose the router with the highest priority. Break a tie by choosing the numerically highest RID from the highest-priority routers.

5. If any routers claim to be the DR, elect the one with the highest priority. In the event of a tie, choose the router with the numerically highest IP address from the highest-priority routers.

6. If no routers claim to be the DR, the newly elected BDR becomes the new DR. Then another election must be held to elect a new BDR.

OSPF Areas

Areas in OSPF break up the internetwork into smaller parts, reducing the amount of information each router must store and maintain. Every router must have complete information about its own area. Information is shared between areas, but the information a router stores about other areas is not as detailed. In addition, routing information can be filtered at area borders, which further reduces the amount of routing information stored by a router.

An area is identified by a number, which is a 32-bit unsigned integer value. Area 0 is reserved for the backbone of the network, and all areas must connect to Area 0 directly. Area numbers can be expressed as decimal integers or in dotted decimal format. Therefore, both Area 0 and Area 0.0.0.0 are valid and in fact equivalent, as are Area 132.24.16.12 and Area 2216169484.

Based on its role in an area, a router can be one or more of the following types:

- *Internal router:* A router whose interfaces are all in the same area.
- *Backbone router:* A router with at least one interface in Area 0.
- *Area Border Router (ABR):* A router with at least one interface in Area 0 and at least one interface in another area.
- *Autonomous System Boundary Router (ASBR):* A router that connects an AS running OSPF to another AS by running another routing protocol, such as RIP or IGRP.

Figure 4-1 displays the different types of OSPF routers and their places in the network.

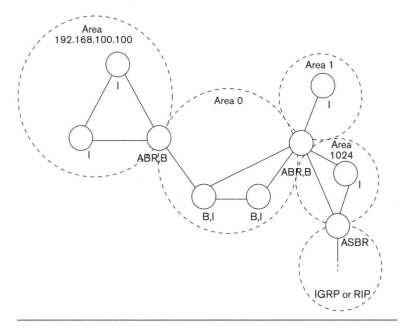

Figure 4-1 *OSPF routers can play one or several roles, depending on their placement within the areas of the internetwork.*

Link State Advertisements

LSAs are the means by which OSPF routers communicate information for the link state database. Routers use the LSAs to build an accurate and complete map of the internetwork, from which they derive routes to use in the routing table.

LSAs come in several types, which are identified by the following type numbers:

Type 1   *Router LSA*: Ever router generates one Router LSA, which includes its RID, along with a list of all of the router's interfaces, including their state and cost. Type 1 LSAs do not traverse ABRs.

Type 2   *Network LSA*: Every DR generates one Network LSA for a multi-access network. A Network LSA includes a list of all routers attached to the multi-access network. Like Type 1 LSAs, Type 2 LSAs are blocked by ABRs and kept within the area in which they were generated.

Type 3   *Network Summary LSA*: Network Summary LSAs carry routing information about one area into another area. They can also contain default routing information. Network Summary LSAs are generated by ABRs to propagate routing information between areas. An ABR generates only one Type 3 LSA for each destination network, no matter how many routes it may know to each destination. Network Summary LSAs are not included in the SPF algorithm run by an OSPF router; instead, they are simply inserted into the routing table. In this respect, OSPF behaves as a distance vector routing protocol between areas.

Type 4   *ASBR Summary LSA*: ASBR Summary LSAs are also generated by ABRs. They are identical to Network Summary LSAs, except they contain routing information about a particular host (an ASBR), rather than about a network. Type 4 LSAs are used in conjunction with Type 5 LSAs to find the best path to an external network.

Type 5   *AS External LSA*: AS External LSAs are originated by an
             ASBR. They advertise routes external to the OSPF AS,
             such as those from other routing protocols or static
             routes. They may also advertise a default route, if the
             default route is external to OSPF. Type 5 LSAs are not
             associated with a particular area, so they are flooded
             throughout the OSPF AS.

Type 6   *Group Membership LSA*: Type 6 LSAs are a part of Mul-
             ticast OSPF (MOSPF), which routes multicast packets.
             MOSPF is not supported by Cisco at this time and is not
             covered in this text.

Type 7   *NSSA External LSA*: NSSA External LSAs are origi-
             nated by ASBRs in not-so-stubby areas (NSSAs). Type 7
             LSAs serve the same function as Type 5 LSAs, except
             they are limited to NSSAs. They are explained further in
             the "Not-So-Stubby Areas" section later in this chapter.

Type 8   *External Attributes LSA*

Type 9   *Opaque LSA (link-local scope)*

Type 10   *Opaque LSA (area-local scope)*

Type 11   *Opaque LSA (AS scope)*

Types 8, 9, 10, and 11 LSAs are proposed but not currently implemented in OSPF.

All LSAs have an age, which is measured in seconds. When generating
an LSA, the router sets its age to zero. As the LSA travels throughout an
internetwork, every router increases the age of an LSA by the *InfTransDelay* of the outgoing interface. By default, the InfTransDelay is 1 for all
interfaces on a Cisco router, and it can be changed by using the command
ip ospf transmit-delay *seconds*.

The age of an LSA is also kept in the link state database and incremented over time. *MaxAge* is the maximum amount of time an LSA can
exist without being refreshed. MaxAge is 3,600 seconds (one hour). If an
LSA in the link state database reaches MaxAge, the router will flush the
LSA from its database. The originating router of an LSA can prematurely

age an LSA by setting the age to MaxAge and flooding the LSA. This causes all other routers to flush the LSA. A router may need to do this if its RID changes or if the LSA has reached the maximum sequence number and must start over with the first sequence number.

The *LSRefreshTime* is the amount of time a router waits before sending out a new copy of the LSA with a higher sequence number. This prevents LSAs from reaching MaxAge and being flushed from each router's link state database. LSRefreshTime is 30 minutes. Prior to IOS 11.3, Cisco used one refresh timer for all LSAs. This allowed the updates to be grouped together in packets, instead of being sent individually. Even though this made the process more efficient, it also caused traffic spikes during the flooding of all of the LSAs.

With IOS 11.3AA, Cisco introduced LSA group pacing. Each LSA has its own refresh timer, but after a timer expires, the router waits for the group-pacing interval to expire before flooding the LSA. This allows LSAs with close timers to still be grouped together in packets, making the flooding more efficient. The default group pacing interval is four minutes, and it can be changed with the command `timers lsa-group-pacing` *seconds*.

LSA Flooding

The operation of OSPF depends upon all routers in an area sharing a common link state database. Therefore, all LSAs need to be flooded throughout the area, and the process must be reliable. Every router that receives an LSA for a particular area will flood that LSA out of all other interfaces that are part of that area. LSAs are not packets on their own; they are contained within *Link State Update* (LSU) packets, and several LSAs may be contained in one LSU. When a router receives an LSU, it does not simply forward the packet. Instead, the router extracts the LSAs from the packet, enters them into its database, and builds its own LSU to forward the new or updated LSAs to its adjacent neighbors.

OSPF uses *Link State Acknowledgements* (LSAcks) to make sure that each LSA is successfully received by its adjacent neighbors. An LSAck contains the headers of the LSAs that it acknowledges, which provide enough information to uniquely identify the LSAs. When a router sends an LSA out of an interface, the LSA is recorded in the retransmit queue of that interface. The router waits *RxmtInterval* (default of five seconds) to receive an LSAck for the LSA. If it does not receive an LSAck, the router retransmits the LSA. Regardless of what type of packet (unicast or multicast) a router uses to send the original LSU, a retransmitted LSU is always a unicast.

Stub Areas

Routers in a nonbackbone area with no ASBRs have only one way to reach any networks outside the OSPF AS—through an ABR. Therefore, routers in these areas do not need to receive Type 5 LSAs, as long as they will send packets destined for unknown hosts to an ABR. This type of area is knows as a *stub area*. In a stub area, all routers must be configured as stub routers. The Hello packet contains a "stub-area characteristic" bit-flag, which must be in common between neighbors.

Caution

Make sure all routers in a stub area are configured as stub routers. Failure to do so prevents routers configured differently from forming neighbor relationships.

ABRs attached to stub areas filter Type 4 and Type 5 LSAs from being advertised into the stub area. Without the Type 4 and Type 5 LSAs, a stub-area router relies on its default route to reach destinations outside of the OSPF AS. As a result, the ABRs must generate a Type 3 LSA for the stub area to advertise the default route. Configuring a stub area conserves memory on the routers in that area because they receive fewer LSAs for their databases.

Because they have no routing information for external routes, the routers in a stub area cannot determine the best route to an external destination. They must route externally destined packets based on the default route, so the cost from each router to the ABRs determines how the packets are forwarded. In some cases, this causes the router to choose a suboptimal route to the final destination, but this may be acceptable for the performance benefits. In addition, virtual links cannot traverse a stub area; full routing information is required for a virtual link.

Totally Stubby Areas

Totally stubby areas are currently Cisco-proprietary. If an area can reach all external destinations by forwarding packets to an ABR, the same is true for all destinations within the OSPF AS but outside the stub area. In addition to blocking Type 4 and Type 5 LSAs, an ABR connected to a totally stubby area also blocks Type 3 LSAs, preventing the propagation of information from other OSPF areas into the totally stubby area. The ABR generates only one Type 3 LSA for the area — the default route.

All routers in a totally stubby area must be configured as stub-area routers. Only the configurations of the ABRs need to be changed to make the area totally stubby.

Not-So-Stubby Areas

Stub area routers do not allow Type 5 LSAs, so an ASBR cannot be part of a stub area. However, it may be desirable to create a stub area that contains an ASBR. The routers in that area would receive external routes from the ASBR in the area, but external routes from other areas would be blocked.

For this reason, *not-so-stubby areas* (*NSSAs*) were invented. In an NSSA, the ASBR generates Type 7 LSAs, instead of Type 5 LSAs. These LSAs are functionally equivalent to Type 5 LSAs, but they are allowed in the NSSA. The ABR cannot pass Type 7 LSAs into the other OSPF areas; it must either block the external routes at the area border, or it can convert the Type 7 LSAs to Type 5 LSAs for the rest of the internetwork. If the ASBR sets the P-bit (an option in the Type 7 LSA), the ABR translates the Type 7 LSA to a Type 5 LSA for other areas. If the P-bit is not set, the ABR simply blocks the LSA.

You can also create totally stubby NSSAs by combining the characteristics of totally stubby areas and NSSAs. This kind of area permits Type 7 LSAs, but the ABR blocks all Types 3, 4, and 5 LSAs from other areas and generates a default route.

OSPF in the Routing Table

The following IP routing table contains OSPF routes:

```
O E2 192.168.100.0/24 [110/20] via 192.168.12.1, 00:03:15, Serial1

O E2 192.168.101.0/24 [110/20] via 192.168.12.1, 00:03:15, Serial1

C    192.168.12.0/24 is directly connected, Serial1

O    192.168.1.0/24 [110/1572] via 192.168.12.1, 00:08:25, Serial1

C    192.168.2.0/24 is directly connected, Ethernet0

O IA 192.168.3.0/24 [110/3134] via 192.168.12.1, 00:08:25, Serial1

O IA 192.168.4.0/24 [110/3144] via 192.168.12.1, 00:08:25, Serial1

O E2 192.168.5.0/24 [110/20] via 192.168.12.1, 00:02:30, Serial1

O IA 192.168.31.0/24 [110/3124] via 192.168.12.1, 00:08:25, Serial1

     192.168.254.0/32 is subnetted, 1 subnets

O IA    192.168.254.4 [110/3135] via 192.168.12.1, 00:08:28, Serial1
```

From this routing table, you can see that the default administrative distance for all OSPF routes is 110. The metric for each OSPF route is the accumulated cost of all outgoing interfaces along that route. The cost of an interface is an unsigned 16-bit integer in the range of 1 through 65,535, and by default, it is calculated by dividing 10^8 by the bandwidth of the link to which the interface is attached. The reference bandwidth (10^8) or the cost of a particular interface can be changed. The cost of a virtual link is the cost to the neighbor.

In the IP routing table, all OSPF routes have an "O" in the far-left column. There are several different types of routes in OSPF, and they are all flagged differently in the routing table (with characters following the O):

- *Intra-area routes* are routes internal to the area(s) to which the router is connected. They are generated from Type 1 and Type 2 LSAs by the SPF algorithm and are not flagged in the routing table.

- *Inter-area routes* are routes that are external to the area but internal to OSPF. They are generated from Type 3 LSAs and are flagged with "IA" in the routing table.

- *External routes* originate in other ASs, rather than from OSPF itself. They are generated by ASBRs, which advertise them using Type 5 LSAs. There are two types of external routes, which vary in the way their cost is calculated by each router. Type 1 external routes, which are flagged "E1" in the routing table, have a cost equal to that assigned by the ASBR plus the cost of the path to the ASBR. Type 2 external routes are flagged "E2" in the routing table. They have a cost equal to that assigned by the ASBR — the cost to the ASBR is not included. Therefore, all routers with a particular E2 route use the same cost. By default, ASBRs make all external routes E2 routes.

- *NSSA external routes* also originate in other ASs, but they are generated by ASBRs within an NSSA. NSSA external routes may be Type 1 or Type 2, which are flagged respectively "N1" and "N2" in the routing table. Their cost is calculated in the same way as that for E1 and E2 routes, respectively.

OSPF Authentication

Authentication can be used in packet exchanges between OSPF neighbors. Neighbors must agree on authentication type, which is included in all packets. The authentication types are (0) no authentication, (1) simple passwords, and (2) MD5 checksums. When configuring simple passwords, only one password is permitted per interface, but every interface may have a different password. Each interface on a particular network must share the same password. Simple passwords are transmitted in clear text in the OSPF packets and could be discovered by capturing packets on that network. MD5 checksums offer an additional level of security, as the passwords are not transmitted in clear text. In addition, multiple MD5 passwords can be configured on the same interface. Each password is assigned a key ID, and as long as the key ID and password match on both neighbors, they can communicate. This allows different keys to be used between different pairs of neighbors on the same network. It also allows easy changeover between old and new passwords, as both can exist on the router concurrently during the changeover.

Configuring OSPF

Getting OSPF running on a network is a fairly easy task. A few simple configuration commands on the routers will have them routing with OSPF in a short time. However, in more complicated environments, the configuration of OSPF can be much more involved. OSPF offers many different options, so it can meet the needs of various networks. In these configuration examples, we start with a basic OSPF configuration and then consider more complicated situations.

Basic OSPF Configuration

To enable OSPF on a router, issue the `router ospf pid` command in global configuration mode, as shown here:

```
R10(config)#router ospf 1
R10(config-router)#
```

This command configures the router to run an OSPF process with process ID (PID) number 1. The PID is only locally significant, so routers do not need to share the same PID. Issuing this command also puts you into OSPF configuration mode. This is where you enter configuration parameters for OSPF. At this time, you must use the `network address wildcard-mask area area-id` command in order to configure OSPF to run on certain interfaces:

```
R10(config-router)#network 192.168.10.0 0.0.0.255 area 1
```

This command will start OSPF on any interfaces with IP addresses in the range 192.168.10.1 through 192.168.10.254. Note that the mask used in the network statement is a wildcard mask, the same as is used in access lists. In a wildcard mask, the 1 bits signify the wildcard bits, and the 0 bits signify the bits that must match exactly. Having one network statement in the OSPF configuration is sufficient to get OSPF running on the router, as long as at least one interface matches the network statement.

Now we will configure OSPF on the routers in the network shown in Figure 4-2. The entire network will part of a single area — Area 1.

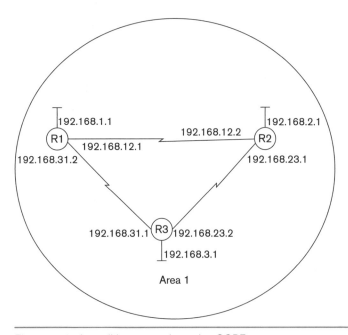

Figure 4-2 *A small internetwork running OSPF*

The routers would be configured as follows:

R1:

```
interface Loopback0
 ip address 192.168.254.1 255.255.255.255
!
interface Ethernet0
ip address 192.168.1.1 255.255.255.0
!
interface Serial0
 ip address 192.168.12.1 255.255.255.0
!
interface Serial1
```

```
 ip address 192.168.31.2 255.255.255.0
!
router ospf 1
 network 192.168.1.1 0.0.0.0 area 1
 network 192.168.12.1 0.0.0.0 area 1
 network 192.168.31.2 0.0.0.0 area 1
```

R2:

```
interface Loopback0
 ip address 192.168.254.2 255.255.255.255
!
interface Ethernet0
 ip address 192.168.2.1 255.255.255.0
!
interface Serial0
 ip address 192.168.23.1 255.255.255.0
!
interface Serial1
 ip address 192.168.12.2 255.255.255.0
!
router ospf 1
 network 0.0.0.0 255.255.255.255 area 1
```

R3:

```
interface Loopback0
 ip address 192.168.254.3 255.255.255.255
!
interface Ethernet0
 ip address 192.168.3.1 255.255.255.0
!
interface Serial0
 ip address 192.168.31.1 255.255.255.0
!
interface Serial1
 ip address 192.168.23.2 255.255.255.0
!
```

```
router ospf 1
network 192.168.0.0 0.0.127.255 area 1
```

Note that we use loopback interfaces here and in most examples in order to make it easy to identify the routers by their RIDs. All interfaces are in Area 1, but each router is configured with different kinds of network statements. The configuration of R1 lists each interface IP address separately in an OSPF network command. It uses a wildcard mask of 0.0.0.0, which indicates that the addresses must match exactly. On the other hand, R2 uses a wildcard mask of 255.255.255.255 to indicate that all interfaces with IP addresses should run OSPF. There is no need to list out any other addresses. Finally, R3 uses another method, specifying a network address with a wildcard mask to enable OSPF only on some interfaces but not all. Because of their network statements, R2 is currently running OSPF on its loopback interface, but R1 and R3 are not running OSPF on their loopback interfaces.

Because all of the routers in the area have an identical link state database, it is sufficient to view only one database here:

```
R2#show ip ospf database

        OSPF Router with ID (192.168.254.2) (Process ID 1)


            Router Link States (Area 1)


Link ID          ADV Router       Age      Seq#       Checksum Link count

192.168.254.1    192.168.254.1    918      0x80000005 0xD3A2   5

192.168.254.2    192.168.254.2    919      0x80000007 0x7373   6

192.168.254.3    192.168.254.3    891      0x80000004 0x2518   5
```

Notice that there are only Router LSAs in this link state database. Network LSAs are only generated by the DR for multi-access networks if they are not a stub network. A stub network (not to be confused with a stub area) has only one OSPF router attached to it. The opposite of a stub network is a transit network, which has more than one router attached. Traffic may transit such a network on its way to the destination. Because a Router LSA lists the router's interfaces, it sufficiently describes any stub networks, eliminating the need for Network LSAs. Therefore, if we attach another router to one of the Ethernet networks, the DR will advertise a Type 2 LSA for that network. Figure 4-3 shows our previous internetwork with an additional router.

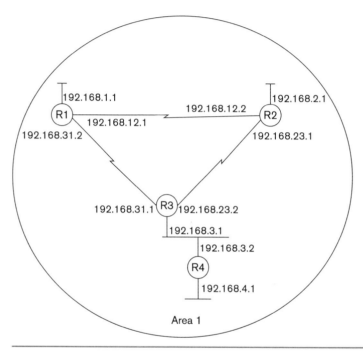

Figure 4-3 *Two or more OSPF routers on a multi-access network make that network a transit network.*

With the addition of R4 to the 192.168.3.0/24 network, the link state database for the area shows the following addition of a Network LSA:

```
R2>show ip ospf database

        OSPF Router with ID (192.168.254.2) (Process ID 1)


            Router Link States (Area 1)


Link ID          ADV Router       Age      Seq#         Checksum Link count
192.168.254.1    192.168.254.1    1020     0x80000005 0xD3A2    5
192.168.254.2    192.168.254.2    1022     0x80000007 0x7373    6
```

```
192.168.254.3    192.168.254.3    5        0x80000005 0x8C6    5
192.168.254.4    192.168.254.4    15       0x80000004 0x93E5   2


                 Net Link States (Area 1)


Link ID          ADV Router       Age      Seq#       Checksum
192.168.3.1      192.168.254.3    5        0x80000001 0xA6E2
```

Because 192.168.3.0/24 is now a transit network, it has a DR and its own LSA. Notice that 192.168.4.0/24 has been added to the internetwork as a stub network, so it does not have its own LSA.

Using Multiple OSPF Areas

A multiple-area network is almost as easily configured as a single-area network, but you must be careful to make sure that interfaces are assigned to the correct areas. ABRs have interfaces in one or more areas, including at least one interface in Area 0. For example, Figure 4-4 shows our sample network reconfigured with four areas.

The three ABRs are configured as follows:

R1:

```
interface Loopback0
 ip address 192.168.254.1 255.255.255.255
!
interface Ethernet0
ip address 192.168.1.1 255.255.255.0
!
interface Serial0
 ip address 192.168.12.1 255.255.255.0
!
interface Serial1
 ip address 192.168.31.2 255.255.255.0
!
router ospf 1
```

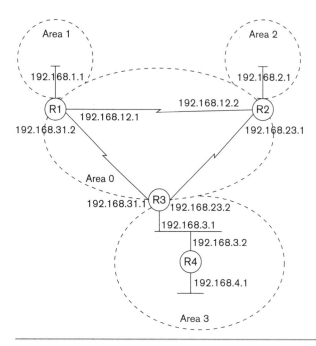

Figure 4-4 *A small OSPF internetwork using multiple areas*

```
network 192.168.1.1 0.0.0.0 area 1
network 192.168.31.2 0.0.0.0 area 0
network 192.168.12.1 0.0.0.0 area 0
```

R2:
```
interface Loopback0
 ip address 192.168.254.2 255.255.255.255
!
interface Ethernet0
 ip address 192.168.2.1 255.255.255.0
!
interface Serial0
 ip address 192.168.23.1 255.255.255.0
!
interface Serial1
```

```
ip address 192.168.12.2 255.255.255.0
!
router ospf 1
 network 192.168.2.1 0.0.0.0 area 2
 network 192.168.12.2 0.0.0.0 area 0
 network 192.168.23.1 0.0.0.0 area 0
```

R3:

```
interface Loopback0
 ip address 192.168.254.3 255.255.255.255
!
interface Ethernet0
 ip address 192.168.3.1 255.255.255.0
!
interface Serial0
 ip address 192.168.31.1 255.255.255.0
!
interface Serial1
 ip address 192.168.23.2 255.255.255.0
!
router ospf 1
 network 192.168.3.1 0.0.0.0 area 3
 network 192.168.23.2 0.0.0.0 area 0
 network 192.168.31.1 0.0.0.0 area 0
```

The configuration commands enable each router to use both of its serial interfaces as part of Area 0 and its Ethernet interface as part of another area. On all three ABRs we used explicit interface addresses in the OSPF network statements, but we could also have used wildcards. It is important to note that a router will process the network area statements in the order given. Overlapping is allowed, so another valid way to configure R3 is as follows:

```
router ospf 1
 network 192.168.3.1 0.0.0.0 area 3
 network 0.0.0.0 255.255.255.255 area 0
```

This configuration assigns only the interface with address 192.168.3.1 to Area 3 and all other interfaces to Area 0.

 Caution

Exercise caution when using wildcards in the OSPF network statements. Interfaces are matched against the statements sequentially, rather than by finding the longest match. When adding network statements, make sure to check that the interface(s) you wish to match with the new statements are not matched by previous statements. If they are, the new statements will not have the desired result.

After creating the four areas, the link state database of R2 will be the following:

```
R2#show ip ospf database

           OSPF Router with ID (192.168.254.2) (Process ID 1)


                Router Link States (Area 0)


Link ID          ADV Router       Age      Seq#       Checksum Link count

192.168.254.1    192.168.254.1    87       0x8000000C 0x9260   4

192.168.254.2    192.168.254.2    72       0x80000007 0xF5F0   4

192.168.254.3    192.168.254.3    83       0x80000008 0x625C   4


                Summary Net Link States (Area 0)


Link ID          ADV Router       Age      Seq#       Checksum

192.168.1.0      192.168.254.1    546      0x80000001 0x877

192.168.2.0      192.168.254.2    89       0x80000001 0x1548

192.168.3.0      192.168.254.3    480      0x80000003 0xFF59

192.168.4.0      192.168.254.3    485      0x80000001 0x5DF2

192.168.254.4    192.168.254.3    485      0x80000001 0x1248
```

```
                     Router Link States (Area 2)


Link ID        ADV Router      Age        Seq#        Checksum Link count
192.168.254.2  192.168.254.2   84         0x80000002 0x6F77    1


                     Summary Net Link States (Area 2)


Link ID        ADV Router      Age        Seq#        Checksum
192.168.1.0    192.168.254.2   69         0x80000001 0x5BE2
192.168.3.0    192.168.254.2   69         0x80000001 0x45F6
192.168.4.0    192.168.254.2   69         0x80000001 0x9E92
192.168.12.0   192.168.254.2   79         0x80000001 0x7DBF
192.168.23.0   192.168.254.2   89         0x80000001 0x42E
192.168.31.0   192.168.254.2   69         0x80000001 0xE623
192.168.254.4  192.168.254.2   69         0x80000001 0x53E7
```

Note that some LSAs exist in the table twice. Because R2 is the ABR, it generates matching LSAs from each area to send into the other areas. The routing table of R2 is now as follows:

```
R2#show ip route
Codes: C - connected, S - static, I - IGRP, R - RIP, M - mobile, B - BGP
       D - EIGRP, EX - EIGRP external, O - OSPF, IA - OSPF inter area
       N1 - OSPF NSSA external type 1, N2 - OSPF NSSA external type 2
       E1 - OSPF external type 1, E2 - OSPF external type 2, E - EGP
       i - IS-IS, L1 - IS-IS level-1, L2 - IS-IS level-2, * - candidate default
       U - per-user static route, o - ODR


Gateway of last resort is not set


C    192.168.12.0/24 is directly connected, Serial1
O IA 192.168.1.0/24 [110/1572] via 192.168.12.1, 00:00:28, Serial1
C    192.168.2.0/24 is directly connected, Ethernet0
O IA 192.168.3.0/24 [110/1572] via 192.168.23.2, 00:00:28, Serial0
O IA 192.168.4.0/24 [110/1582] via 192.168.23.2, 00:00:28, Serial0
O    192.168.31.0/24 [110/3124] via 192.168.23.2, 00:00:28, Serial0
                     [110/3124] via 192.168.12.1, 00:00:28, Serial1
```

```
C    192.168.23.0/24 is directly connected, Serial0
     192.168.254.0/32 is subnetted, 2 subnets
O IA    192.168.254.4 [110/1573] via 192.168.23.2, 00:00:28, Serial0
C    192.168.254.2 is directly connected, Loopback0
```

Notice that there are now inter-area routes (flagged with IA) in the routing table. Although we have changed the network from one area to four areas, the routing table has not changed. Although some of the routes have changed to inter-area routes, the exact same set of routes is listed with the exact same metrics.

Configuring Stub Areas

We are now going to work with a completely new example network, as shown in Figure 4-5. This network is also using RIP, which has routes that the OSPF domain needs to learn. R4 will serve as our ASBR, and it will redistribute the RIP routes into OSPF. Configuring redistribution is covered in Chapter 8.

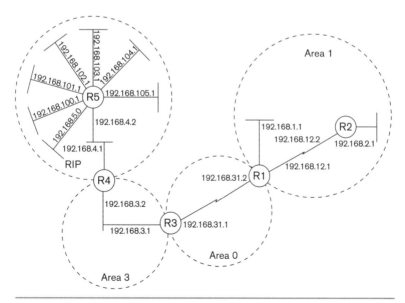

Figure 4-5 *This network with multiple areas is redistributing RIP into OSPF. Use of stub areas and NSSAs will help save resources on this internetwork.*

Running both RIP and OSPF, the routing table of R4 appears as follows:

```
R4#show ip route
Codes: C - connected, S - static, I - IGRP, R - RIP, M - mobile, B - BGP
       D - EIGRP, EX - EIGRP external, O - OSPF, IA - OSPF inter area
       E1 - OSPF external type 1, E2 - OSPF external type 2, E - EGP
       i - IS-IS, L1 - IS-IS level-1, L2 - IS-IS level-2, * - candidate default
       U - per-user static route


Gateway of last resort is not set


R    192.168.104.0/24 [120/1] via 192.168.4.2, 00:00:04, Ethernet1

R    192.168.105.0/24 [120/1] via 192.168.4.2, 00:00:04, Ethernet1

R    192.168.100.0/24 [120/1] via 192.168.4.2, 00:00:05, Ethernet1

R    192.168.101.0/24 [120/1] via 192.168.4.2, 00:00:05, Ethernet1

R    192.168.102.0/24 [120/1] via 192.168.4.2, 00:00:05, Ethernet1

R    192.168.103.0/24 [120/1] via 192.168.4.2, 00:00:05, Ethernet1

O IA 192.168.12.0/24 [110/3134] via 192.168.3.1, 00:09:54, Ethernet0

O IA 192.168.1.0/24 [110/1582] via 192.168.3.1, 00:09:54, Ethernet0

O IA 192.168.2.0/24 [110/3144] via 192.168.3.1, 00:09:54, Ethernet0

C    192.168.3.0/24 is directly connected, Ethernet0

C    192.168.4.0/24 is directly connected, Ethernet1

R    192.168.5.0/24 [120/1] via 192.168.4.2, 00:00:05, Ethernet1

O IA 192.168.31.0/24 [110/1572] via 192.168.3.1, 00:09:55, Ethernet0

     192.168.254.0/32 is subnetted, 1 subnets

C       192.168.254.4 is directly connected, Loopback0
```

The RIP and OSPF routes coexist in the same routing table. R4 is redistributing the RIP routes into OSPF. Under normal conditions, the redistributed routes traverse all areas. Therefore, the routing table of R2 is as follows:

```
R2#show ip route
Codes: C - connected, S - static, I - IGRP, R - RIP, M - mobile, B - BGP
       D - EIGRP, EX - EIGRP external, O - OSPF, IA - OSPF inter area
       N1 - OSPF NSSA external type 1, N2 - OSPF NSSA external type 2
       E1 - OSPF external type 1, E2 - OSPF external type 2, E - EGP
       i - IS-IS, L1 - IS-IS level-1, L2 - IS-IS level-2, * - candidate default
```

```
      U - per-user static route, o - ODR

Gateway of last resort is not set

O E2 192.168.104.0/24 [110/20] via 192.168.12.1, 00:03:15, Serial1

O E2 192.168.105.0/24 [110/20] via 192.168.12.1, 00:03:15, Serial1

O E2 192.168.100.0/24 [110/20] via 192.168.12.1, 00:03:15, Serial1

O E2 192.168.101.0/24 [110/20] via 192.168.12.1, 00:03:15, Serial1

O E2 192.168.102.0/24 [110/20] via 192.168.12.1, 00:03:15, Serial1

O E2 192.168.103.0/24 [110/20] via 192.168.12.1, 00:03:15, Serial1

C    192.168.12.0/24 is directly connected, Serial1

O    192.168.1.0/24 [110/1572] via 192.168.12.1, 00:08:25, Serial1

C    192.168.2.0/24 is directly connected, Ethernet0

O IA 192.168.3.0/24 [110/3134] via 192.168.12.1, 00:08:25, Serial1

O IA 192.168.4.0/24 [110/3144] via 192.168.12.1, 00:08:25, Serial1

O E2 192.168.5.0/24 [110/20] via 192.168.12.1, 00:02:30, Serial1

O IA 192.168.31.0/24 [110/3124] via 192.168.12.1, 00:08:25, Serial1

     192.168.254.0/32 is subnetted, 2 subnets

O IA    192.168.254.4 [110/3135] via 192.168.12.1, 00:08:28, Serial1

C       192.168.254.2 is directly connected, Loopback0
```

Notice that all of the RIP routes show up as Type 2 external routes on R2. By default, Cisco ASBRs generate Type 2 external routes, but they can be configured to generate Type 1 default routes. The summary of the link state database on R2 is the following:

```
R2#show ip ospf database database-summary

          OSPF Router with ID (192.168.254.2) (Process ID 1)
```

Area ID	Router	Network	S-Net	S-ASBR	Type-7	Subtotal	Delete	Maxage
1	2	0	4	1	N/A	7	0	0
AS External						9	0	0
Total	2	0	4	1	0	16		

There are several things to note in this output. First, only Area 1 is listed, because it is the only area in which R2 is participating. Any LSAs from outside Area 1 are Type 3 LSAs, and they fall under the S-Net column. The Type-7 column will always read N/A, except in NSSAs. Finally, external routes are not considered part of any area, so they have a category of their own. R2 has nine Type 5 LSAs in its link state database, even though it must reach all of them through the same router—R1. To save resources within Area 1, configure it as a stub area. To do so, you must enter the following command on every router in the area, including the ABR(s):

```
R2(config-router)#area 1 stub
```

After Area 1 is configured as a stub area, R1 blocks all Type 4 and Type 5 LSAs from Area 1. Therefore, the link state database on R2 now has far fewer entries and appears as follows:

```
R2#show ip ospf database database-summary


        OSPF Router with ID (192.168.254.2) (Process ID 1)


Area ID     Router  Network S-Net   S-ASBR  Type-7  Subtotal Delete Maxage

1           2       0       5       0       N/A     7        0      0

AS External                                         0        0      0

Total       2       0       5       0       0       7
```

Note that R2 has no AS External entries (Type 5 LSAs) or S-ASBR entries (Type 4 LSAs). There is one additional S-Net entry because R1 generates a default route as a Type 3 LSA for the stub area. The routing table for R2 is now much shorter, and it appears as the following:

```
R2#show ip route
Codes: C - connected, S - static, I - IGRP, R - RIP, M - mobile, B - BGP
       D - EIGRP, EX - EIGRP external, O - OSPF, IA - OSPF inter area
       N1 - OSPF NSSA external type 1, N2 - OSPF NSSA external type 2
       E1 - OSPF external type 1, E2 - OSPF external type 2, E - EGP
       i - IS-IS, L1 - IS-IS level-1, L2 - IS-IS level-2, * - candidate default
       U - per-user static route, o - ODR

Gateway of last resort is 192.168.12.1 to network 0.0.0.0
```

```
C    192.168.12.0/24 is directly connected, Serial1
O    192.168.1.0/24 [110/1572] via 192.168.12.1, 00:01:46, Serial1
C    192.168.2.0/24 is directly connected, Ethernet0
O IA 192.168.3.0/24 [110/3134] via 192.168.12.1, 00:01:46, Serial1
O IA 192.168.4.0/24 [110/3144] via 192.168.12.1, 00:01:46, Serial1
O IA 192.168.31.0/24 [110/3124] via 192.168.12.1, 00:01:46, Serial1
        192.168.254.0/32 is subnetted, 2 subnets
O IA    192.168.254.4 [110/3135] via 192.168.12.1, 00:01:46, Serial1
C       192.168.254.2 is directly connected, Loopback0
O*IA 0.0.0.0/0 [110/1563] via 192.168.12.1, 00:01:46, Serial1
```

Notice the last route (the default) is flagged IA because Type 3 LSAs are interpreted as inter-area routes.

Configuring Totally Stubby Areas

Because all inter-area traffic from R2 must go through R1 in the preceding example, R2 does not really need to know about any of the inter-area routes either. Therefore, it can be a totally stubby area, with no loss of routing functionality. You can configure a stub area as a totally stubby area by issuing the following command on the ABR only:

```
R1(config-router)#area 1 stub no-summary
```

Note that the other routers still need to be configured as stub area routers, but they do not require this configuration command. After making this configuration change, the database on R2 has even fewer entries, as shown here:

```
R2#show ip ospf database database-summary
```

```
        OSPF Router with ID (192.168.254.2) (Process ID 1)
```

Area ID	Router	Network	S-Net	S-ASBR	Type-7	Subtotal	Delete	Maxage
1	2	0	1	0	N/A	3	0	0
AS External						0	0	0
Total	2	0	1	0	0	3		

Configuring the area as a totally stubby area eliminates all Type 3 LSAs from Area 1 except for the default route LSA. The routing table for R2 now only has intra-area routes and the default route, as shown here:

```
R2#show ip route
Codes: C - connected, S - static, I - IGRP, R - RIP, M - mobile, B - BGP

       D - EIGRP, EX - EIGRP external, O - OSPF, IA - OSPF inter area

       N1 - OSPF NSSA external type 1, N2 - OSPF NSSA external type 2

       E1 - OSPF external type 1, E2 - OSPF external type 2, E - EGP

       i - IS-IS, L1 - IS-IS level-1, L2 - IS-IS level-2, * - candidate default

       U - per-user static route, o - ODR


Gateway of last resort is 192.168.12.1 to network 0.0.0.0


C    192.168.12.0/24 is directly connected, Serial1

O    192.168.1.0/24 [110/1572] via 192.168.12.1, 00:01:17, Serial1

C    192.168.2.0/24 is directly connected, Ethernet0

     192.168.254.0/32 is subnetted, 1 subnets

C       192.168.254.2 is directly connected, Loopback0

O*IA 0.0.0.0/0 [110/1563] via 192.168.12.1, 00:01:17, Serial1
```

We cannot shorten the routing table of R2 any more than this because it only contains intra-area routes. An OSPF router must by definition have a full database of all routes in its own area, so we cannot eliminate these routes.

Configuring NSSAs

In the network in Figure 4-5, we cannot configure Area 3 as a stub area because it contains an ASBR. Because a stub area does not allow Type 5 LSAs, R4 could not advertise its external routes. However, we can make Area 3 an NSSA if we desire stub behavior and an ASBR in the same area. Before we configure Area 3 as an NSSA, the link state database of R3 contains the following entries:

```
R3#show ip ospf database database-summary


      OSPF Router with ID (192.168.254.3) (Process ID 1)
```

Area ID	Router	Network	S-Net	S-ASBR	Type-7	Subtotal	Delete	Maxage
0	2	0	5	1	N/A	8	0	0
3	2	1	4	1	N/A	8	0	0
AS External						9	0	0
Total	4	1	9	2	0	25		

And the database for R4 is as follows:

```
R4#show ip ospf database database-summary

          OSPF Router with ID (192.168.254.4) (Process ID 1)
```

Area ID	Router	Network	S-Net	S-ASBR	Type-7	Subtotal	Delete	Maxage
3	2	1	4	1	N/A	8	0	0
AS External						9	0	0
Total	2	1	4	1	0	17		

Even though the link state database is small on these routers, it is important to remember that this is a small internetwork. Large internetworks would have significantly larger databases, which could hamper performance. To configure an NSSA, enter the following command on all routers in the area:

```
R3(config-router)#area 3 nssa
```

After making this change, the link state database for R3 lists entries under the Type-7 column for Area 3. The Type 7 LSAs remain within the area in which they were originated, so Area 0 has none, as shown here:

```
R3#show ip ospf database database-summary

          OSPF Router with ID (192.168.254.3) (Process ID 1)
```

Area ID	Router	Network	S-Net	S-ASBR	Type-7	Subtotal	Delete	Maxage
0	2	0	5	0	N/A	7	0	0
3	2	1	4	0	9	16	0	0
AS External						7	0	0
Total	4	1	9	0	9	30		

And the routing table for R3 flags the routes as N2, rather than E2, as shown here because they are in an NSSA:

```
R3#show ip route
Codes: C - connected, S - static, I - IGRP, R - RIP, M - mobile, B - BGP
       D - EIGRP, EX - EIGRP external, O - OSPF, IA - OSPF inter area
       N1 - OSPF NSSA external type 1, N2 - OSPF NSSA external type 2
       E1 - OSPF external type 1, E2 - OSPF external type 2, E - EGP
       i - IS-IS, L1 - IS-IS level-1, L2 - IS-IS level-2, * - candidate default
       U - per-user static route, o - ODR


Gateway of last resort is not set


O IA 192.168.12.0/24 [110/3124] via 192.168.31.2, 00:00:26, Serial0
O N2 192.168.104.0/24 [110/20] via 192.168.3.2, 00:00:26, Ethernet0
C    192.168.31.0/24 is directly connected, Serial0
O N2 192.168.105.0/24 [110/20] via 192.168.3.2, 00:00:26, Ethernet0
O    192.168.4.0/24 [110/20] via 192.168.3.2, 00:00:36, Ethernet0
O N2 192.168.5.0/24 [110/20] via 192.168.3.2, 00:00:26, Ethernet0
O N2 192.168.102.0/24 [110/20] via 192.168.3.2, 00:00:26, Ethernet0
     192.168.254.0/32 is subnetted, 1 subnets
C    192.168.254.3 is directly connected, Loopback0
O IA 192.168.1.0/24 [110/1572] via 192.168.31.2, 00:00:26, Serial0
O N2 192.168.103.0/24 [110/20] via 192.168.3.2, 00:00:26, Ethernet0
O IA 192.168.2.0/24 [110/3134] via 192.168.31.2, 00:00:26, Serial0
O N2 192.168.100.0/24 [110/20] via 192.168.3.2, 00:00:26, Ethernet0
C    192.168.3.0/24 is directly connected, Ethernet0
O N2 192.168.101.0/24 [110/20] via 192.168.3.2, 00:00:27, Ethernet0
```

However, in the routing table on R1, the routes still exist as E2. Routers outside of the NSSA are not aware of the existence of the NSSA, as shown here in the IP routing table of R1:

```
R1#show ip route
Codes: C - connected, S - static, I - IGRP, R - RIP, M - mobile, B - BGP
       D - EIGRP, EX - EIGRP external, O - OSPF, IA - OSPF inter area
       E1 - OSPF external type 1, E2 - OSPF external type 2, E - EGP
```

```
        i - IS-IS, L1 - IS-IS level-1, L2 - IS-IS level-2, * - candidate default

Gateway of last resort is not set

O E2 192.168.104.0 [110/20] via 192.168.31.1, 00:13:23, Serial1

O E2 192.168.105.0 [110/20] via 192.168.31.1, 00:13:23, Serial1

O E2 192.168.100.0 [110/20] via 192.168.31.1, 00:13:23, Serial1

O E2 192.168.101.0 [110/20] via 192.168.31.1, 00:13:23, Serial1

O E2 192.168.102.0 [110/20] via 192.168.31.1, 00:13:23, Serial1

O E2 192.168.103.0 [110/20] via 192.168.31.1, 00:13:23, Serial1

C    192.168.12.0 is directly connected, Serial0

C    192.168.1.0 is directly connected, Ethernet0

O    192.168.2.0 [110/1572] via 192.168.12.2, 00:24:39, Serial0

O IA 192.168.3.0 [110/1572] via 192.168.31.1, 00:24:19, Serial1

O IA 192.168.4.0 [110/1582] via 192.168.31.1, 00:13:27, Serial1

O E2 192.168.5.0 [110/20] via 192.168.31.1, 00:13:23, Serial1

C    192.168.31.0 is directly connected, Serial1

     192.168.254.0 255.255.255.255 is subnetted, 1 subnets

C       192.168.254.1 is directly connected, Loopback0
```

R3, the ABR for Area 3, converted the Type 7 LSAs to Type 5 LSAs when propagating them outside of the NSSA. Issuing the following command on the ASBR can change this behavior:

```
R4(config-router)#summary-address 192.168.5.0 255.255.255.0 not-advertise
```

This command causes the ASBR to set the P-bit in the LSA for 192.168.5.0/24 to tell the ABR not to advertise that route as a Type 5 LSA outside of the NSSA. For more information on the summary-address command, please see the discussion of redistribution in Chapter 8.

With the change of Area 3 to an NSSA, the link state database on R4 is considerably smaller, as you can see here:

```
R4#show ip ospf database database-summary

        OSPF Router with ID (192.168.254.4) (Process ID 1)


Area ID       Router  Network S-Net   S-ASBR  Type-7  Subtotal Delete Maxage
```

3	2	1	4	0	9	16	0	0
AS External						0	0	0
Total	2	1	4	0	9	16		

However, even though the R3 is blocking LSAs, as would the ABR of a stub area, it is not generating a default route into the NSSA. A look at the routing table of R4, shown here, confirms that there is no default route:

```
R4#show ip route
Codes: C - connected, S - static, I - IGRP, R - RIP, M - mobile, B - BGP
       D - EIGRP, EX - EIGRP external, O - OSPF, IA - OSPF inter area
       N1 - OSPF NSSA external type 1, N2 - OSPF NSSA external type 2
       E1 - OSPF external type 1, E2 - OSPF external type 2, E - EGP
       i - IS-IS, L1 - IS-IS level-1, L2 - IS-IS level-2, * - candidate default
       U - per-user static route, o - ODR


Gateway of last resort is not set


O IA 192.168.12.0/24 [110/3134] via 192.168.3.1, 00:01:24, Ethernet0
R    192.168.104.0/24 [120/1] via 192.168.4.2, 00:00:15, Ethernet1
O IA 192.168.31.0/24 [110/1572] via 192.168.3.1, 00:01:31, Ethernet0
R    192.168.105.0/24 [120/1] via 192.168.4.2, 00:00:15, Ethernet1
C    192.168.4.0/24 is directly connected, Ethernet1
R    192.168.5.0/24 [120/1] via 192.168.4.2, 00:00:15, Ethernet1
R    192.168.102.0/24 [120/1] via 192.168.4.2, 00:00:15, Ethernet1
     192.168.254.0/32 is subnetted, 1 subnets
C       192.168.254.4 is directly connected, Loopback0
O IA 192.168.1.0/24 [110/1582] via 192.168.3.1, 00:01:24, Ethernet0
R    192.168.103.0/24 [120/1] via 192.168.4.2, 00:00:15, Ethernet1
O IA 192.168.2.0/24 [110/3144] via 192.168.3.1, 00:01:24, Ethernet0
R    192.168.100.0/24 [120/1] via 192.168.4.2, 00:00:15, Ethernet1
C    192.168.3.0/24 is directly connected, Ethernet0
R    192.168.101.0/24 [120/1] via 192.168.4.2, 00:00:16, Ethernet1
```

The reason for this is that even though an NSSA is similar to a stub area, the NSSA has two ways out of the network—through an ABR or through an ASBR. OSPF does not try to determine which should be the default route. Therefore, it is up to the administrator to configure the network with a default route. If R3 (the ABR) is to generate a default route, it can be configured to do so with the following command:

```
R3(config-router)#area 3 nssa default-information-originate
```

The link state database on R3 now shows one more Type 7 LSA in Area 3, shown here:

```
R3#show ip ospf database database-summary
```

```
        OSPF Router with ID (192.168.254.3) (Process ID 1)
```

Area ID	Router	Network	S-Net	S-ASBR	Type-7	Subtotal	Delete	Maxage
0	2	0	5	0	N/A	7	0	0
3	2	1	4	0	10	17	0	0
AS External						7	0	0
Total	4	1	9	0	10	31		

That LSA is the default route LSA generated by R3, which can be seen in the following routing table of R4:

```
R4#show ip route
Codes: C - connected, S - static, I - IGRP, R - RIP, M - mobile, B - BGP
       D - EIGRP, EX - EIGRP external, O - OSPF, IA - OSPF inter area
       N1 - OSPF NSSA external type 1, N2 - OSPF NSSA external type 2
       E1 - OSPF external type 1, E2 - OSPF external type 2, E - EGP
       i - IS-IS, L1 - IS-IS level-1, L2 - IS-IS level-2, * - candidate default
       U - per-user static route, o - ODR

Gateway of last resort is 192.168.3.1 to network 0.0.0.0

O IA 192.168.12.0/24 [110/3134] via 192.168.3.1, 00:03:04, Ethernet0
R    192.168.104.0/24 [120/1] via 192.168.4.2, 00:00:18, Ethernet1
O IA 192.168.31.0/24 [110/1572] via 192.168.3.1, 00:03:04, Ethernet0
R    192.168.105.0/24 [120/1] via 192.168.4.2, 00:00:18, Ethernet1
C    192.168.4.0/24 is directly connected, Ethernet1
R    192.168.5.0/24 [120/1] via 192.168.4.2, 00:00:18, Ethernet1
R    192.168.102.0/24 [120/1] via 192.168.4.2, 00:00:18, Ethernet1
```

```
        192.168.254.0/32 is subnetted, 1 subnets
C       192.168.254.4 is directly connected, Loopback0
O IA 192.168.1.0/24 [110/1582] via 192.168.3.1, 00:03:04, Ethernet0
R       192.168.103.0/24 [120/1] via 192.168.4.2, 00:00:18, Ethernet1
O IA 192.168.2.0/24 [110/3144] via 192.168.3.1, 00:03:04, Ethernet0
R       192.168.100.0/24 [120/1] via 192.168.4.2, 00:00:18, Ethernet1
C       192.168.3.0/24 is directly connected, Ethernet0
R       192.168.101.0/24 [120/1] via 192.168.4.2, 00:00:19, Ethernet1
O*N2 0.0.0.0/0 [110/1] via 192.168.3.1, 00:03:04, Ethernet0
```

Notice that the route is flagged N2, indicating that it was advertised in a Type 7 LSA. For information on making the ASBR the default route, please see Chapter 8.

If the ABR of an NSSA is also an ASBR, it would normally distribute its own Type 7 LSAs into the NSSA, in addition to distributing Type 5 LSAs into normal areas. To configure the ABR/ASBR to prevent distribution of Type 7 LSAs into the NSSA, use the following command:

```
R4(config-router)#area 3 nssa no-redistribution
```

LSAs for the external routes will be distributed to all areas to which the ABR/ASBR is attached, with the exception of Area 3.

Configuring Totally Stubby NSSAs

If the ABR is the default route for the NSSA, the routers in the NSSA do not necessarily need to know of the inter-area routes. We can make Area 3 from the previous example a totally stubby NSSA. To configure a totally stubby NSSA, issue the following commands on the ABR:

```
R3(config-router)#no area 3 nssa default-information-originate
R3(config-router)#area 3 nssa no-summary
```

Note that this configuration obsolesced our previous area 3 nssa command, so we removed it before entering the new command. Now R3 advertises the default route in a Type 3 LSA. Because all other Type 3

LSAs are blocked at the ABR, only one Type 3 LSA exists in the link state database for Area 3 on R3, as shown here:

```
R3#show ip ospf database database-summary


                OSPF Router with ID (192.168.254.3) (Process ID 1)


Area ID        Router  Network S-Net   S-ASBR  Type-7  Subtotal Delete Maxage
0              2       0       5       0       N/A     7        0      0
3              2       1       1       0       9       13       0      0
AS External                                            7        0      0
Total          4       1       6       0       9       27
```

Because it is contained in a Type 3 LSA, the default route appears in the following routing table of R4 as an inter-area route:

```
R4#show ip route
Codes: C - connected, S - static, I - IGRP, R - RIP, M - mobile, B - BGP
       D - EIGRP, EX - EIGRP external, O - OSPF, IA - OSPF inter area
       N1 - OSPF NSSA external type 1, N2 - OSPF NSSA external type 2
       E1 - OSPF external type 1, E2 - OSPF external type 2, E - EGP
       i - IS-IS, L1 - IS-IS level-1, L2 - IS-IS level-2, * - candidate default
       U - per-user static route, o - ODR


Gateway of last resort is 192.168.3.1 to network 0.0.0.0


R    192.168.104.0/24 [120/1] via 192.168.4.2, 00:00:09, Ethernet1
R    192.168.105.0/24 [120/1] via 192.168.4.2, 00:00:09, Ethernet1
C    192.168.4.0/24 is directly connected, Ethernet1
R    192.168.5.0/24 [120/1] via 192.168.4.2, 00:00:09, Ethernet1
R    192.168.102.0/24 [120/1] via 192.168.4.2, 00:00:09, Ethernet1
     192.168.254.0/32 is subnetted, 1 subnets
C       192.168.254.4 is directly connected, Loopback0
R    192.168.103.0/24 [120/1] via 192.168.4.2, 00:00:09, Ethernet1
R    192.168.100.0/24 [120/1] via 192.168.4.2, 00:00:09, Ethernet1
C    192.168.3.0/24 is directly connected, Ethernet0
R    192.168.101.0/24 [120/1] via 192.168.4.2, 00:00:09, Ethernet1
```

```
O*IA 0.0.0.0/0 [110/11] via 192.168.3.1, 00:01:05, Ethernet0
```

Configuring Summarization

One of the features of OSPF that makes it popular is *route summarization*. Route summarization can take place on inter-area routes and on external routes. Inter-area summarization takes place on ABRs, while external summarization takes place on ASBRs. External summarization is covered in the discussion of redistribution in Chapter 8.

Configuring a stub area conserves resources on the stub area routers, but it does not help the backbone. Route summarization preserves resources on the backbone by advertising a group of network addresses as one summary address. In addition to creating fewer entries in the routing tables on the backbone routers, summarization prevents the propagation of LSAs to other areas when one of the summarized networks goes down or comes up.

The network shown in Figure 4-6 has several contiguous networks that can be summarized.

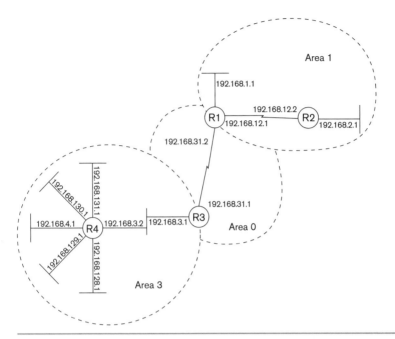

Figure 4-6 *OSPF can summarize contiguous subnets and advertise them with a single LSA.*

You can summarize networks 192.168.128.0/24, 192.168.129.0/24, 192.168.130.0/24, and 192.168.131.0/24 as 192.168.128.0/17. This summarization is performed on the ABR (R3). Before configuring summarization on R3, the routing table of R1 is as follows:

```
R1#show ip route

Codes: C - connected, S - static, I - IGRP, R - RIP, M - mobile, B - BGP

       D - EIGRP, EX - EIGRP external, O - OSPF, IA - OSPF inter area

       E1 - OSPF external type 1, E2 - OSPF external type 2, E - EGP

       i - IS-IS, L1 - IS-IS level-1, L2 - IS-IS level-2, * - candidate default


Gateway of last resort is not set


C    192.168.12.0 is directly connected, Serial0

C    192.168.1.0 is directly connected, Ethernet0

O    192.168.2.0 [110/1572] via 192.168.12.2, 00:51:36, Serial0
```

```
O IA 192.168.3.0 [110/1572] via 192.168.31.1, 00:02:32, Serial1

O IA 192.168.4.0 [110/1582] via 192.168.31.1, 00:02:32, Serial1

C    192.168.31.0 is directly connected, Serial1

     192.168.254.0 255.255.255.255 is subnetted, 2 subnets

O IA    192.168.254.4 [110/1573] via 192.168.31.1, 00:02:32, Serial1

C       192.168.254.1 is directly connected, Loopback0

O IA    192.168.128.0 [110/1573] via 192.168.31.1, 00:02:32, Serial1

O IA    192.168.129.0 [110/1573] via 192.168.31.1, 00:02:32, Serial1

O IA    192.168.130.0 [110/1573] via 192.168.31.1, 00:02:32, Serial1

O IA    192.168.131.0 [110/1573] via 192.168.31.1, 00:02:32, Serial1
```

Each route shows up individually as an inter-area route. However, we can configure summarization by issuing the following command on R3:

```
R3(config-router)#area 3 range 192.168.128.0 255.255.128.0
```

Note that the area listed in this command is the area in which the summarized routes reside. After summarization has been configured, the routing table of R1, shown here, is much shorter:

```
R1#show ip route

Codes: C - connected, S - static, I - IGRP, R - RIP, M - mobile, B - BGP

       D - EIGRP, EX - EIGRP external, O - OSPF, IA - OSPF inter area

       E1 - OSPF external type 1, E2 - OSPF external type 2, E - EGP

       i - IS-IS, L1 - IS-IS level-1, L2 - IS-IS level-2, * - candidate default


Gateway of last resort is not set


C    192.168.12.0 is directly connected, Serial0

C    192.168.1.0 is directly connected, Ethernet0

O    192.168.2.0 [110/1572] via 192.168.12.2, 00:57:06, Serial0

O IA 192.168.3.0 [110/1572] via 192.168.31.1, 00:08:02, Serial1

O IA 192.168.4.0 [110/1582] via 192.168.31.1, 00:08:02, Serial1

C    192.168.31.0 is directly connected, Serial1

     192.168.254.0 255.255.255.255 is subnetted, 1 subnets

C       192.168.254.1 is directly connected, Loopback0

O IA 192.168.128.0 255.255.128.0 [110/1573] via 192.168.31.1, 00:00:18, Serial1
```

Now all of those routes that are within the summarized network address are advertised with one route inter-area route. Not only does this conserve resources in the backbone, but it also conserves resources in other areas without making them stub areas.

Configuring OSPF on NBMA Networks

OSPF on NBMA networks poses a special challenge. A multi-access network requires a DR to flood LSAs through the network and to advertise the multi-access network with its own LSA. However, NBMA networks do not have the ability to discover neighbors by multicasting Hello packets. Therefore, special configuration is required to make OSPF function on NBMA networks.

The OSPF internetwork in Figure 4-7 includes a Frame Relay network between three routers. R1, R2, and R3 are part of a Frame Relay cloud in which R1 has a permanent virtual circuit (PVC) to R2 and to R3, but R2 and R3 are not connected by a PVC.

The following examples show several different ways to configure OSPF on this internetwork.

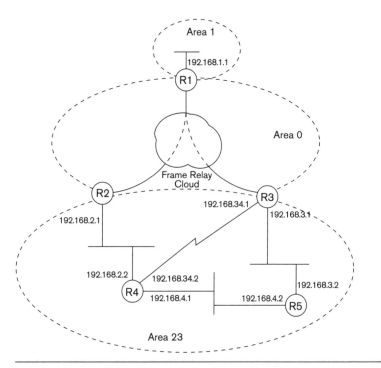

Figure 4-7 *OSPF on an NBMA network*

Configuring the NBMA network with neighbor statements

Because an NBMA network does not allow routers to multicast to discover neighbors, you must manually configure each router to recognize its neighbors. OSPF has a `neighbor` command that simply requires you to specify the IP address of the neighbor. The neighbors need to be configured on all routers on the NBMA network. The following configurations of R1, R2, and R3 include explicitly defined neighbors:

R1:

```
interface Loopback0
 ip address 192.168.254.1 255.255.255.255
```

```
!
interface Ethernet0
 ip address 192.168.1.1 255.255.255.0
!
interface Serial0
 ip address 192.168.123.1 255.255.255.0
 encapsulation frame-relay
 frame-relay map ip 192.168.123.2 102
 frame-relay map ip 192.168.123.3 103
!
router ospf 1
 network 192.168.1.1 0.0.0.0 area 1
 network 192.168.123.1 0.0.0.0 area 0
 neighbor 192.168.123.3
 neighbor 192.168.123.2
```

R2:

```
interface Loopback0
 ip address 192.168.254.2 255.255.255.255
!
interface Ethernet0
 ip address 192.168.2.1 255.255.255.0
!
interface Serial1
 ip address 192.168.123.2 255.255.255.0
 encapsulation frame-relay
 ip ospf priority 0
 frame-relay interface-dlci 201
!
router ospf 1
 network 192.168.2.1 0.0.0.0 area 23
 network 192.168.123.2 0.0.0.0 area 0
 neighbor 192.168.123.1
```

R3:

```
interface Loopback0
  ip address 192.168.254.3 255.255.255.255
!
interface Ethernet0
  ip address 192.168.3.1 255.255.255.0
!
interface Serial0
  ip address 192.168.123.3 255.255.255.0
  encapsulation frame-relay
  ip ospf priority 0
  frame-relay interface-dlci 301
!
interface Serial1
  ip address 192.168.34.1 255.255.255.0
!
router ospf 1
  network 192.168.3.1 0.0.0.0 area 23
  network 192.168.34.1 0.0.0.0 area 23
  network 192.168.123.3 0.0.0.0 area 0
  neighbor 192.168.123.1
```

As you can see, each router was configured with neighbor statements explicitly naming its neighbors. Because they both have a priority of 0 on the NBMA network, R2 and R3 cannot be a DR or BDR. R1 must be the DR because it is the only router to have a connection to both other routers on the Frame Relay network. No BDR is needed; if R1 goes down, R2 and R3 will be unable to communicate anyway. The neighbor table of R1, shown here, illustrates that we have achieved the desired result:

```
R1#show ip ospf neighbor
```

Neighbor ID	Pri	State	Dead Time	Address	Interface
192.168.254.3	0	FULL/ -	0:01:32	192.168.123.3	Serial0
192.168.254.2	0	FULL/ -	0:01:36	192.168.123.2	Serial0

Both R2 and R3 are considered neighbors of R1, and neither is a DR or BDR. The following interface properties of R1 show that it considers itself the DR for the network:

```
R1#show ip ospf interface serial 0
Serial0 is up, line protocol is up
  Internet Address 192.168.123.1 255.255.255.0, Area 0
  Process ID 1, Router ID 192.168.254.1, Network Type NON_BROADCAST, Cost: 1562
  Transmit Delay is 1 sec, State DR, Priority 1
  Designated Router (ID) 192.168.254.1, Interface address 192.168.123.1
  No backup designated router on this network
  Timer intervals configured, Hello 30, Dead 120, Wait 120, Retransmit 5
    Hello due in 0:00:21
  Neighbor Count is 2, Adjacent neighbor count is 2
    Adjacent with neighbor 192.168.254.3
    Adjacent with neighbor 192.168.254.2
```

Note that the network type is NON_BROADCAST and that the priority on this interface is 1, the Cisco default. On R2 and R3, the following output from this same command shows that their priority is 0, and they are neighbors only with R1:

```
R2#show ip ospf interface serial 1
Serial1 is up, line protocol is up
  Internet Address 192.168.123.2/24, Area 0
  Process ID 1, Router ID 192.168.254.2, Network Type NON_BROADCAST, Cost: 1562
  Transmit Delay is 1 sec, State DROTHER, Priority 0
  Designated Router (ID) 192.168.254.1, Interface address 192.168.123.1
  No backup designated router on this network
  Old designated Router (ID) 192.168.254.2, Interface address 192.168.123.2
  Timer intervals configured, Hello 30, Dead 120, Wait 120, Retransmit 5
    Hello due in 00:00:12
  Neighbor Count is 1, Adjacent neighbor count is 1
    Adjacent with neighbor 192.168.254.1 (Designated Router)
  Suppress hello for 0 neighbor(s)
```

R2 only sees one neighbor on the network—the neighbor listed in its configuration. Even though NBMA networks and broadcast networks are both multi-access and need a DR, the neighbor relationships are different due to the architecture of the network. Note that if a PVC were to be added between R2 and R3, each router would have to be told about its new neighbor. In a full-mesh NBMA network, you would not need to manually choose a DR, since all routers could form an adjacency with any chosen DR.

Configuring the NBMA network as a broadcast network

Some NBMA media, such as Frame Relay, can be configured as broadcast media. In these cases, it may be easier to change the network type rather than configure neighbors explicitly. If the network can be configured as a broadcast network, then the discovery of neighbors will be automatic, thereby making configuration of OSPF easier. You can configure Frame Relay to act as a broadcast network, in which case the routers in Figure 4-7 would be configured as follows:

R1:

```
interface Loopback0
 ip address 192.168.254.1 255.255.255.255
!
interface Ethernet0
ip address 192.168.1.1 255.255.255.0
!
interface Serial0
 ip address 192.168.123.1 255.255.255.0
 encapsulation frame-relay
 ip ospf network broadcast
 frame-relay map ip 192.168.123.2 102 broadcast
 frame-relay map ip 192.168.123.3 103 broadcast
!
router ospf 1
 network 192.168.1.1 0.0.0.0 area 1
 network 192.168.123.1 0.0.0.0 area 0
```

R2:

```
interface Loopback0
 ip address 192.168.254.2 255.255.255.255
!
interface Ethernet0
 ip address 192.168.2.1 255.255.255.0
!
interface Serial1
 ip address 192.168.123.2 255.255.255.0
 encapsulation frame-relay
 ip ospf network broadcast
 ip ospf priority 0
 frame-relay map ip 192.168.123.1 201 broadcast
 frame-relay map ip 192.168.123.3 201 broadcast
!
router ospf 1
 network 192.168.2.1 0.0.0.0 area 23
 network 192.168.123.2 0.0.0.0 area 0
```

R3:

```
interface Loopback0
 ip address 192.168.254.3 255.255.255.255
!
interface Ethernet0
 ip address 192.168.3.1 255.255.255.0
!
interface Serial0
 ip address 192.168.123.3 255.255.255.0
 encapsulation frame-relay
 ip ospf network broadcast
 ip ospf priority 0
 frame-relay map ip 192.168.123.1 301 broadcast
 frame-relay map ip 192.168.123.2 301 broadcast
!
```

```
interface Serial1
 ip address 192.168.34.1 255.255.255.0
!
router ospf 1
 network 192.168.3.1 0.0.0.0 area 23
 network 192.168.34.1 0.0.0.0 area 23
 network 192.168.123.3 0.0.0.0 area 0
```

The `neighbor` commands have been removed from each router's configuration, and the Frame Relay network is being treated as a broadcast network. Neighbor relationships are only formed between directly connected routers. The `broadcast` keyword on the Frame Relay map statements allows the multicast packets to traverse the PVCs, but it does not allow the multicast packets to make more than one hop. Therefore, we have configured the serial interfaces on R2 and R3 to have a priority of 0, so that R1 will be the DR, shown here:

```
R1#show ip ospf interface serial 0
Serial0 is up, line protocol is up
  Internet Address 192.168.123.1 255.255.255.0, Area 0
  Process ID 1, Router ID 192.168.254.1, Network Type BROADCAST, Cost: 1562
  Transmit Delay is 1 sec, State DR, Priority 1
  Designated Router (ID) 192.168.254.1, Interface address 192.168.123.1
  No backup designated router on this network
  Timer intervals configured, Hello 10, Dead 40, Wait 40, Retransmit 5
    Hello due in 0:00:01
  Neighbor Count is 2, Adjacent neighbor count is 2
    Adjacent with neighbor 192.168.254.3
    Adjacent with neighbor 192.168.254.2
```

Configuring the NBMA network as a point-to-multipoint network

Another option in configuring OSPF to work over an NBMA network is to change the network type to point-to-multipoint. In this configuration, the point-to-multipoint network is viewed as a collection of point-to-point links. Each router is adjacent with each of its neighbors, and there is

no DR. To create a point-to-multipoint network, configure the routers in
Figure 4-7 as follows:

R1:

```
interface Loopback0
 ip address 192.168.254.1 255.255.255.255
!
interface Ethernet0
 ip address 192.168.1.1 255.255.255.0
!
interface Serial0
 ip address 192.168.123.1 255.255.255.0
 encapsulation frame-relay
 ip ospf network point-to-multipoint
 frame-relay interface-dlci 102
 frame-relay interface-dlci 103
!
router ospf 1
 network 192.168.1.1 0.0.0.0 area 1
 network 192.168.123.1 0.0.0.0 area 0
```

R2:

```
interface Loopback0
 ip address 192.168.254.2 255.255.255.255
!
interface Ethernet0
 ip address 192.168.2.1 255.255.255.0
!
interface Serial1
 ip address 192.168.123.2 255.255.255.0
 encapsulation frame-relay
 ip ospf network point-to-multipoint
 frame-relay interface-dlci 201
!
router ospf 1
```

```
network 192.168.2.1 0.0.0.0 area 23
network 192.168.123.2 0.0.0.0 area 0
```

R3:

```
interface Loopback0
  ip address 192.168.254.3 255.255.255.255
!
interface Ethernet0
  ip address 192.168.3.1 255.255.255.0
!
interface Serial0
  ip address 192.168.123.3 255.255.255.0
  encapsulation frame-relay
  ip ospf network point-to-multipoint
  frame-relay interface-dlci 301
!
interface Serial1
  ip address 192.168.34.1 255.255.255.0
!
router ospf 1
  network 192.168.3.1 0.0.0.0 area 23
  network 192.168.34.1 0.0.0.0 area 23
  network 192.168.123.3 0.0.0.0 area 0
```

The only change to each router in order to make OSPF treat the Frame Relay network as a point-to-multipoint network is to add the statement ip ospf network point-to-multipoint to the interface configurations. OSPF interface detail on R1 shows that the network type is POINT_TO_MULTIPOINT:

```
R1#show ip ospf interface serial 0
Serial0 is up, line protocol is up
  Internet Address 192.168.123.1 255.255.255.0, Area 0
  Process ID 1, Router ID 192.168.254.1, Network Type POINT_TO_MULTIPOINT, Cost:
  1562
  Transmit Delay is 1 sec, State POINT_TO_MULTIPOINT,
```

```
Timer intervals configured, Hello 30, Dead 120, Wait 120, Retransmit 5

  Hello due in 0:00:06

Neighbor Count is 2, Adjacent neighbor count is 2

  Adjacent with neighbor 192.168.254.3

  Adjacent with neighbor 192.168.254.2
```

The interface timers reflect the default values for a point-to-multipoint network. In addition, the state of the interface is listed as POINT_TO_ MULTIPOINT. Both R2 and R3 are neighbors of R1, as seen here:

```
R1#show ip ospf neighbor


Neighbor ID     Pri   State        Dead Time   Address          Interface

192.168.254.3     1   FULL/  -     0:01:34     192.168.123.3    Serial0

192.168.254.2     1   FULL/  -     0:01:33     192.168.123.2    Serial0
```

Note that R2 and R3 are not neighbors and do not form an adjacency in this configuration. Adjacencies are only formed over the PVCs in the Frame Relay network.

Configuring the NBMA network as a collection of point-to-point links using subinterfaces

The final option for configuring OSPF on an NBMA network is to create subinterfaces of the serial interface, each of which is its own point-to-point network. One caveat of this method is that each point-to-point network must have its own subnet, but the classless nature of OSPF allows you to create smaller subnets on the point-to-point links, thereby preserving address space. The routers in Figure 4-7 are now configured as follows:

R1:

```
interface Loopback0

 ip address 192.168.254.1 255.255.255.255

!

interface Ethernet0

ip address 192.168.1.1 255.255.255.0

 !
```

```
interface Serial0

 no ip address

 encapsulation frame-relay

!

interface Serial0.102 point-to-point

 ip address 192.168.123.1 255.255.255.252

 frame-relay interface-dlci 102

!

interface Serial0.103 point-to-point

 ip address 192.168.123.5 255.255.255.252

 frame-relay interface-dlci 103

!

router ospf 1

 network 192.168.1.1 0.0.0.0 area 1

 network 192.168.123.1 0.0.0.0 area 0

 network 192.168.123.5 0.0.0.0 area 0
```

R2:

```
interface Loopback0

 ip address 192.168.254.2 255.255.255.255

!

interface Ethernet0

 ip address 192.168.2.1 255.255.255.0

!

interface Serial1

 no ip address

 encapsulation frame-relay

!

interface Serial1.201 point-to-point

 ip address 192.168.123.2 255.255.255.252

 frame-relay interface-dlci 201

!

router ospf 1

 network 192.168.2.1 0.0.0.0 area 23
```

```
network 192.168.123.2 0.0.0.0 area 0
```

R3:

```
interface Loopback0
 ip address 192.168.254.3 255.255.255.255
!
interface Ethernet0
 ip address 192.168.3.1 255.255.255.0
!
interface Serial0
 no ip address
 encapsulation frame-relay
!
interface Serial0.301 point-to-point
 ip address 192.168.123.6 255.255.255.252
 frame-relay interface-dlci 301
!
interface Serial1
 ip address 192.168.34.1 255.255.255.0
!
router ospf 1
 network 192.168.3.1 0.0.0.0 area 23
 network 192.168.34.1 0.0.0.0 area 23
 network 192.168.123.3 0.0.0.0 area 0
 network 192.168.123.6 0.0.0.0 area 0
```

Each Frame Relay *Data Link Connection Identifier* (*DLCI*) is assigned to a separate subinterface. In addition, the addressing of the interfaces is modified, so each PVC has its own subnet. Notice that the exact same network (192.168.123.0/24) is used, but it has been broken down into smaller subnets. Each subinterface is now a point-to-point network, shown here:

```
R1#show ip ospf interface serial 0
Serial0 is up, line protocol is up
    OSPF not enabled on this interface
R1#show ip ospf interface serial 0.102
Serial0.102 is up, line protocol is up
```

```
Internet Address 192.168.123.1 255.255.255.252, Area 0
Process ID 1, Router ID 192.168.254.1, Network Type POINT_TO_POINT, Cost: 1562
Transmit Delay is 1 sec, State POINT_TO_POINT,
Timer intervals configured, Hello 10, Dead 40, Wait 40, Retransmit 5
  Hello due in 0:00:05
Neighbor Count is 1, Adjacent neighbor count is 1
  Adjacent with neighbor 192.168.254.2
R1#show ip ospf interface serial 0.103
Serial0.103 is up, line protocol is up
  Internet Address 192.168.123.5 255.255.255.252, Area 0
  Process ID 1, Router ID 192.168.254.1, Network Type POINT_TO_POINT, Cost: 1562
  Transmit Delay is 1 sec, State POINT_TO_POINT,
  Timer intervals configured, Hello 10, Dead 40, Wait 40, Retransmit 5
    Hello due in 0:00:02
  Neighbor Count is 1, Adjacent neighbor count is 1
    Adjacent with neighbor 192.168.254.3
```

The router is no longer running OSPF on the physical interface — only on the subinterfaces. OSPF can only run on interfaces with IP addresses assigned, and when using subinterfaces, the physical interface itself is not assigned an IP address. This configuration is easy to maintain, but it does require more work when configuring each router. In addition, using subinterfaces requires more memory, which may be a concern in some networks.

Configuring Virtual Links

All areas in an OSPF internetwork must connect directly to the backbone area. This can severely limit the placement of areas, and it also has the potential of making OSPF unusable on some networks, especially if the network is very wide. To solve the problems that this limitation may cause, virtual links can be used to link a remote area to the backbone through another area. The area across which the virtual link is formed must have full routing information; therefore, it cannot be a stub area.

In the network shown in Figure 4-8, Area 10 is separated from the backbone by Area 1. We will use a virtual link to connect Area 10 to Area 0, thereby meeting the requirement that all areas must connect to the backbone.

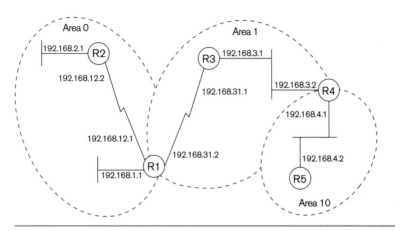

Figure 4-8 *An area that is not physically connected with Area 0 must use a virtual link to connect to the backbone.*

We will configure a virtual link between R4 and R1, thereby making it appear to OSPF that Area 0 and Area 10 are directly connected. Configuring a virtual link is fairly easy, and you only need to configure the two endpoints. In this example, we only configure R1 and R4 for the virtual link. R3 does not need any knowledge of the virtual link, even though all of the virtual link traffic must traverse it. The configuration of R1 and R4 would be the following:

R1:

```
interface Loopback0
 ip address 192.168.254.1 255.255.255.255
!
interface Ethernet0
ip address 192.168.1.1 255.255.255.0
!
interface Serial0
 ip address 192.168.12.1 255.255.255.0
!
interface Serial1
 ip address 192.168.31.2 255.255.255.0
!
```

```
router ospf 1
 network 192.168.1.1 0.0.0.0 area 0
 network 192.168.31.2 0.0.0.0 area 1
 network 192.168.12.1 0.0.0.0 area 0
 area 1 virtual-link 192.168.254.4
```

R4:

```
interface Loopback0
 ip address 192.168.254.4 255.255.255.255
!
interface Ethernet0
 ip address 192.168.3.2 255.255.255.0
!
interface Ethernet1
 ip address 192.168.4.1 255.255.255.0
!
router ospf 1
 network 192.168.3.2 0.0.0.0 area 1
 network 192.168.4.1 0.0.0.0 area 10
 area 1 virtual-link 192.168.254.1
```

To configure the virtual link, you need only specify the area over which the link will operate and the RID of the neighbor router. To view the virtual links on a router, use the command show ip ospf virtual-links, as shown here:

```
R1#show ip ospf virtual-links
Virtual Link OSPF_VL0 to router 192.168.254.4 is up
  Run as demand circuit
  DoNotAge LSA not allowed (Number of DCbitless LSA is 2).
  Transit area 1, via interface Serial1, Cost of using 1572
  Transmit Delay is 1 sec, State POINT_TO_POINT,
  Timer intervals configured, Hello 10, Dead 40, Wait 40, Retransmit 5
    Hello due in 00:00:00
    Adjacency State FULL (Hello suppressed)
```

The virtual link is considered a point-to-point link, and its cost is the cost between the two endpoints of the link. The routers become neighbors and form an adjacency, as long as the timers are the same between them. The other situation in which you would use a virtual link is when two ABRs have only one connection on the backbone. For example, in the network in Figure 4-7, R2 and R3 are only connected by R1, so if R1 or one of the PVCs goes down, R2 and R3 would be unable to communicate. In this network that would not be a concern, as they only connect to the same non-backbone area. However, if an additional area were connected to the network at each router, they could not route between those areas during an outage. In this case, a virtual link between R2 and R3 could be created across Area 23. To create the virtual link, the routers would be configured as follows:

R2:

```
interface Loopback0
 ip address 192.168.254.2 255.255.255.255
!
interface Ethernet0
 ip address 192.168.2.1 255.255.255.0
!
interface Serial1
 no ip address
 encapsulation frame-relay
!
interface Serial1.201 point-to-point
 ip address 192.168.123.2 255.255.255.252
 frame-relay interface-dlci 201
!
router ospf 1
 network 192.168.25.1 0.0.0.0 area 23
 network 192.168.2.1 0.0.0.0 area 23
 network 192.168.123.2 0.0.0.0 area 0
 area 23 virtual-link 192.168.254.3
```

R3:

```
interface Loopback0
```

```
ip address 192.168.254.3 255.255.255.255
!
interface Ethernet0
 ip address 192.168.3.1 255.255.255.0
!
interface Serial0
 no ip address
 encapsulation frame-relay
!
interface Serial0.301 point-to-point
 ip address 192.168.123.6 255.255.255.252
 frame-relay interface-dlci 301
!
interface Serial1
 ip address 192.168.34.1 255.255.255.0
!
router ospf 1
 network 192.168.3.1 0.0.0.0 area 23
 network 192.168.34.1 0.0.0.0 area 23
 network 192.168.123.3 0.0.0.0 area 0
 network 192.168.123.6 0.0.0.0 area 0
 area 23 virtual-link 192.168.254.2
```

The configuration is the same as for the previous virtual link we created. The virtual link configuration command specifies the area over which the virtual link will run and the RID of the neighbor.

Configuring Interface Properties

Many OSPF properties can be customized to suit any network environment. Although most implementations should not require a change to the default values of the timers, some instances occur in which tuning the timers can enhance the efficiency of the protocol. To configure the interface timers, enter interface configuration mode and use the following commands:

```
R1(config-if)#ip ospf dead-interval 45
```

```
R1(config-if)#ip ospf hello-interval 15
R1(config-if)#ip ospf retransmit-interval 10
```

All of these statements take an integer number of seconds as the parameter value. If the HelloInterval and the RouterDeadInterval are not identical on all router interfaces on the same network, the routers cannot become neighbors. The timers on a virtual link can also be changed using the following commands in OSPF configuration mode:

```
R1(config-router)#area 1 virtual-link 192.168.254.4 dead-interval 45

R1(config-router)#area 1 virtual-link 192.168.254.4 hello-interval 15

R1(config-router)#area 1 virtual-link 192.168.254.4 retransmit-interval 10
```

Other properties, such as priority and cost, can be configured for each interface, as well. The following commands can be issued in interface configuration mode:

```
R1(config-if)#ip ospf priority 200

R1(config-if)#ip ospf cost 1

R1(config-if)#ip ospf transmit-delay 18
```

Tip

When using networking equipment from multiple vendors, make sure that their implementations of OSPF work together. For example, all routers must compute interface cost in the same way, or OSPF may not function correctly. You can use the `ip ospf cost <integer>` command to change the interface cost of Cisco routers to match other equipment.

A virtual link does not need a DR, so it has no priority. The cost is calculated based on the path of the virtual link, and it cannot be changed. However, the InfTransDelay of a virtual link can be modified from the default by using the following command in OSPF configuration mode:

```
R1(config-router)#area 1 virtual-link 192.168.254.4 transmit-delay 18
```

Configuring Other OSPF Options

OSPF load balances over equal-cost paths. By default, a router load balances across no more than four paths of equal cost. However, a router will support anywhere from one (no load balancing) to six paths to the same destination in the routing table. To change the maximum paths allowed in the routing table from OSPF, enter the following in OSPF configuration mode:

```
R1(config-router)#maximum-paths 6
```

For interfaces that do not have cost manually assigned with the `ip ospf cost` command, OSPF automatically determines the cost. To compute the cost, OSPF divides a reference bandwidth (by default 10^8, or 100 Mbps) by the bandwidth of the interface. Interfaces with speeds greater than or equal to 100 Mbps all have a cost of 1. For networks with many fast links of various speeds, cost could be meaningless because all links would have a cost of 1. To change the reference bandwidth, issue the following command in OSPF configuration mode:

```
R1(config-router)#ospf auto-cost reference-bandwidth 1000
% OSPF: Reference bandwidth is changed.
     Please ensure reference bandwidth is consistent across all routers.
```

The numeric parameter is the number of Mbps that should be considered the reference bandwidth. The range of valid parameter values is 1 through 4,294,967. Note that the reference bandwidth should be identical on all routers, or the cost of interface is meaningless on the network. The router reminds you of this after you enter the command, as you can see in the sample output.

After receiving a topology change, a router usually waits five seconds before running the SPF algorithm. In addition, it waits ten seconds after running the SPF algorithm before running it again. To modify this behavior, use the following command:

```
R1(config-router)#timers spf 8 16
```

After an LSA refresh timer expires, the router waits for the amount of time specified by the LSA group pacing interval before it sends out the refreshed LSA. This feature enables the router to group multiple LSAs in the LSU packet, if their timers expire within a short time of each other. By default, the group pacing interval is four minutes (240 seconds). You can change the LSA group pacing interval to any number of seconds from 10 to 1,800 with the following command (introduced in IOS 11.3AA):

```
R1(config-router)#timers lsa-group-pacing 360
```

By default, the administrative distance of OSPF is 110. You can change this for OSPF as a whole with the `distance` command, shown here:

```
R1(config-router)#distance 40
```

You also have the option of changing the administrative distance for particular routes, rather than for the routing protocol as a whole. To change the administrative distance based on the source of the route, use the following command:

```
R1(config-router)#distance 25 192.168.254.2 0.0.0.0 18
```

After specifying the distance (25 in this case), enter the RID of the source of the route, followed by a wildcard mask. In this example, all routes from only 192.168.254.2 will be affected. Finally, you can specify a standard IP access list against which the routes should be matched, and we used access list 18 in the example. The access list is an optional parameter, and if it is missing, the statement applies to all routes from the listed source. Note that the `distance` configuration command is not an OSPF-specific command and works with other routing protocols. In addition, the `distance` command only affects the router on which it is entered. Other routers in the internetwork continue to operate with the default distance, even if the routes are learned from a router on which the administrative distance has been changed.

You can also change the administrative distance of OSPF routes based on their type — intra-area, inter-area, and external. Use the following command in OSPF configuration mode:

```
R1(config-router)#distance ospf intra-area 20 inter-area 30 external 40
```

You can specify any or all of the types of routes in this command. Like the other distance commands, the `distance ospf` command affects only the router on which it is issued.

Finally, you can change the cost (metric) of the default route that is distributed by an ABR into a stub area. The default cost is 1, and it can be changed with the following command on the ABR:

```
R1(config-router)#area 1 default-cost 200
```

Note that the cost of the default route on each router in the area will also include the router's cost to the ABR.

Configuring Authentication

To add some extra security to the routing process on your network, you can configure OSPF authentication on the routers. Passwords are assigned to interfaces, and neighbors on a network must use the same password on that network. Passwords do not have to be the same throughout OSPF or even an area.

To configure simple password authentication, specify the password for each interface and configure the area for authentication. If we use simple passwords for Area 0 of the network in Figure 4-7, R1 and R2 would be configured as follows:

R1:

```
interface Loopback0
 ip address 192.168.254.1 255.255.255.255
!
interface Ethernet0
ip address 192.168.1.1 255.255.255.0
!
interface Serial0
 no ip address
 encapsulation frame-relay
!
interface Serial0.102 point-to-point
 ip address 192.168.123.1 255.255.255.252
 ip ospf authentication-key pass12
!
interface Serial0.103 point-to-point
 ip address 192.168.123.5 255.255.255.252
 ip ospf authentication-key pass13
!
router ospf 1
 network 192.168.1.1 0.0.0.0 area 1
```

```
network 192.168.123.1 0.0.0.0 area 0
network 192.168.123.5 0.0.0.0 area 0
area 0 authentication
```

R2:

```
interface Loopback0
 ip address 192.168.254.2 255.255.255.255
!
interface Ethernet0
 ip address 192.168.2.1 255.255.255.0
!
interface Serial1
 no ip address
 encapsulation frame-relay
!
interface Serial1.201 point-to-point
 ip address 192.168.123.2 255.255.255.252
 ip ospf authentication-key pass12
!
router ospf 1
 network 192.168.2.1 0.0.0.0 area 23
 network 192.168.123.2 0.0.0.0 area 0
 area 0 authentication
```

In this configuration, the shared password between R1 and R2 is "pass12", and the password between R1 and R3 is "pass13". If the `ip ospf authentication-key` command specified a password on an interface but the `area 0 authentication` command were missing, the routers would continue to operate without authentication.

To change Area 0 to use MD5 authentication, configure R1 and R2 as follows:

R1:

```
interface Loopback0
 ip address 192.168.254.1 255.255.255.255
!
interface Ethernet0
```

```
ip address 192.168.1.1 255.255.255.0
!
interface Serial0
 no ip address
 encapsulation frame-relay
!
interface Serial0.102 point-to-point
 ip address 192.168.123.1 255.255.255.252
 ip ospf message-digest-key 2 md5 crypt12
!
interface Serial0.103 point-to-point
 ip address 192.168.123.5 255.255.255.252
 ip ospf message-digest-key 2 md5 crypt13
!
router ospf 1
 network 192.168.1.1 0.0.0.0 area 1
 network 192.168.123.1 0.0.0.0 area 0
 network 192.168.123.5 0.0.0.0 area 0
 area 0 authentication message-digest
```

R2:

```
interface Loopback0
 ip address 192.168.254.2 255.255.255.255
!
interface Ethernet0
 ip address 192.168.2.1 255.255.255.0
!
interface Serial1
 no ip address
 encapsulation frame-relay
!
interface Serial1.201 point-to-point
 ip address 192.168.123.2 255.255.255.252
 ip ospf message-digest-key 2 md5 crypt12
!
```

```
router ospf 1

network 192.168.25.1 0.0.0.0 area 23

network 192.168.2.1 0.0.0.0 area 23

network 192.168.123.2 0.0.0.0 area 0

area 0 authentication message-digest
```

The `ip ospf message-digest-key` interface command specifies the key ID (2 in this case) and the password (crypt12). On both routers, the key ID must be the same for the same password, or else the routers will not become neighbors. When specifying the areas in which to use authentication, the keyword `message-digest` is added to indicate that the area is to use MD5 authentication. When viewing the OSPF properties of an interface, MD5 authentication information appears at the bottom, as shown here:

```
R2#show ip ospf interface serial 1.201

Serial1.201 is up, line protocol is up

  Internet Address 192.168.123.2/30, Area 0

  Process ID 1, Router ID 192.168.254.2, Network Type POINT_TO_POINT, Cost: 1562

  Transmit Delay is 1 sec, State POINT_TO_POINT,

  Timer intervals configured, Hello 10, Dead 40, Wait 40, Retransmit 5

    Hello due in 00:00:07

  Neighbor Count is 1, Adjacent neighbor count is 1

    Adjacent with neighbor 192.168.254.1

  Suppress hello for 0 neighbor(s)

  Message digest authentication enabled

    Youngest key id is 2
```

Authentication can also be used on a virtual link. Use one of the two commands below to enable either simple passwords or MD5 authentication on the virtual link:

```
R2(config-router)#area 23 virtual-link 192.168.254.3 authentication-key pw

R2(config-router)#area 23 virtual-link 192.168.254.3 message-digest-key 3 md5 pw
```

Troubleshooting OSPF and Common Pitfalls

As when troubleshooting any routing problem, the first step in troubleshooting OSPF is to determine the exact symptoms of the problem. A careful examination of the symptoms gives you a better indication of where to look for causes. When looking at the routers on your network, you have several options to look for the source of the problem. You can examine the current state of interfaces, neighbors, and databases, or you can use the debug commands to view OSPF activities as they happen.

Viewing Protocol Information

To begin troubleshooting, verify which routing protocols are running on a router. Using the show ip protocols command displays all actively running IP routing protocols. This can be especially helpful when troubleshooting an ASBR, as more than one protocol should be listed along with redistribution information. The output of show ip protocols is as follows:

```
r5#show ip protocols
Routing Protocol is "ospf 1"
  Sending updates every 0 seconds
  Invalid after 0 seconds, hold down 0, flushed after 0
  Outgoing update filter list for all interfaces is not set
  Incoming update filter list for all interfaces is not set
  Redistributing: ospf 1
  Routing for Networks:
    192.168.1.5/32
  Routing Information Sources:
    Gateway         Distance      Last Update
    192.168.254.1        110      16:26:05
    192.168.254.2        110      16:26:05
    192.168.254.4        110       16:26:05
  Distance: (default is 110)
```

Based on this output, we know that OSPF is the only IP routing protocol running on this router. This output also tells us if any protocols are being redistributed into OSPF, the networks on which OSPF is running, and the sources of routing information (LSAs). The command show ip ospf also gives the following detailed information about the OSPF process:

```
r5#show ip ospf

Routing Process "ospf 1" with ID 192.168.254.5

Supports only single TOS(TOS0) routes

It is an area border and autonomous system boundary router

Summary Link update interval is 00:30:00 and the update due in 00:16:59

External Link update interval is 00:30:00 and the update due in 00:20:45

Redistributing External Routes from,

SPF schedule delay 5 secs, Hold time between two SPFs 10 secs

Number of DCbitless external LSA 0

Number of DoNotAge external LSA 0

Number of areas in this router is 2. 1 normal 0 stub 1 nssa

    Area BACKBONE(0)

        Number of interfaces in this area is 1

        Area has no authentication

        SPF algorithm executed 5 times

        Area ranges are

        Link State Update Interval is 00:30:00 and due in 00:15:12

        Link State Age Interval is 00:20:00 and due in 00:05:12

        Number of DCbitless LSA 4

        Number of indication LSA 0

        Number of DoNotAge LSA 0

    Area 2

        Number of interfaces in this area is 0

        It is a NSSA area

        Perform type-7/type-5 LSA translation

        generates NSSA default route with cost 1

        Area has message digest authentication

        SPF algorithm executed 2 times

        Area ranges are

        Link State Update Interval is 00:30:00 and due in 00:00:00

        Link State Age Interval is 00:20:00 and due in 00:16:56
```

```
Number of DCbitless LSA 0
Number of indication LSA 0
Number of DoNotAge LSA 0
```

After providing some global information, the output lists the areas to which the router is attached and quite a bit of information about each area. It indicates how many interfaces are in each area, the area type (such as NSSA), and the authentication type in use. It also displays information about LSA options, such as whether or not NSSA ABRs are translating Type 7 LSAs to Type 5 LSAs, as well as displaying statistics about other LSA options.

Examining OSPF Interfaces

Many OSPF properties are specific to each interface on which OSPF is running. Interfaces must be configured in such a way that they do not break neighbor adjacencies. To view the current configuration and state of an interface, you can use the show ip ospf interface command. Without any parameters, the command lists all interfaces, including those not running OSPF. To look at a particular interface, simply list the interface on the command line, as shown here:

```
R4#show ip ospf interface ethernet 0
Ethernet0 is up, line protocol is up
  Internet Address 192.168.3.2/24, Area 3
  Process ID 1, Router ID 192.168.254.4, Network Type BROADCAST, Cost: 10
  Transmit Delay is 1 sec, State DR, Priority 1
  Designated Router (ID) 192.168.254.4, Interface address 192.168.3.2
  Backup Designated router (ID) 192.168.254.3, Interface address 192.168.3.1
  Timer intervals configured, Hello 10, Dead 40, Wait 40, Retransmit 5
    Hello due in 00:00:01
  Neighbor Count is 1, Adjacent neighbor count is 1
    Adjacent with neighbor 192.168.254.3  (Backup Designated Router)
  Suppress hello for 0 neighbor(s)
  Message digest authentication enabled
    Youngest key id is 1
```

This output shows many useful pieces of information, such as the area and the timers on the interface, which must match for routers to establish a neighbor relationship. The network type indicates how OSPF treats the interface, and the state displays the role that the router plays on that network. On broadcast or NBMA networks, the state shows whether the router is the DR, BDR, or a DRother. Cost, priority, and authentication information (if configured) are also shown. Finally, the command displays the number of neighbors on the interface and which neighbors are adjacent.

Viewing OSPF Neighbors

When routing information is not communicated between two routers, it may be because they have not formed a neighbor relationship. To view the current neighbors of a router, use the `show ip ospf neighbor` command, shown here:

```
R4#show ip ospf neighbor


Neighbor ID     Pri   State        Dead Time   Address       Interface
192.168.254.3    1    FULL/BDR     00:00:39    192.168.3.1   Ethernet0
```

The output lists every neighbor's RID, along with the priority, state, dead time (time since the last Hello packet was received), address, and connected interface. To list only the neighbors on a particular interface, the interface name can be included on the command line. A more detailed look at a neighbor can be seen by issuing the command with a specific neighbor RID, as follows:

```
r5#show ip ospf neighbor 192.168.1.5
 Neighbor 192.168.254.1, interface address 192.168.1.1
    In the area 0 via interface Serial0
    Neighbor priority is 1, State is FULL
    Options 2
    Dead timer due in 00:01:32
```

The output adds the area of the neighbor and the options set in its Hellos.

Examining the Link State Database

The link state database is the source of all OSPF routes in the IP routing table. As a result, many routing problems can be traced back to incorrect or missing information in the link state database. The link state database is a good place to determine which router is the source of a problem. Remember that all routers in an area should have identical link state databases.

The link state database can be viewed in whole or in part, and the various views are displayed using different forms of the show ip ospf database command. To view the entire link state database, use the command without any qualifiers, as shown here:

```
r5#show ip ospf database

        OSPF Router with ID (192.168.254.5) (Process ID 1)


              Router Link States (Area 0)


Link ID         ADV Router      Age     Seq#        Checksum Link count
192.168.254.1   192.168.254.1   161     0x80000032 0xB3E8    4
192.168.254.2   192.168.254.2   1041    0x80000030 0x636E    1
192.168.254.4   192.168.254.4   982     0x80000035 0xD116    3
192.168.254.5   192.168.254.5   163     0x80000032 0x15BB    2


              Summary Net Link States (Area 0)


Link ID         ADV Router      Age     Seq#        Checksum
192.168.1.0     192.168.254.1   161     0x8000002E 0xFCB3
192.168.2.0     192.168.254.2   965     0x8000002E 0x96A2
192.168.4.0     192.168.254.4   983     0x8000002E 0xF9B2
192.168.10.0    192.168.254.1   161     0x8000002F 0x8806
192.168.20.0    192.168.254.2   965     0x8000002E 0xFCC6
192.168.40.0    192.168.254.4   983     0x8000002E 0x2A5E
192.168.140.0   192.168.254.4   983     0x8000002E 0x22E6


              Summary Net Link States (Area 2)
```

```
Link ID          ADV Router       Age       Seq#        Checksum
0.0.0.0          192.168.254.5    57        0x80000025 0x9673


                 Type-7 AS External Link States (Area 2)


Link ID          ADV Router       Age       Seq#        Checksum Tag
0.0.0.0          192.168.254.5    1634      0x80000024 0x6C1A    0
```

All LSAs in the database are listed, along with minor details about each one. For each LSA, the advertising router, age, and sequence number are listed. To view only the LSAs generated by this router, use the show ip ospf database self-originate command. It outputs a list like the one above but includes only the LSAs generated locally. In addition, you can view all LSAs with a particular source by entering show ip ospf database adv-router *x.x.x.x*, where *x.x.x.x* is the RID of the router whose LSAs you are interested in viewing.

Sometimes the list of LSAs can be long and hard to read. If that degree of detail is not needed, you can view a count of the various types of LSAs in the link state database. Use the command show ip ospf database database-summary, as shown here:

```
r5#show ip ospf database database-summary


                 OSPF Router with ID (192.168.254.5) (Process ID 1)


Area ID        Router  Network S-Net   S-ASBR  Type-7  Subtotal Delete Maxage
0              4       0       7       0       N/A     11       0      0
2              0       0       1       0       1       2        0      0
AS External                                            0        0      0
Total          4       0       8       0       1       13
```

In this output, it is easy to see which types of LSAs are present in the database without actually looking at each LSA individually. This option can be particularly useful when trying to see how the link state database changes when a change is made to some part of the network.

If you would rather see more detailed output of LSA information, use the show ip ospf database command with a qualifier. The available qualifiers include the following:

- show ip ospf database router — View Type 1 LSA details
- show ip ospf database network — View Type 2 LSA details
- show ip ospf database summary — View Type 3 LSA details
- show ip ospf database asbr-summary — View Type 4 LSA details
- show ip ospf database external — View Type 5 LSA details
- show ip ospf database nssa-external — View Type 7 LSA details

If one of these commands is entered without any further parameters, the router displays a detailed list of all LSAs of the type specified. If you specify the link ID (IP address) for a particular LSA, only that LSA is displayed.

Debugging OSPF

The debug commands in the Cisco IOS are excellent up-to-the-minute troubleshooting tools, especially because they display information about processes or events that are normally hidden from users. Use the debug commands with caution, as they can easily flood the screen and make it difficult or impossible to enter commands.

Tip

If debug output is making your screen scroll too fast to read any output or what you are typing, carefully enter undebug all and press Enter. That should turn off all debugging (even if it takes a minute for your terminal to stop showing all of the debug output that was already generated).

A common problem is to have two routers on the same network that do not form a neighbor relationship. While the possible reasons for this are many, usually something in the configuration prevents that relationship from forming. It often helps to view the configuration of the routers' inter-faces and see if they match. If you still cannot locate the problem, use the following command to view adjacency events:

```
R3#debug ip ospf adj
OSPF adjacency events debugging is on
```

With adjacency debugging enabled, every Hello packet received generates debug output. If the required properties in the Hello packet match those of the receiving router, normal Hello processing generates output similar to this:

```
OSPF: Rcv hello from 192.168.254.4 area 23 from Serial1 192.168.34.2
OSPF: End of hello processing
```

If two routers do not form a neighbor relationship, one may not be seeing Hellos from the other. However, there may also be a problem with the Hellos. Debugging adjacency events helps determine which is the case. For example, if the interface timers are different, the output may look like this:

```
OSPF: Rcv hello from 192.168.254.5 area 23 from Ethernet0 192.168.3.2
OSPF: Mismatched hello parameters from 192.168.3.2
Dead R 60 C 40, Hello R 15 C 10  Mask R 255.255.255.0 C 255.255.255.0
```

This output clearly states that the Hello parameters do not match. It then lists the parameters, so you can see the problem. In this case, the dead and Hello timers are different.

If the routers are configured to use different areas on the same network, the following debug output may be generated:

```
OSPF: Rcv pkt from 192.168.3.2, Ethernet0, area 0.0.0.23
      mismatch area 0.0.0.24 in the header
```

A difference in the area properties of two routers may be due to a simple configuration error, in which the wrong area was configured on one of the interfaces. However, because the order of the network statements determines area assignment, this problem could have a more subtle cause. Consider the following configuration lines:

```
interface Ethernet 1
 ip address 192.168.2.1
!
router ospf 1
 network 192.168.1.1 0.0.0.0 area 1
```

```
network 192.168.0.0 0.0.255.255 area 0
network 192.168.2.1 0.0.0.0 area 2
```

Ethernet1 should be in Area 2, and an initial look at this configuration seems to indicate that it is configured correctly. However, Ethernet1 will end up in Area 0. Why is this? The interface IP address is compared with the area commands in the order entered. Ethernet1 would start by being checked against the first line and would not match. Then Ethernet1 would be compared to the second statement, at which point it would match, and the interface would be assigned to Area 0. The third statement would never be checked. The solution to this problem is to swap the order of the second and third lines by removing the second line and adding it again, as shown here:

```
R1(config-router)#no network 192.168.0.0 0.0.255.255 area 0
R1(config-router)#network 192.168.0.0 0.0.255.255 area 0
```

When the statement is added back to the configuration, it will be appended to the end of the existing network statements. This should resolve this problem.

If the routers are using authentication, several new potential pitfalls are introduced. One such pitfall is that the routers may be using different authentication types — some could be configured for simple passwords and others for MD5 authentication. If two routers are using different authentication types on the same network, the following message would be generated:

```
OSPF: Rcv pkt from 192.168.123.6, Serial0.103 : Mismatch Authentication type. In
put packet specified type 2, we use type 1
```

If both routers are using simple passwords, but one of them is configured with the wrong password, the debug output would indicate the following message:

```
OSPF: Rcv pkt from 192.168.123.6, Serial0.103 : Mismatch Authentication Key - Cl
ear Text
```

Similarly, if both routers are using MD5 authentication, but they have different passwords for the same key ID, the following message would be displayed:

```
OSPF: Rcv pkt from 192.168.123.6, Serial0.103 : Mismatch Authentication Key - Me
ssage Digest Key 2
```

Finally, two routers using MD5 authentication may not have the same key ID configured, which would be indicated as follows:

```
OSPF: Rcv pkt from 192.168.123.6, Serial0.103 : Mismatch Authentication Key - No
message digest key 3 on interface
```

Another common pitfall occurs in stub areas and NSSAs. In both of these types of areas, all of the routers must be configured with the statement area *area-id* stub or area *area-id* nssa, whichever the case may be. If any router in the area is not configured in this way, it cannot form neighbor relationships with the other routers. In this case, one of the routers should provide debug output similar to this:

```
OSPF: Rcv hello from 192.168.254.5 area 23 from Ethernet0 192.168.3.2
OSPF: Hello from 192.168.3.2 with mismatched Stub/Transit area option bit
```

Finally, adjacency debugging output can also be useful to see DR/BDR election take place or to see the events that occur as two routers form a new neighbor relationship.

Other debug commands enable you to view more of the internal processes that take place in OSPF or some specific aspects of communication between the routers. These commands are probably less likely to indicate common problems, but in certain circumstances, they may be needed. Here is a list of the other debug commands available for OSPF:

- debug ip ospf events
- debug ip ospf flood
- debug ip ospf lsa-generation
- debug ip ospf packet
- debug ip ospf retransmission
- debug ip ospf spf
- debug ip ospf tree

Because they have more niche uses, these commands are not covered here. Feel free to investigate them and use those you find helpful.

Wrap-Up

OSPF can be a very useful routing protocol because of to its scalability and flexibility. It does not have any limitations on network size, but the routers must have enough resources to run it. Even though larger networks require more processing power, the use of areas can help alleviate some of the penalty, allowing OSPF networks to be very large. OSPF adapts to a variety of network types and can be configured for optimal performance and/or efficiency on each individual implementation. Finally, because OSPF is an open standard, equipment from multiple vendors can run the same routing protocol on your network.

The biggest caveat to OSPF is that it is not quite as common to find OSPF-enabled devices as it is RIP-enabled devices. However, OSPF has become prolific and most routers on the market today support it. For those parts of the network that will not support OSPF, redistribution can provide connectivity while preventing you from having to run legacy protocols across your whole network. Network administrators today should consider OSPF as a candidate for the primary routing protocol on their networks.

Chapter 5

Integrated System to Integrated System

Intermediate System to Intermediate System (IS-IS) is an International Organization for Standardization (ISO) protocol for routing Connectionless-mode Network Service (CLNS), the network-layer protocol of the Open Systems Interconnection (OSI) suite.

At the time that ISO was developing IS-IS, the Internet Architecture Board (IAB) was also developing Open Shortest Path First (OSPF) as the preferred IP-routing replacement for Routing Information Protocol (RIP). The Internet Engineering Task Force (IETF) was considering OSPF as the recommended internal IP routing protocol. However, at this time, many thought that the OSI suite would replace TCP/IP as the preferred protocol stack. Therefore, there was a movement to make IS-IS, rather than OSPF, the IETF-recommended standard. Integrated IS-IS was developed as an extension to IS-IS that would allow it to route IP. In this chapter, the term IS-IS is used to refer to what is technically known as Integrated IS-IS.

As you have probably figured out by now, the IETF chose OSPF as the recommended IP routing protocol. Nonetheless, IS-IS and OSPF share many characteristics, no doubt due in part to the interaction of the parties involved in the development of both. Both protocols are reliable and robust link state routing protocols, and both are in wide use today.

Understanding IS-IS

IS-IS is similar to OSPF in many ways, but some significant differences exist as well. Throughout the chapter, various aspects of IS-IS are compared to those of OSPF to aid in understanding the details of IS-IS. Therefore, knowledge of OSPF, which can be gained from Chapter 4, can be helpful when reading this chapter. However, the explanations and examples in this chapter do not rely entirely on knowledge of OSPF and, thus, should be sufficient to gain an understanding of IS-IS independently. The following properties of IS-IS are similar to those of OSPF:

- IS-IS is a link state routing protocol. All routers maintain a link state database, and they use a shortest path first algorithm to calculate routes.

- IS-IS makes use of areas to divide the routed network into more manageable parts and to reduce the resource requirements for the routers. It also uses a two-layer hierarchy to route between areas.

- IS-IS routers use Hello packets to maintain adjacencies with other IS-IS routers.

- IS-IS supports Variable-Length Subnet Masks (VLSM) and summarization at area boundaries.

The differences between IS-IS and OSPF include the following:

- IS-IS routers are part of one area only. Area boundaries fall between routers, rather than within routers, as in OSPF.

- The IS-IS backbone is defined by the use of router types, rather than by the use of a particular Area ID (Area 0 in OSPF).

- IS-IS information is passed between routers using CLNS, rather than IP. Therefore, IS-IS uses protocol data units, not IP packets, to communicate.

As you can see, an understanding of OSPF will help you build an understanding of the basic concepts of IS-IS. However, it is equally important to learn the distinctions between the two protocols, so that there is no problem understanding the behavior of IS-IS.

Starting with IS-IS Basics

IS-IS was originally designed to route CLNS, and it is one of two protocols designed to work together for that purpose. IS-IS dictates how routers (known as *independent systems* in ISO terminology) communicate routing information with each other. The other protocol, ES-IS, specifies communications between hosts (known as *end systems*) and routers. ES-IS allows hosts to discover and communicate with routers on the network. However, ES-IS is not used with IS-IS when routing IP, so it is not covered here.

Like OSPF, IS-IS uses areas to divide the network into smaller parts. An area defines the part of the network about which a router must have complete knowledge. Areas are explained in detail in the next section.

The foundation of IS-IS is CLNS, rather than IP, so it uses ISO-defined protocol data units (PDUs) to communicate between routers. Several types of PDUs are used by IS-IS, including Hello PDUs, link state PDUs (LSPs), and sequence number PDUs (SNPs). Hello PDUs allow IS-IS routers to form adjacencies with each other, discover new routers on the network, and determine when a router is no longer reachable.

IS-IS routers exchange routing information with link state PDUs (LSPs). These LSPs are used to build and maintain a link state database in each router. An LSP identifies each router, along with important information about it, such as its area and connected networks. The LSPs are reliably flooded to all routers through a process that uses sequence number PDUs. All of the PDU types, Hello PDUs, LSPs, and SNPs are explained in detail later in this chapter.

Similar to OSPF, IS-IS calculates routes based on Dijkstra's Shortest Path First (SPF) algorithm. The algorithm must be run whenever there is a change in the network topology. The IS-IS routes are then added to the IP routing table, where they may coexist with routes from other routing protocols.

IS-IS Areas

IS-IS routers are part of one area and one area only, which is a significant difference from OSPF. Rather than assigning different interfaces on a router to different areas (making an Area Boundary Router in OSPF), the area boundaries in IS-IS fall on the network links between routers. Area boundaries are shown in Figure 5-1.

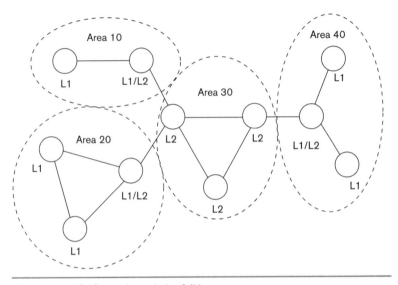

Figure 5-1 *IS-IS area boundaries fall between routers.*

If we compare Figure 5-1 to Figure 4-1, we can see the differences in layout between OSPF areas and IS-IS areas. First of all, the area boundaries no longer cut through routers; they cut through networks. Second, the IS-IS backbone area can be assigned any ID, but the OSPF backbone must be Area 0. Instead of the OSPF nomenclature of Area Border Routers (ABRs), Autonomous System Boundary Routers (ASBRs), internal routers, and backbone routers, IS-IS defines three types of routers:

- Layer 1 (L1) router: A router within a non-backbone area that will only share updates with other L1 routers and L1/L2 routers in its area.

- Layer 2 (L2) router: A router that shares updates with other L2 routers and L1/L2 routers. It will share information with them regardless of area. L2 routers comprise the backbone of the routing domain.

- Layer 1/Layer 2 (L1/L2) router: A router at an IS-IS area boundary that shares updates with all router types. It is responsible for exchanging routing information between its area and the backbone.

Within an area, the L1 routers never receive routing information about networks outside of their area. Routing information does not cross area boundaries as it does in OSPF. Instead, IS-IS areas behave in much the same way as OSPF totally stubby areas, including the generation of a default route within the area to a backbone-attached L1/L2 router.

Network Entity Titles

Although IS-IS can be used to route in an IP-only environment, it is still a CLNS routing protocol at heart. Therefore, some properties of IS-IS stem from necessities of routing CLNS. One such property is the Network Entity Title (NET). The NET uniquely identifies each router on the internetwork, similar to the OSPF Router ID (RID). The NET is a network address that identifies the System ID and the Area ID for the router.

The NET is extremely flexible and can be as simple or complex as the network design requires. For a network running IS-IS independently, a simple NET scheme should be chosen. However, some situations may require GOSIP or OSI NSAP compliance, and parts of the NET may be assigned by outside authorities. A complete description of possible NET formats is beyond the scope of this text, so we will use a simple NET format, shown in Figure 5-2, in our configuration examples.

Figure 5-2 *A simple, valid NET format. This is the format used in the configuration examples in this chapter.*

As you can see in the figure, the fields of the NET are separated by periods. The NET must always start with a single–octet field. Depending on the format of the NET, the meaning of that field can vary. In the examples in this chapter, the first octet represents the Area ID. By definition, the Area ID can be up to two octets long. If your Area ID values fit into one octet, you can use the first octet to represent them. If you want to use any Area ID values greater than 256, you need to use an Area ID field that is two octets long, in which case the first field cannot be used to represent the Area ID. Whether or not the Area ID is the first octet, it must immediately precede System ID. The final octet of the NET is always the NSAP Selector (SEL). The SEL identifies a particular service on a network node. When the SEL is 0x00, it is the address of the node itself. Therefore, the SEL must always be 0x00 when configuring the NET. The System ID can vary in size from one to eight octets, but all routers in the same autonomous system must use the same size for the System ID, and the System IDs must be unique. In the Cisco IOS, the System ID must be six octets. The MAC address of an interface on the router is typically chosen as the System ID.

Although an IS-IS router can be part of only one area, it can be configured with multiple area addresses. When this is done, those area addresses all refer to the same area and will be advertised throughout the area. To configure multiple Area IDs on one router, multiple NETs can be entered, with varying Area IDs. The number of Area IDs configured on a router is limited to three. An example of this is given in the "Configuring Multiple Areas on One Router" section later in this chapter.

IS-IS Network Types

IS-IS supports only two network types: *broadcast* and *point-to-point*. Although it makes IS-IS less flexible than OSPF when it comes to supporting different network configurations, this limited number of choices also makes IS-IS easier to configure. For example, a Frame Relay interface with multiple PVCs can be configured for OSPF in four different ways. In IS-IS, the only option is to break up the interface into several subinterfaces, each of which is a point-to-point network.

The primary difference between broadcast and point-to-point IS-IS networks lies in the adjacencies and Hello PDUs, which are discussed in the following section.

Adjacencies and Hello PDUs

IS-IS routers use Hello PDUs to build and maintain relationships with one another. Using Hello PDUs, the routers can identify their neighbors. Each Hello contains identifying information about the sending router and several parameters that identify how the router will behave. If two neighbors agree on the necessary parameters, they will establish an adjacency. IS-IS adjacencies are similar to those in OSPF, but some significant differences do exist.

One important difference is that the Hello interval and hold time do not need to be the same on neighbors for them to be adjacent. The Hello PDU contains a hold time, which the receiving router uses as the hold time for the neighbor. This enables each neighbor to use a different Hello interval. This behavior differs from that of OSPF, where neighbors must agree on the Hello interval and the hold time.

Routers establish adjacencies at L1 and L2 separately. L1 routers form adjacencies with L1 and L1/L2 routers. L2 routers form adjacencies with L2 and L1/L2 routers. L1/L2 routers maintain two separate sets of adjacencies, one for L1 neighbors and one for L2 neighbors. If two neighbors are both L1/L2 routers, they establish and maintain two independent adjacencies. L1 and L2 neighbors can never become adjacent.

Because a mix of routers (L1, L2, and L1/L2) may exist on a broadcast network, the network may have both types of adjacencies running on it, each with a different set of routers. IS-IS routers use separate L1 and L2 Hello PDUs on broadcast networks to maintain the adjacencies with the different sets of routers. Therefore, an L1/L2 router will need to send and receive both types of Hello PDU.

On the other hand, the two routers on a point-to-point network can only establish adjacencies with each other. Although they may establish two adjacencies (if both are L1/L2 routers), both adjacencies in this case are the same—just two neighbors. Therefore, point-to-point networks require only one Hello PDU, which contains information to establish both L1 and L2 adjacencies if necessary.

Designated IS and Router Priority

IS-IS uses a *Designated IS* (DIS) on broadcast networks to reduce the amount of traffic required to advertise broadcast networks and to flood LSPs on them. The DIS performs similar functions to the Designated Router (DR) in OSPF. The DIS is responsible for advertising the broadcast network to which all of the routers are attached. This prevents the other routers from having to advertise adjacencies with all routers on that network. The DIS advertises a *pseudonode*, which represents the network, and each router advertises just one adjacency—to the pseudonode. Although the pseudonode is actually a network, it appears as a router in the link state database.

The pseudonode has its own LSP, separate from that of the DIS, even though they are both generated by the DIS. The DIS assigns a one-octet Pseudonode ID to the broadcast network, which is concatenated with the System ID of the DIS to form the Local Area Network (LAN) ID. The LAN ID is reported as the source of the LSPs for the pseudonode in the link state database, as described in the next section.

The DIS also plays a role in the flooding of LSPs on the broadcast network. However, this behavior differs from that exhibited by DRs in OSPF. In OSPF, each router on the broadcast network becomes adjacent only with the DR (and the Backup Designated Router, or BDR). Link-State Advertisements (LSAs) are transmitted only between the DR and each router. In IS-IS, each router on the broadcast network becomes adjacent with every neighbor. In addition, the LSPs are multicasted to all of the neighbors, so the DIS does not have to advertise LSPs between routers on the broadcast network. However, the DIS handles the transmission of SNPs to make sure that all neighbors receive all LSPs. The use of SNPs in flooding is described in detail in "LSP Flooding."

Because IS-IS routers establish separate L1 and L2 adjacencies, there is a separate DIS for L1 and for L2 on the same broadcast network. It is possible for one router to fill both roles, but they are still independent. Therefore, there is an L1 pseudonode and an L2 pseudonode if both types of router exist on the same network.

The DIS is elected based on router priority, which is a configurable parameter on each interface and is also separate for L1 and L2 adjacencies. The default priority is 64 on Cisco routers, but it can range from zero to 127. If the priority is zero, that particular router will be ineligible to become the DIS on that network. Ties in priority are broken by choosing the numerically highest System ID. Because routers on point-to-point networks do not elect a DIS, the priority of point-to-point interfaces is always zero.

It is important to note some differences between DR election in OSPF and DIS election in IS-IS. In OSPF, once the DR is chosen, it remains the DR until it is removed from the network. Even if a higher priority router comes up, it cannot become the DR until an election, which is usually caused by the loss of the current DR, takes place. In IS-IS, the router with the highest priority will always assume the role of DIS, even if that means replacing the currently active DIS. Of course, when this happens, new LSPs (reflecting the new LAN ID) must be generated. Another difference between IS-IS and OSPF is that IS-IS does not elect a backup DIS.

Link State PDUs

Every router generates LSPs in the IS-IS autonomous system. Similar to LSAs in OSPF, LSPs are stored in link state databases on every router and are used to build routes using the SPF algorithm. LSPs are flooded throughout an area, and all routers in the area must have an identical view of the network.

On point-to-point networks, neighboring routers send unicast LSPs to each other directly. On broadcast networks, the routers multicast the LSPs, using separate addresses for L1 and L2 LSPs. L1 LSPs are multicasted to the MAC address 0180.C200.0014, known as AllL1ISs. L2 LSPs are sent to the multicast MAC address 0180.C200.0015, known as AllL2ISs.

The following is a link state database from an L1 router:

```
IS-IS Level-1 Link State Database

LSPID                  LSP Seq Num   LSP Checksum  LSP Holdtime  ATT/P/OL

0000.3060.7994.00-00   0x00000023    0x04C0        991           0/0/0

0000.3060.7994.01-00   0x00000002    0x5F45        720           0/0/0

0000.30E2.50ED.00-00*  0x0000000A    0x4F2D        992           0/0/0

0000.30E2.50ED.01-00*  0x00000003    0x2C6D        985           0/0/0

0060.5CF3.FAEE.00-00   0x0000001D    0xA340        991           0/0/0

0060.5CF3.FAEE.01-00   0x00000002    0xE9C2        941           0/0/0
```

The LSPs in the link state database above describe six nodes, which can be determined from the LSPID column. The first six octets in the column are the System ID of the originating router. The next octet is the Pseudonode ID, which is non-zero for all LSPs that represent broadcast networks.. Therefore, three of the nodes in the link state database are pseudonodes, and the other three are routers. Finally, the last octet of the LSPID (following the hyphen) is the LSP Number. This is used when an LSP is so large that it must be fragmented. Each fragment appears in the link state database separately, but they describe the same router or pseudonode. The LSPs originated locally appear in the link state database with asterisks (*).

This table also includes the Sequence Number, Checksum, Remaining Lifetime, and option bits. The Sequence Number tracks the version of the LSP. It starts at one and is incremented for each new instance of the LSP. The Sequence Number is an unsigned 32-bit integer, so the maximum value is 0xFFFFFFFF. If an LSP reaches the maximum, the IS-IS process must shut down for 21 minutes to let the LSP age out of all databases. Although this may seem like a severe limitation, a new instance of the LSP would have to be generated every second for over 136 years to reach that limit.

The Checksum is used to make sure that the LSP arrives intact at each router. If a router receives an LSP with an invalid Checksum, it will purge the LSP from all databases by setting the Remaining Lifetime to zero and flooding it. When this happens, the originator of the LSP generates a new instance of the LSP. This behavior can be disabled, as will be seen in the configuration section of this chapter.

The Remaining Lifetime of an LSP (labeled Holdtime in the link state database above) is similar to the Age in an OSPF LSA. The primary difference is that the Remaining Lifetime starts at the maximum and counts down, rather than counting from zero up to the maximum. The Remaining Lifetime starts with a value of 1200 seconds (20 minutes) by default. When the Remaining Lifetime of an LSP in the link state database reaches zero, the router keeps it for another 60 seconds and then removes it from the database. To prevent this from happening, IS-IS routers refresh their LSPs every 15 minutes by default. (The actual refresh time includes a randomization factor of up to 25 percent.)

The ATT/P/OL column indicates the values of those bits in the LSP. The ATT (attachment) bit indicates that the router is able to route to other areas. (In the LSP, this is actually a four-bit field, indicating which of the metrics are supported by the attachment. However, Cisco routers support only one of the four metrics, so only one bit is shown in the link state database.) The ATT bit is set in LSPs for L1/L2 routers, and L1 routers determine their default route from this bit. The P bit is the Partition bit, which indicates a special capability of the router. Cisco routers do not support this feature, so it should always be 0.

The Overload (OL) bit is a unique feature of IS-IS, used to signal to all other routers that the originating router may be unable to hold the entire link state database. This may occur if a router is low on memory. The other routers in the area realize that a router with the OL bit set may make poor routing decisions, so they will attempt to circumvent the problem by routing around the troubled router. Packets destined for networks directly connected to that router will still be forwarded to it, but it will not be used for transit traffic until the problem has been cleared. The overload condition exists separately for the L1 and L2 databases, and it can be set manually in the configuration.

Flooding LSPs

LSPs are flooded reliably through the use of SNPs. SNPs contain enough information to identify each LSP, without including the entire LSP. There are two types of SNPs: Complete SNPs (CSNPs) and Partial SNPs (PSNPs). As you can guess from their names, CSNPs include all LSPs in the link state database, and PSNPs include only some.

PSNPs are used to acknowledge LSPs on point-to-point networks. When a router sends an LSP (its own or that of another router) to its neighbor on a point-to-point network, it sets a timer to wait for acknowledgement of that LSP. The neighbor is expected to send a PSNP that acknowledges that LSP (and perhaps others as well). If the timer expires before the LSP is acknowledged, the sending router retransmits the LSP. The default timer value is five seconds on Cisco routers, but it can be changed on a per-interface basis.

On broadcast networks, the routers receive multicast LSPs from all of their neighbors. Rather than having each router on the network acknowledge each LSP, the DIS sends CSNPs (that contain LSP) in its link state database. The CSNPs are multicasted on the network every ten seconds by default, but this interval can be changed. L1 CSNPs are sent to the multicast address AllL1ISs, and L2 CSNPs are sent to AllL2ISs.

All of the other routers on the broadcast network compare the CSNP to their link state databases. If a router is missing an LSP that is contained in the CSNP, it multicasts a PSNP containing the LSP that it is missing. The DIS responds to any PSNPs with the requested LSPs.

If a router has an LSP in its database that is missing from the CSNP or is newer than the one that appears in the CSNP, it multicasts the LSP to all of its neighbors. If a router detects that an LSP is missing from the CSNP but another router has already sent out the LSP, it does not send the LSP again.

IS-IS in the Routing Table

The following is a Cisco router IP routing table that includes IS-IS routes:

```
i L1 192.168.100.0/24 [115/20] via 192.168.16.6, Ethernet0
i L1 192.168.101.0/24 [115/20] via 192.168.16.6, Ethernet0
i L1 192.168.102.0/24 [115/20] via 192.168.16.6, Ethernet0
i L1 192.168.103.0/24 [115/20] via 192.168.16.6, Ethernet0
i L2 192.168.34.0/24 [115/20] via 192.168.14.4, Serial1
                    [115/20] via 192.168.13.3, Serial0
C    192.168.13.0/24 is directly connected, Serial0
C    192.168.14.0/24 is directly connected, Serial1
i L2 192.168.5.0/24 [115/40] via 192.168.14.4, Serial1
                    [115/40] via 192.168.13.3, Serial0
i L2 192.168.24.0/24 [115/20] via 192.168.14.4, Serial1
i L2 192.168.25.0/24 [115/30] via 192.168.14.4, Serial1
                    [115/30] via 192.168.13.3, Serial0
C    192.168.16.0/24 is directly connected, Ethernet0
i L2 192.168.23.0/24 [115/20] via 192.168.13.3, Serial0
```

We can learn many things by looking at this routing table. First, the "i" at the start of each line indicates which routes are from the IS-IS routing process. Following the "i" is either "L1" or "L2", depending on the source of the route. L1 routers can only have L1 routes, and L2 routers can only have L2 routes. L1/L2 routers usually have a mix of both.

After the network address in each line, you can see that the default administrative distance for IS-IS is 115. This indicates how preferred

IS-IS is over other IP routing protocols. The number following the administrative distance of every IS-IS route is the metric, which is used to decide between different IS-IS routes to the same destination. The metric is calculated by adding the cost of each outgoing interface along a particular path. The default IS-IS cost of any interface on a Cisco router is 10. Because all interfaces are the same cost by default, the metric behaves like a hop count unless the costs of interfaces are changed. The cost of an interface can be between zero and 63. The maximum cost for an IS-IS path is 1023, so care must be used when increasing the cost of interfaces. Although this metric limit reduces the flexibility of IS-IS, especially in large environments, it makes the SPF algorithm more efficient.

IS-IS actually uses four metrics: default, delay, expense, and error. The default metric must be supported by all routers, but the other three are optional. When multiple metric types are in use, the SPF algorithm must be run for each type of metric, significantly increasing the resources required. For this reason, Cisco routers, along with those from other vendors, only support the default metric. Throughout the rest of this chapter, the term "metric" (without naming an explicit type) refers to the default metric.

IS-IS Authentication

IS-IS allows for a very basic form of authentication. Passwords can be used to authenticate routing information, but they can only be passed in clear text. Therefore, this authentication mechanism does not provide strong security. However, it may be helpful in avoiding problems that can be introduced by attaching a router to a network before necessary configuration changes have been made.

There are three different types of IS-IS passwords:

- Neighbor password: Router interfaces on the same network can share a common password. This password is contained in Hello PDUs and can prevent adjacencies from forming. Separate passwords are used for L1 and L2 neighbors.

- Area password: L1 (and L1/L2) routers in the same area can share a password. In this case, all routers in the area must support authentication and be configured with the same password. This password is contained in L1 LSPs and SNPs; it can prevent L1 LSPs from being accepted by/from all routers in the area.

- Domain password: L2 (and L1/L2) routers in the IS-IS routing domain can share a password. The same password must be configured on all L2 routers. It is contained in L2 LSPs and SNPs, and it can prevent L2 LSPs from being accepted by/from all L2 routers.

Configuration examples of each type of authentication are provided in the "Configuring Authentication" section later in this chapter.

Configuring IS-IS

Configuring IS-IS is fairly simple when used to route only IP. The biggest decisions that must be made are about the structure of the areas. The steps required to configure the routers and their interfaces are usually short and easy. This section starts with a small network running IS-IS, and then it considers some of the issues facing larger networks.

Basic IS-IS Configuration

To start the IS-IS routing process, simply enter the **router isis** command in global configuration mode. This puts you into the configuration mode for IS-IS. While in that mode, you are also required to enter a NET. The NETs used in the following examples are all of the simple form shown previously in Figure 5-2. The System IDs in the examples are always chosen from one of the interfaces of the router being configured. The following two configuration lines start the IS-IS process on R1:

```
R1(config)#router isis
R1(config-router)#net 01.0060.5cf3.faee.00
```

Once the IS-IS routing process has been started, you must configure the interfaces that will participate in IS-IS to route IP. To do so, enter the **ip router isis** interface configuration command. The command must be entered not only on the interfaces that should speak IS-IS, but also on all interfaces whose networks should be advertised in IS-IS. This command is used in the full configuration examples that follow.

We will configure the example network shown in Figure 5-3 to run IS-IS as its IP routing protocol. All three routers will be in the same area, Area 1, with all of their interfaces configured for IS-IS.

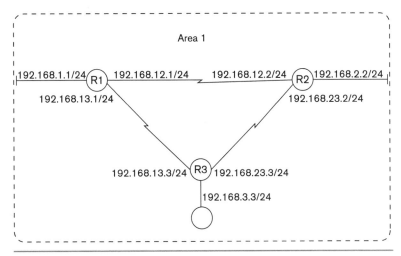

Figure 5-3 *A small one-area IS-IS network with three routers*

In this network, the configuration for R1 is:

```
clns routing
!
interface Ethernet0
 ip address 192.168.1.1 255.255.255.0
 ip router isis
!
interface Serial0
 ip address 192.168.12.1 255.255.255.0
 ip router isis
!
interface Serial1
 ip address 192.168.13.1 255.255.255.0
 ip router isis
!
router isis
 net 01.0060.5cf3.faee.00
```

The configuration for R2 is:

```
clns routing
!
interface Serial0
 ip address 192.168.23.2 255.255.255.0
 ip router isis
!
interface Serial1
 ip address 192.168.12.2 255.255.255.0
 ip router isis
!
interface TokenRing0
 ip address 192.168.2.2 255.255.255.0
 ip router isis
!
router isis
 net 01.0000.30e2.50ed.00
```

The configuration for R3 is:

```
clns routing
!
interface Serial0
 ip address 192.168.13.3 255.255.255.0
 ip router isis
!
interface Serial1
 ip address 192.168.23.3 255.255.255.0
 ip router isis
!
interface TokenRing0
 ip address 192.168.3.3 255.255.255.0
 ip router isis
!
router isis
 net 01.0000.3060.7994.00
```

The first thing to note is that the global configuration command `clns routing` appears in the configuration for all three routers, even though it was not mentioned above. This command is entered automatically by the router when the IS-IS routing process is created with the `router isis` command. It is required and cannot be removed. (Because you need not worry about entering it explicitly, that command will be omitted in the rest of the configuration examples.)

With the routers configured as shown above, R2 establishes adjacencies with both neighbors:

```
R2#show clns is-neighbors


System Id        Interface    State   Type Priority   Circuit Id       Format
0060.5CF3.FAEE Se1           Up      L1L2 0 /0       00               Phase V
0000.3060.7994 Se0           Up      L1L2 0 /0       01               Phase V
```

This output lists the System ID of each neighbor, along with the interface on which it was learned. Also, note that both neighbors are L1/L2 routers, which is the default router type when IS-IS is enabled. Because R2 is also an L1/L2 router, it establishes two adjacencies with each L1/L2 neighbor. R2 also has two link state databases, which are maintained separately:

```
R2#sh isis database
IS-IS Level-1 Link State Database
LSPID                    LSP Seq Num   LSP Checksum   LSP Holdtime   ATT/P/OL
0000.3060.7994.00-00   0x00000023    0x04C0         991            0/0/0
0000.3060.7994.01-00   0x00000002    0x5F45         720            0/0/0
0000.30E2.50ED.00-00*  0x0000000A    0x4F2D         992            0/0/0
0000.30E2.50ED.01-00*  0x00000003    0x2C6D         985            0/0/0
0060.5CF3.FAEE.00-00   0x0000001D    0xA340         991            0/0/0
0060.5CF3.FAEE.01-00   0x00000002    0xE9C2         941            0/0/0


IS-IS Level-2 Link State Database
LSPID                    LSP Seq Num   LSP Checksum   LSP Holdtime   ATT/P/OL
0000.3060.7994.00-00   0x00000025    0xDEE0         993            0/0/0
0000.30E2.50ED.00-00*  0x0000000E    0xEF36         995            0/0/0
0060.5CF3.FAEE.00-00   0x0000001E    0xCB03         991            0/0/0
```

When routing in only one area, there is no need for the routers to maintain two adjacencies for each neighbor. You can use the `is-type level-1` command in IS-IS configuration mode to change the router type to L1:

```
R2(config)#router isis
R2(config-router)#is-type level-1
```

If all three routers are configured to be L1 routers, the link state database maintained by IS-IS becomes much simpler:

```
R2#show isis database

IS-IS Level-1 Link State Database

LSPID                    LSP Seq Num  LSP Checksum  LSP Holdtime  ATT/P/OL

0000.3060.7994.00-00  0x0000002B   0xF1CC        1074          0/0/0

0000.3060.7994.01-00  0x00000003   0x5D46        521           0/0/0

0000.30E2.50ED.00-00* 0x00000019   0x2F40        1070          0/0/0

0000.30E2.50ED.01-00* 0x00000004   0xD369        761           0/0/0

0060.5CF3.FAEE.00-00  0x0000002B   0x8552        1075          0/0/0

0060.5CF3.FAEE.01-00  0x00000003   0xE7C3        879           0/0/0
```

Now only one adjacency per neighbor and one link state database is maintained by R2, with no loss of routing information.

 Tip

Whenever possible, change IS-IS routers from the default type of L1/L2 to either L1 or L2 explicitly. This minimizes the resources required, because the router needs to maintain only one link state database.

The routing table for R2 has all of the subnets in its IP routing table:

```
R2#show ip route

Codes: C - connected, S - static, I - IGRP, R - RIP, M - mobile, B - BGP
       D - EIGRP, EX - EIGRP external, O - OSPF, IA - OSPF inter area
       N1 - OSPF NSSA external type 1, N2 - OSPF NSSA external type 2
       E1 - OSPF external type 1, E2 - OSPF external type 2, E - EGP
       i - IS-IS, L1 - IS-IS level-1, L2 - IS-IS level-2, * - candidate default
       U - per-user static route, o - ODR
```

```
Gateway of last resort is not set

C    192.168.12.0/24 is directly connected, Serial1
i L1 192.168.13.0/24 [115/20] via 192.168.23.3, Serial0
                     [115/20] via 192.168.12.1, Serial1
i L1 192.168.1.0/24 [115/20] via 192.168.12.1, Serial1
C    192.168.2.0/24 is directly connected, TokenRing0
i L1 192.168.3.0/24 [115/20] via 192.168.23.3, Serial0
C    192.168.23.0/24 is directly connected, Serial0
```

Notice that there are two equal-cost routes to 192.168.13.0/24, one from each neighbor. Because the routes are equal-cost, they are both installed in the routing table, which would be the case with up to six equal-cost routes by default.

Configuring Multiple IS-IS Areas on One Router

A significant difference between OSPF and IS-IS is the structure of their areas. While OSPF allows routers to participate in more than one area, an IS-IS router can be in only one area. However, a router can be configured with multiple Area IDs by using more than one NET. This causes all of the Area IDs to be used in the same area.

Using the example network shown in Figure 5-3 above, we leave the configurations of R1 and R2 unchanged. However, adding a second NET to R3 results in the following configuration:

```
interface Serial0
 ip address 192.168.13.3 255.255.255.0
 ip router isis
!
interface Serial1
 ip address 192.168.23.3 255.255.255.0
 ip router isis
!
interface TokenRing0
```

```
ip address 192.168.3.3 255.255.255.0

ip router isis

!

router isis

 net 01.0000.3060.7994.00

 net 03.0000.3060.7994.00

 is-type level-1
```

This results in R3 using two Area IDs — 1 and 3. You can see this in the output of the show clns protocol command:

```
R3#show clns protocol

IS-IS Router: <Null Tag>

  System Id: 0000.3060.7994.00  IS-Type: level-1

  Manual area address(es):

        01

        03

  Routing for area address(es):

        01

        03

  Interfaces supported by IS-IS:

        TokenRing0 - IP

        Serial1 - IP

        Serial0 - IP

  Redistributing:

    static

  Distance: 110
```

From this output, you can see that R3 recognizes that it is configured with Area 1 and Area 3. Issuing the same command on R1 results in even more interesting information:

```
R1#sh clns protocol

IS-IS Router: <Null Tag>

  System Id: 0060.5CF3.FAEE.00  IS-Type: level-1

  Manual area address(es):

        01
```

```
Routing for area address(es):
     01
     03
Interfaces supported by IS-IS:
     Ethernet0 - IP
     Serial1 - IP
     Serial0 - IP
Redistributing:
   static
Distance: 110
```

R1 recognizes Area 1 and Area 3 as well. The output states explicitly that R1 is configured only with Area 1, but it is still routing for Area 3 at the same time. The same results would be seen on R2.

This feature of IS-IS can be useful for migrating to a new area-numbering scheme or for splitting an existing area into multiple areas. You can do such migrations gradually, rather doing than an immediate cutover, as OSPF requires. Whenever a router is configured with multiple Area IDs, it treats them as the same area, and it notifies its neighbors of the additional Area IDs. This fact is also important when troubleshooting IS-IS. A misconfigured router can cause two areas to be treated as one.

Because each router can be part of only one area at a time, multiple NETs will normally only be assigned to a router during a transitional period. In a stable IS-IS network, all routers should have only one NET.

Routing through Multiple IS-IS Areas

Even though a stable routing environment would not usually use multiple Area IDs on the same router, it is likely that a larger network would use multiple areas throughout the IS-IS routing domain. Use of multiple areas will help minimize the memory required to maintain link state databases on the routers in each area.

Although the network shown in Figure 5-4 is not very large, we will use it as an example for configuration of multiple IS-IS areas.

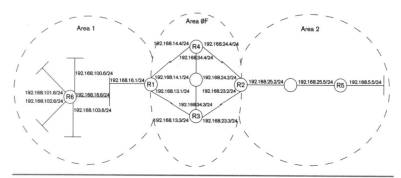

Figure 5-4 *An IS-IS network with multiple areas*

Area 0F is the backbone area, so the routers within the area are L2 routers (R3 and R4). The routers that have links to the Area 0F routers need to be L1/L2 routers (R1 and R2). All other routers are L1 routers (R5 and R6). The following is the configuration of R1:

```
interface Ethernet0
 ip address 192.168.16.1 255.255.255.0
 ip router isis
!
interface Serial0
 ip address 192.168.13.1 255.255.255.0
 ip router isis
!
interface Serial1
 ip address 192.168.14.1 255.255.255.0
 ip router isis
!
router isis
 net 01.0060.5cf3.faee.00
```

Notice that within the router process, the **is-type** command does not appear. This is because it is set to its default value (L1/L2), so it is not shown in the configuration. The configuration of R3 would look like this:

```
interface Serial0
 ip address 192.168.13.3 255.255.255.0
```

```
 ip router isis
!
interface Serial1
 ip address 192.168.23.3 255.255.255.0
 ip router isis
!
interface TokenRing0
 ip address 192.168.34.3 255.255.255.0
 ip router isis
!
router isis
 net 0f.0000.3060.7994.00
 is-type level-2-only
```

Notice that R3 is specifically configured as an L2 router. If this were not done, R3 would establish two adjacencies with R4, since they are both in the same area. Configuring the routers in the backbone area as L2 routers will offer the same performance advantages as configuring routers in other areas as L1 routers.

As a backbone router, R3 will have the entire internetwork in its link state database and in its IP routing table:

```
R3#show ip route
Codes: C - connected, S - static, I - IGRP, R - RIP, M - mobile, B - BGP
       D - EIGRP, EX - EIGRP external, O - OSPF, IA - OSPF inter area
       N1 - OSPF NSSA external type 1, N2 - OSPF NSSA external type 2
       E1 - OSPF external type 1, E2 - OSPF external type 2, E - EGP
       i - IS-IS, L1 - IS-IS level-1, L2 - IS-IS level-2, * - candidate default
       U - per-user static route, o - ODR

Gateway of last resort is not set

i L2 192.168.100.0/24 [115/30] via 192.168.13.1, Serial0
i L2 192.168.101.0/24 [115/30] via 192.168.13.1, Serial0
i L2 192.168.102.0/24 [115/30] via 192.168.13.1, Serial0
i L2 192.168.103.0/24 [115/30] via 192.168.13.1, Serial0
```

```
C    192.168.34.0/24 is directly connected, TokenRing0
C    192.168.13.0/24 is directly connected, Serial0
i L2 192.168.14.0/24 [115/20] via 192.168.13.1, Serial0
                     [115/20] via 192.168.34.4, TokenRing0
i L2 192.168.5.0/24 [115/30] via 192.168.23.2, Serial1
i L2 192.168.24.0/24 [115/20] via 192.168.34.4, TokenRing0
                     [115/20] via 192.168.23.2, Serial1
i L2 192.168.25.0/24 [115/20] via 192.168.23.2, Serial1
i L2 192.168.16.0/24 [115/20] via 192.168.13.1, Serial0
C    192.168.23.0/24 is directly connected, Serial1
```

Notice that all IS-IS routes are L2 routes. The routing table for R4 would be very similar to that of R3. In contrast, the routing table for R2 has all of the routes as well, but it differentiates between those from within its area and those from the backbone:

```
R2#show ip route
Codes: C - connected, S - static, I - IGRP, R - RIP, M - mobile, B - BGP
       D - EIGRP, EX - EIGRP external, O - OSPF, IA - OSPF inter area
       N1 - OSPF NSSA external type 1, N2 - OSPF NSSA external type 2
       E1 - OSPF external type 1, E2 - OSPF external type 2, E - EGP
       i - IS-IS, L1 - IS-IS level-1, L2 - IS-IS level-2, * - candidate default
       U - per-user static route, o - ODR


Gateway of last resort is not set

i L2 192.168.100.0/24 [115/40] via 192.168.23.3, Serial0
                      [115/40] via 192.168.24.4, Serial1
i L2 192.168.101.0/24 [115/40] via 192.168.23.3, Serial0
                      [115/40] via 192.168.24.4, Serial1
i L2 192.168.102.0/24 [115/40] via 192.168.23.3, Serial0
                      [115/40] via 192.168.24.4, Serial1
i L2 192.168.103.0/24 [115/40] via 192.168.23.3, Serial0
                      [115/40] via 192.168.24.4, Serial1
i L2 192.168.34.0/24 [115/20] via 192.168.23.3, Serial0
                     [115/20] via 192.168.24.4, Serial1
```

```
i L2 192.168.13.0/24 [115/20] via 192.168.23.3, Serial0

i L2 192.168.14.0/24 [115/20] via 192.168.24.4, Serial1

i L1 192.168.5.0/24 [115/20] via 192.168.25.5, TokenRing0

C    192.168.24.0/24 is directly connected, Serial1

C    192.168.25.0/24 is directly connected, TokenRing0

i L2 192.168.16.0/24 [115/30] via 192.168.23.3, Serial0

                     [115/30] via 192.168.24.4, Serial1

C    192.168.23.0/24 is directly connected, Serial0
```

R2 tags the routes with either an L1 or an L2 designation, indicating whether they were learned from within the area or from outside the area. The routing table of R1 would also have both L1 and L2 routes. In contrast, R5 does not have routes for any networks outside of Area 2:

```
R5#show ip route
Codes: C - connected, S - static, I - IGRP, R - RIP, M - mobile, B - BGP
       D - EIGRP, EX - EIGRP external, O - OSPF, IA - OSPF inter area
       N1 - OSPF NSSA external type 1, N2 - OSPF NSSA external type 2
       E1 - OSPF external type 1, E2 - OSPF external type 2, E - EGP
       i - IS-IS, L1 - IS-IS level-1, L2 - IS-IS level-2, * - candidate default
       U - per-user static route, o - ODR

Gateway of last resort is 192.168.25.2 to network 0.0.0.0

C    192.168.25.0/24 is directly connected, TokenRing0
i L1 192.168.24.0/24 [115/20] via 192.168.25.2, TokenRing0
C    192.168.5.0/24 is directly connected, Ethernet0
i L1 192.168.23.0/24 [115/20] via 192.168.25.2, TokenRing0
i*L1 0.0.0.0/0 [115/10] via 192.168.25.2, TokenRing0
```

All IS-IS routes learned by R5 are L1 routes, and they are only those networks that are directly connected to R2 (the only other router in Area 2). Notice that R5 has a default route pointing to R2. This is the reason why R5 does not need every route in the IS-IS routing domain; R5 creates the default route when it sees that the ATT bit is set in the LSP from R2, indicating that R2 is attached to other networks.

Tip

Sometimes the default route will not automatically appear in the routing tables of L1 routers. The results differ based on the IOS version in use. If you do not see a default route, but the ATT bit is set in an LSP, try enabling CLNS routing on the interfaces, in addition to IP routing. Simply enter `clns router isis` in interface configuration mode.

Configuring Summarization

The use of IS-IS areas prevents some routing information from reaching the non-backbone areas, thereby reducing the amount of memory used by the IS-IS routing process. However, the backbone routers must still learn and store information about all subnets in their link state databases and in their routing tables. In a well-structured network, summarization can be used to reduce the amount of network information that an L1/L2 router passes on to the backbone. In addition, a summary address will prevent updates from going to the backbone when one of the summarized routes changes state.

Consider the network shown in Figure 5-4 once again. The four subnets attached to R6 are 192.168.100.0/24, 192.168.101.0/24, 192.168.102.0/ 24, and 192.168.103.0/24. All four of these subnets can be summarized by the network 192.168.100.0/22. To advertise this summarized network to the backbone from R1, use the **summary-address** command in IS-IS configuration mode:

```
R1(config)#router isis
R1(config-router)#summary-address 192.168.100.0 255.255.252.0
```

With the summary address configured on R1, it advertises only the summarized route to the backbone. Therefore, the routing table on R2 now looks like this:

```
R2#show ip route
Codes: C - connected, S - static, I - IGRP, R - RIP, M - mobile, B - BGP
       D - EIGRP, EX - EIGRP external, O - OSPF, IA - OSPF inter area
       N1 - OSPF NSSA external type 1, N2 - OSPF NSSA external type 2
       E1 - OSPF external type 1, E2 - OSPF external type 2, E - EGP
```

```
     i - IS-IS, L1 - IS-IS level-1, L2 - IS-IS level-2, * - candidate default
     U - per-user static route, o - ODR

Gateway of last resort is not set

i L2 192.168.34.0/24 [115/20] via 192.168.23.3, Serial0
                     [115/20] via 192.168.24.4, Serial1
i L2 192.168.13.0/24 [115/20] via 192.168.23.3, Serial0
i L2 192.168.14.0/24 [115/20] via 192.168.24.4, Serial1
i L1 192.168.5.0/24 [115/20] via 192.168.25.5, TokenRing0
C    192.168.24.0/24 is directly connected, Serial1
C    192.168.25.0/24 is directly connected, TokenRing0
i L2 192.168.16.0/24 [115/30] via 192.168.23.3, Serial0
                     [115/30] via 192.168.24.4, Serial1
C    192.168.23.0/24 is directly connected, Serial0
i L2 192.168.100.0/22 [115/40] via 192.168.23.3, Serial0
                      [115/40] via 192.168.24.4, Serial1
```

Notice that when compared to the routing table listed for R2 earlier, all of the stub networks attached to R6 are now missing. They have been replaced with the summarized route to 192.168.100.0/22. Note also that this does not affect L1 routers in other areas (such as R5) because they never receive routes from other areas anyway.

Configuring Interface Properties

Several IS-IS interface properties can be used to modify the behavior of IS-IS on the router. Some of the more important and/or common ones are covered in this section.

Tip

You can always find out other IS-IS interface configuration options by using context sensitive help. Most of them will be displayed by entering `isis ?` in interface configuration mode.

The time period between sending Hello PDUs can be configured with the `hello-interval` command. The value entered is a number of seconds between 0 and 65,535, with a default value of 10. Because L1 and L2 Hellos are independent on broadcast networks, the Hello interval is set separately for L1 and L2. For example, to set the L1 Hello interval to 20 seconds, the following command would be issued:

```
R3(config-if)#isis hello-interval 20 level-1
```

If the level is not specified, the router assumes that it is the L1 setting and automatically appends `level-1` to the command.

Caution

Over a point-to-point network, a router sends only one Hello PDU, which can establish both the L1 and L2 adjacencies. The router uses the `level-1` configuration to determine the properties of the point-to-point Hello PDU. Therefore, on point-to-point interfaces, always set the `level-1` Hello properties as desired. There is no need to specify `level-2` configuration parameters, even if the router is an L2 router.

In addition to the Hello interval, you can modify the amount of time that a router tells its neighbor to wait for the next Hello. The hold time is advertised in the Hello PDU, so the neighbor knows how long to wait between Hellos. The hold time is determined by multiplying the Hello interval by the Hello multiplier, the default value of which is three. The valid range of values is between three and 1000. To change the Hello multiplier to five, the command would be entered as follows:

```
R3(config-if)#isis hello-multiplier 5 level-1
```

As with the Hello interval, the Hello multiplier can be different for L1 and L2 Hellos. The router assumes that the `level-1` setting is being configured if none is specified. On point-to-point interfaces, the `level-1` setting is the only one used.

To make a router more or less preferred to be the DIS on a broadcast network, use the `isis priority` interface configuration command. The default priority value is 64, and the valid range is between zero and 127. The higher the priority value, the more likely the router is to become the DIS. The priority is configured separately for L1 and L2 adjacencies as well. This command will change the priority of the router to 100 on this particular network for L1 adjacencies:

```
R3(config-if)#isis priority 100 level-1
```

If no level is specified, the router assumes `level-1`. The priority value on point-to-point interfaces will always be zero, despite any changes made to the configuration.

To change the cost of an interface from the default value of 10, use the `isis metric` command. The cost can range from zero to 63 and is set separately for L1 and L2 routes. To set the cost of an interface to 20 for L1 routes, use the command as follows:

```
R3(config-if)#isis metric 20 level-1
```

As with the other commands above, if no level is specified, the router adds `level-1`. Metrics other than the default metric can also be changed with this command, but these metrics are not currently implemented by Cisco.

When a router forwards an LSP to a neighbor on a point-to-point network, it starts a timer. If the LSP is not acknowledged with a PSNP before the interval has passed, it is retransmitted. The default value is five seconds, but it may be set to any value between zero and 65,535. To change the retransmit interval, use the following command:

```
R3(config-if)#isis retransmit-interval 10
```

This setting has no impact on broadcast networks because each LSP is not individually acknowledged. Instead, the DIS uses CSNPs to make sure that all routers have a complete link state database. The default CSNP interval is 10 seconds, but it may range from zero to 65,535 seconds. It is configured separately for L1 and L2 CSNPs, using this command:

```
R3(config-if)#isis csnp-interval 20 level-1
```

If the level is not specified, the router assumes `level-1` and adjusts the configuration accordingly.

The `isis lsp-interval` and `isis retransmit-throttle-interval` commands can be used to regulate the LSP traffic on an interface. Use `isis lsp-interval` to specify the amount of time between

LSP transmissions on the interface in milliseconds. The default value is 33 milliseconds. Note that this sets the amount of time that must be waited between transmitting any LSPs, not necessarily the same LSP. The `isis retransmit-throttle-interval` command works similarly to the `isis lsp-interval` command, except it is specific to retransmissions of LSPs. If not configured explicitly, the retransmit interval defaults to the time specified with the `isis lsp-interval` command. The use of these two commands is shown here:

```
R3(config-if)#isis lsp-interval 150
R3(config-if)#isis retransmit-throttle-interval 300
```

These two commands can be used to exert tight control over the IS-IS traffic on an interface. Bear in mind that changing these values can impact the convergence time of IS-IS when a topology change occurs.

Finally, you can modify the type of adjacencies formed via a certain interface with the `isis circuit-type` command. You can specify that the interface should form only L1 adjacencies, only L2 adjacencies, or both (which is the default). The command is used as follows:

```
R3(config-if)#isis circuit-type level-1
```

The valid parameters are `level-1, level-1-2` (the default value), and `level-2-only`. Although it can be used on any router, using this command only makes sense on L1/L2 routers.

Configuring Other IS-IS Properties

In addition to being able to configure interface properties for IS-IS, you can modify many global IS-IS properties. Some of these are standard protocol configuration commands, which can be used when configuring several or all of the IP routing protocols. The important configuration commands specific to IS-IS are covered here.

Tip

You can learn other IS-IS configuration commands by using context-sensitive help. After entering the configuration mode for IS-IS, enter **?** on the command line to be presented with a list of commands.

You can specify the minimum amount of time a router must wait between successive SPF calculations. This can help alleviate performance problems during times of heavy LSP traffic. By default, a router will not run the SPF algorithm for five seconds after completing a calculation. You can change the interval can to any number of seconds between zero and 120 by using the following command:

```
R3(config-router)#spf-interval 10
```

As shown, this command will make the interval between all SPF calculations (L1 and L2) 10 seconds. It can also be changed for L1 and L2 SPF calculations individually, using the following two commands:

```
R3(config-router)#spf-interval level-1 8
R3(config-router)#spf-interval level-2 16
```

When an LSP with an invalid Checksum is received, the receiving router normally sets the Remaining Lifetime to zero and floods the updated LSP, thereby purging it from the link state databases of the entire area. This causes the originating router to create a new instance of the LSP. To prevent routers from purging LSPs that they receive with invalid checksums, enter the following command:

```
R3(config-router)#ignore-lsp-errors
```

With this setting enabled, the router just drops the LSP from its link state database without purging it from the network. At this point, it is treated as an LSP that was never received. The router should still receive a retransmitted copy of the LSP, due to the use of SNPs in the reliable flooding process.

By default, LSPs are generated with a Remaining Lifetime of 1200 seconds (20 minutes). To change the maximum lifetime, use the `max-lsp-lifetime` command. The maximum lifetime can range from 1 to 65,535 seconds (approximately 18 hours). To set it to double its default value, enter the following:

```
R3(config-router)#max-lsp-lifetime 2400
```

In order to prevent an LSP from reaching zero lifetime and being removed from the link state database of all receiving routers, the originating router refreshes the LSP by sending a new instance every 15 minutes by default. The refresh interval can be changed, which makes the most sense when the max:mum lifetime has been changed. For example, to change the refresh interval to 30 minutes, use the following command:

```
R3(config-router)#lsp-refresh-interval 1800
```

An LSP is fragmented if it is too large. The maximum size of an LSP is normally determined by the Maximum Transmission Unit (MTU) of the network medium. To manually set the maximum size of an LSP, use the lsp-mtu command. The maximum size of an LSP may be set anywhere between 128 and 4352 bytes, using the syntax shown here:

```
R3(config-router)#lsp-mtu 4000
```

The OL bit is used to signal other IS-IS routers that a particular router is low on resources and cannot store the entire link state database. Other routers try to avoid transiting the overloaded router to route traffic to any networks other than those directly connected to that router. If there is some reason this behavior desired, a router can be manually configured to set the OL bit in its LSPs as follows:

```
R3(config-router)#set-overload-bit
```

Configuring Authentication

Although IS-IS authentication is very simplistic and will not offer much security, it can be useful to prevent accidental introduction of incorrect or undesirable routing information. In an environment where routers will move around a lot and need to be reconfigured before speaking IS-IS, authentication can be a big help.

Configuring subnet authentication

Subnet authentication involves sharing a password with IS-IS neighbors. This is an interface property, so the command must be entered in interface configuration mode. To configure subnet authentication on the Ethernet network to which R1 is attached, use the following commands:

```
R1(config)#interface Ethernet 0
```

```
R1(config-if)#isis password password level-1
```

With this configuration entered on R1, it does not establish an adjacency with any other L1 IS-IS router on its Ethernet network unless the same password is configured. The same can be done for L2 using the `level-2` keyword. If neither keyword is specified, the router will automatically add `level-1` to the command.

Configuring area authentication

All L1 (and L1/L2) routers in an area can share a common password. To configure area authentication, the `area-password` command must be issued in IS-IS configuration mode, as shown here:

```
R1(config)#router isis
R1(config-router)#area-password password
```

Remember that because a router is part of only one area, there is no need to tie the area password to a particular area. With area authentication enabled, routers with different passwords do not exchange LSPs.

Configuring domain authentication

All L2 (and L1/L2) routers throughout the IS-IS routing domain can also authenticate each other using a domain password. The domain password is entered in the sub-configuration mode for IS-IS. The command is as follows:

```
R1(config)#router isis
R1(config-router)#domain-password password
```

With this command enabled, L2 routers with different passwords do not exchange LSPs.

Troubleshooting IS-IS

When encountering problems with IS-IS routing for IP, several commands are available in the Cisco IOS to aid in troubleshooting. The most useful troubleshooting commands are shown and explained here.

Tip

To find other debug and show commands that are available for use with IS-IS, use the context-sensitive help. In particular, try viewing some of the help available by entering the following commands: show isis ?, show clns ?, debug isis ?, and debug clns ?.

Viewing Protocol Information

As with other IP routing protocols, a good place to start troubleshooting IS-IS problems is with general information about the routing process itself. The show ip protocols command provides information about all IP routing protocols, including IS-IS. The output of the command on a router running only IS-IS is shown here:

```
R1#show ip protocols
Routing Protocol is "isis"
  Sending updates every 0 seconds
  Invalid after 0 seconds, hold down 0, flushed after 0
  Outgoing update filter list for all interfaces is not set
  Incoming update filter list for all interfaces is not set
  Redistributing: isis
  Address Summarization:
    192.168.100.0/255.255.252.0 into level-2
  Routing for Networks:
    Ethernet0
    Serial0
    Serial1
  Routing Information Sources:
    Gateway         Distance      Last Update
    192.168.14.4        115       00:07:49
    192.168.13.3        115       00:07:49
    192.168.16.6        115       00:07:49
  Distance: (default is 115)
```

This output displays several useful pieces of information, including the presence of filters, whether IS-IS is redistributing any other protocols, whether summarization is being used, which networks are being routed, and which neighbors are providing routing information. This information can be particularly helpful in analyzing how IS-IS is interacting with other routing protocols on the same router.

The `show clns protocol` command also presents information about the IS-IS routing process. The System ID of the router is displayed, giving a piece of vital information for understanding link state databases. In addition, the IS type is shown, clarifying the behavior of the router. The area is also displayed, including all Area IDs for the area, even those that are configured only on other routers. (You can see an example of this in the "Configuring Multiple IS-IS Areas on One Router" section.) The output looks like this:

```
R1#show clns protocol
IS-IS Router: <Null Tag>
   System Id: 0060.5CF3.FAEE.00  IS-Type: level-1-2
   Manual area address(es):
        01
   Routing for area address(es):
        01
   Interfaces supported by IS-IS:
        Serial1 - IP
        Serial0 - IP
        Ethernet0 - IP
   Redistributing:
     static
   Distance: 110
```

The interface support and redistribution information shown by the `show ip protocols` command are also displayed here.

Troubleshooting Adjacencies

Because adjacencies are required before any routing information is exchanged, problems forming adjacencies can have far-reaching effects. Fortunately, the requirements for adjacencies are not as strict for IS-IS as they are for OSPF. For example, the timers between neighbors do not have to be the same. Instead, an IS-IS router advertises its own hold time in its

Hello PDUs and sets the hold time in an outgoing LSP. Therefore, even if routers have different timers configured, they will still interact correctly.

When looking for information on IS-IS neighbors, two similar commands can be useful. The first of these is `show clns is-neighbors`. The output of this command is shown here:

```
R1#show clns is-neighbors


System Id       Interface   State  Type Priority  Circuit Id        Format

0000.0C3F.F382 Et0          Up     L1   64         0060.5CF3.FAEE.01 Phase V

0000.30E2.AC02 Se1          Up     L2   0          00                Phase V

0000.3060.7994 Se0          Up     L2   0          00                Phase V
```

It lists the System ID of every neighbor, the interface on which that neighbor was learned, the state and type of the adjacency, and the neighbor's priority, along with some other information. Similar information is shown with the `show clns neighbors` command:

```
R1#show clns neighbors


System Id       SNPA            Interface   State  Holdtime  Type Protocol

0000.0C3F.F382 0000.0c3f.f382   Et0          Up     24        L1   IS-IS

0000.30E2.AC02 *HDLC*           Se1          Up     29        L2   IS-IS

0000.3060.7994 *HDLC*           Se0          Up     27        L2   IS-IS
```

The most useful piece of additional information provided here is the hold time of the neighbor, which decreases until another Hello is received. Note that for both commands, the Type column lists the type of adjacency formed with the neighbor, rather than the IS type of the neighbor. Therefore, an L1/L2 neighbor shows up in the neighbor table as L1 when viewed from an L1 router.

To see additional information about each neighbor, you can include the `detail` keyword after either of these two commands. This causes an additional three lines of output to be generated for each neighbor, listing the Area ID(s), IP address(es), and uptime. For example:

```
R1#show clns is-neighbors Serial 0 detail


System Id     Interface   State  Type Priority  Circuit Id        Format
```

```
0000.3060.7994 Se0        Up    L2   0         00              Phase V
   Area Address(es): 0f
   IP Address(es):  192.168.13.3*
   Uptime: 04:49:34
```

If a particular interface is not specified, then this information is shown for all neighbors. The `detail` keyword causes the same additional information to be displayed for both `show clns is-neighbors` and `show clns neighbors`.

If a neighbor that should be showing up in the neighbor table is missing, you may wish to view information about Hello PDUs as they arrive. To do so, use the following command in privileged EXEC mode:

```
R1#debug isis adj-packets
IS-IS Adjacency related packets debugging is on
```

This debug command causes every Hello PDU to generate output. Typical output looks like this:

```
ISIS-Adj: Sending L1 IIH on Ethernet0
ISIS-Adj: Sending serial IIH on Serial1
ISIS-Adj: Rec serial IIH from *HDLC* on Serial0, cir type 2, cir id 00
ISIS-Adj: rcvd state 0, old state 0, new state 0
ISIS-Adj: Action = 2, new_type = 0
ISIS-Adj: Rec serial IIH from *HDLC* on Serial1, cir type 2, cir id 00
ISIS-Adj: rcvd state 0, old state 0, new state 0
ISIS-Adj: Action = 2, new_type = 0
ISIS-Adj: Rec L1 IIH from 0000.0c3f.f382 (Ethernet0), cir type 1, cir id 0060.5C
F3.FAEE.01
ISIS-Adj: Sending serial IIH on Serial0
ISIS-Adj: Sending L2 IIH on Ethernet0
```

You can see in this output the Hellos received from all three neighbors, along with all those sent. If an L1 neighbor were configured with the incorrect area ID, the following error output would be seen:

```
ISIS-Adj: Rec L1 IIH from 0000.0c3f.f382 (Ethernet0), cir type 1, cir id 0060.5C
F3.FAEE.01
ISIS-Adj: Area mismatch, level 1 IIH on Ethernet0
```

After the message indicating the Hello is received, there is a message warning of an area mismatch. Similarly, if there is a subnet password mismatch, the following message is seen on the neighbor(s) with a password configured:

```
ISIS-Adj: Rec L1 IIH from 0000.0c3f.f382 (Ethernet0), cir type 1, cir id 0060.5C
F3.FAEE.01
ISIS-Adj: Authentication failed
```

If the passwords on two neighbors are different, this message should be generated on both. However, if authentication is failing because one neighbor has no password configured at all, this message is only seen on the router with the password. The router without a password attempts to form an adjacency and lists the neighbor in its neighbor table:

```
R1#show clns is-neighbors Ethernet 0
```

System Id	Interface	State	Type	Priority	Circuit Id	Format
0000.0C3F.F382	Et0	Init	L1	128	0060.5CF3.FAEE.01	Phase V

The neighbor is in the Init state, and it stays that way until this router knows that the remote router recognizes it as a neighbor. But authentication is failing because this router has no password configured, so that will never happen. This neighbor remains in the Init state indefinitely. The priority value of 128 simply indicates that these two routers have not finished exchanging information.

Viewing the Link State Database and Updates

When you have problems routing with IS-IS, the link state database should be able to provide valuable clues to the source. The LSPs listed in the link state database contain all of the information known to the IS-IS routing process; they are the source of all IS-IS routes in the IP routing table.

The show isis database command lists the LSPs in the link state database(s). Without any other parameters, the command lists all LSPs in summary form:

```
R1#show isis database
IS-IS Level-1 Link State Database
```

LSPID	LSP Seq Num	LSP Checksum	LSP Holdtime	ATT/P/OL
0000.0C3F.F382.00-00	0x0000009B	0x5A71	968	0/0/0
0060.5CF3.FAEE.00-00*	0x00000013	0x39AB	1054	1/0/0
0060.5CF3.FAEE.01-00*	0x0000000F	0x03F6	1000	0/0/0

```
IS-IS Level-2 Link State Database
```

LSPID	LSP Seq Num	LSP Checksum	LSP Holdtime	ATT/P/OL
0000.3060.7994.00-00	0x00000091	0xF023	416	0/0/0
0000.30E2.50ED.00-00	0x00000086	0xCCA0	1115	0/0/0
0000.30E2.AC02.00-00	0x00000089	0x787D	1094	0/0/0
0000.30E2.AC02.01-00	0x0000007E	0x251A	1156	0/0/0
0060.5CF3.FAEE.00-00*	0x00000097	0xD573	1063	0/0/0

The L1 and L2 link state databases are maintained and displayed separately. Any LSPs generated locally are marked with an asterisk, including all parts of fragmented LSPs and any LSPs generated on behalf of a pseudonode, as in the preceding output. The Sequence Number, Checksum, and hold time are also shown. The states of the ATT, P, and OL bits are displayed at the end of the line.

The show isis database command takes many optional parameters. You can look at one LSP in particular or only L1 or L2 LSPs. To view more information about each LSP, use the detail keyword. For example, to view detailed information about the L1 LSPs above, enter the following:

```
R1#show isis database detail level-1
IS-IS Level-1 Link State Database
```

LSPID	LSP Seq Num	LSP Checksum	LSP Holdtime	ATT/P/OL
0000.0C3F.F382.00-00	0x0000009B	0x5A71	728	0/0/0

```
  Area Address: 01
  NLPID:      0xCC
  IP Address:  192.168.103.6
  Metric: 10 IP 192.168.16.0 255.255.255.0
  Metric: 10 IP 192.168.100.0 255.255.255.0
  Metric: 10 IP 192.168.101.0 255.255.255.0
  Metric: 10 IP 192.168.102.0 255.255.255.0
  Metric: 10 IP 192.168.103.0 255.255.255.0
```

```
Metric: 10 IS 0000.0C3F.F382.05

Metric: 10 IS 0000.0C3F.F382.04

Metric: 10 IS 0000.0C3F.F382.03

Metric: 10 IS 0000.0C3F.F382.02

Metric: 10 IS 0060.5CF3.FAEE.01

Metric: 0  ES 0000.0C3F.F382

0060.5CF3.FAEE.00-00* 0x00000013   0x39AB      814          1/0/0

Area Address: 01

NLPID:      0xCC

IP Address:  192.168.14.1

Metric: 10 IP 192.168.16.0 255.255.255.0

Metric: 10 IP 192.168.13.0 255.255.255.0

Metric: 10 IP 192.168.14.0 255.255.255.0

Metric: 10 IS 0060.5CF3.FAEE.01

Metric: 0  ES 0060.5CF3.FAEE

0060.5CF3.FAEE.01-00* 0x0000000F   0x03F6      759          0/0/0

Auth:       Length: 7

Metric: 0  IS 0060.5CF3.FAEE.00

Metric: 0  IS 0000.0C3F.F382.00
```

For each LSP, you can see the area and routing information about all of the networks. This information allows you to determine whether or not the router knows the information in question.

Sometimes looking at the link state database is not enough to determine a problem, especially if a route or LSP is missing from the database. Using debug commands can help determine what information the router is receiving. To view the LSPs and the SNPs that are received and sent by the router, enter the following command in privileged EXEC mode:

```
R6#debug isis update-packets
IS-IS Update related packet debugging is on
```

With update packet debugging enabled, the router prints messages for every LSP sent and received. The following lines show the result of one updated LSP being received and one being sent:

```
ISIS-Update: Rec L1 LSP 0000.0C3F.F382.00-00, seq 9C, ht 1092,
ISIS-Update: from SNPA 0060.5cf3.faee (Ethernet0)
```

```
ISIS-Update: LSP newer than database copy
ISIS-Update: Sending L1 LSP 0000.0C3F.F382.00-00, seq 9D, ht 1199 on Ethernet0
```

If there is a problem with the area password or domain password, it appears in this debug output. When two routers are configured with different area or domain passwords, they still become adjacent. However, LSPs fail to pass the authentication test, as seen here:

```
ISIS-Update: Rec L1 LSP 0060.5CF3.FAEE.01-00, seq C, ht 629,
ISIS-Update: from SNPA 0060.5cf3.faee (Ethernet0)
ISIS-Update: LSP authentication failed
```

Update packet debugging generates many lines of output when the router needs to build a new LSP. In addition, it shows some basic information about SNPs sent and received. For example, the following output shows a PSNP acknowledging a particular LSP sent over a point-to-point link:

```
ISIS-SNP: Rec L2 PSNP from 0000.30E2.AC02 (Serial1)
ISIS-SNP: PSNP entry 0060.5CF3.FAEE.00-00, seq 99, ht 1197
```

On broadcast networks, the DIS generates a message when sending a CSNP:

```
ISIS-Update: Sending L1 CSNP on Ethernet0
```

Other routers on the broadcast network also print a message upon receiving the CSNP:

```
ISIS-SNP: Rec L1 CSNP from 0060.5CF3.FAEE (Ethernet0)
```

Although this information about SNPs can be helpful, it is not very detailed. To view more detailed information about SNPs, issue the following debug command:

```
R6#debug isis snp-packets
IS-IS CSNP/PSNP packets debugging is on
```

With SNP debugging enabled, the receipt of CSNPs, along with the decisions that follow, is displayed:

```
ISIS-SNP: Rec L1 CSNP from 0060.5CF3.FAEE (Ethernet0)
ISIS-SNP: CSNP range 0000.0000.0000.00-00 to FFFF.FFFF.FFFF.FF-FF
```

```
ISIS-SNP: Same entry 0000.0C3F.F382.00-00, seq 9B

ISIS-SNP: Same entry 0060.5CF3.FAEE.00-00, seq 13

ISIS-SNP: Same entry 0060.5CF3.FAEE.01-00, seq F
```

In addition to confirming that the CSNP was received, this output shows that when compared to the link state database, all of the LSPs matched those in the CSNP. When an updated LSP is flooded to a neighbor, a PSNP is received to acknowledge the new LSP:

```
ISIS-SNP: Rec L2 PSNP from 0000.30E2.AC02 (Serial1)

ISIS-SNP: PSNP entry 0060.5CF3.FAEE.00-00, seq 9D, ht 1193

ISIS-SNP: Same entry 0060.5CF3.FAEE.00-00, seq 9D
```

Gathering Information about SPF Calculations

Checking the regularity and cause of SPF calculations can help determine if there is a problem on the network. In a stable network, periodic SPF calculations should take place once every fifteen minutes. In an unstable network, the SPF algorithm will be run much more often. The show isis spf-log command displays the last 20 SPF calculations, as shown here:

```
R6#show isis spf-log


    Level 1 SPF log

    When   Duration  Nodes  Count    Last trigger LSP   Triggers
    01:41:17     0      1      2   0060.5CF3.FAEE.01-00  LSPEXPIRED
    01:33:58     0      1      1                         PERIODIC
    01:20:12     0      1      2   0060.5CF3.FAEE.01-00  LSPEXPIRED
    01:18:58     0      1      1                         PERIODIC
    01:03:58     0      1      1                         PERIODIC
    00:59:02     0      1      2   0060.5CF3.FAEE.01-00  LSPEXPIRED
    00:50:55     0      1      1   0000.0c3f.f388   TLVCODE
    00:50:51     4      3      2   0060.5CF3.FAEE.01-00  LSPHEADER
    00:49:32     0      3      1   0060.5CF3.FAEE.00-00  TLVCODE
    00:48:58     0      3      1                         PERIODIC
    00:37:21     0      1      2   0000.0C3F.F382.00-00  DBCHANGED NEWLSP
    00:37:16     4      3      4   0060.5CF3.FAEE.01-00  NEWADJ NEWLSP TLVCONTENT
```

00:33:58	0	3	1		PERIODIC
00:27:04	0	2	3	0000.0C3F.F382.00-00	IPQUERY NEWLSP TLVCONTENT
00:25:30	4	3	2	0000.0C3F.F382.00-00	NEWADJ TLVCONTENT
00:18:59	0	3	1		PERIODIC
00:16:23	0	2	3	0000.0C3F.F382.01-00	IPQUERY TLVCONTENT
00:15:02	4	3	2	0000.0C3F.F382.00-00	NEWADJ TLVCONTENT
00:03:59	0	3	1		PERIODIC

The first column, labeled When, lists the amount of time that has passed since each SPF calculation. The Duration column lists the number of milliseconds required to complete the calculation. The Nodes column tells the number of nodes (including pseudonodes) that were included in the SPF calculation. The Count indicates the number of triggers that caused the calculation. The Last trigger LSP column indicates the last LSP received that caused the calculation. If multiple LSPs were received before the calculation, this column only indicates one of them. Finally, the Triggers column gives the reason(s) for the calculation. Some of the trigger values you are likely to see include the following:

- PERIODIC: Full SPF calculations are run every 15 minutes. In a stable IS-IS network, this should be the most common trigger value seen.
- IPQUERY: The `clear ip route` command was issued on the router, or there has been an interface state change. The `clear ip route` command causes the entire IP routing table to be cleared, resulting in all routing processes recalculating their routes or waiting for routes to be received from the neighbors.
- DBCHANGED: The `clear isis *` command was issued on the router. This command clears the IS-IS link state database and all adjacencies.
- NEWADJ: This router has created a new adjacency with another router.
- NEWLSP: A new LSP from a new router or broadcast network (pseudonode) has been received.
- TLVCODE: A newer version of an LSP, containing a different set of data fields, has been received.
- TLVCONTENT: A newer version of an LSP has been received, with one or more of the data field contents being changed. This often indicates that an adjacency has gone down or come up somewhere.

To gain a complete picture of the processing taking place during an SPF calculation, issue the following debug command in privileged EXEC mode:

```
R1#debug isis spf-events
IS-IS SPF events debugging is on
```

SPF event debugging tends to generate a lot of output when an SPF calculation is triggered. Most of the information is too detailed to discuss at length, but some of it can be interesting. For example, the following lines show the routes derived from the SPF calculation that will be inserted into the IP routing table:

```
ISIS-SPF: Add 192.168.16.0/255.255.255.0 to IP route table, metric 20
ISIS-SPF: Next hop 0000.0C3F.F382/192.168.16.6 (Ethernet0) (rejected)
ISIS-SPF: Add 192.168.100.0/255.255.255.0 to IP route table, metric 20
ISIS-SPF: Next hop 0000.0C3F.F382/192.168.16.6 (Ethernet0) (accepted)
ISIS-SPF: Add 192.168.101.0/255.255.255.0 to IP route table, metric 20
ISIS-SPF: Next hop 0000.0C3F.F382/192.168.16.6 (Ethernet0) (accepted)
ISIS-SPF: Add 192.168.102.0/255.255.255.0 to IP route table, metric 20
ISIS-SPF: Next hop 0000.0C3F.F382/192.168.16.6 (Ethernet0) (accepted)
ISIS-SPF: Add 192.168.103.0/255.255.255.0 to IP route table, metric 20
ISIS-SPF: Next hop 0000.0C3F.F382/192.168.16.6 (Ethernet0) (accepted)
```

On the other hand, a route is rejected if it already exists in the IP routing table from a source with a better administrative distance than IS-IS. This output shows such an occurrence:

```
ISIS-SPF: Add 192.168.13.0/255.255.255.0 to IP route table, metric 20
ISIS-SPF: Next hop 0000.3060.7994/192.168.13.3 (Serial0) (rejected)
```

This debug command displays a lot of information that is hard to decipher without intimate knowledge of the SPF algorithm. In addition, it is difficult to sort through all of the information to pick out anything valuable. This command may not be the best troubleshooting tool, especially when time is of the essence. It may be a good idea to log the output through the telnet client or to copy and paste it for later review.

To view information about SPF calculation triggers as they happen, use the following debug command:

```
R6#debug isis spf-triggers
IS-IS SPF triggering events debugging is on
```

With trigger debugging enabled, messages are generated whenever an SPF calculation is run. The messages are brief and contain similar information to that displayed by the show isis spf-log command. This example output is generated when the 15-minute period calculation interval passes:

```
ISIS-SPF-TRIG: L1, periodic SPF
```

The following lines of output indicate other possible trigger events that could cause an SPF calculation. These include an interface state change, a new adjacency, an updated LSP, and a new LSP, respectively:

```
ISIS-SPF-TRIG: L1, IP query
ISIS-SPF-TRIG: L1, new adjacency
ISIS-SPF-TRIG: L1, 0060.5CF3.FAEE.01-00 TLV contents changed, code 2
ISIS-SPF-TRIG: L1, new LSP 0 0000.0C3F.F382.04-00
```

If you are interested in finding out the timing and size details of SPF calculations as they happen, enable SPF statistic debugging with the following command:

```
R6#debug isis spf-statistics
IS-IS SPF Timing and Statistics Data debugging is on
```

With SPF statistic debugging enabled, all SPF calculations generate output that indicates the time it took to compute, the number of nodes, and the number of links. This can be used to monitor the timing and duration of SPF calculations, which may indicate the need for a faster router in a large environment. The following output is typical of this debug command:

```
ISIS-Stats: Compute L1 SPT
ISIS-Stats: Complete L1 SPT, Compute time 0.000, 4 nodes, 3 links on SPT, 0
suspends
```

Wrap-Up

As a link state protocol, IS-IS can be a convenient choice for IP routing because of its simplicity. If the network environment in place requires the use of areas to limit routing information, IS-IS is a good choice. Because of its simplicity, it can be easier to configure than OSPF in some environments. However, this simplicity comes at a price — less flexibility. For example, use of subinterfaces for a Frame Relay network may not be an option in some environments. Finally, in mixed environments where CLNS is used alongside IP, IS-IS is an ideal choice, because only one routing protocol would be required on the network. IS-IS is a very stable and robust routing protocol, as is OSPF, so the choice may be more or less academic in many cases. As always, the needs of any network should be considered individually when choosing a routing protocol.

Chapter 6

Border Gateway Protocol Version 4

In the previous chapters, we have looked at various interior gateway protocols (IGPs). However, these protocols, with their frequent updates and methods for propagating routes, are not suitable for very large environments. For example, the size of the Internet has exploded in such a way that the routing technologies we have covered previously do not have the global scalability necessary for efficient routing and route management at that magnitude. Therefore, we turn our focus to the Border Gateway Protocol (BGP), an exterior gateway protocol (EGP).

This chapter begins with an overview of BGP, its history, and the basics of its operation. Next, we begin configuring BGP in a simple environment. This will include a basic BGP configuration, a discussion of BGP attributes, aggregating addresses, creating route maps, defining peer groups, and modifying other parameters. Once the basics of BGP configuration have been explained, we will move on to more advanced and complex topics. The advanced section will go over route filtering, communities, confederations, and route reflectors. Finally, we cover troubleshooting techniques, sample configurations, and things to watch out for when implementing a BGP environment.

This chapter does not cover all of the specifics of how BGP works. For that, many references are available, and we are encourage you to read them. The RFCs (Request for Comments) on BGP, and *Internet Routing Architectures* by Bassam Halabi are excellent sources of BGP information.

BGP Overview

BGP is the exterior gateway protocol utilized on the Internet today. BGP, currently in its fourth version as specified in RFC 1771, has evolved along with the Internet to provide loop-free inter-domain routing. The many enhancements to BGP over the years have allowed it to continue to be the routing protocol that drives the operation of the Internet. The latest BGP enhancements include support for Classless Interdomain Routing (CIDR) and route and path aggregation. These added functions have enabled BGP-4 to better deal with the tremendous growth of the Internet by more effectively managing the size of the global routing table.

BGP-4 provides a new set of mechanisms for supporting classless inter-domain routing. These mechanisms include support for advertising an IP prefix and elimination of the concept of network 'class' within BGP. BGP-4 also introduces mechanisms that allow the aggregation of routes.

Similar to the Routing Information Protocol (RIP), and the Interior Gateway Routing Protocol (IGRP), BGP is a distance-vector routing protocol. However, BGP has a lot of added functionality over these interior gateway protocols. What makes BGP really stand apart from other routing protocols is its ability to provide robust policy-routing capabilities.

To aid in the reliability of BGP, the protocol makes use of the host router's transport control protocol (TCP) stack to provide reliable connections. By operating through TCP, BGP does not need to provide its own reliable transport for its update traffic. More specifically, BGP uses TCP port 179 for its communication. For this reason, stable routing already needs to be established between the intended BGP routers. Directly connected links, an internal routing protocol, or static routes can handle this. Once a BGP session is established, routing updates are incremental; only information regarding changes is propagated throughout the BGP domain. This is in contrast to other distance-vector protocols, which broadcast the entire routing table at regular intervals. By only transmitting incremental updates, bandwidth on the link is conserved, as is the router's processing power.

BGP divides the Internet up into a collection of autonomous systems. RFC 1711 defines an Autonomous System (AS) in this manner:

The classic definition of an Autonomous System is a set of routers under a single technical administration, using an interior gateway protocol and common metrics to route packets within the AS, and using an exterior gateway protocol to route packets to other ASs. Since this classic definition was developed, it has become common for a single AS to use several interior gateway protocols and sometimes several sets of metrics within an AS. The use of the term Autonomous System here stresses the fact, even when multiple IGPs and metrics are used, the administration of an AS appears to other ASs to have a single coherent interior routing plan and presents a consistent picture of what destinations are reachable through it.

Figure 6-1 illustrates the concept of Autonomous Systems. The Internet is made up of many interconnected autonomous systems.

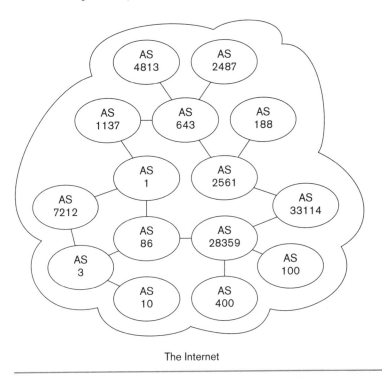

The Internet

Figure 6-1 *The Internet is made up of many Autonomous Systems.*

The primary function of a BGP speaking system is to exchange network reachability information with other BGP systems. This information is named *Network Layer Reachability Information*, or *NLRI*; it includes information on the list of ASs that reachability information traverses. Each NLRI update consists of a network number, a list of ASs that the information has passed through (called the AS path), and a list of other path attributes.

NLRI information is used to construct a graph of network connectivity that is used to remove routing loops. Routing policies are also applied to this graph when selecting the best path to a destination. There are many ways that BGP can control routing updates and apply policies, including techniques such as route filtering, path filtering, and community filtering, to name a few. BGP also provides mechanisms for consolidating routing information with route aggregation.

Understanding the History of BGP

BGP's predecessor, the Exterior Gateway Protocol (EGP), was first introduced in 1982 in RFC 827, and was formalized in 1984 in RFC 904. It was becoming apparent, at the time, that in order for the 'internet' to grow, routers needed to be divided into separate administrative domains with only a small number of routers actually attached to the core network. Each domain administrator would manage his or her own routers and routing protocols, while routing between domains would be provided through another method. EGP was created in order to address these issues by providing some means to manage routing between administrative domains.

At this time, it was already expected that the Internet would be divided up into administrative domains or Autonomous Systems, with some of these ASs actually used as a transport for traffic between different autonomous systems. It was mainly for this reason that EGP was created, to give the administrators of these transit ASs more control over the traffic that was passing through their network.

It also became painfully evident that several serious scaling problems were looming on the horizon. The use of classes in the division of the IP network space was causing a lack of class B networks. Class C networks were too small, so many times Class B networks were used, with many addresses being wasted. The Internet routing table was growing beyond the capabilities of the routing software used at the time.

For these reasons, a more robust routing protocol with better mechanisms for dealing with addressing problems was needed.

Note the duplicate usage of the acronym EGP. Although the same term is used twice, be aware that one usage refers to a generic gateway protocol type, and the other usage is actually the name of the specific gateway protocol.

Understanding BGP Operation

This section contains a brief overview of the BGP protocol operation, which will provide you with a good BGP foundation for the configuration tasks.

Before it exchanges information with an external AS, BGP ensures that networks within the AS are reachable. This is done by a combination of internal BGP peering among routers within the AS, and by redistributing BGP routing information to IGPs that run within the AS, such as IGRP, Information System to Information System (IS-IS), RIP, and Open Shortest Path First (OSPF).

All BGP speakers within an AS must establish peer relationships with one another. This full logical mesh is required to prevent loops from being created within an AS. BGP-4 provides two techniques that alleviate the requirement for a logical full mesh: confederations and route reflectors. We cover these techniques later in the chapter.

To start off the BGP process, two BGP speaking systems initiate a connection between themselves using the TCP.

Any two routers that have opened a TCP connection to each other for the purpose of exchanging routing information are known as *peers* or *neighbors*. BGP uses this information to construct a loop-free map of ASs. Note that within an AS, BGP peers do not have to be directly connected.

BGP peers initially exchange their full BGP routing tables. Thereafter, BGP peers send incremental updates only. BGP peers also exchange keepalive messages to ensure that the connection is up, and notification messages in response to errors or special conditions. There are several kinds of notification messages used in BGP. These are outside the scope of this book, however, so you are urged to examine this information in RFC 1771.

Preparing to Implement BGP

There are several reasons to implement BGP in your network. If your network has grown so large that your IGP is no longer suitable, you can use BGP to divide it and make it more scalable. If you have a multihomed Internet site, you can use BGP to provide redundancy and load balancing to your network. If you are acting as a transit AS for other Internet users, you must use BGP to provide connectivity. Route policies or Quality of Service (QoS) policies may also necessitate running BGP in your environment.

The most effective way to implement BGP in your environment is to follow a *best practice* method of deploying BGP. First, configure BGP. Next, to aid in the stability of Internet routing, generate a stable aggregate route. This ensures BGP route stability by avoiding route flapping, and helps keep the size of the BGP table small by using an aggregate address instead of many smaller network addresses. Route flapping is a term used to describe an unstable route. If the route is frequently going up and down, it is said to be flapping. This topic will be discussed in more detail in the section titled "Route Dampening."

To further aid in BGP stability, and the stability of your own AS, set inbound and outbound routing policies. And finally, where applicable, configure link load-sharing and multihoming. You want to implement inbound policies because they allow you to modify the routing information, such as adding a recognizable community value to routing updates that may be used in outbound filters or other route policies. The local-preference of a route may also be modified to override the default value of 100. Multihoming and load sharing configurations are also reasons to implement inbound policies.

Implementing an outbound policy prefix filter helps protect against routing mistakes that may have serious consequences in the global Internet. Agreements with your ISP may also require you to tag communities on BGP routes as they are propagated. We discuss the topic of BGP communities more thoroughly in the section titled "Understanding BGP Communities" later in this chapter.

Before you actually deploy BGP in your environment, some administrative tasks must be completed in preparation. The operation of BGP requires that an Autonomous System Number (ASN) be assigned to your administrative domain. How this number gets assigned depends on how you are planning to implement BGP.

Private Autonomous System Numbers

In some BGP implementations, you can use an Autonomous System Number (ASN) that comes from a private pool of numbers. Your ISP will assign one of these numbers to you. Because they are private, they will only be seen by your upstream provider and will not be propagated beyond that.

These numbers are in the range of 64512 to 65335. They are set aside in the BGP specification specifically for autonomous systems that are required to run BGP for various reasons, but do not need their AS present on the Internet. An example of this would be implementing a routing policy between your AS and your ISP.

Public Autonomous System Numbers

For most implementations of BGP, a public ASN will need to be assigned. The Internet Assigned Numbers Authority (`www.iana.org`), along with the regional Internet registries, oversee the assignment of these numbers. The American Registry for Internet Numbers, or ARIN (`www.arin.net`), is the registry for the Americas, the Caribbean, and Africa. Reseaux IP Europeens, or RIPE (`www.ripe.net`), is the registry for Europe. Asian Pacific Network Information Center, or APNIC (`www.apnic.net`), is the registry for Asia and the Pacific Rim. To get an ASN assigned, you will need to contact the appropriate registry for your area and complete an application.

The public ASNs are taken out of the range from 1 to 64511. Certain criteria must be met, however, when requesting a public ASN. A requesting organization must provide verification that it has the following:

- A unique routing policy (its policy differs from its border gateway peers
- A multihomed site

Installing the Equipment

Due to its complexity and the size of its routing tables, BGP requires a powerful router with adequate memory. Because BGP requires more horsepower, it is important to ensure that you have the right kind of equipment available for the method of BGP connectivity that you plan on using. With BGP, there are usually three different methods to communicate with ISPs: default route only, default route and routes of the ISP's customers, and the full Internet route table. Due to the size of the current Internet routing table, a router with a minimum of 64 MB of RAM is required.

The *default route only* method is the easiest way to connect to your ISP. This method consumes a low amount of memory, and does not use much of the router's processing power. This is because it does not have to make many routing decisions, as nearly all traffic will be destined for the default route. It works by the provider injecting itself as the default route and then advertising that route to your BGP speaker. Paths to this exit point, sometimes called the *default gateway*, are determined inside your network by IGP metrics.

The *customer and default routes* method tends to use a medium amount of memory and requires more CPU utilization. In practice, this tends to be the most efficient method. The best path to customers of your ISP is chosen from the routes existing in the BGP routing table of your routers. Other routes will follow the default route, which is usually the best path, as most ISPs are not far off the Internet backbone. This usually equates to the same amount of hops between your site and the nearest network access point. The local-preference BGP attribute can be used to override the route based on prefix, as-path, or community. IGP metrics are used to determine the best exit point for all other destinations.

Obtaining the full Internet routing table from all providers is the most detailed and most resource-intensive method for determining routes. All destinations are usually reached by following the best path, which is usually the shortest AS path from your router. The routes can still be manually tuned using BGP attributes such as local-preference, as-path, communities, or matches based on network prefix.

Routes need to exist before BGP can work. BGP is not meant to establish routes between individual routers. In many cases, the BGP speaker interfaces will exist on the same network and reachability won't be much of an issue. If this is not the case, however, it can be remedied either by using an IGP to establish a route between the BGP routers, or by utilizing static routes. This is a requirement because BGP establishes its connections at the transport (TCP) layer of the TCP/IP protocol suite. Just like any TCP/IP application, TCP ports will be opened on the neighbor routers through which the BGP communication process will occur. This cannot be the case if no route to the neighbor exists. Once the session is established, it alone cannot maintain the route to the neighbor router. If the route to the neighbor router no longer exists in the routing table, the BGP session will fail.

Gathering Information about the BGP Peers

To implement BGP, you need to know some information in order to configure the BGP process on your router. You must know the ASN of the neighboring AS, and you must know the IP address of the BGP speaker to which you will be communicating. It is also important to collect other information, such as communities, etc, if you plan on implementing policy routing with BGP.

Basic BGP Configuration

Now that you have a basic understanding of how BGP operates, we will apply this knowledge to configure BGP routing on a Cisco router. This section also introduces some of the more common BGP topics.

Considering how complex a protocol BGP is, it is surprisingly easy to initially configure. Making BGP operational only requires a few configuration steps, but the advanced filtering and manipulation available in BGP makes it a challenging protocol to implement. These more advanced topics will be covered in the next section.

Getting Started

We see in Figure 6-2 two autonomous systems that want to communicate using BGP. We will build our BGP connection over the serial interfaces that exist on the border routers, and advertise the networks that exist on the Ethernet interfaces of those routers.

Figure 6-2 *Two Autonomous Systems*

We will start by configuring BGP on the example network shown in Figure 6-3. This network is comprised of just two routers in a simple BGP connection. This is the most basic BGP configuration. We will start here and work our way towards more difficult and challenging configuration tasks.

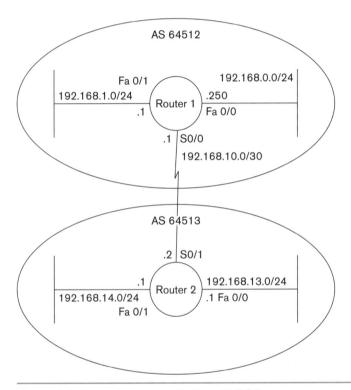

Figure 6-3 *Two routers communicating with BGP*

First we begin by configuring the interfaces as shown, and then assigning IP addresses to them.

On Router 1, our interface configuration looks like this:

```
interface FastEthernet0/0
 ip address 192.168.0.250 255.255.255.0
interface FastEthernet0/1
 ip address 192.168.1.1 255.255.255.0
interface Serial0/0
```

```
ip address 192.168.10.1 255.255.255.252
```

Once we have configured Router 2 and verified that our interfaces are up, we will then proceed to configure BGP between the routers. Here is the interface configuration sample from Router 2:

```
interface FastEthernet0/0
 ip address 192.168.13.1 255.255.255.0
interface FastEthernet0/1
 ip address 192.168.14.1 255.255.255.0
interface Serial0/1
 ip address 192.168.10.2 255.255.255.252
```

Now that the interfaces on both routers are configured, we want to verify that they are working before we proceed to our next step. The easiest way to do this is to utilize the show ip interface brief command available in the Cisco Internetwork Operating System (IOS):

```
Router1#show ip interface brief

Interface      IP-Address      OK? Method Status Protocol

Ethernet0/0    192.168.0.250 YES manual up      up

Serial0/0      192.168.10.1  YES manual up      up

Ethernet0/1    192.168.1.1   YES manual up      up


Router2#show ip interface brief

Interface      IP-Address      OK? Method Status Protocol

Ethernet0/0    192.168.13.1  YES manual up      up

Serial0/1      192.168.10.2  YES manual up      up

Ethernet0/1    192.168.14.1  YES manual up      up
```

From the output, we can see that the interfaces are up and running. Now we are ready to set up our simple BGP connection.

Defining the BGP Process

To enable BGP routing, we must first establish the BGP routing process. In global configuration mode, we start out by entering the router command, followed by the protocol type. Once we have entered the command `router bgp` in configuration mode, we then define the Autonomous System of the BGP process:

```
Router1(config)#router bgp ?

  <1-65535>  Autonomous system number
```

We will use AS number 64512 for this example. The command we enter at the router configuration prompt looks like this:

```
Router1(config)#router bgp 64512
Router1(config-router)#
```

You can see that we have now dropped into the router configuration prompt.

Once we repeat this process on Router 2 by assigning its ASN, we continue to enter commands that will apply to this specific BGP process.

Assigning BGP Neighbors

The next part of the BGP configuration process is to form the BGP neighbor, or peer, relationship. Because BGP is meant to be a globally scalable routing protocol, it can't afford to advertise its presence using the methods of IGPs. For BGP to work, it must completely understand the relationship it has with its neighbor. This requires a bit more work when initially setting it up, but allows it to operate on a much larger scale.

Because the networks are defined and the interfaces are up, we can establish the BGP neighbor association and then we should see the fruits of our effort in the IP routing table. The neighbor statement takes these arguments:

```
neighbor address remote-as remote-as-number
```

So following this template, we then enter the IP address of Router 2's serial interface, and the ASN that we have assigned it:

```
Router1(config-router)#neighbor 192.168.10.2 remote-as 64513
```

Because the BGP neighbor relationship is bidirectional, we also need to configure Router 2 in the same manner:

```
Router2(config-router)#neighbor 192.168.10.1 remote-as 64512
```

Although our peer relationship is now built, we will not begin to see routes appear in the routing table until we have configured the routers to advertise networks into BGP. We cover this topic later, in "Advertising Networks."

To simplify peering with a large number of neighbors, a router running BGP can be configured to peer with many BGP speakers based on an access list instead of configuring each neighbor explicitly as shown above.

This feature can be enabled by entering the following command in router configuration mode:

```
neighbor any access-list-number/name
```

If a neighbor attempts to initiate a BGP connection, its address must be accepted by the access list in order for the connection to be accepted. If no access list is specified, connections from any BGP speaker are accepted. If this option is configured, however, the router will not attempt to initiate a BGP connection to these neighbors, so the neighbors must be explicitly configured to initiate the BGP connection.

Advertising Networks

Because we want this router to advertise the networks attached to its Ethernet interfaces, we need to define these networks in the BGP routing process. BGP provides three methods for an AS to originate networks: by redistributing static routes defined on the router, by redistributing dynamic routes learned from another routing protocol, or by using the `network` command to explicitly define which routes the router will advertise. The network command method is the preferred method, because redistributing routes from other routing protocols into BGP can cause instability. Routes being redistributed into BGP that are frequently disappearing and reappearing in the routing table can cause this instability. This will result in routes flapping in the global routing table and can cause severe problems that may possibly affect the whole Internet. Redistributing BGP into IGPs is also not recommended, as it can result in routes being redistributed back into BGP. This causes routes to be advertised as originating from your AS, also causing potentially severe routing problems. Using the explicit `network` command gives you more control over what you are advertising to your BGP peer.

Redistributing static and dynamic routes is covered in Chapter 8. Right now, we are concerned with advertising networks via the `network` command. When used with BGP, the `network` command specifies the networks that the AS originates.

Now we will enter the networks we want advertised into the BGP process:

```
Router1(config-router)#network 192.168.0.0
Router1(config-router)#network 192.168.1.0
```

You may notice that no network masks were entered with the network statements. By default, the network statements will be entered into the BGP process at the classful network boundary. If you want to inject into BGP a network that does not exist at a classful network boundary, you can use the `mask` option of the network command:

```
Router1(config-router)#network 192.168.0.0 ?
  backdoor    Specify a BGP backdoor route
  mask        Network mask
  route-map   Route-map to modify the attributes
  weight      Set BGP weight for network
  <cr>
```

We cover the other options later in the chapter. If we wanted to enter the network on which the serial interfaces reside in the BGP process, we would use the mask command because that network does not exist on a classful network boundary. The input at the router configuration prompt would look like this:

```
Router1(config-router)#network 192.168.10.0 mask 255.255.255.252
```

Now that we have our networks defined on Router 1, let us catch up to where we are on Router 2 so that we may continue with defining our BGP neighbors:

```
Router2(config)#router bgp 64513
Router2(config-router)#network 192.168.13.0
Router2(config-router)#network 192.168.14.0
```

Networks that are advertised by the BGP speaker with the network configuration command must exist in the IP routing table before they will be advertised. These routes will be advertised as originating in the BGP speaker's AS. The BGP origin attribute of these routes will have a value of IGP. The network commands should list all networks in your AS that you want to advertise, not just those directly connected to the BGP speaker. This is a bit different from configuring the IGPs in that the network command does not start up BGP on certain interfaces. Instead, it indicates to BGP which networks it should originate from this router.

 Caution

Cisco IOS versions 11.3 and earlier limited the number of network commands that could be entered in the BGP process to 200. This limit does not exist in IOS version 12.0 and later

Resetting the BGP Session

When changes are made to the configuration of either BGP peer, we need to reset the BGP connection in order to have the BGP process reflect the change. This is necessary when any parameter of the BGP protocol is changed, so the neighbor association can be reestablished and any protocol options can be renegotiated. This is accomplished by entering the following command at the privileged EXEC prompt:

```
Router1#clear ip bgp *
```

This instructs the router to reset all BGP connections, and then reestablish them. There are also options for this command to reset only certain connections. The options available to this command are as follows:

```
Router1#clear ip bgp ?
  *                Clear all peers
  <1-65535>        Clear peers with the AS number
  A.B.C.D          BGP neighbor address to clear
  dampening        Clear route flap dampening information
  external         Clear all external peers
  flap-statistics  Clear route flap statistics
  peer-group       Clear all members of peer-group
```

When the BGP connection is reset, routes are withdrawn from the routing table, and updates are sent once the conversation is again established. This can cause instability if many routes are being withdrawn and reinserted into the routing table. In order to prevent this resetting of the BGP session, the Cisco IOS offers a command that does a *soft reconfiguration*. This applies changes to the BGP process without closing the BGP session.

```
Router1#clear ip bgp * soft out
```

This command instructs the router to do a soft reset on the outbound BGP updates. There is also an option to soft reset inbound BGP updates.

Viewing the Status of the BGP Connection

Now that we have configured a rudimentary BGP, let's take a look at what changes we can now see.

The Cisco IOS has several commands we can use to check the status of the BGP conversation. The first command we will use will give us an overview of the BGP routing process:

```
Router1#sho ip bgp summary
BGP router identifier 192.168.10.1, local AS number 64512
BGP table version is 5, main routing table version 5
4 network entries and 4 paths using 532 bytes of memory
3 BGP path attribute entries using 156 bytes of memory
1 BGP AS-PATH entries using 24 bytes of memory
0 BGP route-map cache entries using 0 bytes of memory
0 BGP filter-list cache entries using 0 bytes of memory
BGP activity 4/0 prefixes, 4/0 paths


Neighbor       V  AS    MsgRcvd MsgSent  TblVer InQ OutQ Up/Down  State/PfxRcd
192.168.10.2   4 64513 6       6        5      0   0    00:01:18  2
```

We can see from this command output that Router 1 recognizes Router 2 as a BGP neighbor.

Using the show ip route command, we should be able to see our newly created BGP routes appear in the routing tables of our two routers:

```
Router1#sho ip route
Codes: C - connected, S - static, I - IGRP, R - RIP, M - mobile, B - BGP
       D - EIGRP, EX - EIGRP external, O - OSPF, IA - OSPF inter area
```

```
        N1 - OSPF NSSA external type 1, N2 - OSPF NSSA external type 2

        E1 - OSPF external type 1, E2 - OSPF external type 2, E - EGP

        i - IS-IS, L1 - IS-IS level-1, L2 - IS-IS level-2, ia - IS-IS inter area

        * - candidate default, U - per-user static route, o - ODR

        P - periodic downloaded static route


Gateway of last resort is not set


B    192.168.13.0/24 [20/0] via 192.168.10.2, 03:29:59

B    192.168.14.0/24 [20/0] via 192.168.10.2, 03:29:59

     192.168.10.0/30 is subnetted, 1 subnets

C       192.168.10.0 is directly connected, Serial0/0

C    192.168.0.0/24 is directly connected, Ethernet0/0

C    192.168.1.0/24 is directly connected, Ethernet0/1
```

This output shows all the routes that Router 1 knows about, including the BGP routes and directly connected routes. To view only the BGP routes, we can enter the command as such:

```
Router1#sho ip route bgp

B    192.168.13.0/24 [20/0] via 192.168.10.2, 03:31:28

B    192.168.14.0/24 [20/0] via 192.168.10.2, 03:31:28
```

And the same on Router 2.

```
Router2#sho ip route bgp

B    192.168.0.0/24 [20/0] via 192.168.10.1, 03:33:32

B    192.168.1.0/24 [20/0] via 192.168.10.1, 03:33:32
```

Now that we have verified that our neighbor relationships exist and that the routes have propagated into both routers, our work is done.

Interior versus Exterior BGP

BGP supports two kinds of neighbors: internal and external. *Internal neighbors* are in the same autonomous system; *external neighbors* are in different autonomous systems. Normally, external neighbors are adjacent to each other and share a subnet, while internal neighbors may be anywhere in the same autonomous system.

The type of BGP that we configured in the previous example is External-BGP (EBGP). Figure 6-4 shows a diagram of what EBGP looks like logically.

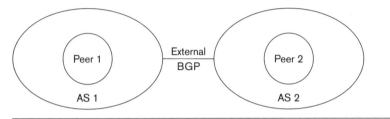

Figure 6-4 *External BGP occurs between Autonomous Systems.*

If Router 1 and Router 2 were in the same autonomous system, then Internal BGP (IBGP) would have been configured, as shown in Figure 6-5.

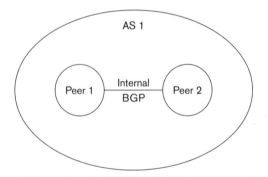

Figure 6-5 *Internal BGP occurs within an Autonomous System.*

There are differences in the way that EBGP and IBGP behave. Whereas External BGP forwards routing information that it has learned along to other neighbors, IBGP does not. Routes learned via IBGP are never forwarded to other IBGP neighbors. That it is why it is crucial that all BGP routers in your network have full mesh Internal BGP connections. Without this, it is possible that some routers will not know all of the routes, and this will have an adverse affect on traffic traveling through your network. This behavior is caused by the fact that BGP is a distance vector protocol, and uses split horizon to prevent routing loops. For a detailed discussion on split horizon, you can read about another distance vector protocol, Routing Information Protocol (RIP), covered in Chapter 2.

While processing routing updates, another difference occurs in the way that IBGP and EBGP handle the next hop parameter. EBGP peers are usually directly connected, so the router sending the updates sets the next hop parameter to itself. IBGP peers are in the same AS, and do not modify the next hop parameter when they are advertising reachability information to each other.

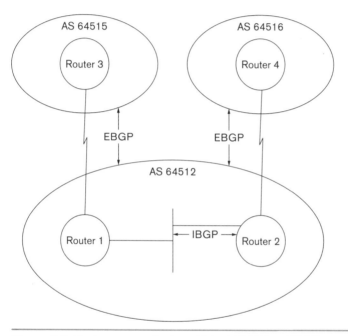

Figure 6-6 *Routers communicating with both EBGP and IBGP*

Authenticating BGP Peers

To add some security to your BGP connection, you can use MD5 authentication between two BGP peers. Because BGP only requires that the IP address of the neighbor be configured before the session is begun, it is possible that another router is masquerading as the peer you are expecting, or is modifying the route data and re-routing traffic. Traffic interception like this could cause sensitive data to be transmitted right into the hands of a network intruder. As unlikely as this scenario seems, it is still a good idea to configure BGP authentication.

BGP authentication uses the MD5 hash algorithm on the TCP connection between peers. Authentication only requires adding one line per neighbor to the routing process configuration. Invoking authentication causes the Cisco IOS software to generate and check the MD5 digest of every segment sent on the TCP connection. This feature must be configured with the same password on both BGP peers; otherwise, they will not establish a connection.

Authentication is entered using this format:

```
neighbor ip-address/peer-group password password-string
```

We will establish authentication between our two routers by entering the following line in router configuration mode:

```
Router1(config-router)# neighbor 192.168.10.2 password 2403rsf2p9
```

The IP address following the neighbor statement corresponds to the address of the BGP peer. In order for authentication to work, the same password must be entered on both routers and applied to the appropriate neighbor.

Digging Deeper into BGP

Let us revisit our configuration in a little bit more detail. There was much information presented to us while we were verifying our BGP configuration with the show command in the previous section. We need to get a better understanding of this information to help us continue on with more advanced BGP configuration tasks.

The first command that we will take a look at again is the show ip bgp summary command. We used this command to verify that our neighbor relationship was established once we were finished configuring the BGP process on both routers:

```
Router1#sho ip bgp summary
BGP router identifier 192.168.10.1, local AS number 64512
BGP table version is 5, main routing table version 5
4 network entries and 4 paths using 532 bytes of memory
3 BGP path attribute entries using 156 bytes of memory
```

```
1 BGP AS-PATH entries using 24 bytes of memory

0 BGP route-map cache entries using 0 bytes of memory

0 BGP filter-list cache entries using 0 bytes of memory

BGP activity 4/0 prefixes, 4/0 paths


Neighbor       V  AS   MsgRcvd MsgSent  TblVer InQ OutQ Up/Down  State/PfxRcd

192.168.10.2   4 64513 6       6        5      0   0    00:01:18 2
```

As you can see, this command gives us a lot of information about BGP. The first line tells us the BGP router identifier and the local ASN. If you remember, we explicitly defined the local ASN when we created the BGP process. The router identifier, on the other hand, is a value picked automatically by the IOS to identify the router. This becomes more important later on in our discussion. This value is chosen by the IOS from the numerically largest IP address assigned to an interface on the router. It may be necessary to modify this value at some point. For example, the router identifier is used as a tie breaker when choosing a path when equal-cost paths exist. This may cause traffic to follow an unexpected path.

We can also look at the `show ip bgp` command to get information about the routes we are receiving.

```
Router1#sho ip bgp

BGP table version is 4, local router ID is 192.168.1.1

Status codes: s suppressed, d damped, h history, * valid, > best, i - internal

Origin codes: i - IGP, e - EGP, ? - incomplete


   Network         Next Hop         Metric LocPrf Weight Path

*> 192.168.1.0     0.0.0.0          0             32768  i

*> 192.168.13.0    192.168.10.2     0             0      64513 i

*> 192.168.14.0    192.168.10.2     0             0      64513 i
```

From this show output, we see the routes that Router 1 is learning via BGP. We also see other information about these routes: the metric, the local preference, the weight, and the AS path. These values are covered in detail in the following sections.

BGP Attributes

BGP gets it flexibility from the parameters it allows the network administrator to configure. These parameters are called *attributes* in the BGP world, and they come in several different values. BGP attributes are classified into four categories; well-known mandatory, well-known discretionary, optional transitive, and optional non-transitive.

Well-known attributes are those that must be implemented in all BGP routers. Mandatory attributes must be present in all update messages; otherwise, the BGP connection is incompatible, and it will fail. The discretionary attributes may or may not be present in all update messages; but if they are present, they must be recognized by all implementations of BGP.

Optional attributes are those that do not have to be recognized by all BGP implementations. The type of optional attribute determines whether or not this information is passed on to other peers if the attribute is unrecognized. Transitive optional attributes are passed on to other peers. If the attribute is unrecognized, then the partial bit in the update is set to inform other peers receiving the update that a router in the path does not understand that attribute. If the optional attribute is non-transitive and it is unrecognized, then the attribute is ignored, and it is not passed on to other BGP peers.

These attributes are used by BGP when determining the best path to a destination, in addition to other BGP parameters. In this section, we cover some of the BGP attributes that are used in the decision process.

AS path

The AS-path attribute is a list of all the autonomous systems that a routing update has traveled through. Whenever an update passes through an AS, BGP prepends its AS number onto the existing AS path in the update. The AS Path can be enumerated in two ways: AS-SET, which is an unordered mathematical set of all the ASs that have been traversed, or AS-SEQUENCE, which is an ordered set.

Origin

This attribute provides information about the source of the BGP update. The value of this attribute can be IGP, EGP, or Incomplete.

A value of IGP denotes that the route originated within the AS of the advertising router.

When the origin attribute has a value of EGP, it has been learned via another router using an exterior gateway protocol.

Incomplete reveals that the origin of the route has been learned by some means other than via an EGP or redistributed from an IGP.

These values can be displayed by using the `show ip bgp` command at the router console. They appear at the far right hand side of the BGP route entry, and display as *i* for an origin of IGP, *e* for EGP, and *?* for Incomplete.

Tip

Always use a route-map to override set origin IGP, the origin attribute. In making the origin of all routes equal, other criteria can be used to choose the best route.

Next hop

In order to tell a BGP peer what next hop to use to reach a particular AS, the router sending the update adjusts the value of the next hop attribute. For EBGP, this attribute is usually the IP address of the BGP neighbor. For IBGP, this is usually the address of the EBGP peer in the neighboring AS. In the case of multi-access media, the next hop might be a third router that exists on the same subnet. This behavior is used to better optimize routing.

Weight

This is a Cisco proprietary attribute that was added to the BGP protocol to assist in the BGP-path-selection process. Adjustments of the weight attribute can affect which route is preferred when multiple paths to the same destination exist. This attribute is only present on the local router, and is not propagated to other BGP peers. Routes originated by the router are assigned a weight of 32768, while other paths that it learns are assigned a value of zero. A larger weight value is preferred when selecting paths.

Local preference

Local preference is another way to affect the path selection process. Unlike weight, local preference is an attribute that is propagated to other routers in the AS in routing updates. The path with the highest preference is the preferred path, with paths being assigned a local preference value of 100 by default.

Multi-exit discriminator

The multi-exit discriminator, or MED, is a non-transitive attribute that is used to convey the relative preference of entry points into an AS. By default, the MED is assigned a value of 0 when an update is generated, with lower values being preferred.

The MED attribute, unlike local preference, is exchanged between ASs. Because it is non-transitive, however, the MED value for that destination is reset to zero when it leaves the neighboring AS, unless it is explicitly configured to propagate MED information to other ASs.

MED values for the same destination that are received from multiple ASs are only usable if the receiving router has the command `bgp always-compare-med` configured. Otherwise the MED value of these routing updates will not be used in the path selection process.

Community

Communities are a way to group destinations into a logical unit to make it easier to apply routing policies. A community is a group of networks that share a common attribute. It is easier to apply routing policies to a community than it is to apply them to each destination individually. This grouping also crosses AS boundaries, so other ASs can also use the community value.

Using Loopback Interfaces

The loopback interface is a virtual interface, which is always up on the router, , and can be a useful tool when configuring advanced functions of the router. It provides a reliable interface to use for BGP updates, and is most often used with IBGP. It gives your IBGP routing design more stability by allowing the BGP connection to choose multiple paths to the destination neighbor. For instance, if a router is using its Ethernet 1 interface as the source of its BGP connections and that interface goes down, the BGP session will be broken. However, if the loopback interface is used for the BGP connection, should Ethernet 1 interface go down, the session will be able to continue through another interface on that router. This method isn't used as often with EBGP because configuring a loopback interface requires using another network for the loopback address. One example of where you would use loopbacks with EBGP is when you are trying to load balance traffic across multiple serial links. We cover this example later, when we discuss Multihoming BGP.

You can see from Figure 6-7 that there are multiple paths between the BGP peers. If the physical interface addresses were used to establish the BGP connection, and one of those interfaces failed, BGP communication would fail. Using the loopback address allows the BGP connection to follow the other path to the neighbor router.

Loopback Address

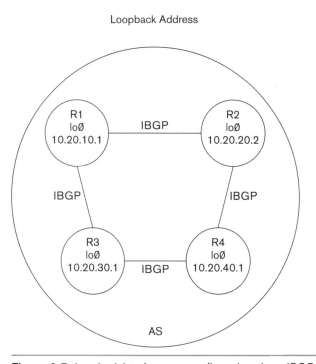

Figure 6-7 *Loopback interfaces are configured on these IBGP peers.*

EBGP neighbors are usually directly connected; in contrast, IBGP neighbors are often not directly connected. If a special situation prevents the EBGP neighbors from being directly connected, the ebgp-multihop option of the neighbor command is used:

```
neighbor ip-address ebgp-multihop
```

This command specifically applies to EBGP, and is not used for IBGP connections. One situation where you might use this command is when you're using a loopback interface as the source of your EBGP updates. This is most often seen in a configuration for load balancing. Usually this is unnecessary when BGP neighbors are directly connected, because the conversation will fail anyway, once connectivity is lost. Multi-hop neighbors should use loopback addresses, especially if multiple paths exist between them. This way, if one path fails, the conversation can continue over a different path. When the neighbor association is tied to a specific interface and that interface goes down, the conversation will stop. Be aware that loopback interfaces require another network address range, and these addresses must be advertised via a routing protocol or static routes.

 Caution

To prevent possible route instability, the multi-hop session will not be established if the only route to the multi-hop peer's address is the default route.

There are other useful applications of the loopback interface. If you find it necessary to adjust the value of the router identifier, you can do so by altering the IP addresses of the interfaces on the router to increase its value, or you can define a loopback address on the router. To illustrate, we have configured the loopback interface on Router 1.

```
Router1(config)#int lo0
Router1(config-if)#ip address 192.168.200.254 255.255.255.255
```

When we show the current configuration of the router, this is what the loopback interface will look like:

```
!
interface Loopback0
 ip address 192.168.200.254 255.255.255.255
 no ip directed-broadcast
!
```

The loopback interface is configured with a /32 netmask because no other devices are actually configured on that network, so the loopback interface only needs one address. We can also use this same method to configure the rest of the loopback interfaces in the network. Using this technique, you can configure 254 routers, and use only one Class C address space.

To configure BGP to initiate the connection from the loopback interface, use the following command syntax:

```
neighbor ip-address update-source interface interface-number
```

To configure the router to use the loopback address, we would enter the command specifying the loopback interface:

```
neighbor 192.168.10.2 update-source loopback 0
```

Now that we have reset the BGP session between Router 1 and Router 2 in Figure 6-7, we should be able to see the change in the router identifier reflected in the BGP summary.

```
Router1#sho ip bgp summary
BGP router identifier 192.168.200.254, local AS number 64512
```

As you can see, the configuration of the loopback interface worked, and the router identifier has indeed been altered.

BGP Synchronization with IGPs

When an AS provides transit service to other Ass, and there are non-BGP routers in the AS, transit traffic might be dropped if the intermediate non-BGP routers have not learned routes for that traffic via an IGP. To prevent this from happening, BGP must wait until the IGP has propagated routing information across the autonomous system. This causes BGP to be *synchronized* with the IGP.

Synchronization is a behavior of BGP that is enabled by default on Cisco routers. This means that BGP will not advertise any routes from your autonomous system until the Interior Gateway Protocol that is running inside your administrative domain has stabilized. This is important because if your AS were to advertise a route before all routers in your network had learned about the route, your autonomous system could receive traffic that some routers cannot yet route, causing that traffic to be lost.

Synchronization is not always a requirement, however. There are a couple of cases in which it is possible to disable this behavior. If you are not acting as a transit network between different autonomous systems, or if all of the routers in your network are running BGP, you do not need to synchronize BGP with your IGP. This will allow BGP to converge more quickly.

Disabling synchronization is as simple as typing the following command at the config-router prompt:

```
Router1(config-router)#no synchronization
```

Aggregating Addresses

To minimize the size of the IP routing table, you may want to aggregate several networks into one supernet, provided the path to them follows the same next hop. There are two ways that you can place aggregates into your routing table. One way is to redistribute an aggregated route into BGP from an IGP or static route. Another option is to use the aggregation feature that is provided by the Cisco IOS with the `aggregate-address` command. Using this method, an aggregate address will be added to the BGP table if there is a more specific entry that already exists in the table.

Aggregation combines several routes into one larger route. The aggregate is used to reduce the number of prefixes in the Internet routing table and to increase stability. It adds to the stability because even though the more specific routes may appear or disappear in the routing table, as long as at least one specific route exists, the aggregate will always stay up.

You can configure the router to advertise the aggregate and the original, more specific routes, or to only advertise the aggregate itself.

Tip

Consider using a combination of aggregates, network, and null routes to solidify the advertisement of the aggregates.

The following configuration example illustrates the usage of the `aggregate-address` command:

```
Router2(config-router)#aggregate-address 192.168.8.0 255.255.248.0 summary-only
```

```
Router1#sho ip route
     192.168.14.0/30 is subnetted, 1 subnets
C       192.168.14.0 is directly connected, Serial0
C    192.168.1.0/24 is directly connected, Ethernet0
B    192.168.8.0/21 [20/0] via 192.168.14.2, 00:02:34
```

We can see from this example that the networks 192.168.10.0 and 192.168.11.0 from Router 2 have been aggregated into 192.168.8.0/21.

Without using the `summary-only` option, we can see that the original routes are still in the routing table, plus the new aggregate address.

```
     192.168.14.0/30 is subnetted, 1 subnets
C       192.168.14.0 is directly connected, Serial0
```

```
B    192.168.10.0/24 [20/0] via 192.168.14.2, 00:00:30
B    192.168.11.0/24 [20/0] via 192.168.14.2, 00:00:30
C    192.168.1.0/24 is directly connected, Ethernet0
S*   0.0.0.0/0 [1/0] via 192.168.1.2
B    192.168.8.0/21 [20/0] via 192.168.14.2, 00:00:01
```

If you want the router to modify the value of a BGP attribute when it propagates the aggregate route, use an attribute map, as demonstrated by the following commands:

```
route-map SETORIGIN permit 10
set origin igp
!
aggregate-address 192.168.8.0 255.255.248.0 attribute-map SETORIGIN
```

When aggregates are generated from more specific routes, all of the AS-path information of the more specific routes are combined to form one large set of AS paths called the AS SET. This set is useful for preventing routing information loops.

When routes are aggregated, the atomic_aggregate BGP attribute is added to the NLRI for those routes. Its presence indicates that some AS-path information was lost in the process of aggregation. If the `as-set` keyword is used in the configuration of the command, however, this attribute is not set, and the AS-path information of the more specific routes are combined into an AS set of the AS-path attribute. The AS-path attribute and the community attribute will carry information about the specific routes.

The aggregator attribute will also be set when this option is used. It identifies the IP address and autonomous system number of the router generating the aggregate. This can be helpful when troubleshooting routing problems, as it identifies the source of the route aggregation.

Route Maps

Route-maps are a very important part of the implementation of BGP. They are used to control and modify BGP routing updates between ASs. Route maps can be configured on a per-neighbor basis and applied to either inbound or outbound updates. Route maps take specific criteria that are set by the route-map creator, and then try to match BGP updates against it. If one of these updates matches a criterion in the route map, then a predetermined action is taken against the update. The format of the route map is:

```
Route-map map-tag permit/deny sequence-number
```

This command is issued in global configuration mode. The `map-tag` entry is a user-specified route map name, usually something that describes what the map does. The permit and deny directives are used to control the behavior of the route map. If permit is issued as the route map directive and a condition is matched, then the actions specified by the route map are applied to the update, and the route map is then finished. If deny is issued as the directive and an update matches the condition of the deny statement, then the update is not accepted, and the route map exits.

From this router output, you can see the options available to the `match` and `set` route map commands.

```
Router1(config-route-map)#match ?
  as-path      Match BGP AS path list
  clns         CLNS information
  community    Match BGP community list
  interface    Match first hop interface of route
  ip           IP specific information
  length       Packet length
  metric       Match metric of route
  route-type   Match route-type of route
  tag          Match tag of route


Router1(config-route-map)#set ?
  as-path         Prepend string for a BGP AS-path attribute
  automatic-tag   Automatically compute TAG value
  clns            OSI summary address
  comm-list       set BGP community list (for deletion)
  community       BGP community attribute
  dampening       Set BGP route flap dampening parameters
  default         Set default information
  interface       Output interface
  ip              IP specific information
```

```
level              Where to import route

local-preference   BGP local preference path attribute

metric             Metric value for destination routing protocol

metric-type        Type of metric for destination routing protocol

origin             BGP origin code

tag                Tag value for destination routing protocol

weight             BGP weight for routing table
```

The sequence number is used to determine where in the route map a set of instructions resides. The lowest instances of the route map are applied first, and if a match is not found, then it continues on to the next instance. If an update does not apply to any of the route map conditions, it is not accepted. It is for this reason that you must remember to have your final sequence number permit all routes if you want to accept routes that are not explicitly defined in the route map.

Route maps can set the following values: as-path, community-list, community, dampening, local-preference, metric, nlri, origin, weight, and ip next hop.

Conditions are applied to route maps by using the match and set keywords. The match keyword specifies the conditions to be met, and the set keyword specifies the actions that are taken on the matching update.

Here we see a simple example of a route map. We have named the map SAMPLEMAP, told it to permit the BGP update, and given it the sequence number of 10.

```
route-map SAMPLEMAP permit 10

match ip address 192.168.14.0

set metric 20

route-map SAMPLEMAP permit 20
```

When an update matches the destination ip address 192.168.14.0, BGP will set the metric for the update as 20. It will then accept the update, and exit the route map series. For any route that doesn't match the IP address specified, the second sequence will accept all routes, and no changes will be made to them before the route map exits.

Route maps are applied to a neighbor using this template:

```
Neighbor ip-address/peer-group-name route-map route-map-name in/out
```

Cisco IOS supports matching based on three attributes: AS path, community number, and network number. To match an autonomous system, use an as-path access-list. Community-based matching requires the `community-list` command, and to match on a network, use an ip access-list.

Caution

Route maps cannot be used to filter inbound updates when matching based on the ip address of the destination.

Peer Groups

A BGP peer group is a group of BGP neighbors that share the same update policies. Route maps, distribution lists, and filter lists usually set update policies. Instead of defining the same policies for each individual neighbor, you define a peer group name and assign policies to the peer group. Peer groups help ease the configuration process of many BGP peers. If many peers are configured with the same update policies, you can simplify the process by using BGP peer groups. This can conserve many configuration lines and prevent possible mistakes. It will also conserve processing power on the BGP router by not having to process all of the policies individually for each neighbor. With peer groups, the router creates the update once, based on the policies of the peer group. It then distributes the update to all of the peers in the peer group.

Because most BGP peers of a router are IBGP peers, this is where you will most commonly find peer groups configured. However, if EBGP peers are configured with peer groups, some restrictions apply:

- The router distributing the updates cannot be a transit router, distributing the routes it learns to other EBGP peers. This is because updates from an EBGP neighbor of a peer group could be passed on to other EBGP neighbors in the same peer group

- All EBGP peers in the peer group should belong to the same logical network.

There are certain cases in which a peer group member could have slightly different policies than the rest of the peer group. If this is the case, additional policies can be configured on the member, in addition to those already applied to it by the peer group. If there is a conflicting parameter, the individually assigned parameter will take precedence on that neighbor. However, peer group members will always inherit the following parameters: remote-as, version, update-source, out-route-map, out-filter-list, out-dist-list, minimum-advertisement-interval, and next-hop-self.

Members of a peer group inherit all of the configuration options of the peer group. Peer group members can also be configured to override configuration options if the options do not affect outgoing updates.

There are three steps to follow when configuring a peer group. Create the peer group, configure peer group parameters, and finally, assign neighbors to the peer group.

Creating the peer group

To create a BGP peer group, use the following command in router configuration mode:

```
neighbor peer-group-name peer-group
```

The peer group name can be any descriptive name that makes it easier to understand the purpose of the grouping.

Configuring peer group parameters

Options are assigned to the peer group by using the neighbor command similarly to how it was used above with an IP address. The context-sensitive help listing below shows the commands that are available to assign to neighbors using a peer group name.

```
Router1(config-router)#neighbor PEERGROUP ?
  advertise-map          specify route-map for conditional advertisement
  advertisement-interval Minimum interval between sending EBGP routing updates
  default-originate      Originate default route to this neighbor
  description            Neighbor specific description
  distribute-list        Filter updates to/from this neighbor
  ebgp-multihop          Allow EBGP neighbors not on directly connected
                         networks
  filter-list            Establish BGP filters
  maximum-prefix         Maximum number of prefix accept from this peer
  next-hop-self          Disable the next hop calculation for this neighbor
  password               Set a password
  peer-group             Configure peer-group
```

prefix-list	Filter updates to/from this neighbor
remote-as	Specify a BGP neighbor
remove-private-AS	Remove private AS number from outbound updates
route-map	Apply route map to neighbor
route-reflector-client	Configure a neighbor as Route Reflector client
send-community	Send Community attribute to this neighbor
shutdown	Administratively shut down this neighbor
soft-reconfiguration	Per neighbor soft reconfiguration
timers	BGP per neighbor timers
unsuppress-map	Route-map to selectively unsuppress suppressed routes
update-source	Source of routing updates
version	Set the BGP version to match a neighbor
weight	Set default weight for routes from this neighbor

Assigning neighbors to the peer group

Finally, to configure a BGP neighbor to be a member of that BGP peer group, use the following command in router configuration mode, using the same peer group name:

neighbor *ip-address* peer-group *peer-group-name*

You can disable a BGP peer or peer group without removing all the configuration information using the neighbor shutdown command. To disable an existing BGP neighbor or neighbor peer group, use the following command in router configuration mode:

neighbor *ip-address/peer-group-name* shutdown

This does not delete the neighbor configuration, but only suppresses it until the command is entered again, negating it with the no prefix.

Modifying Next Hop Processing

When processing updates for most media types, the value of the next hop attribute is usually the address of the BGP speaker that propagated the update. When multiple BGP speakers are connected to the same multi-access media, this causes the traffic to traverse more router hops than necessary, when the value of the next hop attribute could just be set to the router used to forward traffic to that destination. The Cisco IOS can automatically determine the value for this attribute when on a multi-access media, and set it appropriately. This value is also set to the address of the third-party router, regardless of the AS that it belongs to.

Another exceptional case arises when multiple BGP speakers are attached to a nonbroadcast multiaccess (NBMA) network such as Frame Relay or X.25. Although multiple routers can exist on the same multi-access network, it may not always be possible for them to contact each other directly, depending on the provisioning of the circuits.

A sample of this is shown in Figure 6-8.

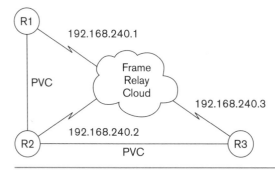

Next Hop Processing

Figure 6-8 *BGP routers on an NBMA network*

This diagram illustrates the impact of next hop processing. Although all three of these routers exist on the same IP network, permanent virtual circuits (PVCs) only exist between Router 1 and Router 2, and Router 2 and Router 3. BGP expects them to be able to communicate with each other. So, when Router 2 sends updates to Router 1 regarding the routes that Router 3 can reach, the next hop attribute of the update will be assigned the IP address of Router 3. Router 1 will not be able to reach Router 3, because there is no direct PVC connection between the two.

You can configure the Cisco IOS to disable next hop processing for BGP updates to a neighbor.

To disable next hop processing and provide a specific address to be used instead of the next hop address, use the following command in router configuration mode:

```
neighbor {ip-address | peer-group-name} next-hop-self
```

Configuring this command causes the current router to advertise itself as the next hop for the specified neighbor. Therefore, other BGP neighbors will forward to it packets for that address. This is useful in a non-meshed environment, because you know that a path exists from the present router to that address.

Using route maps is less cumbersome than configuring a specific address to be the next hop for BGP routes.

To configure the neighbor-peering address to be used for the next hop address, use the following route map configuration command:

```
set ip next-hop ip-address [peer-address]
```

Disabling Automatic Summarization

By default, automatic network summarization is enabled in the BGP routing process. With this enabled, when a subnet is redistributed from an IGP into BGP, only the network route is entered into the BGP table. To disable this behavior, use this command when configuring the routing process:

```
no auto-summary
```

Disabling this will allow more control over which networks are advertised. Otherwise, BGP will always generate network summaries, possibly causing routing inconsistencies.

Changing Local Preference

By default, routes that are advertised into IBGP from a BGP speaker are given a local preference value of 100. It is possible to define a particular path as more or less preferable than other paths by changing this default value. Local preference is a mandatory attribute that is local to the AS.

Assigning a local preference value

A local preference value can be assigned to all routes that are propagated into IBGP from a particular router. To assign a different default local preference value for all routes, enter this command in router configuration mode:

```
bgp default local-preference local-preference-value
```

This method affects all routes that are distributed by that router.

```
router bgp 64512
neighbor 192.168.14.2 remote-as 64513
bgp default local-preference 150
```

This configuration causes all routes advertised from this router into IBGP to have a local preference value of 150. You could use a similar configuration on another BGP router with a different local preference value assigned to choose which router is used for the default exit point of traffic. Because local preference is exchanged within the AS, other IBGP routers will see both routers advertising the same network with different local preferences, and will choose the router with the highest local preference value.

Using a route map to set local preference

You can also use route maps to change the local preference of specific paths. Route maps provide more flexibility than the `bgp default local-preference` configuration command.

An example of route map usage is shown here:

```
route-map SetLocalPref permit 10
match ip address 192.168.15.0
set local-preference 200
route-map SetLocalPref permit 20
```

With this configuration, network 192.168.15.0 is assigned a local preference of 200. All other routes are accepted, and their attributes are unchanged.

Advanced BGP Configuration

We have looked at fundamental BGP topics in the previous section. In this section, we look at the more advanced topics of BGP, which make the protocol very flexible and more difficult to configure. We start off by looking at the different methods available to apply policies on BGP routing updates. Other topics covered are different methods to scale Internal BGP, and utilizing BGP attributes to enforce routing policy.

Defining BGP Routing Policies

The power of BGP comes from its ability to apply filters and policies on traffic and routing updates that enter its domain. BGP supports transit policies via controlled distribution of routing information. There are several different ways to filter updates:

- using IP access lists with the `neighbor distribute-list` command
- using prefix lists with the `neighbor prefix-list` command
- using AS-path access lists with the `neighbor filter-list` command
- applying route maps with the `neighbor route-map` command

All of these methods have basically the same end result, with preference, familiarity, and special requirements being the biggest factors in choosing a method. The first three methods are discussed in this section. The last method, route maps, was discussed in the "Route Maps" section earlier in the chapter.

Using IP access lists

To restrict the routing information that the router learns or advertises, you can filter based on routing updates to or from a particular neighbor. The filter consists of an access list that is applied to updates to or from a neighbor. The filtering of routing information can be applied on a per-neighbor or per-peer-group basis. This filtering can be used with both inbound and outbound routing traffic.

In order to filter routes using the `distribute-list` command, you must first create a filter using an IP access list. This access list is then assigned to the BGP neighbor with the `neighbor`configuration command, and all updates are then filtered by that access list, with matching entries permitted, and other updates denied.

Once the IP access list is created, apply it to the neighbor or peer group with the following command in router configuration mode:

```
neighbor ip-address/peer-group-name distribute-list access-list-number/name in/out
```

Tip

The `distribute-list` command is used only with IP access lists, and not AS-path or prefix lists.

Note the following configuration example:

```
Router1(config)#access-list 1 permit 192.168.10.0 0.0.0.255
Router1(config)#router bgp 64512
Router1(config-router)#distribute-list 1 in
```

By assigning access list 1 to incoming updates, the BGP process will only accept routes that match the network specified in the access list. Therefore, only destination 192.168.10.0 will be accepted, and all other routes will be denied implicitly.

Using access lists to filter aggregates is a bit trickier. Assume, for example, that a router has different subnets of 192.168, and you want to advertise the aggregate of 192.168 only. The use of a standard access list will permit the aggregate, and all of the subnets.

To filter everything out except for the supernet, you must use an extended access list. The following sample access list illustrates the usage:

```
access-list 150 permit ip 192.168.0.0 0.0.255.255 255.255.0.0 0.0.255.255
```

The first address and wildcard mask pair specifies the supernet that is going to be permitted by the access list, and the second address and wildcard mask determine the exact prefix length to be allowed. This access list will only allow routes from 192.168 that have a subnet mask of 16 bits.

Configuring BGP filtering using prefix lists

Another method available when filtering routing updates is the use of prefix lists. Prefix lists are a more advanced method of filtering than access lists, and they offer several advantages. Prefix lists offer a performance improvement over access lists, they support filtering on incremental updates, and they offer greater flexibility when filtering on IP network numbers.

 Caution

Prefix lists and distribute lists cannot be used at the same time with the same BGP peer.

Using prefix lists to filter updates involves matching destination networks with networks that are programmed into the prefix list. Processing a prefix list is similar to processing a route map. When a match is found, the route is either permitted or denied, depending on the configuration of the prefix list. If the prefix list is empty, then all prefixes are permitted by default. If a route does not match any of the entries in the prefix list and there is no empty prefix list, then the prefix is implicitly denied.

As with route maps, the routing process starts searching through the prefix list at the smallest sequence number. The first match is the match to be used, and the router then applies the rule and stops processing the update. Because prefix lists are processed from lowest to highest, it is best to place the criteria that are applied most often toward the beginning of the prefix list to alleviate excessive processing.

To create a prefix list entry, use the following command in router configuration mode:

```
ip prefix-list list-name seq seq-number permit/deny network/len [ge ge-value]
[le le-value]
```

The optional keywords ge (greater than or equal) and le (less than or equal) can be used to specify a range of prefixes to be matched. The range is assumed to be from the ge value to 32 if only the ge option is used, and from 'len' (length) to the le-value if only the le attribute is used.

The values of the variable relate to each other in this manner:

```
len < ge-value <= le-value <= 32
```

Apart from deleting a whole prefix list, it is also possible to delete entries from a prefix list individually. To do so, specify the sequence number of the prefix list in this manner:

```
no ip prefix-list seq sequence-number
```

Specifying a sequence number when creating a prefix list is not required, as the router will automatically generate a sequence number for the prefix-list entry. These sequences are generated in increments of 5 by default.

If this behavior is unwanted, it is possible to disable this automatic generation of sequence numbers using the following command:

```
no ip prefix-list sequence number
```

If this is configured, sequence numbers must be explicitly specified when creating entries using the IP prefix-list command.

Regular expressions

Besides filtering based on IP network numbers such as the ones we have looked at in the previous methods, routing updates can also be filtered on BGP AS-paths. Using regular expressions to match against the AS-path attribute does this. The use of regular expressions makes AS-path filtering very powerful and flexible. The next few paragraphs will serve as a brief introduction to regular expressions.

Regular expressions are used to match patterns of characters. This can be a single character pattern, or a pattern of multiple characters. To create a pattern, uppercase and lowercase letters, numbers, and keyboard symbols are used. Certain keyboard symbols have certain meanings in regular expressions; we will cover these next. The use of the alphabet is case sensitive, so it is important to be aware of what case you are trying to match.

Special characters allow us to create more flexible regular expressions, by matching on wildcards, or special conditions of the pattern we are matching. Commonly used symbols are shown below:

- . (period) — matches any single character, including white space
- * (asterisk) — matches 0 or more occurrences of the pattern
- + (plus) — matches one or more occurrences of the pattern
- ? (question mark) — matches 0 or 1 occurrences of the pattern
- ^ (caret) — marks the beginning of the string
- $ (dollar sign) — marks the end of the string
- _ (underscore) — matches the beginning of the string, the end of the string, white space, or a delimiter (comma, braces, parenthesis)
- [ ] (brackets) — designate a range of single character patterns
- - (hyphen) — specify a range of characters
- ( ) (parentheses) — BGP specific symbols, parentheses designate a pattern as a confederation name

If one of these characters exists in a string that you wish to match on, you can escape the symbol by using the backslash (\). If a backslash precedes a character, it will match on that character, instead of using the special meaning. For example, below is shown the usage of the backslash to match certain characters:

```
\?
\$
```

Using the brackets, a range of characters can be specified to match on one position in the string. For instance, to match a string that contains the numbers 0, 1, and 2, you could use the following syntax:

```
[012]
```

Or, to match on a string of characters that contain any letter, uppercase or lowercase, we could use the hyphen to specify a range, rather than enter all of the possibilities.

```
[a-zA-Z]
```

This regular expression would match any letter in the alphabet, uppercase or lowercase.

These symbols can also be used in combination:

```
.*
```

This regular expression would match any pattern.

When used with AS paths, numbers are the primary characters that are being matched on, and the special modifiers are used to filter certain ASs. A few examples of matching AS paths are shown here:

```
^$          Matches any paths originating in own AS
^100$       Matches paths from directly connected AS 100
_200_       Matches any path that has transited AS 200
_300$       Matches all paths originating in AS 300
^400_       Match paths transiting directly connected AS 400
_[1234]00_  Matches any path that has transited AS 100, 200, 300 or 400
```

These are only a few examples of the possible uses of regular expressions with regard to BGP. A more detailed discussion of regular expressions is available in the "Regular Expression" Appendix of the *Cisco Documentation Dial Solutions Command Reference*.

Configuring AS-path access lists

Knowing how regular expressions work, we can configure AS-path access lists on both incoming and outgoing updates. To do this, define an AS-path access list and apply it to particular neighbors or peer-groups. You can filter on AS paths by adhering to the following procedure. First, the AS-path access list is created using the following global configuration command:

```
ip as-path access-list list-number permit/deny regular-expression
```

This access list is then applied using the neighbor router configuration command:

```
Neighbor ip-address/peer-group filter-list list-number in/out/weight weight-value
```

To verify that the regular expression you created is going to work like you intended, you can test it using this show command at the router's privileged exec prompt:

```
show ip bgp regexp regular-expression
```

The router then displays all of the paths that match the specified regular expression.

Understanding BGP communities

We covered the community attribute briefly in the section about BGP attributes. We will now discuss it in more detail.

To review, communities are groups of network destinations that are used to make it easier to apply routing policies. They can be applied to neighbors or peer groups, and the attribute is carried across AS boundaries. Networks can also be members of multiple communities. This method simplifies the configuration of routing policies on a BGP speaking router.

Communities are another way to filter incoming and outgoing routes. The distribute lists and prefix lists discussed in the previous section would be cumbersome to configure for a large network with a complex routing policy. For example, individual neighbor statements and access lists or prefix lists would need to be configured for each neighbor on each router that was involved in the policy. BGP communities allow routers to tag routes with an indicator (the community attribute) so other routers can make decisions based on that tag. BGP communities are used for destinations and routes that share common properties and therefore share common policies. Routers act on the community rather than the individual route. Communities are not restricted to one network or AS. By default, all destinations belong to the general Internet community.

Based on the community, you can control which routing information to accept, prefer, or distribute to other neighbors. A BGP speaker can set, append, or modify the community of a route when it learns, advertises, or redistributes routes.

You can use community lists to create groups of communities to use in a match clause of a route map. Just like an access list, a series of community lists can be created. Statements are checked until a match is found. As soon as one statement is satisfied, the test is concluded.

The community attribute is represented by a 32-bit value. The upper 16 bits indicate the AS number that defined the community. The lower 16 bits are the community number itself. This value can be written as a decimal number, or in the newer two-part AS-number:community-number format. By default, the community value is displayed as a decimal representation. You can display the community value with the `show ip bgp community` command.

To display BGP communities in the new format, use the following command in global configuration mode:

```
ip bgp-community new-format
```

To set the value of the community attribute, you can configure it in a route map using the following syntax:.

```
set community community-number additive none
```

The additive option specifies that the community number be added to the communities to which this route is already a member. The "none" option removes the community attribute from any updates that match the route map.

Four pre-defined communities can substitute for the community number:

- no-export, which instructs the router not to advertise this route to any EBGP peers

- no-advertise, which instructs to not advertise this route to any peer

- local-AS, which is only to be distributed inside the local AS

- Internet, the default community to which all routers belong

Because the community attribute is an optional, transitive attribute, it will pass it on to the next router if it is not understood. If, on the other hand, the router does understand communities, then it must be configured to propagate the community explicitly, otherwise the attribute will be stripped in outgoing updates. The following command will configure the router to pass on community information to the peer or peer group.

```
neighbor ip-address/peer-group-name send-community
```

To filter based on communities in route maps, use this command:

```
ip community-list community-list-number permit/deny community-number
```

The community list is used in the route map with the following syntax:

```
match community community-list-number exact
```

This exact option means that only the communities present in the community list can be present in the community attribute of an update.

When routes are aggregated, the resulting aggregate has a community attribute that contains all of the communities from the original routes.

It is also possible to delete the community attribute from inbound and outbound updates. A route map is used to match the updates and delete the community values. That route map command is as follows:

```
set comm-list list-num delete
```

Tip

In order to delete a BGP community using this method, the community list used in the route map should list only one community.

BGP and Weights

Cisco has implemented a feature that is not a part of the original BGP standard: assigning weights to routes. This gives you more control over the path selection process. These weights, however, are local to the router they are configured on. They are not propagated, and will not affect the behavior of other routers. The value of these weights can be between 0 and 65535, with the higher number being the preferred route. The paths originated by the local router running the Cisco IOS software by default have a weight of 32768. Paths originated by other sources will have a weight of zero.

The weight attribute can be set by using AS-path access lists, route maps, or by configuring the `neighbor weight` command in router configuration mode.

Assigning weights by BGP AS-path attribute

One way of adjusting the value of the weight attribute is to configure an AS-path access list and assign it to a particular BGP peer. A given weight becomes the weight of the route if the AS path is accepted by the access list. You would apply it to the neighbor in this manner:

```
neighbor ip-address/peer-group-name filter-list list-number weight weight-value
```

Using a route map to Set the Weight Attribute

Using the `set weight` command in a route map to adjust the value of the weight attribute is another method.

A sample configuration is shown here:

```
route-map SAMPLEMAP permit 10
match ip address 192.168.14.0
set weight 400
route-map SAMPLEMAP permit 20
```

This route-map will match on the destination IP address 192.168.14.0 and set the weight of the route to 400.

Assigning weights by neighbor

To configure BGP administrative weights based on the neighbor, use this syntax at the router configuration prompt:

```
neighbor ip-address/peer-group-name weight weight-value
```

By entering this command, you are telling the router to assign the configured weight value to all routes received from that peer.

Scaling IBGP

As the size of the IBGP network grows, the number of IBGP router sessions increases at a very rapid rate. In order to satisfy the requirement of a fully meshed IBGP network, IBGP sessions increase at a rate of n(n-1)/2.

This means on the order of hundreds or thousands of IBGP connections in large networks. Two extensions have been created to deal with this problem: BGP Confederations and Route Reflectors.

Implementing BGP Confederations

The first method we cover is the implementation of a BGP Confederation. BGP Confederations are a way to divide an Autonomous System into many smaller sub-ASs, and group them into a single confederation. This way, the number of connections inside the AS is reduced. To the rest of the BGP world, the confederation looks like it is a single AS, but on the inside it is made up of many smaller ASs.

You use confederations to divide the AS into multiple mini-ASs and assign the mini-ASs to a confederation. Each mini-AS is fully meshed internally, and IBGP is run among its members. Each mini-AS has a connection to the other mini-ASs within the confederation. Even though the mini-ASs have EBGP peers to other mini-ASs within the confederation, they exchange routing updates as if they were using IBGP. That is, the next hop, MED, and local preference information is preserved. To the outside world, the confederation looks like a single AS.

The first step in configuring the confederation is to configure the BGP routing process by using the confederation sub-AS number, rather than the ASN that has been assigned to you.

```
Router1(Config)# router bgp sub-AS number
```

The next step in configuring a BGP confederation is to set up the confederation identifier. This identifier is common throughout the confederation, and corresponds to the ASN by which the outside views you. Although your AS is split up into multiple sub-ASs, it will still look like a single AS to any external peers.

To configure the BGP confederation identifier, input the following command in router configuration mode:

```
bgp confederation identifier autonomous-system
```

Next, identify the sub-ASs that you have configured by their internal ASN; configure the following command in the BGP routing protocol configuration:

```
bgp confederation peers autonomous-system autonomous-system ...
```

Next, list all of the numbers that you will be using inside of your confederation, so BGP knows which ASs it must make exceptions for in EBGP sessions.

When neighbor commands are entered into the BGP routing process with other intra-domain peers, their new sub-ASNs are used as their remote ASN. External peers are still entered using their original ASN.

In the example shown in Figure 6-9, there are 6 routers in the autonomous system. Using the $n(n-1)/2$ formula , you can see that this would require 15 IBGP sessions be established in the AS. Using BGP confederations, we are able to decrease this to 5 IBGP sessions.

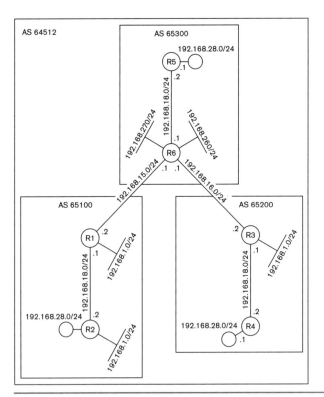

Figure 6-9 *BGP confederations implemented in an Autonomous System*

To give an example of how this is done, we will show configuration samples from a few of the routers.

R1:

```
router bgp 65100
 bgp confederation identifier 64512
 bgp confederation peers 65200 65300
 network 192.168.1.0
 network 192.168.14.0
 network 192.168.15.0
 neighbor 192.168.14.2 remote-as 65100
 neighbor 192.168.15.1 remote-as 65300
```

R5:

```
router bgp 65300
 bgp confederation identifier 64512
 bgp confederation peers 65100 65200
 network 192.168.28.0
 network 192.168.18.0
 neighbor 192.168.18.1 remote-as 65300
```

R6:

```
router bgp 65300
 bgp confederation identifier 64512
 bgp confederation peers 65100 65200
 network 192.168.15.0
 network 192.168.16.0
 network 192.168.18.0
 network 192.168.26.0
 network 192.168.27.0
 neighbor 192.168.15.2 remote-as 65100
 neighbor 192.168.16.2 remote-as 65200
 neighbor 192.168.18.2 remote-as 65300
```

The important things to take note of are the AS used in the router bgp command, the bgp confederation configuration commands, and the ASs used in the neighbor configuration.

Although Routers 1, 3 and 6 are external neighbors, the BGP routing process is still aware that they are in the same autonomous system. We can verify this by using the show ip bgp neighbors command.

```
Router6#sho ip bgp neighbors

BGP neighbor is 192.168.15.2, remote AS 65100, external link

 Index 1, Offset 0, Mask 0x2

  BGP version 4, remote router ID 192.168.15.2

  Neighbor under common administration

<output removed>
```

The last line is what we are interested in. The link is specified as external BGP, but we can see that the router notates this with neighbor under common administration.

Configuring BGP route reflectors

Another technique to reduce the size of the IBGP mesh is by using route reflectors. This method is usually preferred over BGP confederations, because it offers the ability to slowly migrate routers over to the new scheme. Routers that are configured in the route-reflector design, and those that are not, can coexist in the AS.

This allows easy, gradual migration from the old BGP model to the route reflector model. Initially, you could create a single cluster with a route reflector and a few clients. All the other IBGP speakers could be non-client peers to the route reflector, and then more clusters could be created gradually.

 Tip

To facilitate an effective design, the route reflector topology should follow the physical network topology.

When you use route reflectors, the rule that IBGP routes are not redistributed to other IBGP peers is relaxed; therefore, all IBGP speakers do not need to be fully meshed. This technique requires an IBGP peer to be configured as a route reflector. This router, called a route reflector server, is responsible for redistributing routes learned via IBGP to other internal peers.

Internal peers that have been specifically configured to communicate with a route reflector are called *client peers*. The remaining routers that have not been configured as route reflector clients are called *non-client peers*. The router configured as the route reflector "reflects" the routes between these two groups of routers. The route reflector and the routers configured as its clients constitute a route reflector cluster. Peers in the cluster do not need to have a full IBGP mesh with each other. The only requirement is that they have an IBGP session established to the route reflector. Non-client peers are still required to be fully meshed with other non-client peers, and those routers must be configured as route reflectors. Clients can only communicate with their route reflector, not with non-clients.

The way a route reflector handles routing an update depends on the type of neighbor that it receives the update from. If the update comes from an external peer, the update is propagated to all peers, client and non-client. If the route comes from a non-client peer, it is then advertised only to the reflector's clients. If the route comes from one of its clients, the route reflector, it then advertises it to all the remaining clients, and to its non-client peers.

Configuring route reflection takes place mostly on the router that has been designated as the route reflector server. The only change made to the clients is that they peer with only one internal peer, the route reflector.

To configure a route reflector to designate a peer as a route reflector client, use the following neighbor configuration command:

```
neighbor ip-address route-reflector-client
```

This configuration command tells the router to advertise IBGP routes to this particular peer. The route reflector client command must also be entered after the `neighbor remote-as` command and any peer-group commands.

An Autonomous System can have multiple route reflectors. Because route reflectors treat each other just as they would any other IBGP peer, they must be fully meshed with each other.

A standard route reflector design divides the BGP AS into multiple clusters. The route reflectors will have a full mesh between them, and the clients are configured with only one IBGP session, with the route reflector in their cluster.

Normally a cluster has a single route reflector. It is possible, however, to configure redundancy between multiple route reflectors in a single cluster. In this configuration, all of the route reflectors in the cluster must be configured with a new identifier, the cluster ID. With this new identifier, route reflectors can recognize updates that have been distributed by the other route reflectors in the same cluster. Cluster ID becomes a BGP attribute that is used with updates in the cluster. All of the route reflectors in the cluster must be fully meshed, and they should have identical configurations of client and non-client peers.

Caution

To avoid route maps modifying attributes and possibly creating routing loops, "set" modifications of outbound route maps are disabled for routes reflected to IBGP peers.

Entering the following command in router configuration mode configures the cluster ID:

```
bgp cluster-id id
```

Tip

The cluster-id must be assigned to the router before any route reflector clients are configured.

The `show ip bgp` command will display the Router ID of the originating router and the list of cluster attributes.

By default, route reflector clients are not fully meshed, and the routes from a client are reflected to other clients. If the clients are fully meshed, however, the route reflector does not need to reflect routes to clients. To disable client-to-client route reflection, enter this command on each client router in router configuration mode:

```
no bgp client-to-client reflection
```

Caution

The clients of a route reflector cannot be members of a peer group if client-to-client route reflection is being used.

To better understand the configuration of route reflectors, examine the diagram shown in Figure 6-10.

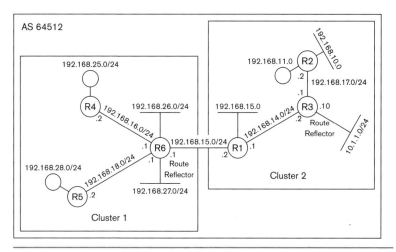

Figure 6-10 *An Autonomous System designed with route reflectors*

Following are the configurations of the two routers designated as the route reflectors, Router 3 and Router 6, and one of the route reflector clients, Router 1. Note that although they should have been used, loopback interfaces were not utilized in this example.

R1 (Route Reflector Client):

```
router bgp 64512
 network 192.168.1.0
 network 192.168.14.0
 network 192.168.15.0
 neighbor 192.168.14.2 remote-as 64512
```

R3 (Route Reflector):

```
router bgp 64512
 bgp cluster-id 2
 network 192.168.17.0
```

```
network 192.168.14.0

network 10.1.1.0 mask 255.255.255.0

neighbor 192.168.14.1 remote-as 64512

neighbor 192.168.14.1 route-reflector-client

neighbor 192.168.15.1 remote-as 64512

neighbor 192.168.17.2 remote-as 64512

neighbor 192.168.17.2 route-reflector-client
```

R6 (Route Reflector):
```
router bgp 64512

 bgp cluster-id 1

 network 192.168.15.0

 network 192.168.16.0

 network 192.168.18.0

 network 192.168.26.0

 network 192.168.27.0

 neighbor 192.168.14.2 remote-as 64512

 neighbor 192.168.16.2 remote-as 64512

 neighbor 192.168.16.2 route-reflector-client

 neighbor 192.168.18.2 remote-as 64512

 neighbor 192.168.18.2 route-reflector-client
```

The configurations above also include the cluster-ID command to demonstrate how they are configured in the BGP process.

Using show commands, we can verify that the route reflector process is indeed working. Under normal circumstances, only routes that were originated by an IBGP peer would be advertised to another IBGP peer. Routes learned from one IBGP peer are not redistributed to the other IBGP peers. This is not the case with route reflectors, as shown by this output:

```
Router1#sho ip bgp

BGP table version is 12, local router ID is 192.168.15.2

Status codes: s suppressed, d damped, h history, * valid, > best, i - internal

Origin codes: i - IGP, e - EGP, ? - incomplete
```

```
  Network              Next Hop          Metric LocPrf Weight Path
* i10.1.1.0/24         192.168.14.2           0    100      0 i
*> 192.168.1.0         0.0.0.0                0          32768 i
*>i192.168.10.0        192.168.17.2           0    100      0 i
*>i192.168.11.0        192.168.17.2           0    100      0 i
* i192.168.14.0        192.168.14.2           0    100      0 i
*>                     0.0.0.0                0          32768 i
*> 192.168.15.0        0.0.0.0                0          32768 i
*>i192.168.16.0        192.168.15.1           0    100      0 i
*>i192.168.17.0        192.168.14.2           0    100      0 i
*>i192.168.18.0        192.168.15.1           0    100      0 i
*>i192.168.25.0        192.168.16.2           0    100      0 i
*>i192.168.26.0        192.168.15.1           0    100      0 i
*>i192.168.27.0        192.168.15.1           0    100      0 i
```

We can see that although Router 1 only peers with one other router, it has learned all of the routes internal to the Autonomous System.

It is evident from this short configuration example that the technique of using route reflectors is easier to configure than BGP confederations. No changes need to be made on those BGP speakers that are designated as route reflector clients, and only a couple of extra changes are needed for those routers configured as route reflectors.

Backdoor Routes

Depending on the topology of your network, EBGP routes may be preferred over IGP routes. Even if the same route is being learned through both EBGP and an IGP, and the EBGP route is less optimal, the router will still choose the EBGP route because it has the more favorable administrative distance.

One possible solution is to adjust the administrative distances assigned to the protocols. However, since this would affect all of the routes on the router, this method is not recommended.

The IOS offers an option to remedy this problem. It is the backdoor-configuration command.

```
network network-address backdoor
```

This causes this network to be treated as a locally assigned network. By default, locally assigned networks have an administrative distance of 200, and this causes the IGP route to be preferred, because the IGP route will now have a lower administrative distance. Although the network is treated as a local network, it will not be advertised in any BGP updates.

Using Figure 6-11, we can illustrate the control over routing that the backdoor command gives the administrator.

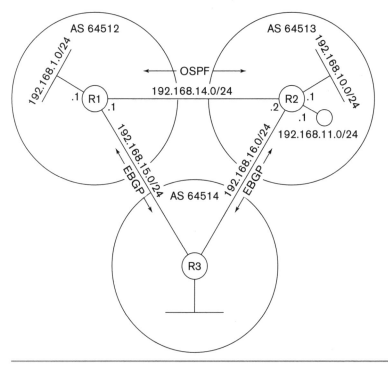

Figure 6-11 *A backdoor route is used to reach the 192.168.10.0 network using fewer hops.*

The BGP configuration of Router 1 contains this line:

```
network 192.168.10.0 backdoor
```

Using show commands, we'll display the effect that adding this config-uration line has on the routing table. Remember that EBGP has a smaller administrative distance than does OSPF. This means that the same destination will use the route specified by EBGP, as a lower administrative distance is preferred.

```
Router1#sho ip route
Codes: C - connected, S - static, I - IGRP, R - RIP, M - mobile, B - BGP
       D - EIGRP, EX - EIGRP external, O - OSPF, IA - OSPF inter area
       N1 - OSPF NSSA external type 1, N2 - OSPF NSSA external type 2
       E1 - OSPF external type 1, E2 - OSPF external type 2, E - EGP
       i - IS-IS, L1 - IS-IS level-1, L2 - IS-IS level-2, * - candidate default
       U - per-user static route, o - ODR

Gateway of last resort is 192.168.1.2 to network 0.0.0.0

     192.168.14.0/30 is subnetted, 1 subnets
C       192.168.14.0 is directly connected, Serial0
     192.168.15.0/30 is subnetted, 1 subnets
C       192.168.15.0 is directly connected, Serial1
O    192.168.10.0/24 [110/74] via 192.168.14.2, 00:00:24, Serial0
B    192.168.11.0/24 [20/0] via 192.168.15.1, 00:06:02
C    192.168.1.0/24 is directly connected, Ethernet0
```

As you can see, due to the backdoor command, the OSPF advertisement of the 192.168.10.0 network had a lower administrative value than the BGP advertisement, and was therefore installed into the routing table.

Setting Administrative Distances

Administrative distance is a way to set the order of preference of different routing protocols. When there is a matching network route in multiple routing protocols, the route from the protocol with the lowest administrative distance is installed in the IP routing table. There are three administrative distances associated with BGP: external, internal, and local. Routes that are learned from EBGP peers are assigned the external, routes that are learned from IBGP peers are assigned the internal, and routes that are generated locally are assigned the local administrative distance.

The default administrative distances for BGP are 20 for external routes, 200 for internal routes, and 200 for local routes.

It is possible to change the default administrative distances that are assigned to routes learned through BGP. Depending on the network design, this may be necessary in certain topologies, though it is generally considered bad practice and not recommended. The distance of external routes should be lower than any other dynamic routing protocol in order to prevent routing loops. Likewise, the internal and external distances should have a value greater than any of the other dynamic routing protocols.

To change the default administrative distance, enter this command in router configuration mode:

```
distance bgp external-distance internal-distance local-distance
```

 Tip

Administrative distance is not used to influence the selection of BGP routes during the route selection process. It is used when selecting routes to install in the IP routing table.

Advertising the Default Route

The advertisement of the default network in BGP is not turned on automatically. If you want to inject the default route, you must explicitly configure it on the router. To do so, use the following command in router configuration mode:

```
default-information originate
```

Two routers have been configured as BGP peers for this example. In the configuration we have constructed for our example, in order to get Router 1 to inject the default route to Router 2, we must first configure a default route by entering a static route, and then redistribute the static routes into BGP.

```
Router1(config)# ip route 0.0.0.0 0.0.0.0 192.168.1.2
Router1(config)# router bgp 64512
Router1(config-router)# redistribute static
Router1(config-router)# default-information originate
```

We can see that once the configuration is complete, Router 2 is receiving the default router from Router 1.

```
Router2#show ip route
Gateway of last resort is 192.168.14.1 to network 0.0.0.0

     192.168.14.0/30 is subnetted, 1 subnets
C       192.168.14.0 is directly connected, Serial0
C    192.168.10.0/24 is directly connected, Ethernet0
B    192.168.1.0/24 [20/0] via 192.168.14.1, 00:02:56
B*   0.0.0.0/0 [20/0] via 192.168.14.1, 00:01:18
```

Adjusting BGP Timers

BGP uses two timers to control certain functions of the protocol. The keepalive interval is the maximum time the router will wait between routing updates. The holdtime is the amount of time that the router will keep a route after the keepalive timer has expired. The default values of 60 seconds for keepalive, and 180 seconds for holdtime are adjustable.

The values of these timers are negotiated when a BGP connection is initiated. The smaller of the values between the routers is chosen during the negotiation process.

The following command is entered in router configuration mode to adjust the default values of the timers:

```
timers bgp keepalive-value holdtime-value
```

Timers can also be adjusted on a per-neighbor basis. To adjust the timers for a specific neighbor, enter this command in router configuration mode:

```
neighbor ip-address/peer-group timers keepalive holdtime
```

 Caution

Neighbor or peer-group-specific timers override the values configured with the `timers bgp` command.

Handling Link Failure

When the physical link between external BGP neighbors goes down, this does not affect the BGP session until the keepalive timer expires. The

Cisco IOS, however, offers a configuration option to cause the BGP session to immediately reset once a down state of the link is detected. To enable this, enter this command in router configuration mode:

```
bgp fast-external-fallover
```

This allows the BGP router to more quickly discover unavailable routes, instead of waiting for the keepalive timer to expire.

Multihoming BGP

A popular aspect of BGP is its ability to add redundancy to critical network connections for both inbound and outbound traffic. BGP can also be used to load balance traffic across multiple links. This is possible when a BGP speaker learns two EBGP paths for an IP prefix from a neighboring AS. Typically, the BGP routing process will choose the path with the lowest router ID to install into the IP routing table. In order for BGP to take advantage of these multiple links, the BGP multipath must be enabled, and then multiple routes can be installed in the IP routing table. The `maximum-paths` configuration command controls the number of identical paths to be installed in the IP routing table.

To enable multiple paths, enter this command in router configuration mode:

```
maximum-paths number
```

BGP can support a maximum of eight parallel paths.

When configuring multiple paths for inbound traffic, it is considered better practice to use *advertise maps*, than to adjust the length of the AS path when advertising the AS.

An advertise map is a route map that is applied to a neighbor with the following command:

```
Neighbor ip-address/peer-group advertise-map exist-map-name non-exist-map
non-exist-name
```

The BGP speaker will advertise the prefix specified in map 1 to the neighbor for which this configuration is applied. Should a problem occur with the prefix in map 1, and it is no longer present in the IP routing table, the prefix specified in map 2 will then be advertised to the neighbor.

An example of this configuration is shown here:

```
access-list 10 permit 192.168.215.0
access-list 20 permit 192.168.0.0
neighbor 10.10.1.1 advertise-map map1 non-exist-map map2
route-map map1 permit 10
match ip address 10
route-map map2 permit 10
match ip address 20
```

This example will advertise the prefix 192.168.215.0 to the neighbor at IP address 10.10.1.1 until the route for 192.168.215.0 disappears from the IP routing table. Once this occurs, the prefix specified by the non-exist-map, in this case 192.168.0.0, will be advertised to the neighbor.

In Figure 6-12, you can see the application of load balancing with BGP. Following are the configurations of the routers that accomplished this:

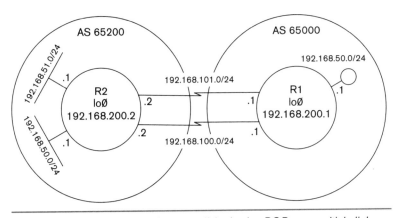

Figure 6-12 *Load balancing is accomplished using BGP over multiple links.*

R1:

```
interface Loopback0
 ip address 192.168.200.1 255.255.255.255
!
interface Serial0
 ip address 192.168.100.1 255.255.255.0
```

```
 bandwidth 1544

 clockrate 1300000

!

interface Serial1

 ip address 192.168.101.1 255.255.255.0

 bandwidth 1544

 clockrate 1300000

!

interface TokenRing0

 ip address 192.168.150.1 255.255.255.0

 ring-speed 16

!

router ospf 1

 network 192.168.200.1 0.0.0.0 area 0

 network 192.168.100.0 0.0.0.255 area 0

 network 192.168.101.0 0.0.0.255 area 0

!

router bgp 65000

 network 192.168.150.0

 neighbor 192.168.200.2 remote-as 65200

 neighbor 192.168.200.2 ebgp-multihop 255

 neighbor 192.168.200.2 update-source Loopback0

 maximum-paths 4
```

R2:

```
interface Loopback0

 ip address 192.168.200.2 255.255.255.255

!

interface Ethernet0

 ip address 192.168.50.1 255.255.255.0

 no keepalive

 media-type 10BaseT

!

interface Ethernet1

 ip address 192.168.51.1 255.255.255.0
```

```
 no keepalive
 media-type 10BaseT
!
interface Serial0
 ip address 192.168.100.2 255.255.255.0
 bandwidth 1544
!
interface Serial1
 ip address 192.168.101.2 255.255.255.0
 bandwidth 1544
!
router ospf 1
 network 192.168.100.0 0.0.0.255 area 0
 network 192.168.101.0 0.0.0.255 area 0
 network 192.168.200.2 0.0.0.0 area 0
!
router bgp 65200
 network 192.168.50.0
 network 192.168.51.0
 neighbor 192.168.200.1 remote-as 65000
 neighbor 192.168.200.1 ebgp-multihop 255
 neighbor 192.168.200.1 update-source Loopback0
 maximum-paths 4
```

From these configuration examples you can see that loopback interfaces were configured on both routers. BGP was set up to advertise BGP routes using the loopback interface as the update source and to establish the neighbor relationship with the loopback interface of the peer router. The ebgp-multihop command was also required because the loopback interface is considered to be behind the physical interface.

Route Dampening

The concept of route dampening was introduced into BGP to ease the effects of an unstable route on the global routing table. A "flapping" route is one that is frequently going up and down; a flapping route can cause major instabilities by forcing frequent update and withdrawal messages to be generated in the Internet backbone.

When a route is considered dampened, the peer is no longer accepting updates from it. It will stay in this state for a period of time, until it has stabilized and a predetermined threshold has been met.

Tip

Resetting a BGP connection does not cause a dampening penalty to be applied to the route.

A route is given a penalty of 1000 for each time it flaps. It is also placed into the *history state*, which means that this is no longer the best path to the destination. This penalty accumulates each time it flaps, and decreases by half for each half-life period. When the penalty accumulates to the point that the value of penalty exceeds the suppress limit, the route is suppressed. At this point, the route is considered *dampened*. The default value for the suppress limit is 2000. The route will continue to be suppressed until the half-life decay decreases the value enough so that the penalty becomes less than the reuse limit. The default half-life value is 15 minutes. Once the penalty is less than the reuse limit, the route is advertised again. The reuse limit has a default value of 750. A route cannot be suppressed for more time than the maximum suppress limit, which is usually 4 times the half-life time.

In order to avoid routing loops, external routes that are learned through IBGP are not dampened when they flap. This prevents IBGP peers from having a higher penalty than external peers for external routes.

Activating BGP dampening on a Cisco router requires that this command be entered into its configuration:

```
bgp dampening
```

Once route dampening is configured, it is also possible to change the default values that are associated with dampening. The following command illustrates the correct syntax for adjusting these default values:

```
bgp dampening half-life-time reuse-limit suppress-limit maximum-suppress-limit
route-map map-name
```

Caution

The route dampening statistics for a route are cleared when a BGP peer connection is reset.

Using show commands, you can display route-dampening statistics. These statistics display which routes are dampened, and how much time remains before the route is unsuppressed.

```
show ip bgp dampened-paths
```

Route-dampening statistics can also be cleared, and suppressed routes will be unsuppressed by entering this command:

```
clear ip bgp dampening network-address subnet-mask
```

All dampened routes can be cleared and unsuppressed. Entering the network number and the subnet mask in the command can clear specific routes.

Disabling AS Path Comparison

The BGP-4 RFC 1771 did not include the use of the as-path attribute to influence the BGP decision algorithm. However, the Cisco IOS software uses the as-path attribute to resolves ties in the path selection process. In order to force the router to follow the RFC exactly, the IOS software includes a command to prevent the influence of as-path during path selection. Enter this command in router configuration mode to force compliance with the RFC:

```
bgp bestpath as-path ignore
```

Troubleshooting

Troubleshooting BGP involves making use of the many show and debug commands that are available to you in the command-line interface. Much information can be gleaned from these commands, and they are very useful in tracking down the source of routing problems.

The BGP Path Selection Process

In order to troubleshoot BGP routes that are not propagating as expected, it is necessary to understand how BGP selects the routes it uses. Most of the routing decisions that BGP makes are based on the values of the different attributes. There is a particular order in which BGP checks these attributes when choosing the best route for sending traffic. As soon as a criterion is met, the route is selected. If the criterion is not met, the path selection process continues down the list until it is able to select the best path. RFC 1771 specifies most of these criteria. A couple have been added by the Cisco IOS software to handle the Cisco proprietary attributes and functions.

1. Ensure the next hop is accessible.

2. For internal paths, if synchronization is enabled, the route must exist in the IGP for the route to be chosen.

3. The path with the largest weight is chosen as the preferred route. (This is a Cisco proprietary criterion.)

4. The route with the highest local preference value is selected.

5. The route originated by the local router is chosen.

6. Prefer the route with the shortest AS path. (This criterion was not specified by RFC 1771 and can be turned off, as covered previously.)

7. Prefer the route with the lowest origin code.

8. Select the route with the lowest MED attribute.

9. Prefer the EBGP path over the IBGP path.

10. Select the route with the lowest IGP metric (the shortest path inside the AS).

11. If "maximum-paths" is enabled, multiple paths can be inserted into the routing table at this point, if they are both external routes, and they originate from the same neighboring AS.

12. Otherwise, select the route with the lowest Router ID (RID).

Displaying BGP Statistics with Show Commands

The show ip bgp command has many options associated with it, and it can also be used by itself. Following are the options available to the command and their results:

```
Router#show ip bgp ?
  A.B.C.D          Network in the BGP routing table to display
  cidr-only        Display only routes with non-natural netmasks
  community        Display routes matching the communities
  community-list   Display routes matching the community-list
  dampened-paths   Display paths suppressed due to dampening
  filter-list      Display routes conforming to the filter-list
  flap-statistics  Display flap statistics of routes
  inconsistent-as  Display only routes with inconsistent origin ASs
  neighbors        Detailed information on TCP and BGP neighbor connections
  paths            Path information
  peer-group       Display information on peer-groups
  regexp           Display routes matching the AS path regular expression
  summary          Summary of BGP neighbor status
  <cr>
```

Here is a sample show ip bgp output.

```
Router1#sho ip bgp
BGP table version is 5, local router ID is 192.168.14.1
Status codes: s suppressed, d damped, h history, * valid, > best, i - internal
Origin codes: i - IGP, e - EGP, ? - incomplete


   Network          Next Hop        Metric LocPrf Weight Path
*> 0.0.0.0          192.168.1.2          0        32768 ?
*> 192.168.1.0      0.0.0.0              0        32768 i
*> 192.168.10.0     192.168.14.2         0            0 64513 i
*> 192.168.11.0     192.168.14.2         0            0 64513 i
```

We are able to obtain a lot of information using this command regarding the BGP routes that the router has learned. Note that the static route that was redistributed into BGP has been assigned the origin value of incomplete.

The summary option of the command will display other information regarding the BGP process.

```
Router1#sho ip bgp summary

BGP router identifier 192.168.200.254, local AS number 64512

BGP table version is 5, main routing table version 5

4 network entries and 4 paths using 532 bytes of memory

3 BGP path attribute entries using 156 bytes of memory

1 BGP AS-PATH entries using 24 bytes of memory

0 BGP route-map cache entries using 0 bytes of memory

0 BGP filter-list cache entries using 0 bytes of memory

BGP activity 12/8 prefixes, 12/8 paths


Neighbor       V AS    MsgRcvd MsgSent TblVer InQ OutQ Up/Down  State/PfxRcd
192.168.10.2   4 64513 35      35      5      0   0    00:12:35   2
```

This output shows the results of configuring a loopback address on the router, which we covered earlier in the chapter.

On the second line of the summary, we see an entry that states the version of the BGP table and the main routing table. This illustrates an important concept with Cisco routers. There are two tables associated with BGP. One is the BGP table itself, which is built from updates received from other BGP routers. These routes are then inserted into the main routing table once all the routes are compared and filtered. It is possible for the BGP table and main routing table versions to be different. But because we only have one routing process running on this router, the main routing table will not be changed unless the BGP table is changed. (Static routes do not affect the main-routing-table version). If the router were also running an IGP, updates to the IGP would change the version of the main routing table.

At the bottom of the output, we can see the IP address of the neighbor interface we configured. Note some statistics associated with this. The "V" column is the version column, showing which version of BGP the neighbor is running. This will be Version 4 in most cases, as that is the current standard on the Internet, though it is possible to run into older versions in some environments.

The next two columns show the number of update messages that have been received and sent by the router. Following that is the BGP table version as reported by the neighbor router. These version numbers are usually synchronized once the neighbor association is created. Next we see the In Queue and the Out Queue, depicting the number of update messages queued up to be sent or received. You will usually see this value increase if a link is congested, and routing updates are being generated faster than they can be sent out.

The Up/Down column shows the time elapsed since the session was created. When communication is lost, or the BGP session is reset, this clock will also be reset. Finally we see the State/PfxRcd column. This column serves two purposes. During the negotiation process, this column reflects the current state of the session. This will be, in order, the following states: Idle, Active, OpenSent, OpenConfirm and Established. They represent the different stages of the BGP neighbor negotiation process.

The Idle stage fits its name, as the BGP process is currently doing nothing. When in Active state, the BGP process is preparing to establish the connection. It then sends an "open" request to the neighbor router. Once this request is acknowledged, it then sends an acknowledgement back to the neighbor router. Once the neighbor router has acknowledged that it is also ready, the session is in the Established state.

Once the session is established, this column will then display the number of route prefixes that have been received from that neighbor. Here we see that it is displaying 2. This is indicative that our configuration is correct; we configured the two Ethernet interfaces on the neighbor router, and entered those two networks into the BGP process.

The neighbors option displays a good deal of low level information, useful for troubleshooting tough problems that deal with the neighbor relationship.

```
Router1#sho ip bgp neighbors
BGP neighbor is 192.168.10.2,  remote AS 64513, external link
  BGP version 4, remote router ID 192.168.14.1
  BGP state = Established, up for 00:16:04
  Last read 00:00:06, hold time is 180, keepalive interval is 60 seconds
  Neighbor capabilities:
```

```
Route refresh: advertised and received
  Address family IPv4 Unicast: advertised and received
  Received 494 messages, 0 notifications, 0 in queue
  Sent 494 messages, 0 notifications, 0 in queue
  Route refresh request: received 0, sent 0
  Minimum time between advertisement runs is 30 seconds

For address family: IPv4 Unicast
  BGP table version 13, neighbor version 13
  Index 1, Offset 0, Mask 0x2
  2 accepted prefixes consume 72 bytes
  Prefix advertised 16, suppressed 0, withdrawn 0

  Connections established 8; dropped 7
  Last reset 00:16:28, due to Peer closed the session
Connection state is ESTAB, I/O status: 1, unread input bytes: 0
Local host: 192.168.10.1, Local port: 179
Foreign host: 192.168.10.2, Foreign port: 11012

Enqueued packets for retransmit: 0, input: 0  mis-ordered: 0 (0 bytes)

Event Timers (current time is 0xBED1660):
Timer          Starts    Wakeups          Next
Retrans           20         0            0x0
TimeWait           0         0            0x0
AckHold           19        18            0x0
SendWnd            0         0            0x0
KeepAlive          0         0            0x0
GiveUp             0         0            0x0
PmtuAger           0         0            0x0
DeadWait           0         0            0x0

iss: 3659046196  snduna: 3659046684  sndnxt: 3659046684      sndwnd:  15897
irs:   19006821  rcvnxt:   19007309  rcvwnd:      15897 delrcvwnd:      487
```

```
SRTT: 1198 ms, RTTO: 2874 ms, RTV: 239 ms, KRTT: 0 ms

minRTT: 676 ms, maxRTT: 1740 ms, ACK hold: 200 ms

Flags: passive open, nagle, gen tcbs


Datagrams (max data segment is 1460 bytes):

Rcvd: 40 (out of order: 0), with data: 19, total data bytes: 487

Sent: 38 (retransmit: 0), with data: 19, total data bytes: 487
```

There are a few important things to take note of.

Using this command, we can obtain more information about the remote router than we could with the other commands we have used. This output shows the ASN of the remote router (which we should already know), the IP address of the remote router, and, more importantly, the kind of link that is established with this neighbor, either External or Internal.

Next we see the remote router ID, and the BGP version number that is running on that neighbor. Following that, we see that the connection is in the Established state, and we can view the amount of time that this session has been up.

Under that, we can see the holdtime values and the keepalive values that are being used for this link. Shown are the default settings, but the user can also change these values. They can be changed to help in troubleshooting, or when the connection is being established in an environment that requires it.

Clearing the BGP Database

BGP statistics and tables can be cleared using the `clear ip bgp` command. It has the following syntax:

```
clear ip bgp address/*
```

Using the asterisk will clear the BGP info for all routes. This command can also be used to clear the information for a peer group using the command with the **peer-group** keyword.

```
clear ip bgp peer-group group-name
```

Debugging BGP

A few debugging options are available in the Cisco IOS for troubleshooting BGP.

```
Router1#debug ip bgp ?
  A.B.C.D       BGP neighbor address
  dampening     BGP dampening
  events        BGP events
  keepalives    BGP keepalives
  updates       BGP updates
  <cr>
```

Following is an example usage of the debug ip bgp events command. After it was entered, we cleared the BGP routing process to force it to re-establish its peering. You can see the steps that the BGP process takes when it is establishing a connection with its neighbor.

```
Router1#debug ip bgp events
Router1#clear ip bgp *
Router1#
01:54:58: BGP: reset all neighbors due to User reset
01:54:58: BGP: 192.168.15.1 went from Active to Idle
01:54:59: BGP: 192.168.15.1 went from Idle to Active
01:54:59: BGP: 192.168.15.1 went from Idle to Active
01:55:18: BGP: 192.168.15.1 went from Active to Idle
01:55:18: BGP: 192.168.15.1 went from Idle to Connect
01:55:18: BGP: 192.168.15.1 went from Connect to OpenSent
01:55:18: BGP: 192.168.15.1 went from OpenSent to OpenConfirm
01:55:19: BGP: 192.168.15.1 went from OpenConfirm to Established
01:55:19: BGP: 192.168.15.1 computing updates, neighbor version 0, table version
1, starting at 0.0.0.0
01:55:19: BGP: 192.168.15.1 update run completed, ran for 0ms, neighbor version
0, start version 1, throttled to 1, check point net 0.0.0.0
01:55:34: BGP: scanning routing tables
01:55:47: BGP: 192.168.15.1 computing updates, neighbor version 1, table version
3, starting at 0.0.0.0
```

```
01:55:47: BGP: 192.168.15.1 update run completed, ran for 0ms, neighbor version
1, start version 3, throttled to 3, check point net 0.0.0.0
01:56:34: BGP: scanning routing tables
```

Updates from specific neighbors can be debugged to examine what routes are being advertised. Here is output from a BGP router when it is debugging debug ip bgp based on the IP address of a neighbor router:

```
Router1#debug ip bgp 192.168.15.1 updates
BGP updates debugging is on for neighbor 192.168.15.1
Router1#clear ip bgp *
Router1#
02:24:05: BGP: 192.168.15.1 computing updates, neighbor version 0, table version
1, starting at 0.0.0.0
02:24:05: BGP: 192.168.15.1 update run completed, ran for 0ms, neighbor version
0, start version 1, throttled to 1, check point net 0.0.0.0
02:24:05: BGP: 192.168.15.1 rcv UPDATE w/ attr: nexthop 192.168.15.1, origin i,
path 64514 64513
02:24:05: BGP: 192.168.15.1 rcv UPDATE about 192.168.10.0/24
02:24:05: BGP: 192.168.15.1 rcv UPDATE about 192.168.11.0/24 -- DENIED due to:
distribute/prefix-list;
02:24:35: BGP: 192.168.15.1 computing updates, neighbor version 1, table version
2, starting at 0.0.0.0
02:24:35: BGP: 192.168.15.1 update run completed, ran for 0ms, neighbor version
1, start version 2, throttled to 2, check point net 0.0.0.0
```

This debug command displays the updates that are being received from neighbor 192.168.15.1. We can see that the router, due to a distribute-list that we configured earlier, has denied one of the updates.

Using the debug ip bgp updates command would output the same debug information as shown above, but for all peers.

Logging Neighbor Changes

The Cisco IOS offers a command that enables the logging of the states of BGP neighbors. Messages will be generated whenever the state of a neighbor changes, and this command will log these messages, helping in troubleshooting connections. To activate this function, enter this command in router configuration mode:

```
bgp log-neighbor-changes
```

To read these messages, use the show log command at the console. These messages will also be sent to a syslog server, if one is configured on the router.

Wrap-Up

With the Internet growing in importance daily, from both an individual and a business perspective, proper operation of networks and network services is becoming very critical. BGP makes it possible to ensure reliable routing with its support for route aggregation, multihoming, and policy routing. It also offers means to cost-effectively increase the bandwidth available to an organization. Although BGP is a complicated protocol, it is this flexibility that gives it its power. BGP has a very steep learning curve, but once you have the protocol mastered, there is no end to its applications. It can provide solutions at all levels, from a small business looking to increase the reliability of its network services so they are always available to its customers, to the large multi-national corporation looking to scale its internal network. Apart from implementations on the Internet, BGP is also a viable option for a private network that has grown to such a size that none of the available IGPs available are adequate.

Chapter 7

Static and Default Routing

Static and default routing are perhaps the most misunderstood concepts in all of routing. This is due in large part to their names. *Static* and *default* suggest that they are somehow "simple" or "trivial" to configure. However, this could not be further from the truth. Static and default routing must be carefully understood and configured in a routing environment. Failure to do so can result in problems ranging from routing loops and routing black holes, to, most often, sub-optimal routing. Realize that static and default routing are not "routing protocols" in the strictest sense of the word. But don't let this technicality detract from the importance you assign to the subject. Static and default routing are as prevalent in networking environments today as any "true" IP routing protocol. This chapter is divided into two parts: The first half is devoted to static routing, and the latter half covers default routing and its interaction with the other IP routing protocols.

Overview of Static Routing

So far, we have spent our time discussing and configuring dynamic routing protocols. Another type of routing, *static routing,* can do the same job as its dynamic siblings, albeit with a bit more effort. Instead of allowing the dynamic protocols to build the routing table according to their routing algorithms, we as administrators can explicitly define what should be included in the table. Because you are explicitly telling the router the networks to be contained in the routing table, these static routes have a very low administrative distance. Recall that administrative distance (AD) is a measure of how believable a routing source is, and the lower the AD the more believable the source. The router takes direct input from you in the form of static routes as the most believable source possible, and consequently assigns an AD of either 1 or 0. This AD will be less (more believable) than any other routing protocols or sources we will discuss. Review Figure 1-2 for a list of routing sources and their accompanying ADs. Static routing can be both a blessing and a curse, depending on the specific routing situation you encounter; both instances are covered next.

Figure 7-1 shows a simple configuration in which Router B is connected to the Internet via an ISP.

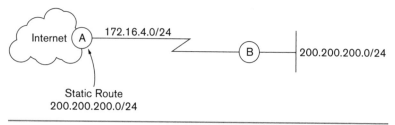

Figure 7-1 *A small company network connecting up to the Internet via an ISP router*

If we configured dynamic routing, we would need to send, in some fashion, the entire Internet routing table, some 77,000+ routes, down the serial link into the small router. This would not work, of course, as the small router wouldn't have the capacity to hold so many routes. The alternative and more feasible solution is to use a combination of static and default routing. The large Internet router would have a single static route to network 200.200.200.0/24 while the small router would have a default route pointing toward the ISP router. Don't worry about the exact configuration at this point; it's covered in the next section. For now, understand that this use of static routing enables you to completely avoid the need for dynamic routing, with relatively little configuration overhead. However, in a large routing environment with multiple routers and multiple paths, configuring static routes becomes administratively burdensome, as illustrated in Figure 7-2.

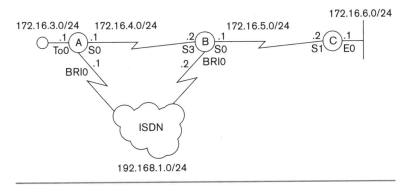

Figure 7-2 *A small network requiring several static routes for full connectivity*

From this simple network with only three routers, you would need to configure several static routes to networks 172.16.3.0/24, 172.16.4.0/24, 172.16.5.0/24, 172.16.6.0/24, and 192.168.1.0/24 in each router. Remember, routers by nature have knowledge of their directly connected networks, and thus it is only necessary to configure static routes for networks not local to the routers. It is easy to see that as your network grows in complexity in terms of number of routers and number of links, the administrative requirements to maintain the static routing can become overwhelming. Every time you bring up a new network, you would have to add a new route to that new network in every single router in your environment.

Configuring Basic Static Routes

Working with the simple three-router diagram in Figure 7-2, let's examine the static routes that would be necessary for Router A:

```
RA(config)# ip route 172.16.5.0 255.255.255.0 172.16.4.2
RA(config)# ip route 172.16.6.0 255.255.255.0 172.16.4.2
```

As you can see, the static routes are entered from global configuration mode, one static route at a time. After the command ip route, the remote network is entered along with the subnet mask, and finally the next hop logical address to get to that network. The next hop logical address is the same as the "via" address that shows up in the routing table. In other words, to get a packet to network 172.16.5.0/24 I must hand off the packet to Router B at address 172.16.4.2 to which I am directly connected without my Serial 0 interface.

An alternative to the above static routes configuration is as follows:

```
RA(config)# ip route 172.16.5.0 255.255.255.0 Serial 0
RA(config)# ip route 172.16.6.0 255.255.255.0 Serial 0
```

This configuration has much the same information, except the next hop logical address is now an interface. Instead of routing to a next hop logical address, you are saying, for example, send all packets destined for network 172.16.5.0/24 out Serial 0. While both methods accomplish the task of routing connectivity there is a slight difference in outcome as it relates to administrative distance. The AD for a static route to a "next hop logical" address is 1; and the AD for a static route to an interface is 0. Additionally, as covered in Chapter 9, static routes are often redistributed automatically if they are static routes to an interface and are not automatically redistributed if the next hop logical address is used.

Another method of static route configuration is presented here for Router A in Figure 7-2:

```
RA(config)# ip route 172.16.5.0 255.255.255.0 192.168.1.2
RA(config)# ip route 172.16.6.0 255.255.255.0 172.16.5.0
```

Notice that the static route for 172.16.5.0/24 is as we might expect, only this time we've elected to point traffic for 172.16.5.0/24 toward the BRI0 interface of Router B using the next hop logical address of 192.168.1.2. Perhaps the primary serial link between Router A and Router B is down and we now want to reconfigure the routers to use the ISDN link. The route to 172.16.6.0/24, however, is quite strange. We've pointed this route to another network, specifically 172.16.5.0/24. This situation is called *recursive route table lookup*. The second line of the preceding configuration says that to get to network 172.16.6.0/24, recursively look in your routing table for a route to 172.16.5.0/24 and send the information there. In this case, information destined for network 172.16.6.0/24 will be forwarded out the BRI0 interface toward 192.168.1.2. Of course, configuring the router to perform potentially several recursive lookups adds overhead to the routing process, but this may be an acceptable trade-off. What is gained is the capability to shape or model traffic flow for one given network using the characteristic of a second network. That is to say, the flow of routing for one network can be used as the directive of how to route another independent network.

Static routes require that the next hop logical address or interface they are tied to be available before the route(s) will be installed in the routing table. Examine the following routes:

```
RA(config)# ip route 172.16.5.0 255.255.255.0 Serial 0
RA(config)# ip route 172.16.6.0 255.255.255.0 172.16.4.2
```

In order for the preceding routes to appear in the routing table of router A, the Serial 0 interface and the next hop logical address 172.16.4.2 must be reachable and up. The above two routes are not dependent on each other; rather, they are different examples showing a similar concept. If, for example, the first route, network 172.16.5.0/24, were in the table and interface Serial 0 went down because of a cable failure, the route would immediately be removed from the routing table. This behavior can sometimes be undesirable. It may be the case, for routing table stability, that you want the route to remain in the table regardless of whether the interface or next hop logical address is available. This effect can be accomplished as follows:

```
RA(config)# ip route 172.16.6.0 255.255.255.0 172.16.4.2 permanent
```

By attaching the keyword "permanent" to the end of a static route command, the route will remain in the table regardless of whether the interface or next hop is up and reachable. Use caution when applying this command. There is a high potential for packet loss if your router continues forwarding packets towards a downed interface.

Configuring Advanced Static Routes

To this point, the static routing we've configured has been fairly straightforward. The following sections take a look at some of the finer details of static routing.

Floating static routes

A *floating static route* is a special type of static route that doesn't go directly into the routing table; rather, it sits in the background until called into duty. Examine again the router diagram in Figure 7-2.

Currently, Router A is configured as shown below, with static routes pointing traffic destined for networks 172.16.5.0/24 and 172.16.6.0/24 toward the next hop logical address of 172.16.4.2 through Serial 0.

```
RA(config)# ip route 172.16.5.0 255.255.255.0 172.16.4.2
RA(config)# ip route 172.16.6.0 255.255.255.0 172.16.4.2
```

Recall that static routes using a next hop logical address are installed in the routing table with an administrative distance of 1. Recall also that should two competing routing sources be telling a router about a particular network, the source with the *lowest* administrative distance will be preferred and, consequently, installed in the routing table. That said, consider the following additional commands that have been added to Router A:

```
RA(config)# ip route 172.16.5.0 255.255.255.0 192.168.1.2 25
RA(config)# ip route 172.16.6.0 255.255.255.0 192.168.1.2 25
```

These particular static routes are for the same networks just described: however, they have a next hop logical address of 192.168.1.2, which funnels traffic out the ISDN BRI0 port. Additionally, the tag 25 on the end of the routes alters the administrative distance. This manipulation of the AD causes the router to install static routes for the original networks out the Serial 0 interface of Router A. This happens because, when faced with equal static routes for a given network, the router chooses the one with the lowest AD. Should Serial 0 go down or become otherwise unavailable, the original routes would have to be removed from the table. At this point, the second set of static routes for the ISDN link would "float" into place in the routing table and back up the originals. The logic is thatbeing, a static route out the ISDN BRI0 with an AD of 25 is better than no route at all. Should the Serial 0 interface again become active and usable, the ISDN routes to 192.168.1.2 would be immediately superseded in the routing table, replaced by the original two static routes.

Summary static routes

A *summary static route* is a specific type of static route that gives you a mechanism for shrinking routing tables. A summary route enables you to do just what it says, summarize two or more specific routes into one statement. The overall result is that full connectivity is maintained and the number of total networks in the routing table is reduced. Figure 7-3 shows an example of where summary static routes are beneficial.

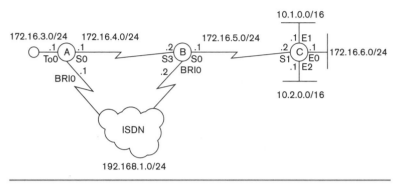

Figure 7-3 *A network configured to utilize summary static routes*

Notice that two additional Ethernet networks, to network 10.1.0.0/16 and 10.2.0.0/16, have been added to Router C. In order for those networks to be reachable from Router A or B, normally two additional static routes would be necessary in each router's configuration, as shown here:

```
RA(config)# ip route 10.1.0.0 255.255.0.0 172.16.4.2
RA(config)# ip route 10.2.0.0 255.255.0.0 172.16.4.2
```

Assuming Router C is fully configured, IP connectivity would be complete with the above additional routes. However, in an effort to optimize the routing table of Router A, consider the following single route, which would replace the above two routes:

```
RA(config)# ip route 10.0.0.0 255.0.0.0 172.16.4.2
```

This static route says, send any packets destined for network 10.0.0.0/8 toward 172.16.4.2. This means that packets destined for any subnet of the major network 10.0.0.0/8, in our case networks 10.1.0.0/16 and 10.2.0.0/16, will be forwarded toward 172.16.4.2. In this manner, with one static route, we have summarized all known subnets of the major network 10.0.0.0/8. We must mention that summarization is most effective in c ontiguous networks. That is to say, using the above configuration, all subnets of 10.0.0.0/8 must be in the direction of Router B from Router A's perspective. If this were not the case, Router A would potentially begin forwarding packets for a subnet of 10.0.0.0/8 in the wrong direction.

Load balancing using static routes

Load balancing is a process by which two separate paths can be utilized to reach a single destination. Routing protocols are most often configurable to support multiple path load balancing, and this is often very desirable. If you have more than one route to a destination, you may want to utilize the second link, unless of course, it is an expensive backup link. The decision to load-balance using routing protocols is keyed off of a metric or set of metrics. Recall that a metric is used to describe the desirability, different from believability, of a route. The metric enables us to assign a value or cost for a given route. Using these metrics some of the routing protocols can load-balance between equal and unequal cost routes for a given destination. Static routes do not employ the concept of a metric and, as such, only support equal cost load sharing. Consider for a moment the network shown in Figure 7-4.

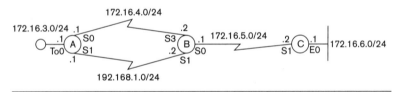

Figure 7-4 *A network configured for load balancing using static routes*

Router A and Router B have between them two identical serial links. To configure Router A for load balancing across these links for the networks belonging to Router C, observe the following commands:

```
RA(config)# ip route 172.16.6.0 255.255.255.0 172.16.4.2
RA(config)# ip route 172.16.6.0 255.255.255.0 192.168.1.2
```

Notice that two static routes have been configured with identical destination networks and different next hop logical addresses. The routing table output for the now configured load balancing on Router A is shown here:

```
RA#sh ip route

Gateway of last resort is not set

C    192.168.1.0/24 is directly connected, Serial1
     172.16.0.0/24 is subnetted, 3 subnets
C        172.16.4.0 is directly connected, Serial0
S        172.16.6.0 [1/0] via 172.16.4.2
                     [1/0] via 192.168.1.2
C        172.16.3.0 is directly connected, TokenRing0
```

It's important to note that the capability to load-balance does not necessitate load balancing. Should one of the interfaces or next hop logical addresses go down or become unavailable, the availability of the route as a whole doesn't fail. Instead, the route will no longer be load-balanced due to the failure of one of the networks, and only a single route to the destination network will remain.

A router usually handles load balancing in one of two ways: either per destination or per packet. There are many different ways a router can switch packets between interfaces, but the two most common and most used methods are *fast switching* and *process switching*. Fast switching is the default for IP and works as follows: When a packet arrives for a destination, the router performs a normal route table lookup and from that lookup selects an outbound interface. In order for the routed packet to leave the outbound interface, a frame must be created for the media type used, say Ethernet for example. We now have an association between a destination network and an outbound frame type. That information, or pre-built frame header, is stored in fast-cache and the next packet that arrives destined for the same remote network does not have to be routed, but can instead be fast-switched using the pre-built frame. In short, when load balancing is configured with fast switching enabled, the packets are load-balanced on a per-destination basis. All traffic for one destination is sent over the first load-balanced link, and traffic for a second destination is sent over the second link. When load balancing is configured and the router is process switching, the router must send every single packet through the routing table and thus makes a decision on a packet-by-packet basis, causing a round-robin effect on the links.

Clearly, process switching is far more processor- and overhead-intensive than fast switching, and should be avoided whenever possible.

Static routes to Null0

The Null0 interface is a software-only interface inside the router that can be used as a place to route unwanted packets. A static route to Null0 is often used in place of the access list that would perform filtering of certain networks. Routing a packet to the "bit bucket" is far less processor-intensive than first routing a packet to an interface and then dropping the packet because of the access list filter in place.

In Figure 7-5, we want to configure Router B such that all packets for network 172.16.0.0/16 as their best match will be "dropped" or routed to Null0.

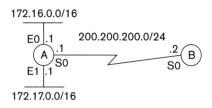

Figure 7-5 *A network configured using static routes to Null0*

To configure Router B to use a static route to Null0, the following command is entered:

```
RB(config)# ip route 172.16.0.0 255.255.0.0 null0
```

Use caution when using this command in place of an access list. The static route applies to the whole router as opposed to just a single interface as is often the case with an access list. This means that any packet matching 172.16.0.0/16 will be routed to the bit bucket, versus, for example, dropping packets that are routed just to an individual interface.

Overview of Default Routing

A default route is a special type of static route that says, "If all else fails, send it here." The capability to have a last resort in the routing table can be a tremendous saving in terms of processor utilization and memory requirements. Default routing is often needed because of a key behavior of routers: If a router does not have a route for a packet, the packet must be dropped. Because this behavior of dropping packets to "unknown" destinations is often not desirable, in order for a router to be fully connected it must have a route to every single network in the world. Recall from the beginning of the chapter that there are currently over 77,000 routes in the Internet, a number far larger than most routers can handle. To help solve the problem of not recording every single route in the table while still maintaining full connectivity, default routing is used. With default routing, we can specify a single route that says "all other routes." Referring back to Figure 7-1 earlier in the chapter, we see the classic example of when default routing is used. Router B is a small router with very little RAM and accordingly cannot support the entire Internet routing table that Router A holds. The next section covers the different ways of configuring default routing to solve not only the problem presented with Figure 7-1 but many other default routing challenges as well.

Configuring Basic Default Routes

Configuring basic default routes is relatively simple; understanding their ramifications and behaviors in complex routing environments is another story. Consider the network shown in Figure 7-6. For this section we have configured full local connectivity using only static routes. We discuss default routing as it relates and interacts with other IP routing protocols in the section "Configuring Advanced Default Routes" later in this chapter.

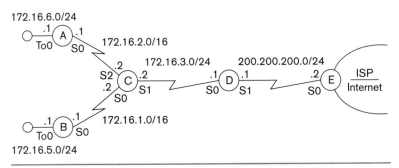

Figure 7-6 *A classic hub and spoke network design*

In this classic hub and spoke configuration, the hub Router C has a connection to the border Router D, which has a connection to the Internet and is running a default static route toward the provider. The configuration of the default route is shown here:

```
RD(config)# ip route 0.0.0.0 0.0.0.0 200.200.200.2
```

The default static route is configured with exactly the same syntax as a regular static route. Notice that the network portion is defined as 0.0.0.0 as is the subnet portion of the mask. A common configuration error is to use a mask of 255.255.255.255. This mask defines a static host route to the IP address of 0.0.0.0, which you are not able to assign to any machine. If you think of the 255.255.255.255 mask as defining a very specific route, the 0.0.0.0 mask does just the opposite it defines something very general. Looking at the following routing table for Router D, we can see that a route toward 200.200.200.2 has been installed as the *gateway of last resort:*

```
RD#sh ip route

Gateway of last resort is 200.200.200.2 to network 0.0.0.0

     172.16.0.0/24 is subnetted, 5 subnets
S       172.16.5.0 [1/0] via 172.16.3.2
S       172.16.6.0 [1/0] via 172.16.3.2
S       172.16.1.0 [1/0] via 172.16.3.2
S       172.16.2.0 [1/0] via 172.16.3.2
C       172.16.3.0 is directly connected, Serial0
C     200.200.200.0/24 is directly connected, Serial1
S*    0.0.0.0/0 [1/0] via 200.200.200.2
```

In addition to using a static default route, the `ipdefault-network` command can be used to configure default routing. This command configures a major classful network to be used as the default network. The following output shows the configuration for Router C:

```
RC(config)#ip default-network 200.200.200.0
```

This command instructs the router to search the routing table for a route to network 200.200.200.0 and, if found, to install that route, and corresponding "via" address, as the gateway of last resort. The following routing table output from Router C shows that 200.200.200.0 is flagged as a candidate default and is also installed as the gateway of last resort:

```
RC#sh ip route


Gateway of last resort is 172.16.3.1 to network 200.200.200.0


S*    200.200.200.0/24 [1/0] via 172.16.3.1

      172.16.0.0/24 is subnetted, 5 subnets

S        172.16.5.0 [1/0] via 172.16.1.1

S        172.16.6.0 [1/0] via 172.16.2.1

C        172.16.1.0 is directly connected, Serial0

C        172.16.2.0 is directly connected, Serial3

C        172.16.3.0 is directly connected, Serial1
```

Remember from our discussion above that the `ip default-network` command is a classful network statement. Figure 7-7 shows the same network we were configuring before only the link between Router D and the upstream router, Router E, has been changed to be included in the 172.16.0.0 major network: in this example, network 172.16.10.0.

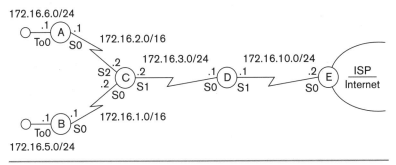

Figure 7-7 *A classic hub and spoke design with all subnets part of the same major network*

When configuring the `ip default-network` command on Router C, the temptation is to enter the following:

```
RC(config)# ip default-network 172.16.10.0
```

This default network statement violates the classful nature of the statement. Additionally, the router does not interpret correctly the given configuration and converts the above statement to the following:

```
ip route 172.16.0.0 255.255.0.0 172.16.10.0
```

The command is interpreted as a static route to the major classful network with a next hop address of the subnet you were trying to specify as the default network in the first place. Obviously this would not be the intended result for this scenario. After receiving these arcane results there may be a temptation to then specify the major classful network as the default network as follows:

```
RC(config)# ip default-network 172.16.0.0
```

The following output shows the routing table of Router C after this command is implemented:

```
RC#sh ip route

Gateway of last resort is not set

*    172.16.0.0/24 is subnetted, 6 subnets
C       172.16.10.0 [1/0] via 172.16.3.1
S       172.16.5.0 [1/0] via 172.16.1.1
S       172.16.6.0 [1/0] via 172.16.2.1
C       172.16.3.0 is directly connected, Serial1
C       172.16.1.0 is directly connected, Serial0
C       172.16.2.0 is directly connected, Serial2
```

As you can see from the routing table output, the heading for the major network 172.16.0.0/16 has been flagged as a candidate default route but no network has been installed as the gateway of last resort. This situation details an acute problem of the `ip default-network` command. The command itself is classful and thus any major network to which you are connected using a subnet of that major network becomes invalid as a potential default network.

Making the situation even more complicated is the following: When using `ip default-network`, if the network used is directly connected to the router, this will not suffice as a default network and subsequently will not be installed as the gateway of last resort for that router. That is not to say it will not distribute a default route to other routers as a result of the command: It will. However, no gateway of last resort will be installed for the router that has the ip default-network command. Conversely, if the network used in the ip default-network command is a known network but not directly connected, the default network will be installed as a gateway of last resort in addition to being propagated to other routers.

Configuring Advanced Default Routes

Up until this point, our discussions of default routing have dealt with configuring defaults in a static environment; that is to say, we were not using any IP routing protocols. We wanted to approach the concept of default routing using a building block approach, starting out with basics and adding more complexity in a structured manner. This section examines the nuances of default routing in a true IP routing environment, stepping through each of the major IP routing protocols.

Understanding ip classless

The ramifications of ip classless or more accurately no ip classless as it pertains to default routing behavior are extensive but far too often misunderstood. When the following condition exists, no ip classless configures the router to not forward or drop packets: The packet is destined to a subnet for which the router does not have a specific route, but the packet does have knowledge of other subnets in the same major network. Figure 7-8 and the corresponding routing table output from Router A show how a network seemingly configured for default routing can still fail because of classful routing.

```
RA#sh ip route

Gateway of last resort is 172.16.3.2 to network 0.0.0.0

     172.16.0.0/24 is subnetted, 3 subnets
C       172.16.1.0 is directly connected, TokenRing0
C       172.16.2.0 is directly connected, TokenRing0
```

```
C       172.16.3.0 is directly connected, Serial0

S*   0.0.0.0/0 [1/0] via 172.16.3.2

S    172.0.0.0/8 [1/0] via 172.16.3.2
```

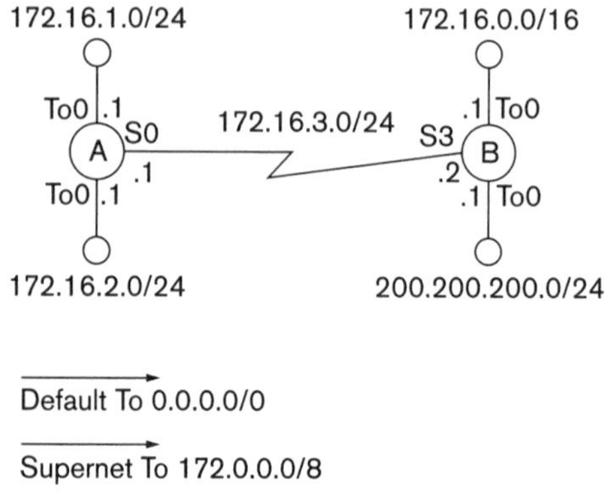

172.16.1.0/24   172.16.0.0/16

To0 .1   .1 To0
    S0   172.16.3.0/24   S3
(A)   (B)
To0 .1   .1   .2
                            .1 To0

172.16.2.0/24   200.200.200.0/24

Default To 0.0.0.0/0

Supernet To 172.0.0.0/8

Figure 7-8 *A sample network showing the ramifications of classless versus classful routing*

We can see that Router A has knowledge of the 172.16.0.0/16 major network and we see that it has been subnetted an additional 8 bits. The router has three interfaces connected to subnets of this major network, 172.16.1.0/24, 172.16.2.0/24, and 172.16.3.0/24. There is also a static default route that has been configured and installed as the gateway of last resort toward Router B. Finally, a static route to the supernet of 172.16.0.0/ 24, in this case 172.0.0.0/8 has been installed again toward Router B, in an effort to configure connectivity to network 172.16.4.0/24:

```
RA#ping 172.16.4.1


Type escape sequence to abort.

Sending 5, 100-byte ICMP Echos to 172.16.4.1, timeout is 2 seconds:

.....

Success rate is 0 percent (0/5)
```

With no `ip classless` configured, we can see from the ping above that the address 172.16.4.1 is not accessible. A ping to 172.16.4.1 fails despite the apparent existence of both a default and supernet route because no `ip classless` will not allow you to match, and subsequently forward, a packet to a supernet or a default route for networks you know about in some granular manner in the routing table. That is, because the router has directly connected interfaces to the 172.16.0.0/16 major network, the router assumes, with no `ip classless` configured, that it knows all the subnets of 172.16.0.0/16 and as such a packet for network 172.16.4.0/24 must not exist and should be dropped, even with the presence of default and supernet routes. It is clearly bad practice to divide up a major network this way.

Despite this behavior for connected major networks, a ping will succeed, through use of the default route, for major networks the router has no granular knowledge of. In the scenario detailed in Figure 7-8 we can see that a ping to 200.200.200.1 succeeds from Router A:

```
RA#ping 200.200.200.1

Type escape sequence to abort.
Sending 5, 100-byte ICMP Echos to 200.200.200.1, timeout is 2 seconds:
!!!!!
Success rate is 100 percent (5/5), round-trip min/avg/max = 1/3/4 ms
```

The default starting in IOS 11.3, `ip classless`, configures the router to match the best supernet available and that supernet may be any default route, including 0.0.0.0/0. Simply put, the router makes a decision independent of the major network class and tries to select the overall best match. With `ip classless` now configured, we can see that ping to 172.16.4.1 succeeds using the supernet route to 172.0.0.0/8:

```
RA#ping 172.16.4.1

Type escape sequence to abort.
Sending 5, 100-byte ICMP Echos to 172.16.4.1, timeout is 2 seconds:
!!!!!
Success rate is 100 percent (5/5), round-trip min/avg/max = 4/4/4 ms
```

The vast majority of the time, it never hurts you to configure all your routers with `ip classless` as it will often save you headaches down the road. This is especially true since the advent of classless interdomain routing (CIDR). However, remember that with `ip classless` configured, any packet coming into a router will be forwarded toward the default if a more specific match cannot be found. This may put an undue burden on the receiving router, so consider carefully whether this situation is acceptable in your environment.

Configuring RIP and 0.0.0.0

Routing Information Protocol (RIP) is very tolerant, and chatty, about the default 0.0.0.0/0 network. That is, if a router running RIP has a default route configured, either through a static default route or use of the `ip default-network` command, RIP will advertise 0.0.0.0/0 to its neighbors. The 0.0.0.0/0 will be automatically advertised even when static redistribution into the RIP domain is not configured. Figure 7-9 shows us again the network we will be examining. Assume we are running RIP among routers A through E on all interfaces shown.

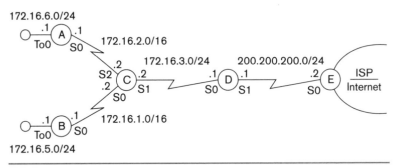

Figure 7-9 *A network using default routes and various routing protocols*

To enable default routing, we have elected to configure Router D as follows:

```
RD(config)# ip route 0.0.0.0 0.0.0.0 200.200.200.2
```

In this configuration, we have used a static default route statement on Router D, which will automatically redistribute a default network into Routers A, B, and C and funnel the information toward Router D. Examining the routing table output from Routers D, C, and A, we can see that default routing has been correctly installed:

```
RD#sh ip route

Gateway of last resort is 200.200.200.2 to network 0.0.0.0

     172.16.0.0/24 is subnetted, 5 subnets
R       172.16.5.0 [120/2] via 172.16.3.2, 00:00:25, Serial0
R       172.16.6.0 [120/2] via 172.16.3.2, 00:00:25, Serial0
R       172.16.1.0 [120/1] via 172.16.3.2, 00:00:25, Serial0
R       172.16.2.0 [120/1] via 172.16.3.2, 00:00:25, Serial0
C       172.16.3.0 is directly connected, Serial0
C     200.200.200.0/24 is directly connected, Serial1
S*    0.0.0.0/0 [1/0] via 200.200.200.2


RC#sh ip route

Gateway of last resort is 172.16.3.1 to network 0.0.0.0

R     200.200.200.0/24 [120/1] via 172.16.3.1, 00:00:25, Serial1
     172.16.0.0/24 is subnetted, 5 subnets
R       172.16.5.0 [120/1] via 172.16.1.1, 00:00:26, Serial0
R       172.16.6.0 [120/1] via 172.16.2.1, 00:00:14, Serial2
C       172.16.1.0 is directly connected, Serial0
C       172.16.2.0 is directly connected, Serial2
C       172.16.3.0 is directly connected, Serial1
R*    0.0.0.0/0 [120/1] via 172.16.3.1, 00:00:25, Serial1


RA#sh ip route

Gateway of last resort is 172.16.2.2 to network 0.0.0.0

     172.16.0.0/24 is subnetted, 5 subnets
R       172.16.5.0 [120/2] via 172.16.2.2, 00:00:07, Serial0
C       172.16.6.0 is directly connected, TokenRing0
R       172.16.1.0 [120/1] via 172.16.2.2, 00:00:07, Serial0
C       172.16.2.0 is directly connected, Serial0
R       172.16.3.0 [120/1] via 172.16.2.2, 00:00:07, Serial0
```

```
R    200.200.200.0/24 [120/2] via 172.16.2.2, 00:00:07, Serial0
R*   0.0.0.0/0 [120/2] via 172.16.2.2, 00:00:07, Serial0
```

Using the `trace` command that follows, we can see that a trace from Router A to 200.200.200.2 successfully traverses the network through first Router C, then Router D, and finally Router E using default routing. Remember from our previous configurations that all this connectivity was established using only one simple default static route:

```
RA#trace 200.200.200.2

Type escape sequence to abort.
Tracing the route to 200.200.200.2

  1 172.16.2.2 4 msec 4 msec 4 msec
  2 172.16.3.1 4 msec 4 msec 4 msec
  3 200.200.200.2 92 msec * 88 msec
```

In the case of RIP, the `ip default-network` command can be used as described in the preceding section; however, note what default information is actually generated from the router housing the `ip default-network` command. In Figure 7-9, if we configured Router D with an `ip default-network` statement to accomplish default routing, no matter what network we specify, the RIP updates sent toward Router C are changed to network 0.0.0.0/0. So despite configuring a specific network as the default, the RIP routing process will always propagate the 0.0.0.0/0 default. This effect can be seen in the following Router D output and RIP debugging capture:

```
RD#sh run
Building configuration...

Current configuration:
!
version 11.2
no service password-encryption
no service udp-small-servers
no service tcp-small-servers
!
```

```
hostname RD
!
interface Serial0
 ip address 172.16.3.1 255.255.255.0
 no fair-queue
!
interface Serial1
 ip address 200.200.200.1 255.255.255.0
 clockrate 2000000
!
router rip
 network 172.16.0.0
 network 200.200.200.0
!
no ip classless
ip default-network 200.200.200.0
!
line con 0
line aux 0
line vty 0 4
 login
!
end
```

In the preceding configuration, notice that we have only configured an `ip default-network` command and not an explicit static route to 0.0.0.0/0. As described in the preceding section, a gateway of last resort would *not* be installed for Router D due to the fact that the `ip default-network` command is configured to a directly connected network. However, despite the lack of an installed gateway of last resort, the default network is generated and propagated as shown here:

```
RD#debug ip rip
RIP protocol debugging is on
RD#clear ip route *
```

```
RD#

RIP: sending general request on Serial0 to 255.255.255.255

RIP: sending general request on Serial0 to 224.0.0.9

RIP: sending general request on Serial1 to 255.255.255.255

RIP: sending general request on Serial1 to 224.0.0.9

RIP: received v1 update from 172.16.3.2 on Serial0

     172.16.1.0 in 1 hops

     172.16.2.0 in 1 hops

RIP: sending v1 update to 255.255.255.255 via Serial0 (172.16.3.1)

     default, metric 1

     network 200.200.200.0, metric 1

RIP: sending v1 update to 255.255.255.255 via Serial1 (200.200.200.1)

     default, metric 1

     network 172.16.0.0, metric 1
```

IGRP and 0.0.0.0

Interior Gateway Routing Protocol (IGRP) handles default routing, and its propagation, much the same way as RIP does except for one major difference. IGRP will not advertise the 0.0.0.0/0 default network to neighbors, even if a default static route to 0.0.0.0/0 is configured on the IGRP router. This does not mean it will not install a route to 0.0.0.0/0 as the gateway of last resort; rather, it won't advertise the fact. The solution when using IGRP is to use the ip default-network command with some legitimate classful network. Remember from our discussions earlier in the chapter that the ip default-network command must be configured to a classful network and the network must be known in the routing table. Again, we will be using Figure 7-9 in our examination of IGRP and default routing.

With the entire network now configured to use IGRP, we first try to configure default routing by configuring Router D as follows:

```
RD(config)# ip route 0.0.0.0 0.0.0.0 200.200.200.2
```

While this configuration will install a gateway of last resort for Router D toward Router E, the default information will not be propagated backward toward the other routers. To successfully configure defaults for the network we must also configure Router D as follows:

```
RD(config)# ip default-network 200.200.200.0
```

Remember that when configuring the ip default-network command, the network must be both classful and present in the routing table. In this case, both conditions are met. The routing table output below from Router A shows that default routing is now working in the network:

```
RA#sh ip route

Gateway of last resort is 172.16.2.2 to network 200.200.200.0

     172.16.0.0/24 is subnetted, 5 subnets
I       172.16.5.0 [100/43312] via 172.16.2.2, 00:00:43, Serial0
C       172.16.6.0 is directly connected, TokenRing0
I       172.16.1.0 [100/43062] via 172.16.2.2, 00:00:43, Serial0
C       172.16.2.0 is directly connected, Serial0
I       172.16.3.0 [100/43062] via 172.16.2.2, 00:00:43, Serial0
I*  200.200.200.0/24 [100/45062] via 172.16.2.2, 00:00:43, Serial0
```

In order to make default routing work in the preceding scenario, both a default static route and the ip default-network command had to be used on Router D. The 0.0.0.0/0 static route installs a gateway of last resort for Router D toward E, and the ip default-network 200.200.200.0 command flags the 200.200.200.0/24 network as a candidate default in Router D's IGRP updates to its neighbors. The following code shows the conditions just described:

```
RD#sh run
Building configuration...

Current configuration:
!
version 11.2
no service password-encryption
no service udp-small-servers
no service tcp-small-servers
!
hostname RD
```

```
!
!
!
interface Serial0
 ip address 172.16.3.1 255.255.255.0
 no fair-queue
!
interface Serial1
 ip address 200.200.200.1 255.255.255.0
 clockrate 2000000
!
router igrp 1
 network 172.16.0.0
 network 200.200.200.0
!
ip classless
ip default-network 200.200.200.0
ip route 0.0.0.0 0.0.0.0 200.200.200.2
!
!
line con 0
 exec-timeout 0 0
line aux 0
line vty 0 4
 login
!
end
```

EIGRP and 0.0.0.0

Enhanced Interior Gateway Routing Protocol (EIGRP) is touted by many as the most complex routing protocol available and, as such, supports a robust default routing option. Unlike its predecessor IGRP, EIGRP does support the 0.0.0.0/0 default route. However, in order for the default network command to be propagated in EIGRP updates, redistribution of static routes must be manually configured. For a complete discussion of route redistribution, please see Chapter 8. As with the other protocols we have examined thus far regarding their behavior with defaults, we will be using Figure 7-9, now configured for EIGRP routing.

The following text shows the configuration for Router D with the bolded output showing the configuration of a static default route and static redistribution:

```
RD#sh run
Building configuration...

Current configuration:
!
version 11.2
no service password-encryption
no service udp-small-servers
no service tcp-small-servers
!
hostname RD
!
interface Serial0
 ip address 172.16.3.1 255.255.255.0
 no fair-queue
!
interface Serial1
 ip address 200.200.200.1 255.255.255.0
 clockrate 2000000
!
router eigrp 1
 redistribute static metric 1000 10 255 1 1500
 network 172.16.0.0
 network 200.200.200.0
!
ip classless
ip route 0.0.0.0 0.0.0.0 200.200.200.2
!
line con 0
```

```
line aux 0

line vty 0 4

 login

 !

end
```

With this configuration in place on Router D, we can see from the routing table of Router C that default routing information is now being propagated downstream:

```
RC#sh ip route

Gateway of last resort is 172.16.3.1 to network 0.0.0.0

D    200.200.200.0/24 [90/2681856] via 172.16.3.1, 01:31:56, Serial1
     172.16.0.0/24 is subnetted, 5 subnets
D       172.16.5.0 [90/2233856] via 172.16.1.1, 01:32:49, Serial0
D       172.16.6.0 [90/2233856] via 172.16.2.1, 01:32:49, Serial2
C       172.16.1.0 is directly connected, Serial0
C       172.16.2.0 is directly connected, Serial2
C       172.16.3.0 is directly connected, Serial1
D*EX 0.0.0.0/0 [170/3074560] via 172.16.3.1, 00:04:16, Serial1
```

The other option for configuring default routing in our environment is to use the ip default-network command in conjunction with the explicit static default route. The following configuration of Router D shows this variation of default routing:

```
RD#sh run

Building configuration...

Current configuration:

!

version 11.2

no service password-encryption

no service udp-small-servers
```

```
no service tcp-small-servers
!
hostname RD
!
interface Serial0
 ip address 172.16.3.1 255.255.255.0
 no fair-queue
!
interface Serial1
 ip address 200.200.200.1 255.255.255.0
 clockrate 2000000
!
router eigrp 1
 network 172.16.0.0
 network 200.200.200.0
!
ip classless
ip default-network 200.200.200.0
ip route 0.0.0.0 0.0.0.0 200.200.200.2
!
line con 0
line aux 0
line vty 0 4
 login
!
end
```

Note that the default route sent by Router D and subsequently installed by Router C is not an external route as is the case when redistributing statics in the prior example. This may seem trivial, but it must be considered if, for example, the network is filtering external networks at some point. The following routing table from Router C shows a default route being installed as a gateway of last resort.

```
RC#sh ip route


Gateway of last resort is 172.16.3.1 to network 200.200.200.0
```

```
D*   200.200.200.0/24 [90/2681856] via 172.16.3.1, 00:08:12, Serial1
     172.16.0.0/24 is subnetted, 5 subnets
D       172.16.5.0 [90/2233856] via 172.16.1.1, 01:42:23, Serial0
D       172.16.6.0 [90/2233856] via 172.16.2.1, 01:42:23, Serial2
C       172.16.1.0 is directly connected, Serial0
C       172.16.2.0 is directly connected, Serial2
C       172.16.3.0 is directly connected, Serial1
```

OSPF/IS-IS and 0.0.0.0

Open Shortest Path First (OSPF) and IS-IS handle default routing exactly the same way, but in a manner very different from RIP, IGRP, and EIGRP. The discussion that follows uses OSPF as the primary protocol but the discussion is virtually interchangeable with IS-IS as well. An OSPF router will not inject a default route automatically to its neighbors even if a default has been configured and installed in the router. Figure 7-10 shows how we have configured our network to use OSPF.

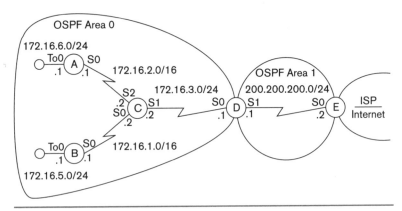

Figure 7-10 *A network using default routes and the OSPF routing protocol*

The following configuration of Router D shows that OSPF and a static default route have been configured toward Router E:

```
RD(config)#router ospf 1
RD(config-router)#network 172.16.0.0 0.0.255.255 area 0
```

```
RD(config-router)#network 200.200.200.0 0.0.0.255 area 1
```

```
RD(config)#ip route 0.0.0.0 0.0.0.0 200.200.200.2
```

Taking a look at the routing table from Router A, we can see that the router has complete knowledge of the network and there is no candidate default network or gateway of last resort:

```
RA#sh ip route
```

```
Gateway of last resort is not set
```

```
     172.16.0.0/24 is subnetted, 7 subnets
O       172.16.5.0 [110/153] via 172.16.2.2, 00:22:39, Serial0
C       172.16.6.0 is directly connected, TokenRing0
O       172.16.1.0 [110/128] via 172.16.2.2, 00:22:39, Serial0
C       172.16.2.0 is directly connected, Serial0
O       172.16.3.0 [110/128] via 172.16.2.2, 00:22:39, Serial0
O IA 200.200.200.0/24 [110/192] via 172.16.2.2, 00:22:39, Serial0
```

In order for OSPF to send a default into the OSPF domain the `default-information originate` command is used. This command is necessary under the OSPF process because in order for the default to be redistributed, the 0.0.0.0 network must be advertised as a type 5 LSA. A type 5 LSA is generated by an Autonomous System Boundary Router (ASBR), and the `default-information originate` command instructs the router that it is in fact an ASBR. For a complete discussion of OSPF, please see Chapter 4. The `default information-originate` command will configure the ASBR to inject a 0.0.0.0/0 route provided a default route is installed in the ASBR itself. If a default network is configured in the ASBR and it is injecting a default route into the domain, the route will cease to be advertised should the default network become unavailable. This behavior may not be desirable if your network experiences a high degree of fluctuation because a flapping of the default network will cause a flapping of the OSPF injected default route throughout the entire domain. The solution to this issue is to use the keyword "always" as shown here:

```
RD(config)#router ospf 1
RD(config-router)#default-information originate always
```

This instructs the OSPF process to inject a 0.0.0.0/0 default into the OSPF domain regardless of whether a viable default is configured and installed on the generating router. A point of confusion often associated with this command is that the existence of this command on a router does not cause a default route to be installed. That is to say, a default route, of some sort, must be manually configured on the router for that router to have the default installed; the `default-information originate` command does not accomplish this task. In our network, we have added the above command for Router D under the OSPF process.

This command configures Router D to inject a 0.0.0.0/0 default toward Routers A, B, and C. And as the following routing table output from Router A shows, the default information has successfully been propagated throughout the network:

```
RA#sh ip route

Gateway of last resort is 172.16.2.2 to network 0.0.0.0

     172.16.0.0/24 is subnetted, 5 subnets

O       172.16.5.0 [110/153] via 172.16.2.2, 00:58:13, Serial0
C       172.16.6.0 is directly connected, TokenRing0
O       172.16.1.0 [110/128] via 172.16.2.2, 00:58:13, Serial0
C       172.16.2.0 is directly connected, Serial0
O       172.16.3.0 [110/128] via 172.16.2.2, 00:58:13, Serial0
O IA 200.200.200.0/24 [110/192] via 172.16.2.2, 00:58:13, Serial0
O*E2 0.0.0.0/0 [110/1] via 172.16.2.2, 00:58:14, Serial0
```

As with other routing protocols, to complete the default routing configuration successfully, remember that the router generating the default route to the rest of the IGP must have its own default route configured. The following code output for Router D shows this to be the case:

```
RD#sh run
Building configuration...
```

```
Current configuration:
!
version 11.2
no service password-encryption
no service udp-small-servers
no service tcp-small-servers
!
hostname RD
!
interface Serial0
 ip address 172.16.3.1 255.255.255.0
 no fair-queue
!
interface Serial1
 ip address 200.200.200.1 255.255.255.0
 clockrate 2000000
!
router ospf 1
 network 172.16.3.1 0.0.0.0 area 0
 network 200.200.200.1 0.0.0.0 area 1
 default-information originate always
!
ip classless
ip route 0.0.0.0 0.0.0.0 200.200.200.2
!
!
line con 0
 exec-timeout 0 0
line aux 0
line vty 0 4
 login
!
end
```

BGP and 0.0.0.0

Border Gateway Protocol (BGP), as described in Chapter 6, is primarily used as a way of interconnecting large autonomous systems. For purposes of interaction between BGP and your IGP, it is a rule of thumb to never redistribute information between the two. With that said, we have configured our network as shown in Figure 7-11.

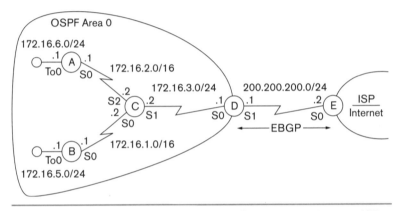

Figure 7-11 *A network running OSPF as the IGP and connection to an ISP with BGP*

In this network, we are running single area OSPF as the IGP, and EBGP on Router D with our upstream ISP on Router E. The OSPF network has been configured for default routing as described in the prior section with Router D using the `default-information originate` command under the OSPF router process. This causes default traffic from Routers A, B, and C to funnel toward Router D. However, Router D does not install a gateway of last resort in its own routing table. In order to configure a default route on Router D, a couple of options exist. A default static route could be configured on Router D toward Router E as described several times in previous sections. Additionally, as this example will show, a default route can be generated by the ISP router via BGP and sent to Router D. The configuration of Router E is shown here:

```
RE#sh run

Building configuration...
```

```
Current configuration:
!
version 11.2
no service password-encryption
no service udp-small-servers
no service tcp-small-servers
!
hostname RE
!
interface Serial0
 ip address 200.200.200.2 255.255.255.0
 bandwidth 256
 no fair-queue
!
interface Serial1
 ip address 192.168.100.1 255.255.255.0
 bandwidth 256
 clockrate 2000000
!
router bgp 1
 no synchronization
 neighbor 200.200.200.1 remote-as 1
 neighbor 200.200.200.1 default-originate
!
ip classless
ip route 172.16.0.0 255.255.0.0 200.200.200.1
!
!
line con 0
 exec-timeout 0 0
line aux 0
line vty 0 4
 login
!
end
```

Configuring a default route to be sent to a BGP neighbor is accomplished with only one line under the BGP routing process: `neighbor 200.200.200.1 default-originate` as shown in bold above. The IP routing table from Router D shows that the default BGP route is now present and installed as the gateway of last resort:

```
RD#sh ip route


Gateway of last resort is 200.200.200.2 to network 0.0.0.0


     172.16.0.0/24 is subnetted, 3 subnets
O       172.16.1.0 [110/128] via 172.16.3.2, 00:15:16, Serial0
O       172.16.2.0 [110/128] via 172.16.3.2, 00:15:16, Serial0
C       172.16.3.0 is directly connected, Serial0
C    200.200.200.0/24 is directly connected, Serial1
B*   0.0.0.0/0 [200/0] via 200.200.200.2, 00:28:41
```

Wrap-Up

As we conclude this chapter, we hope that you now have a greater respect for static and default routing. Over the years, this subject has been given a low level of importance relative to other routing subjects. This indifference about static and default routing has resulted in an industry of people who think that they know everything about the subject but don't. This chapter was meant to empower you with the knowledge to go and explore your networks and fix the inevitable problems that exist with default and static routing. Learning how to correctly massage static default information in any networking scenario takes a while to master. Practicing and experimenting with default and static routing are truly the best methods to becoming a guru at what is more aptly called an art than a science.

Chapter 8

Redistributing Routes

Route redistribution is the process by which routes learned from a routing protocol, static routes, or directly connected routes are transferred into another routing protocol, and from there, are advertised into the second protocol's domain. Although not always considered to be an ideal network design solution, redistribution is often necessary, and all network administrators should understand the concepts behind it.

A few situations may require the implementation of redistribution. Migrating a network from one routing protocol to another requires redistribution between the two protocols until the new protocol is completely implemented. Merging two networks running different routing protocols may require redistribution if routers need to know about the availability of routes in the other network.

Because redistribution of routes can be such a fluid thing, one can almost think of it as more of an art form than a science. A lot of variables are involved, and a thorough understanding of the routing protocols in question is essential to comprehend the idiosyncrasies you may encounter. Often, you can accomplish the same result through several different means.

Redistribution Basics

Redistribution is such a challenging task because some routing protocols support variable length subnet masks (VLSM), whereas some do not; and each routing protocol uses different metrics. Translating these metrics between protocols is not an intuitive or easy task, and it is somewhat arbitrary. Because one routing protocol does not understand the metrics of another routing protocol, the administrator must choose with care the metrics assigned during redistribution in order to achieve the desired routing behavior.

Administrative Distances

Administrative distance (AD) is used to choose between routes from different routing protocols. It is based upon the assumption that more sophisticated routing protocols are more likely to have an optimal and accurate route than some of the older, less sophisticated protocols. A route with a lower administrative distance value is considered the better route, so when there are two routes to the same destination through different routing protocols, the one with the lower administrative distance will be chosen.

To show how administrative distances work, let us look at the example shown in Figure 8-1.

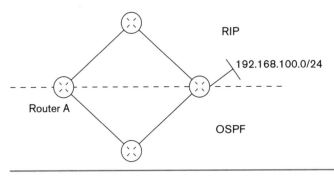

Figure 8-1 *This simple network illustrates the concept behind administrative distances.*

In this example, a router is running both the RIP and OSPF routing protocols. Both of these protocols have a route to the same destination network. However, because OSPF has the lower AD, its route will be the one that is entered into the routing table.

Router A can learn about network 192.168.100/24 through both the RIP routing domain and the OSPF routing domain. Without administrative distances, Router A wouldn't know which one to choose because the metric associated with RIP, *hop count*, is not comparable to the metric that

OSPF uses, *cost*. Some method must be used to choose which routing protocol will be preferred. Cisco developed the administrative distances that you see in Table 8.1.

Table 8.1 *Default Administrative Distances in Cisco Routers*

Route Source	Distance Value
Connected Interface	0
Static Route	1
EIGRP Summary Route	5
External BGP Route	20
Internal EIGRP Route	90
IGRP	100
OSPF	110
IS-IS	115
RIP	120
EGP (Exterior Gateway Protocol)	140
External EIGRP Route	170
Internal BGP Route	200
Unknown Source	255

Using this table, we can compare the AD between RIP and OSPF. OSPF has an AD of 110, and RIP has an AD of 120. Because a lower value is preferred, the OSPF route will be entered into the IP routing table.

When configuring routers, there are a lot of different parameters to remember. With some parameters, a higher number is preferred, as with priority; with others, a lower number is preferred, as with administrative distance. The best way to remember which is more favorable with administrative distance is to associate it with traveling. A shorter distance is usually better than a longer distance, so you would favor the shorter path. It is not always as easy as Figure 8-1 depicts it, however. The routing protocol with the better AD may not always be the preferred route to the destination. We can see an example of this in Figure 8-2. We have taken the network from Figure 8-1 and added more routers in the path in the OSPF domain.

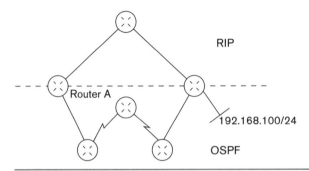

Figure 8-2 *Route selection by administrative distance does not always result in the better route.*

Router A will learn about the network 192.168.100/24 through both the RIP and OSPF routing protocols. From the picture, we can see that due to the number of routers and serial links in the OSPF path, the RIP path would be a better choice. The router, on the other hand, will still choose the OSPF route because the AD is preferred. To remedy a situation like this, more tools are required. These are discussed in the section "Filtering Routes" later in this chapter.

Metrics

When comparing routes in the same routing protocol in order to choose the best route, the router will use the metrics of that protocol. Metrics vary from protocol to protocol, and pose an interesting problem when configuring redistribution. Without an accurate means of translating metrics from one protocol to another, this task falls to the administrator, who must manually configure a metric that is assigned to redistributed routes.

Some routing protocols will not redistribute unless some metric is explicitly configured. For this reason, it is important that default metrics are assigned when performing redistribution. OSPF automatically assigns a metric of 20 to any route that is redistributed into it if no default metric is configured. All other protocols assign a default metric of 0. IS-IS is able to redistribute routes, advertising a cost of 0. RIP, IGRP, and EIGRP, however, will not work with a metric of zero. A default metric greater than zero needs to be assigned to get these protocols to advertise the redistributed routes.

In general, one metric will be assigned to all of the routes imported from a particular routing protocol. For this reason, it is important that the default metric value assigned differs enough from the internal metrics so that internal and redistributed routes can be distinguished from one another. For instance, routes redistributed into RIP may be assigned a default metric of 4 to make it easy to tell the routes apart and to prevent redistributed routes from appearing more appealing than a route to the same destination through the internal network.

One of the challenges to this method, however, is the limited metrics of some routing protocols. RIP routes are only reachable at distances of up to 15, which does not give you much room to play with when configuring default metrics. IS-IS routes are limited to metrics of 1023. While this is not as limiting as RIP, it can still cause issues in some network designs.

Configuring Redistribution

Redistribution is easy to configure, but hard to get working exactly the way you want. In this section, we will cover the steps required to get redistribution operating on a router. The following points are important to remember when configuring redistribution:

- Determine what routing protocol is the source of the routes, and what routing protocol is the destination, or target protocol—the routing protocol that will advertise these newly learned routes.

- Default metrics must also be assigned to the redistributed routes.

- Classful and classless capabilities are also important when redistributing routes. This topic is covered in the section "Route Summarization and Redistributing Between Classful and Classless Protocols."

With these points in mind, we can build our first redistribution configuration using the diagram shown in Figure 8-3.

Route redistribution is constructed in the configuration of the target protocol. We want to advertise routes from another protocol into this protocol. The source protocol is determined by the `redistribute` router configuration command.

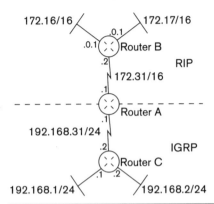

Figure 8-3 *A basic redistribution design, redistributing between RIP and IGRP*

Once the network is configured as depicted in Figure 8-3, we will need to configure redistribution on Router A.

Before redistribution is configured, we should examine the routing table on Router A to ensure that it has learned the routes from the other routers:

```
RouterA#sho ip route
Codes: C - connected, S - static, I - IGRP, R - RIP, M - mobile, B - BGP
       D - EIGRP, EX - EIGRP external, O - OSPF, IA - OSPF inter area
       N1 - OSPF NSSA external type 1, N2 - OSPF NSSA external type 2
       E1 - OSPF external type 1, E2 - OSPF external type 2, E - EGP
       i - IS-IS, L1 - IS-IS level-1, L2 - IS-IS level-2, * - candidate default
       U - per-user static route, o - ODR


Gateway of last resort is not set


C    192.168.31.0/24 is directly connected, Serial1
R    172.17.0.0/16 [120/1] via 172.31.1.2, 00:00:24, Serial0
R    172.16.0.0/16 [120/1] via 172.31.1.2, 00:00:24, Serial0
     172.31.0.0/16 is variably subnetted, 2 subnets, 2 masks
C       172.31.1.2/32 is directly connected, Serial0
C       172.31.0.0/16 is directly connected, Serial0
I    192.168.1.0/24 [100/8486] via 192.168.31.2, 00:01:08, Serial1
I    192.168.2.0/24 [100/8486] via 192.168.31.2, 00:01:08, Serial1
```

We can see here that Router A has learned about routes from Router B via RIP, and Router C via IGRP. Our next step is to configure redistribution on Router A. Once configured, we should see Router B's routes show up on Router C, and vice versa. We will configure redistribution by going into each routing protocol and entering the `redistribute` command followed by the protocol we are redistributing, and the metrics we are assigning. Our configuration is as follows:

```
RouterA(config)#router rip

RouterA(config-router)#redistribute igrp 1 metric 1

RouterA(config-router)#exit

RouterA(config)#router igrp 1

RouterA(config-router)#redistribute rip metric 1000 100 255 1 1500
```

In the RIP routing process, we configured IGRP process 1 for redistribution, and we assigned it a RIP metric of one. In the IGRP 1 process, we enabled redistribution from the RIP routing process, entering metrics for bandwidth, delay, reliability, load, and maximum transmission unit (MTU). These metrics are covered in detail in Chapter 3.

By displaying the routing tables on both Router B and Router C, we can see that the redistributed routes are being advertised:

```
RouterB#sho ip route


R    192.168.31.0/24 [120/1] via 172.31.1.1, 00:00:11, Serial0/0

C    172.17.0.0/16 is directly connected, FastEthernet0/1

C    172.16.0.0/16 is directly connected, FastEthernet0/0

     172.31.0.0/16 is variably subnetted, 2 subnets, 2 masks

C       172.31.1.1/32 is directly connected, Serial0/0

C       172.31.0.0/16 is directly connected, Serial0/0

R    192.168.1.0/24 [120/1] via 172.31.1.1, 00:00:11, Serial0/0

R    192.168.2.0/24 [120/1] via 172.31.1.1, 00:00:11, Serial0/0


RouterC#sho ip route


     192.168.31.0/24 is variably subnetted, 2 subnets, 2 masks

C       192.168.31.1/32 is directly connected, Serial0/0
```

```
C      192.168.31.0/24 is directly connected, Serial0/0

I    172.17.0.0/16 [100/12100] via 192.168.31.1, 00:00:47, Serial0/0

I    172.16.0.0/16 [100/12100] via 192.168.31.1, 00:00:47, Serial0/0

I    172.31.0.0/16 [100/10476] via 192.168.31.1, 00:00:47, Serial0/0

C    192.168.1.0/24 is directly connected, FastEthernet0/0

C    192.168.2.0/24 is directly connected, FastEthernet0/1
```

The configuration on Router A looks like this:

```
router rip
 redistribute igrp 1 metric 1
 network 172.31.0.0


router igrp 1
 redistribute rip metric 1000 100 255 1 1500
 network 192.168.31.0
```

Remember the two points that were covered at the beginning of this section. In the first part of Router A's configuration, RIP is the target routing protocol, and IGRP is the source protocol, meaning routes learned from IGRP are going to be advertised via the RIP process. In the second part of the configuration, IGRP is the target protocol, and RIP is the source protocol.

The type of redistribution we just configured is called *two-way*, or *mutual*, redistribution. When a router redistributes routes in a bidirectional manner between two different routing protocols it is called mutual redistribution. Route filters should be used with mutual redistribution to prevent route feedback. Feedback occurs when a route is redistributed from one routing protocol into a second routing protocol, and then back into the first routing protocol.

One-way redistribution only redistributes routes from one routing protocol into another and is not reciprocated in the other direction. For instance, a router running RIP and IGRP could redistribute the IGRP routes into RIP, but does not redistribute the RIP routes into IGRP.

Which one you use depends on your topology and what you wish to accomplish with redistribution.

Also note that metrics were configured when the source protocol was being specified. Since metrics differ from protocol to protocol, a metric that the target protocol understands must be configured. The exception to this is redistributing between IGRP and EIGRP. These protocols use the same metrics. We will discuss an example of this in the section "Redistributing Between IGRP and EIGRP" later in the chapter.

There are two ways to configure a redistribution metric. In our configuration, we chose to assign a metric directly in the `redistribute` command. When configured like this, the metric will only be applied to routes that are being learned from that particular routing protocol. If we were to redistribute routes from a third routing protocol, a metric would have to be explicitly configured on that protocol also. You can also configure a default metric in the target protocol with the `default-metric` command. When done this way, redistributed routes will be assigned the default metric and do not need to have a metric explicitly configured in the `redistribute` command. You can also use a combination of both commands. Metrics assigned in the `redistribute` command take precedence over metrics assigned with the `default-metric` command. It is also possible to assign metrics using route maps and the `set metric` command. This offers greater flexibility but also adds to the complexity of the metric assignment.

An example configuration utilizing the first two methods for assigning metrics is shown here:

```
router rip
 redistribute igrp 1 metric 4
 redistribute ospf 1
 redistribute eigrp 2 metric 3
 redistribute isis
 default-metric 2
```

Routes learned from OSPF or ISIS will be assigned the default metric of 2, while EIGRP and IGRP will take on the metric values configured in the `redistribute` statement.

The following router output illustrates the various options that are available to the `redistribute` command:

```
RouterA(config-router)#redistribute ?
  bgp        Border Gateway Protocol (BGP)
  connected  Connected
  egp        Exterior Gateway Protocol (EGP)
```

```
eigrp       Enhanced Interior Gateway Routing Protocol (EIGRP)

igrp        Interior Gateway Routing Protocol (IGRP)

isis        ISO IS-IS

iso-igrp    IGRP for OSI networks

mobile      Mobile routes

odr         On Demand stub Routes

ospf        Open Shortest Path First (OSPF)

rip         Routing Information Protocol (RIP)

static      Static routes
```

There are many sources that routes can be redistributed from, as shown by the keywords available to the `redistribute` command. Besides the IP routing protocols, take note of the keywords, `static` and `connected`. The `static` keyword gives you the capability to redistribute static routes that are configured locally on the router. These static routes are those that are configured with the IP address of the next hop router. Static routes that are configured with an interface instead of a next hop IP require the use of the `redistribute connected` command. When a static route is configured with an interface, it is considered by the router to be a directly connected network.

Different routing protocols have different options when configuring the `redistribute` command. For instance, when redistributing from IS-IS, the level from which the routes are to be redistributed must be specified:

```
RouterA(config-router)#redistribute isis ?

  level-1     IS-IS level-1 routes only

  level-1-2   IS-IS level-1 and level-2 routes

  level-2     IS-IS level-2 routes only

  metric      Metric for redistributed routes

  route-map   Route map reference

  <cr>

  WORD        ISO routing area tag
```

When redistributing from OSPF, you can specify whether to redistribute internal or external OSPF routes, and what external type of route to redistribute. This is accomplished using the `match` keyword with the `redistribute` command:

```
RouterA(config-router)#redistribute ospf 1 match ?
  external       Redistribute OSPF external routes
  internal       Redistribute OSPF internal routes
  nssa-external  Redistribute OSPF NSSA external routes


RouterA(config-router)#redistribute ospf 1 match external ?
  1              Redistribute external type 1 routes
  2              Redistribute external type 2 routes
  external       Redistribute OSPF external routes
  internal       Redistribute OSPF internal routes
  match          Redistribution of OSPF routes
  metric         Metric for redistributed routes
  nssa-external  Redistribute OSPF NSSA external routes
  route-map      Route map reference
  <cr>
```

Apart from the metric keyword discussed earlier in this section, you are also given the option of passing routes through a routemap when redistributing. This gives you very granular control over what routes are being redistributed; it is covered later in this chapter in the section "Filtering Routes."

Route Summarization and Redistributing between Classful and Classless Protocols

Configuring route redistribution between classful routing protocols (RIP, IGRP),and classless routing protocols (OSPF, EIGRP, IS-IS, BGP) can be quite a challenge, depending on the topology.

Remember from Chapter 2 that RIP is a classful routing protocol, and it cannot route between discontiguous subnets. Subnetting and supernetting are also a challenge to classful routing protocols. Since a classful routing protocol has no facility to advertise a subnet mask with a network, routes that do not lie on a classful network boundary may be unreachable. The only exception to this is a classful router that has directly connected networks that are not on a classful network boundary. In this situation, the router may learn of other subnetted networks, but only if they have the same subnet mask as its own directly connected networks.

The classless routing protocols have summarization facilities to help redistributing routes into classful routing protocols.

A carefully planned addressing scheme will allow for the effective use of route summarization. Route summarization has several benefits:

- Routes can be summarized at the major network boundaries for redistribution into a classful routing protocol.

- Summarizing routes decreases the size of the IP routing table by advertising fewer routes, thus easing the burden on the router's processing power.

- Route summarization hides internal network instability. When more specific networks become unavailable or malfunction, route summarization prevents this instability from being propagated further.

By default, EIGRP does not advertise the subnetworks of one major network into another major network. This is important to remember if routes are not being redistributed as you would expect them to be. You can disable this behavior with the no auto-summary command in the EIGRP router configuration mode.

Unlike the other classless routing protocols, EIGRP summary addresses are configured on the interface instead of in the routing process. This gives you the capability to advertise different summary routes from different interfaces. An example of this is shown here:

```
RouterA(config-if)#ip summary-address eigrp 1 172.16.0.0255.255.0.0
```

This command will now advertise one route pointing to 172.16/16, instead of the individual, more specific routes. This command is very useful when advertising into a classful routing protocol. Assuming that no IP addressing conflicts occur, you could use it to summarize a set of networks into one major network, and advertise it to the classful routing protocol with a prefix it understands.

When summarizing addresses into IS-IS, the level to which the summarizations are advertised must be configured. Similarly, when redistributing IS-IS routes into another protocol, you must specify the IS-IS level from which the routes are redistributed. For example, a network that exists entirely inside an IS-IS domain may only need to learn about the Level 1 IS-IS routes, and the Level 2 routes can be blocked.

For RIP, which does not have a summarization command, configure a static route consisting of the desired summary address and the address of the next hop router, and add the `redistribute static` command to the RIP routing process.

Filtering Routes

More often than not, you will not be configuring redistribution on routers to redistribute all of the routes they have learned. You will want to filter routes so that only the routes that you are interested in are being redistributed.

This accomplishes two things:

- When redistributing routes, if care is not taken as to which routes are redistributed, there is a high probability that routing loops will occur. By limiting the redistributed routes to a few that are deliberately configured, you are adding to the stability of your internetwork.

- Route filtering also reduces the number of routes a router has to keep track of, thus conserving its resources and processing time.

There are a couple of different options when configuring route filters: access lists and route maps.

Using access lists

By combining access lists with the `distribute-list` command, it is possible to filter routes from specific routing protocols when doing route redistribution. To filter routes using `distribute-lists` when redistributing routes, first configure an access list controlling the routes that you are concerned with. This can be either a `deny` or `permit` action, depending on what your redistribution needs are. The next step is to enter the `distribute-list` command in the routing process that you are redistributing routes into. The syntax is slightly different than configuring a distribute list to filter routes advertised out an interface:

```
distribute-list access-list-number out protocol
```

The distribute list must use the `out` keyword because it is not possible to filter routes into a protocol from which you are exporting routes. Next, instead of an interface, you specify the protocol that is exporting the routes.

The routes from this protocol pass through the access list filter before they are imported into the routing process.

An example of code is shown here:

```
router eigrp 1
 redistribute ospf 1 metric 1000 100 255 1 2500
 network 172.16.0.0
 network 172.17.0.0
 network 172.18.0.0
 distribute-list 10 out ospf 1

router ospf 1
 redistribute eigrp 1 metric 20 metric-type 1 subnets
 network 10.0.0.0 0.255.255.255 area 0
 distribute-list 20 out eigrp 1

access-list 10 permit 10.1.0.0 0.0.255.255
access-list 10 permit 10.3.0.0 0.0.255.255
access-list 10 deny any
access-list 20 permit 172.16.0.0 0.0.255.255
access-list 20 permit 172.17.0.0 0.0.255.255
access-list 20 deny any
```

In this sample configuration, we are filtering routes redistributed between an EIGRP routing process and an OSPF process. The EIGRP process includes the command `distribute-list 10 out ospf 1`. This applies access list 10 to any routes that are redistributed from OSPF. By examining access list 10, you can see that only two networks are going to be allowed to be redistributed: 10.1/24 and 10.3/24. Any other routes will be denied. We configured a deny any access list entry in access list 10, but remember that access lists contain an implicit deny any.

If we wanted to only deny a particular route, and allow all others, we would need to explicitly permit all routes in the last entry:

```
access-list 30 deny 172.16.0.0 0.0.255.255
access-list 30 permit any
```

When combined with the `distribute-list` command, this access list would deny 172.16/24, but would permit all other routes to be redistributed.

Likewise, the routes redistributed into the EIGRP domain would be limited to 172.16/16 and 172.17/16 as configured in the `distribute-list` command.

Using access lists and the `distribute-list` command is very useful for filtering routes, but when you want to be more sophisticated by matching on criteria other than the destination network, or you want to modify routing information when it is redistributed, you need to make use of a route map.

Using route maps

Route maps provide a much more flexible means of controlling route redistribution than distribute lists. Route maps were explained in Chapter 6, but this section focuses on the use of route maps with redistribution.

Route maps offer a lot of power for controlling route redistributions. The following samples of the IOS 'context-sensitive help' show the commands that are available with route maps. By examining these, you can see that they offer a lot of granularity when filtering routes. They can be used to merely filter routes, similar to what we demonstrated using `distribute-lists`, but more importantly, route maps enable you to modify the routing information as it is being imported into the target protocol.

The `match` commands are used to examine the route, looking for specific criteria in order to perform some specified action. The `match` commands available in the Cisco IOS are shown here:

```
RouterSouth(config-route-map)#match ?
  as-path     Match BGP AS path list
  clns        CLNS information
  community   Match BGP community list
  interface   Match first hop interface of route
  ip          IP specific information
  length      Packet length
  metric      Match metric of route
  route-type  Match route-type of route
  tag         Match tag of route
```

Many of the match commands have additional options, as shown by the context-sensitive help of the `match ip` route map command:

```
RouterSouth(config-route-map)#match ip ?
  address       Match address of route or match packet
  next-hop      Match next-hop address of route
  route-source  Match advertising source address of route
```

After the route map has found a match, you can then use the `set` command to modify the route in some fashion. Some of the more useful set commands are `set metric, set metric-type` and `set ip next-hop`. A list of the available set commands is shown here.

```
RouterSouth(config-route-map)#set ?
  as-path           Prepend string for a BGP AS-path attribute
  automatic-tag     Automatically compute TAG value
  clns              OSI summary address
  comm-list         set BGP community list (for deletion)
  community         BGP community attribute
  dampening         Set BGP route flap dampening parameters
  default           Set default information
  interface         Output interface
  ip                IP specific information
  level             Where to import route
  local-preference  BGP local preference path attribute
  metric            Metric value for destination routing protocol
  metric-type       Type of metric for destination routing protocol
  origin            BGP origin code
  tag               Tag value for destination routing protocol
  weight            BGP weight for routing table
```

Like the `match` commands, many `set` commands have additional options:

```
RouterSouth(config-route-map)#set ip ?
  default   Set default information
  next-hop  Next hop address
```

```
precedence  Set precedence field

tos         Set type of service field
```

To configure a route map with redistribution, use the following command syntax in the target protocol:

```
redistribute source-protocol route-map route-map-tag
```

In order to demonstrate the use of route maps, we will construct the network that is illustrated in Figure 8-4.

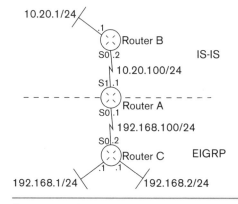

Figure 8-4 *This network utilizes route maps to control redistributed routes.*

In this example, we will redistribute the EIGRP routes into IS-IS. When we do that, we are going to take advantage of the capabilities of a route map and modify the level of IS-IS routes that these redistributed routes are translated to. We want to redistribute network 192.168.1/24 as an IS-IS Level 1 route, and 192.168.2/24 as an IS-IS Level 2 route.

Once our network is configured, we need to build the route map. To do this, we must first create the access lists that will be used by our route map. Since we are only matching against the network address of the destination route, we need only configure standard access lists that correspond to each network. The configuration would look like this:

```
access-list 1 permit 192.168.1.0 0.0.0.255
access-list 2 permit 192.168.2.0 0.0.0.255
```

After the access lists are configured, we can create the route map. A route map is configured with the `route-map` global configuration command. The syntax for the command looks like this:

```
route-map route-map-tag permit/deny sequence-number
```

For this demonstration, we will create a route map with the name CHANGELEVEL, which is a descriptive name reflecting what the route map does. Once this command is entered, we are greeted with the route map configuration prompt:

```
RouterA(config)#route-map CHANGELEVEL permit 10

RouterA(config-route-map)#
```

From here, we can enter our match and set commands:

```
RouterA(config-route-map)#match ip address 1

RouterA(config-route-map)#set level level-1
```

Since we are performing two different actions, we want two sequences to the route map:

```
RouterA(config)#route-map CHANGELEVEL permit 20

RouterA(config-route-map)#match ip address 2

RouterA(config-route-map)#set level level-2
```

Route maps are similar to access lists in that if a default action is not explicitly configured, all remaining traffic will be denied. Since we want any other route that passes through this list to be treated normally, we create another permit sequence to this access list, but we do not need to configure any match or set commands.

Once we are finished configuring Router A for redistribution with a route-map, the configuration looks like this:

```
interface Serial1

 ip address 10.20.100.1 255.255.255.0

ip router isis


router eigrp 1

 network 192.168.100.0
```

```
router isis

 redistribute eigrp 1 metric 10 route-map CHANGELEVEL metric-type internal

 level-2

 net 01.0000.0c5d.6f99.00


access-list 1 permit 192.168.1.0 0.0.0.255

access-list 2 permit 192.168.2.0 0.0.0.255

route-map CHANGELEVEL permit 10

 match ip address 1

 set level level-1


route-map CHANGELEVEL permit 20

 match ip address 2

 set level level-2


route-map CHANGELEVEL permit 30
```

Without the `route-map` command applied, the routing table of Router B looks like this:

```
RouterB#sho ip route

Codes: C - connected, S - static, I - IGRP, R - RIP, M - mobile, B - BGP

       D - EIGRP, EX - EIGRP external, O - OSPF, IA - OSPF inter area

       N1 - OSPF NSSA external type 1, N2 - OSPF NSSA external type 2

       E1 - OSPF external type 1, E2 - OSPF external type 2, E - EGP

       i - IS-IS, L1 - IS-IS level-1, L2 - IS-IS level-2, * - candidate default

       U - per-user static route, o - ODR


Gateway of last resort is not set


     10.0.0.0/24 is subnetted, 2 subnets

C       10.20.1.0 is directly connected, Ethernet0

C       10.20.100.0 is directly connected, Serial0

i L2 192.168.1.0/24 [115/20] via 10.20.100.1, Serial0

i L2 192.168.2.0/24 [115/20] via 10.20.100.1, Serial0
```

```
         192.168.100.0/24 is variably subnetted, 2 subnets, 2 masks
i L2     192.168.100.0/24 [115/20] via 10.20.100.1, Serial0
i L2     192.168.100.2/32 [115/20] via 10.20.100.1, Serial0
```

Notice that without the route map, all routes are redistributed into IS-IS as Level 2 routes.

To prove that our route map works, we can compare the routing table before the route map to the routing table after the route map. You can see the result of applying our route map to the redistribution command:

```
RouterB#sho ip route
Codes: C - connected, S - static, I - IGRP, R - RIP, M - mobile, B - BGP
       D - EIGRP, EX - EIGRP external, O - OSPF, IA - OSPF inter area
       N1 - OSPF NSSA external type 1, N2 - OSPF NSSA external type 2
       E1 - OSPF external type 1, E2 - OSPF external type 2, E - EGP
       i - IS-IS, L1 - IS-IS level-1, L2 - IS-IS level-2, * - candidate default
       U - per-user static route, o - ODR

Gateway of last resort is not set

         10.0.0.0/24 is subnetted, 2 subnets
C        10.20.1.0 is directly connected, Ethernet0
C        10.20.100.0 is directly connected, Serial0
i L1 192.168.1.0/24 [115/20] via 10.20.100.1, Serial0
i L2 192.168.2.0/24 [115/20] via 10.20.100.1, Serial0
         192.168.100.0/24 is variably subnetted, 2 subnets, 2 masks
i L2     192.168.100.0/24 [115/20] via 10.20.100.1, Serial0
i L2     192.168.100.2/32 [115/20] via 10.20.100.1, Serial0
```

Router B's routing table shows that our route map example indeed works. The network 192.168.1/24 is being advertised as an IS-IS Level-1 route, and 192.168.2/24 is being advertised as an IS-IS Level-2 route.

It is easy to tell from this example how flexible and powerful route maps are. Using them enables you to fine-tune your network and route redistribution.

Redistributing into OSPF

Redistributing routes into OSPF has its own challenges, as you will see in this section.

By default, OSPF will only redistribute networks that exist on a class boundary, similar to the auto-summary performed by EIGRP. When redistributing into OSPF, it is important to include the `subnets` keyword. Specifying `subnets` tells the routing process to include all networks, even those that have been further subnetted.

We will use the network shown in Figure 8-5 to illustrate the impact of the `subnets` keyword when redistributing into OSPF.

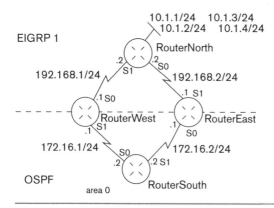

Figure 8-5 *Redistributing from EIGRP into OSPF*

In Figure 8-5, RouterWest is redistributing routes from EIGRP into OSPF, and these OSPF routes are being received by RouterSouth.

RouterWest's configuration looks like this:

```
router eigrp 1
 network 192.168.1.0

router ospf 1
 redistribute eigrp 1 metric 10
 network 172.16.0.0 0.0.255.255 area 0
```

The IP routing information shows the status of RouterSouth's routing table, when the `subnets` keyword is not used during redistribution:

```
RouterSouth>sho ip route
Codes: C - connected, S - static, I - IGRP, R - RIP, M - mobile, B - BGP
       D - EIGRP, EX - EIGRP external, O - OSPF, IA - OSPF inter area
       N1 - OSPF NSSA external type 1, N2 - OSPF NSSA external type 2
       E1 - OSPF external type 1, E2 - OSPF external type 2, E - EGP
       i - IS-IS, L1 - IS-IS level-1, L2 - IS-IS level-2, * - candidate default
       U - per-user static route, o - ODR


Gateway of last resort is not set


     172.16.0.0/16 is variably subnetted, 4 subnets, 2 masks
C       172.16.1.1/32 is directly connected, Serial0
C       172.16.1.0/24 is directly connected, Serial0
C       172.16.2.0/24 is directly connected, Serial1
C       172.16.2.1/32 is directly connected, Serial1
O E2 192.168.1.0/24 [110/10] via 172.16.1.1, 00:00:57, Serial0
O E2 192.168.2.0/24 [110/10] via 172.16.1.1, 00:00:57, Serial0
O E2 192.168.3.0/24 [110/10] via 172.16.1.1, 00:00:57, Serial0
```

Some versions of the Cisco Internetwork Operating System (IOS) will also warn you when you have not added the `subnets` keyword.

```
RouterWest(config-router)#redistribute eigrp 1 metric 10
% Only classful networks will be redistributed
```

However, when the `subnets` keyword is added, we will see the appearance of the 10.1.x network routes that do not exist on a classful network boundary.

```
router eigrp 1
 network 192.168.1.0
!
router ospf 1
 redistribute eigrp 1 metric 10 subnets
 network 172.16.0.0 0.0.255.255 area 0
```

RouterWest's configuration has been changed, adding the `subnets` keyword as we see above. Now the rest of the EIGRP routes show up in the OSPF routing table:

```
RouterSouth>sho ip route
Codes: C - connected, S - static, I - IGRP, R - RIP, M - mobile, B - BGP
       D - EIGRP, EX - EIGRP external, O - OSPF, IA - OSPF inter area
       N1 - OSPF NSSA external type 1, N2 - OSPF NSSA external type 2
       E1 - OSPF external type 1, E2 - OSPF external type 2, E - EGP
       i - IS-IS, L1 - IS-IS level-1, L2 - IS-IS level-2, * - candidate default
       U - per-user static route, o - ODR

Gateway of last resort is not set

     172.16.0.0/16 is variably subnetted, 4 subnets, 2 masks
C       172.16.1.1/32 is directly connected, Serial0
C       172.16.1.0/24 is directly connected, Serial0
C       172.16.2.0/24 is directly connected, Serial1
C       172.16.2.1/32 is directly connected, Serial1
     10.0.0.0/24 is subnetted, 4 subnets
O E2    10.1.3.0 [110/10] via 172.16.1.1, 00:00:30, Serial0
O E2    10.1.2.0 [110/10] via 172.16.1.1, 00:00:30, Serial0
O E2    10.1.1.0 [110/10] via 172.16.1.1, 00:00:30, Serial0
O E2    10.1.4.0 [110/10] via 172.16.1.1, 00:00:30, Serial0
     192.168.1.0/24 is variably subnetted, 2 subnets, 2 masks
O E2    192.168.1.0/24 [110/10] via 172.16.1.1, 00:05:53, Serial0
O E2    192.168.1.2/32 [110/10] via 172.16.1.1, 00:00:30, Serial0
     192.168.2.0/24 is variably subnetted, 2 subnets, 2 masks
O E2    192.168.2.0/24 [110/10] via 172.16.1.1, 00:05:55, Serial0
O E2    192.168.2.1/32 [110/10] via 172.16.1.1, 00:00:32, Serial0
O E2 192.168.3.0/24 [110/10] via 172.16.1.1, 00:05:55, Serial0
```

Notice that the redistributed routes are marked as OSPF Type 2 external routes. By default, when a route is redistributed into OSPF, it is tagged as a Type 2 external route. Recall from Chapter 4 that Type 2 external routes do not accumulate additional cost when they are traversing the OSPF network.

For large OSPF networks doing redistribution, this can result in suboptimal routing. In general, you want to make sure that you are redistributing routes into OSPF as Type 1 external routes, which have their metric modified each time they pass through an OSPF router. This can be accomplished by using the following command when configuring redistribution:

```
RouterEast(config-router)#redistribute eigrp 1 metric-type 1
```

This command redistributes EIGRP routes into the OSPF process, and sets the routes to Type 1 external routes.

To illustrate this, we will again use the network from Figure 8-5. This time, both RouterEast and RouterWest will be redistributing EIGRP routes into OSPF. First we will look at the routing table of RouterSouth when Type 2 routes are used; then we will compare this to the routing table with the routes redistributed as Type 1 routes.

Here is the configuration of RouterEast:

```
router eigrp 1
 network 192.168.2.0


router ospf 1
 redistribute eigrp 1 metric 40 subnets
 network 172.16.0.0 0.0.255.255 area 0
```

A metric of 40 was assigned to these routes to reflect the distance between RouterNorth and RouterEast.

This is the configuration of RouterWest. The distance between Router-West and RouterNorth is shorter, so a metric of 10 was assigned to these routes:

```
router eigrp 1
 network 192.168.1.0
!
router ospf 1
 redistribute eigrp 1 metric 10 subnets
 network 172.16.0.0 0.0.255.255 area 0
```

Look at the costs associated with the links to RouterSouth in Figure 8-5. From the diagram, it is obvious that we would want traffic that is destined for any of the 10.1.x networks reachable through RouterNorth to flow through RouterEast. However, since we are redistributing these routes as OSPF external Type 2 routes, the links to RouterSouth are not going to be taken into account, and the path to RouterWest will be taken. This is reinforced by looking at the routing table of RouterSouth:

```
     10.0.0.0/24 is subnetted, 4 subnets
O E2    10.1.3.0 [110/10] via 172.16.1.1, 00:02:54, Serial0
O E2    10.1.2.0 [110/10] via 172.16.1.1, 00:02:54, Serial0
O E2    10.1.1.0 [110/10] via 172.16.1.1, 00:02:54, Serial0
O E2    10.1.4.0 [110/10] via 172.16.1.1, 00:02:54, Serial0
```

Note that the next hop router for these routes is RouterWest, and that the metric of these routes is the value that was assigned to them during redistribution.

If we change the redistribution to import these routes as Type 1 routes, we see a difference in the routing table of RouterSouth.

RouterWest's OSPF configuration now looks like this:

```
router ospf 1
 redistribute eigrp 1 metric 10 metric-type 1 subnets
 network 172.16.0.0 0.0.255.255 area 0
```

And RouterEast's configuration has changed similarly:

```
router ospf 1
 redistribute eigrp 1 metric 40 metric-type 1 subnets
 network 172.16.0.0 0.0.255.255 area 0
```

The changes we have made should be reflected in the routing table of RouterSouth. If everything goes as planned, the routes to the 10.1.x networks should now go through RouterEast, and by looking at the cost associated with the link in Figure 8-5, the cost of each path should be 140.

These routing entries from the routing table of RouterSouth will verify our assumption:

```
     10.0.0.0/24 is subnetted, 4 subnets
O E1    10.1.3.0 [110/140] via 172.16.2.1, 00:00:12, Serial1

O E1    10.1.2.0 [110/140] via 172.16.2.1, 00:00:12, Serial1

O E1    10.1.1.0 [110/140] via 172.16.2.1, 00:00:12, Serial1

O E1    10.1.4.0 [110/140] via 172.16.2.1, 00:00:12, Serial1
```

The values of the metric and next-hop router affirm that everything has worked the way that we expected it.

Routers that are redistributing routes into OSPF are considered Autonomous System Boundary Routers (ASBRs). This is important depending on where the redistribution is configured. For instance, redistribution cannot be configured on a router in a stub area. External routes are advertised in Type 5 LSAs, and these LSA are not propagated through a stub area. A workaround to this is to configure a not-so-stubby area (NSSA). This will then redistribute the external routes as Type 7 LSAs. Type 7 LSAs can then be converted to Type 5 LSAs at the NSSA ABR, and advertised to the rest of the OSPF domain.

For a more detailed discussion of LSAs and area types, see Chapter 4.

Redistributing between IGRP and EIGRP

Since IGRP and EIGRP understand each other's metrics, a default metric does not have to be configured when redistributing between these two protocols. This is also true when redistributing between different processes of the same protocol; for example, two IGRP processes on the same router are redistributing each other's routes, or two EIGRP processes on the same router are redistributing each other's routes.

Since the EIGRP metrics are larger than IGRP metrics, an IGRP metric is multiplied by a constant of 256 when compared to EIGRP, to make the metrics comparable.

EIGRP and IGRP processes running on the same router with the same AS number will also automatically redistribute routes between each other. When EIGRP and IGRP perform automatic redistribution, AD will be ignored, and only the metrics will be taken into account. This is possible because IGRP and EIGRP use the same metrics.

We will demonstrate this using Figure 8-6 as an example.

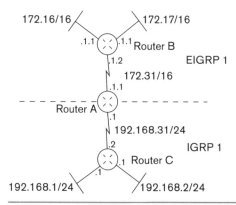

172.16/16   172.17/16

.1.1   .1.1 Router B

.1.2   EIGRP 1

172.31/16

.1.1

Router A

.1

192.168.31/24

.2   IGRP 1

.1 Router C

192.168.1/24   192.168.2/24

Figure 8-6 *Redistributing between IGRP and EIGRP processes with the same Autonomous System number*

In the network in Figure 8-6, Router A is running both EIGRP and IGRP with the same process number. In IGRP and EIGRP, this is also known as the *Autonomous System Number*. The configuration on Router A looks like this:

```
router eigrp 1
 network 172.31.0.0


router igrp 1
 network 192.168.31.0
```

Notice that no redistribution has been explicitly configured in either routing process. But by looking at the routing tables of Router B and Router C, we can see that routes are still being redistributed on Router A:

```
RouterB#sho ip route
Codes: C - connected, S - static, I - IGRP, R - RIP, M - mobile, B - BGP
       D - EIGRP, EX - EIGRP external, O - OSPF, IA - OSPF inter area
       N1 - OSPF NSSA external type 1, N2 - OSPF NSSA external type 2
       E1 - OSPF external type 1, E2 - OSPF external type 2, E - EGP
       i - IS-IS, L1 - IS-IS level-1, L2 - IS-IS level-2, ia - IS-IS inter area
       * - candidate default, U - per-user static route, o - ODR
       P - periodic downloaded static route
```

```
Gateway of last resort is not set


D EX 192.168.31.0/24 [170/2681856] via 172.31.1.1, 00:05:33, Serial0/0

C    172.17.0.0/16 is directly connected, FastEthernet0/1

C    172.16.0.0/16 is directly connected, FastEthernet0/0

C    172.31.0.0/16 is directly connected, Serial0/0

D EX 192.168.1.0/24 [170/2684416] via 172.31.1.1, 00:05:33, Serial0/0

D EX 192.168.2.0/24 [170/2684416] via 172.31.1.1, 00:05:33, Serial0/0
```

In EIGRP, redistributed routes are tagged as EIGRP external routes. In the preceding IP routing table printout, the routes being redistributed from IGRP are annotated as being external routes.

```
RouterC#sho ip route

Codes: C - connected, S - static, I - IGRP, R - RIP, M - mobile, B - BGP

       D - EIGRP, EX - EIGRP external, O - OSPF, IA - OSPF inter area

       N1 - OSPF NSSA external type 1, N2 - OSPF NSSA external type 2

       E1 - OSPF external type 1, E2 - OSPF external type 2, E - EGP

       i - IS-IS, L1 - IS-IS level-1, L2 - IS-IS level-2, ia - IS-IS inter area

       * - candidate default, U - per-user static route, o - ODR

       P - periodic downloaded static route


Gateway of last resort is not set


C    192.168.31.0/24 is directly connected, Serial0/0

I    172.17.0.0/16 [100/10486] via 192.168.31.1, 00:00:54, Serial0/0

I    172.16.0.0/16 [100/10486] via 192.168.31.1, 00:00:54, Serial0/0

I    172.31.0.0/16 [100/10476] via 192.168.31.1, 00:00:54, Serial0/0

C    192.168.1.0/24 is directly connected, FastEthernet0/0

C    192.168.2.0/24 is directly connected, FastEthernet0/1
```

Router B's networks are also appearing in the routing table of Router C due to the automatic redistribution on Router A. IGRP does not distinguish between internal and external routes, so the tags that were displayed with the EIGRP routes on Router B are not present.

If we were to change the IGRP domain number to 2 instead of 1, we would no longer see this automatic redistribution. Here is the configuration of Router A after this change:

```
router eigrp 1
 network 172.31.0.0

router igrp 2
 network 192.168.31.0
```

And now the routes no longer show up on Router B and Router C.

```
RouterB#sho ip route
Codes: C - connected, S - static, I - IGRP, R - RIP, M - mobile, B - BGP
       D - EIGRP, EX - EIGRP external, O - OSPF, IA - OSPF inter area
       N1 - OSPF NSSA external type 1, N2 - OSPF NSSA external type 2
       E1 - OSPF external type 1, E2 - OSPF external type 2, E - EGP
       i - IS-IS, L1 - IS-IS level-1, L2 - IS-IS level-2, ia - IS-IS inter area
       * - candidate default, U - per-user static route, o - ODR
       P - periodic downloaded static route


Gateway of last resort is not set


C    172.17.0.0/16 is directly connected, FastEthernet0/1
C    172.16.0.0/16 is directly connected, FastEthernet0/0
     172.31.0.0/16 is variably subnetted, 2 subnets, 2 masks
C       172.31.0.1/32 is directly connected, Serial0/0
C       172.31.0.0/16 is directly connected, Serial0/0


RouterC#sho ip route
Codes: C - connected, S - static, I - IGRP, R - RIP, M - mobile, B - BGP
       D - EIGRP, EX - EIGRP external, O - OSPF, IA - OSPF inter area
       N1 - OSPF NSSA external type 1, N2 - OSPF NSSA external type 2
       E1 - OSPF external type 1, E2 - OSPF external type 2, E - EGP
       i - IS-IS, L1 - IS-IS level-1, L2 - IS-IS level-2, ia - IS-IS inter area
       * - candidate default, U - per-user static route, o - ODR
       P - periodic downloaded static route


Gateway of last resort is not set
```

```
     192.168.31.0/24 is variably subnetted, 2 subnets, 2 masks
C       192.168.31.1/32 is directly connected, Serial0/0
C       192.168.31.0/24 is directly connected, Serial0/0
C     192.168.1.0/24 is directly connected, FastEthernet0/0
C     192.168.2.0/24 is directly connected, FastEthernet0/1
```

It is important to be aware of the automatic redistribution between EIGRP and IGRP. Be careful not to inadvertently configure both routing protocols with the same AS number on the same router, if you do not want to be redistributing routes between them.

Redistribution and BGP

It is usually considered a bad idea to redistribute routes between BGP and an interior gateway protocol. There are two reasons for this. Redistributing your IGP routes into BGP can cause global instability if one of your IGP routes starts malfunctioning. Similarly, when redistributing BGP routes into your IGP, instability in the global BGP routing tables can have adverse effects on your internal network by causing frequent updates.

When you want to advertise your routes into BGP, list these networks in the BGP process with the network router configuration command. Any routes specified with the network command that exist in the IP routing table are advertised into BGP.

If your design requires redistribution into BGP, you can redistribute into BGP in two ways — from a static route or from a dynamic routing protocol. Static routes are the preferred method, since they are stable, and they allow more control over what is advertised.

If you do redistribute into BGP, however, remember that due to the administrative distance, BGP is susceptible to the same routing loops that we discussed earlier. You may be advertising your IGP routes into BGP, and a second router may be learning routes from both BGP and your IGP. Since BGP has a more favorable administrative distance, it will actually route to these destinations externally, instead of the more efficient path inside your network.

The "origin" attribute discussed in Chapter 6 is very important when dealing with redistribution into BGP. This is also helpful for troubleshooting. When advertised with the network command, routes have their origin attribute set to IGP. When redistributed from another protocol into

BGP, this attribute has a value of incomplete. EGP routes redistributed into BGP have an origin of EGP.

In general, you do not want to redistribute most BGP routes into your IGP. A common design is to redistribute one or two routes and to make them exterior routes in the IGP, or have your BGP speaker generate a default route for your autonomous system. When redistributing from BGP into IGP, only the routes learned using EBGP get redistributed.

Troubleshooting

Troubleshooting route redistribution involves using a lot of the protocol-specific show commands and debug commands that have been covered in previous chapters. Check the contents of the routing table of each router to determine where the problem has occurred. Watch the debug messages of the routing protocols, looking for anything out of the ordinary. Make certain that the router that is performing the redistribution is actually receiving the routes that you want redistributed. The router cannot redistribute routes that it does not know about.

It is important to remember the classless and classful nature of the routing protocols that are being used. Are you redistributing into RIP a route with a subnet that RIP doesn't understand?

Debugging specific protocols may also be necessary when troubleshooting redistribution. The syntax for this is shown here:

```
debug ip protocol options
```

or

```
debug isis options
```

For instance, in the following debug output, you can see that there is a problem sending IS-IS hellos (IIH).

```
RouterA#debug isis adj-packets
IS-IS Adjacency related packets debugging is on
00:02:18: ISIS-Adj: Encapsulation failed on serial IIH (Serial0)
```

Without using debugging, we would only notice that an IS-IS neighbor adjacency is not being established. Using the debugging command, we can tell that there is a problem encapsulating the Connectionless-mode Network Service (CLNS) packet for transmission out interface Serial0. On closer inspection of the router configuration, it becomes evident that PPP encapsulation is being used on that interface, which is incompatible with CLNS. Once encapsulation is changed to High-level Data Link Control (HDLC), the adjacency forms normally.

There are many options available with the debug commands. It is not feasible to cover all the options here, and the reader is encouraged to become familiar with them. Try reading the *Cisco Router Troubleshooting Handbook* by Peter Rybaczyk (IDG Books Worldwide, Inc.)Remember to approach debugging with care. Debugging router operations places a burden on the router, so be careful you don't interfere with normal routing operations.

Understanding the IP Routing Table

It is important to understand the route selection process and the IP routing table. The router may be aware of several routes to a particular destination, but only the route that meets the best criteria will actually be entered into the routing table. The best route is determined by comparing metrics, policies, or administrative distances.

The IP route table displays a lot of information pertinent to route redistribution, namely, the codes that are assigned to routes. There are quite a few available codes to familiarize yourself with. Let's examine this routing table from one of our previous examples:

```
RouterB#sho ip route

Codes: C - connected, S - static, I - IGRP, R - RIP, M - mobile, B - BGP

       D - EIGRP, EX - EIGRP external, O - OSPF, IA - OSPF inter area

       N1 - OSPF NSSA external type 1, N2 - OSPF NSSA external type 2

       E1 - OSPF external type 1, E2 - OSPF external type 2, E - EGP

       i - IS-IS, L1 - IS-IS level-1, L2 - IS-IS level-2, ia - IS-IS inter area

       * - candidate default, U - per-user static route, o - ODR

       P - periodic downloaded static route


Gateway of last resort is not set


     192.168.31.0/24 is variably subnetted, 2 subnets, 2 masks
```

```
D EX    192.168.31.2/32 [170/2681856] via 172.31.1.1, 00:03:16, Serial0/0

D EX    192.168.31.0/24 [170/2681856] via 172.31.1.1, 00:03:16, Serial0/0

C    172.17.0.0/16 is directly connected, FastEthernet0/1

C    172.16.0.0/16 is directly connected, FastEthernet0/0

     172.31.0.0/16 is variably subnetted, 2 subnets, 2 masks

C       172.31.0.1/32 is directly connected, Serial0/0

C       172.31.0.0/16 is directly connected, Serial0/0

D EX 192.168.1.0/24 [170/2684416] via 172.31.1.1, 00:03:16, Serial0/0

D EX 192.168.2.0/24 [170/2684416] via 172.31.1.1, 00:03:16, Serial0/0
```

A lot of the information here is pertinent to troubleshooting redistribution. The far-left column tells us the means by which the router learned of the route. This corresponds to the codes listed at the start of the listing. Using these codes, we can see that we have routes learned both from connected routes and EIGRP external routes.

The next portion of each routing table entry lists the actual network and its subnet mask prefix. Because we are doing redistribution to learn about these routes, we want to make sure the correct route and mask are being advertised. A missing route could be the result of a misconfigured redistribution or, in the case of classless to classful redistribution, a subnet mask that is not understood by the router.

The portion of the routing table entry in brackets is comprised of the administrative distance of the route, followed by the route metric. By comparing the administrative distance with Table 8.1, we can see that the AD value matches up with the default administrative distance of an external EIGRP route. The composite metric of EIGRP is also shown here. The metric was carried through the redistribution process from IGRP and this metric was further modified by EIGRP.

Next is the IP address of the next-hop router. This information can be used to follow the flow of traffic, in order to trace incorrectly routed traffic.

Displayed next is the amount of time that the route has been in the routing table. This can be an indication of the stability of a route. A short lifetime can be indicative of a route that is constantly disappearing and reappearing in the routing table.

Finally, the interface on which traffic to that destination is transmitted is displayed.

When a route is discovered to be a problem, it may be reflected in the routing table. This extract from a routing table shows that a problem has occurred:

```
R    10.0.0.0/8 is possibly down,routing via 192.168.1.2,Serial0
```

The router has noticed a routing malfunction, and the route has been put into holddown to prevent the router from learning incorrect information.

External Routes

An *external route* is one that has been learned from some means other than the routing processes on the router, usually through redistribution. RIP does not distinguish between internally and externally learned routes. Although this simplifies the configuration process, it can be a hindrance when trying to troubleshoot routing issues.

EIGRP, OSPF, and IS-IS track routes according to where they have been learned. These protocols assign an "external" tag to any route that has been learned from someplace other than its routing domain. This is helpful when troubleshooting routing issues. A problem route marked "external" can be tracked to the redistribution boundary, where an issue may lie in the routing domain that it is being redistributed from.

Wrap-Up

Redistribution is easy enough to configure, but it is difficult to fully understand the ramifications of redistribution designs. Be sure to plan your redistribution implementations wisely and thoroughly. Misbehaving routes can lead to suboptimal routing, or quite possibly, routing loops, and the inability to reach some destinations at all.

Due to the volatility inherent in route redistribution, it is important that you keep tight controls on where the routes are being advertised. Make sure that you are only redistributing the routes that you need to, filtering out any others, and using route summaries when possible to aid in the stability and efficiency of the routing table.

Chapter 9

Dial-on-Demand Routing

Despite the constantly shrinking costs of data services, many organizations cannot afford to lease dedicated connections between all of their locations. This is especially true for large organizations with many sites, small organizations with budget limits, and any organizations with offices in hard-to-reach areas where dedicated data services may be expensive or unavailable. For these situations, dial services are often used in place of a dedicated connection.

A dial-up connection can offer significant savings over d edicated connections. In most cases, organizations pay based on the usage time of the connection. Therefore, if the link is down when not in use, it does not cost anything at those times. At the same time, most organizations do not want to sacrifice functionality by implementing a dial-based connection. For this reason, dial-on-demand routing (DDR) is important. It gives organizations access to full routing capabilities, while providing the cost advantages of a nondedicated connection.

Configuring ISDN

In order to take advantage of the DDR features in Cisco routers, you first need to set up a dial-up connection of some sort. Several different types of dial-up connections exist, but one of the most common is *Integrated Subscriber Digital Network* (*ISDN*). ISDN offers dial features similar to those of a traditional phone line, but it offers greater bandwidth than an analog modem can achieve. In addition, the base cost of ISDN is relatively low because providers charge based on usage. These properties make ISDN a good candidate for use in DDR environments. Because of its widespread use for DDR, this section focuses only on ISDN. Bear in mind that the DDR configurations that follow in the later sections can usually be applied to other types of dial-capable interfaces, as well as ISDN.

Many configuration commands are associated with ISDN. The purpose of this section is to provide enough information to create an ISDN connection. It covers the basic commands required to make a successful ISDN connection, along with some additional common features, such as authentication. This is not intended to be a thorough discussion of ISDN, but the information contained here should suffice to begin most installations, and it may be enough to completely configure many installations.

Basic ISDN Configuration

Only a few commands are required to make an ISDN connection operate correctly. First of all, you need to specify the ISDN switch type that your carrier uses. Because the various switch types communicate in different ways, it is critical to your ISDN setup to configure this correctly.

To configure the ISDN switch type, use the following command in global configuration mode:

```
R1(config)#isdn switch-type ?
  basic-1tr6     1TR6 switch type for Germany
  basic-5ess     AT&T 5ESS switch type for the U.S.
  basic-dms100   Northern DMS-100 switch type
  basic-net3     NET3 switch type for UK and Europe
  basic-ni       National ISDN switch type
  basic-ts013    TS013 switch type for Australia
  ntt            NTT switch type for Japan
  vn3            VN3 and VN4 switch types for France
  <cr>
```

Only a few of the switch types available are used in the United States. If you are working on a router outside the United States, only one switch type may be available in that area, making the choice much easier. In the United States, the carrier (usually your local telephone company) must tell you the switch type.

In older IOS versions, you had to use the same switch type for all ISDN interfaces. With newer IOS versions, you can actually use the `isdn switch-type` command in interface configuration mode, as well as global configuration mode. This enables each interface to use a different switch type, a feature only required in specialized installations. When you enter the `isdn switch-type` global configuration command in an IOS that supports it on each interface, the router automatically copies the global command to each ISDN interface configuration. Then you can change each interface as needed.

After the switch type is entered in global configuration mode, most of the commands required to set up ISDN are entered in interface configuration mode. Some switch types require you to specify service provider IDs (SPIDs). For example, the National ISDN switch (`basic-ni`) requires SPIDs, but the AT&T 5ESS switch (`basic-5ess`) does not. Where SPIDs are needed, it is usually the responsibility of the end device (the router, in our examples) to know the SPIDs associated with the line to which it is connected. Sometimes they can be auto-detected, but it is usually a good idea to enter them manually. Like the switch type, your carrier also provides the SPIDs.

ISDN Basic Rate Interface (BRI) consists of two 64-Kbps B-channels and one 16-Kbps D-channel. The D-channel is used for signaling and call setup/teardown, and the two B-channels are used for data. The B-channels are often used together for a combined speed of 128 Kbps. However, they can be used individually to place ISDN calls, so each has its own SPID (when required) and a phone number associated with it. That phone number is often the basis for the SPID of that channel. If you configure a router that has B-channels associated with the phone numbers (555) 555-1000 and (555) 555-1001, and the SPIDs 55555510000101 and 55555510010101, you need to be enter the following in interface configuration mode:

```
R1(config)#interface bri 0
R1(config-if)#isdn spid1 55555510000101
R1(config-if)#isdn spid2 55555510010101
```

When the SPIDs are configured correctly, you establish a connection with the carrier switch. If you have Plain Old Telephone Service (POTS) lines available on your ISDN router, you can verify this by checking for a dial tone. Otherwise, the `show isdn status` command should confirm that layer one is active. See the "Troubleshooting DDR" section later in this chapter for more details on this command. Note that the other examples in this chapter use the AT&T 5ESS switch and, therefore, do not require SPIDs.

In Figure 9-1, an ISDN link connects two routers. Their BRI interfaces are on the same IP subnet, and they need to dial each other automatically when they have traffic destined for each other.

Figure 9-1 *A simple ISDN network*

The first step is to assign the network address to the BRI interface, as shown here:

```
R1(config)#interface bri 0
R1(config-if)#ip address 192.168.254.1 255.255.255.0
```

To get this ISDN network operating, you need to enable one or both routers to place a call to the other. The `dialer string` interface configuration command specifies a number to call in order to connect with the remote router. Because R2 can be reached at 555-2000, enter the following command:

```
R1(config-if)#dialer string 5552000
```

In addition, the router needs to know when to call the remote router. Because the network 192.168.254.0/24 is attached to the BRI0 interface, traffic destined for that network is routed to that interface, but it does not automatically connect the line. In order for the router to bring up the interface, we must define interesting traffic on the router. *Interesting traffic* causes the router to dial a down connection or to reset the idle timer on an up connection. If the router receives uninteresting traffic that is destined for the other side of the DDR connection while it is down, it drops the traffic. If it receives uninteresting traffic while the connection is up, it forwards the but traffic does not reset the idle timer.

To define interesting traffic, enter the `dialer-list` command in global configuration mode. You can restrict the traffic as much as needed with the dialer list by using access lists. For simplicity in these examples, the dialer list allows all IP traffic, but the needs of each network should be evaluated individually. The dialer list is applied to the interface by issuing the `dialer-group` interface configuration command. These commands are entered as follows:

```
R1(config)#dialer-list 1 protocol ip permit
R1(config)#interface bri 0
R1(config-if)#dialer-group 1
```

Our DDR configuration is now complete. Putting all the pieces together, the configuration of R1 is the following:

```
isdn switch-type basic-5ess
!
interface BRI0
 ip address 192.168.254.1 255.255.255.0
 dialer string 5552000
 dialer-group 1
!
dialer-list 1 protocol ip permit
```

And the configuration of R2 is as follows:

```
isdn switch-type basic-5ess
!
interface BRI0
 ip address 192.168.254.2 255.255.255.0
 dialer string 5551000
 dialer-group 1
!
dialer-list 1 protocol ip permit
```

With the above configurations, either router can dial the ISDN connection. A ping from one router to the BRI0 interface of the remote router brings up the ISDN line. If you try to ping 192.168.254.2 from R1, it dials R2 over the ISDN connection. (It may take a moment for the line to come up, so some of the ping packets may timeout.) It is important to remember that at this point you cannot ping other networks because they do not show up in the routing table. You can see the status of the connection with the show dialer command, shown here:

```
R1#show dialer

BRI0 - dialer type = ISDN

Dial String     Successes   Failures   Last called   Last status
5552000             7          2        00:00:11      successful   Default
0 incoming call(s) have been screened.
0 incoming call(s) rejected for callback.


BRI0:1 - dialer type = ISDN
Idle timer (120 secs), Fast idle timer (20 secs)
Wait for carrier (30 secs), Re-enable (15 secs)
Dialer state is data link layer up
Dial reason: ip (s=192.168.254.1, d=192.168.254.2)
Time until disconnect 110 secs
Current call connected 00:00:11
Connected to 5552000


BRI0:2 - dialer type = ISDN
Idle timer (120 secs), Fast idle timer (20 secs)
Wait for carrier (30 secs), Re-enable (15 secs)
Dialer state is idle
```

From the output, you can see that BRI0:1 is connected to 555-2000, but BRI0:2 is idle. These two logical interfaces correspond to the B-channels of the BRI0 interface. They cannot be configured individually—they both rely on the BRI0 configuration.

Note that the dial reason provided for BRI0:1 is an IP packet with a source address of 192.168.254.1 and a destination of 192.168.254.2. This information is particularly helpful when traffic from another device on the network causes the line to be brought up.

Configuring Dialer Map Statements

Thus far, our ISDN configuration is limited, and in most cases you will want to accomplish more. One problem with this configuration is that you can specify only one dial string per physical interface. To use this in a hub-and-spoke topology would require one physical BRI interface for each remote site. However, you can configure one BRI interface to connect with multiple remote sites by configuring dialer map statements. The `dialer map` command associates a dial string with a network address and specifies some additional properties of the individual connection.

The `dialer map` command accepts several parameters, but only a few of them will concern you in most situation, and those are covered here. To use dialer maps in an existing configuration, you must first enter the `no dialer string` command because dialer strings and dialer maps are mutually exclusive. Issue the following two commands on R1 to change to dialer map configuration:

```
R1(config-if)#no dialer string 5552000
R1(config-if)#dialer map ip 192.168.254.2 5552000
```

Dialer map statements are most useful when configuring a router to dial several different peers, based on network address. They also provide the flexibility to specify a remote name, which you can use to configure authentication, and to allow broadcasts, which are necessary in order to use some routing protocols on the connection. Other options available with dialer map statements include the specification of map classes, modem scripts, and the speed of the link. We do not cover these three options in this text, as they are not required for DDR and are not used as commonly as the other options.

Configuring PPP and Authentication

One valid concern about the current configuration is that the routers would accept a connection from any source. Clearly, you do not usually want unidentified routers dialing your network, especially as this could cause your router to send traffic to the unknown site. Therefore, some form of authentication is needed. High-level Data Link Control (HDLC), the default encapsulation for a BRI interface, does not allow authentication, so start by configuring the Point-to-Point Protocol (PPP) as the encapsulation of the

BRI interface. In interface configuration mode, use the `encapsulation ppp` command, shown here:

```
R1(config-if)#encapsulation ppp
```

The encapsulation type must match on both routers in order for a valid connection to be established and for traffic to traverse the link. By changing the encapsulation to PPP on both routers and by making no other changes, the routers continue to operate as they did with HDLC.

Once you are using PPP encapsulation, you can configure the routers to authenticate each other when establishing a connection. Cisco supports the following three standard authentication protocols:

- *Password Authentication Protocol (PAP)*: One router sends the password across the ISDN link in plain text for the other to check.

- *Challenge-Handshake Authentication Protocol (CHAP)*: One router sends a challenge, and the other router returns a response, which is computed from the configured password and the challenge. The receiving router performs the same computation and verifies that the result matches. Neither router transmits the password at any time in the process.

- *Microsoft CHAP (MS-CHAP)*: This is a modified version of CHAP that is supported as of IOS 12.0 for interoperability with Microsoft systems.

For connections between Cisco routers, CHAP is simple to configure. Because CHAP is superior to PAP from a security standpoint, there is almost no reason to use PAP between two Cisco routers. Because CHAP is a standard protocol, it can be used with most non-Cisco devices as well. Whenever possible, use CHAP, but in some cases, PAP may be required. The following authentication example uses CHAP.

To configure CHAP authentication on the routers, use the `ppp authentication` command in interface configuration mode, as shown here:

```
R1(config-if)#ppp authentication chap
```

You must also configure a common password on both routers. The global configuration command `username` accomplishes this. On R1, configure a username of R2; on R2, configure a username of R1. Both need to have the same password. On R1, enter the following:

```
R1(config)#username R2 password isdn
```

Once the username and password are established, the dialer map statement must be told which password to use when establishing a connection. To do this, simply specify the name to associate with the dialer connection. In interface configuration mode, enter the following:

```
R1(config-if)#dialer map ip 192.168.254.2 name R2 5552000
```

Notice that the dialer map statement has not changed, except for the addition of the name parameter. After making all of the changes to this point, the configuration of R1 is now as follows:

```
username R2 password 0 isdn
!
interface BRI0
 ip address 192.168.254.1 255.255.255.252
 encapsulation ppp
 dialer map ip 192.168.254.2 name R2 5552000
 dialer-group 1
 ppp authentication chap
!
dialer-list 1 protocol ip permit
```

And the configuration of R2 is the following:

```
username R1 password 0 isdn
!
interface BRI0
 ip address 192.168.254.2 255.255.255.252
 encapsulation ppp
 dialer map ip 192.168.254.1 name R1 5551000
 dialer-group 1
 ppp authentication chap
!
dialer-list 1 protocol ip permit
```

Notice that the username command contains a zero that we did not enter. This specifies the encryption level, and the router automatically adds it.

Making Use of Both Channels

Earlier we noticed that a dialer connection only used one of the two B-channels available. This provides you with 64 Kbps of bandwidth. However, if you can use both channels between two routers, you will double your available bandwidth. PPP enables you to bind channels together to provide that additional bandwidth. To enable an interface to use both channels, add the ppp multilink command to the BRI interface configuration.

Configuring the router to use both B-channels also requires you to determine a load threshold. This gives you the opportunity to configure the router to bring up the second channel only when needed. The load threshold can be any integer in the range of 1 through 255, and it is based on a fraction of 255. For example, a load threshold of 50 percent is entered as 128, whereas a load threshold of 25 percent is entered as 64. To have the router bring up the second channel immediately, set the load threshold to 1 — the lowest possible value.

Finally, you need to decide if the load threshold applies to inbound traffic, outbound traffic, or either. In this example, we apply it to traffic in either direction. To achieve this configuration, issue the following commands in interface configuration mode:

```
R1(config-if)#ppp multilink
R1(config-if)#dialer load-threshold 1 either
```

With these commands entered, the router brings up both B-channels immediately on dialing. A look at the following output from the show dialer command verifies this:

```
R1#show dialer


BRI0 - dialer type = ISDN


Dial String     Successes   Failures   Last called   Last status
5552000               33          0     00:00:13      successful
0 incoming call(s) have been screened.
0 incoming call(s) rejected for callback.


BRI0:1 - dialer type = ISDN
```

```
Idle timer (120 secs), Fast idle timer (20 secs)

Wait for carrier (30 secs), Re-enable (15 secs)

Dialer state is data link layer up

Dial reason: ip (s=192.168.254.1, d=192.168.254.2)

Time until disconnect 106 secs

Connected to 5552000 (R2)


BRI0:2 - dialer type = ISDN

Idle timer (120 secs), Fast idle timer (20 secs)

Wait for carrier (30 secs), Re-enable (15 secs)

Dialer state is data link layer up

Dial reason: Dialing on overload

Time until disconnect 106 secs

Connected to 5552000 (R2)
```

Notice that the dial reason given for BRI0:1 is an IP packet (as before). However, the dial reason for BRI0:2 is "Dialing on overload." R1 interpreted the traffic amount as high enough to bring up the second channel because we specified such a low dialer load threshold.

Changing the Timers

Several different timers are associated with ISDN connections. These timers include those shown in the show dialer command output: the idle timer, the fast-idle timer, the wait-for-carrier timer, and the reenable timer. They can all be changed using various forms of the dialer command in interface configuration mode.

The timer most commonly changed is the *idle timer*, the timer that determines how long the ISDN connection stays active when no interesting traffic is traversing the link. Because ISDN customers usually pay based on connection time, the idle timer is important. Although it is desirable to have the link disconnect as soon as traffic stops flowing over it, any traffic that arrives while the link is down will have to wait for the link to be reestablished. This causes delay with the first few packets to require the DDR connection. Therefore, a compromise should be found between the cost to keep the connection up and the time to reestablish the connection when traffic arrives.

The idle timer is specified in seconds, and the default value is 120 seconds. If you wish to configure the router to timeout after 30 minutes of idle time, enter the following command:

```
R2(config-if)#dialer idle-timeout 1800
```

The other timers can be configured using the `dialer` command as well, although this is not usually necessary. For example, the following commands reset the other times to their default values (in seconds):

```
R1(config-if)#dialer enable-timeout 15

R1(config-if)#dialer fast-idle 20

R1(config-if)#dialer wait-for-carrier-time 30
```

The *reenable* timer determines how long the router waits after the connection is dropped to reenable the interface for dialing. The *fast-idle timer* is like the idle timer, except that it is used when interesting traffic destined for an alternate peer needs the interface. Finally, the *wait-for-carrier timer* determines the amount of time the router waits for a connection after attempting to dial before giving up.

Configuring Dialer Profiles

The previous configuration examples use a technique known as *legacy configuration*; they apply configuration commands directly to the physical BRI interface. Even though dialer map statements allow some properties to be set based on the connection, most legacy configuration commands affect the interface as a whole. For example, the IP address, encapsulation type, authentication type, and timers always apply to the interface in legacy configuration.

To get around the limitations of legacy configuration, use *dialer profiles*. With dialer profiles, you create logical dialer interfaces, to which you then apply the interface configuration commands. The dialer interfaces must be tied to physical BRI interfaces, but several of them can use a single BRI interface. Few interface configuration commands need to be applied to the BRI interface. Dialer profiles are powerful and provide much finer control over configurations with multiple dial-up connections that share an interface.

In a small network of only two routers, you do not lose any functionality by using legacy configuration. However, it is wise to use dialer profiles even in small installations so that the configuration is flexible if the topology changes. In this example, the configurations of R1 and R2 from the earlier examples are converted to dialer profile configuration. The same functionality is preserved with these configurations. With dialer profiles, the configuration of R1 is as follows:

```
username R2 password 0 isdn
!
interface BRI0
 no ip address
 encapsulation ppp
 dialer pool-member 6
 ppp authentication chap
!
interface Dialer0
 ip address 192.168.254.1 255.255.255.0
 encapsulation ppp
 dialer remote-name R2
 dialer idle-timeout 1800
 dialer string 5552000
 dialer load-threshold 1 either
 dialer pool 6
 dialer-group 1
 ppp authentication chap
 ppp multilink
!
dialer-list 1 protocol ip permit
```

Notice that most of the configuration information has been removed from the BRI0 interface on each router. The exceptions are the encapsu-lation ppp and ppp authentication chap commands. Both the phys-ical and logical interfaces require them for CHAP to work with the dialer profile. The only additional configuration required for the BRI0 interface is to put it into a pool with the dialer pool-member command. By assign-ing physical interfaces to a pool, the logical interfaces that use that pool can choose any of the available physical interfaces when making a connection. The logical interface is tied to the pool with the dialer pool command.

With the exception of the `dialer pool` command, no new commands are needed for the dialer interface. Note that with dialer interfaces, we have started using the `dialer string` command again, since dialer maps are not needed. Instead of using dialer maps to connect to multiple sites, you can use a separate dialer interface for each remote site.

The configuration of R2 is changed in the same manner as that of R1, which is shown here:

```
username R1 password 0 isdn
!
interface BRI0
 no ip address
 encapsulation ppp
 dialer pool-member 6
 ppp authentication chap
!
interface Dialer0
 ip address 192.168.254.2 255.255.255.0
 encapsulation ppp
 dialer remote-name R1
 dialer idle-timeout 1800
 dialer string 5551000
 dialer load-threshold 1 either
 dialer pool 6
 dialer-group 1
 ppp authentication chap
 ppp multilink
!
dialer-list 1 protocol ip permit
```

With dialer profiles, the output of the `show dialer` command looks different. It now displays information about the physical BRI interfaces and the logical dialer interfaces. The following output shows a connection currently established:

```
R1#show dialer


BRI0 - dialer type = ISDN


Dial String      Successes    Failures    Last called    Last status
0 incoming call(s) have been screened.
0 incoming call(s) rejected for callback.


BRI0:1 - dialer type = ISDN
Idle timer (120 secs), Fast idle timer (20 secs)
Wait for carrier (30 secs), Re-enable (15 secs)
Dialer state is data link layer up
Dial reason: ip (s=192.168.254.1, d=192.168.254.2)
Interface bound to profile Dialer0
Time until disconnect 69 secs
Current call connected 00:00:19
Connected to 5552000


BRI0:2 - dialer type = ISDN
Idle timer (120 secs), Fast idle timer (20 secs)
Wait for carrier (30 secs), Re-enable (15 secs)
Dialer state is data link layer up
Dial reason: Dialing on overload
Interface bound to profile Dialer0
Time until disconnect 100 secs
Current call connected 00:00:21
Connected to 5552000


Dialer0 - dialer type = DIALER PROFILE
Load threshold for dialing additional calls is 1
Idle timer (120 secs), Fast idle timer (20 secs)
Wait for carrier (30 secs), Re-enable (15 secs)
Dialer state is data link layer up


Dial String      Successes    Failures    Last called    Last status
5552000              2            0        00:00:21       successful    Default
```

The information about the BRI interface B-channels includes the same information as before, including the dial reason, dial string, and timers. In addition, both interfaces now indicate that they are bound to profile Dialer0. This binding only lasts until the call ends because another dialer interface may use the physical interface next.

ISDN Wrap-Up

Many additional ISDN properties can be configured with both legacy configuration and dialer profiles. Those properties are beyond the scope of this text, but it is advisable to investigate all options available so that you can take advantage of all of the features your router offers. The properties can result in more efficient use of your ISDN connection, which could result in significant cost savings.

Using DDR as a Primary Link

Thus far, our DDR configurations have only allowed the router on either side of the link to reach the remote router. These configurations are of limited use, as they would not enable routing to the remote networks. If you go to the trouble to set up ISDN, you certainly want to route traffic over the link, and there are many options available to do this.

When a DDR connection is the only link between two sites, the routers on each side of the link need to know how to route traffic destined for any network on the other side of the link. A few methods exist to implement this, and the best choice for a particular environment depends on the properties of that network environment. Static routes are appropriate for environments where no routing protocol is needed over the link, such as small networks or sites at the edge of larger networks. Snapshot routing is suitable for networks that run Routing Information Protocol (RIP) or Interior Gateway Routing Protocol (IGRP) and need to be able to send and receive routing protocol updates over the DDR connection. Finally, Open Shortest Path First (OSPF) networks can use the OSPF demand circuit option to route over a DDR connection.

Implementing DDR with Static Routes

The simplest configuration of DDR consists of static routes that point to a next hop on the other side of the DDR connection. In small environments, especially with only two or three sites, this is the most desirable configuration. In large environments, this method is useful for DDR connections to spoke sites. If a routing protocol is in use throughout the network, with only a few DDR-connected sites at the edges, static routes can be used to route to those sites. Those static entries can then be redistributed into the routing protocol, enabling all sites to reach the DDR sites.

Using static routes alone

Returning to the example network shown in Figure 9-1, static routes are used to implement DDR between the two sites. Once the ISDN connection is set up correctly and able to dial the remote router, the routers simply need to be told how to reach the networks on the other side of the connection. In this network, that requires only one additional command on each router — the creation of a static route to the remote network. In global configuration mode, enter the following static route on R1:

```
R1(config)#ip route 192.168.2.0 255.255.255.0 192.168.254.2
```

And enter the following static route on R2:

```
R2(config)#ip route 192.168.1.0 255.255.255.0 192.168.254.1
```

When each router receives traffic destined for the other side of the DDR connection, it forwards it to the next hop, which is attached to its Dialer0 interface. If the connection is down, then the traffic must be defined as interesting to reach the other side.

Using static routes along with a routing protocol

Although static routes can be used with networks of any size, the configuration of the static routes can become burdensome in large networks. When using a routing protocol across the rest of the wide area network (WAN), static routes can still be used to connect DDR sites to the rest of the network. As an example, consider the network shown in Figure 9-2.

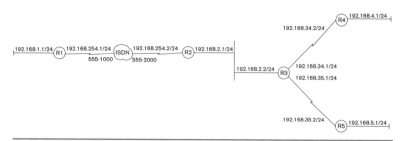

Figure 9-2 *A large network with a DDR connection to a remote site*

In the diagram, R1 is in a remote office that connects to the rest of the network via ISDN. The rest of the network uses serial links, so the connections are permanent. To minimize the overhead created by network changes, RIP is run throughout the network. To prevent the ISDN connection from staying up all of the time with routing updates, a static route is configured for the remote network attached to R1. This static route is configured on R2, and it is redistributed into RIP for propagation to the rest of the network, as shown here:

```
username R1 password 0 isdn
!
interface BRI0
 no ip address
 encapsulation ppp
 dialer pool-member 6
 ppp authentication chap
!
interface Dialer0
 ip address 192.168.254.2 255.255.255.0
 encapsulation ppp
 dialer remote-name R1
 dialer string 5551000
 dialer load-threshold 1 outbound
 dialer pool 6
 dialer-group 1
 ppp authentication chap
 ppp multilink
```

```
!
router rip
 redistribute static
 passive-interface Dialer0
 network 192.168.254.0
 network 192.168.2.0
!
ip route 192.168.1.0 255.255.255.0 192.168.254.1
!
dialer-list 1 protocol ip permit
```

Note that the Dialer0 interface has been made passive in the configuration of RIP. Otherwise, the routing table broadcasts would traverse the link and keep it up at all times. With redistribution of static routes configured, every router in the RIP network has a route to 192.168.1.0/24. For example, the routing table of R4 contains the following:

```
R4#sh ip route
Codes: C - connected, S - static, I - IGRP, R - RIP, M - mobile, B - BGP
       D - EIGRP, EX - EIGRP external, O - OSPF, IA - OSPF inter area
       N1 - OSPF NSSA external type 1, N2 - OSPF NSSA external type 2
       E1 - OSPF external type 1, E2 - OSPF external type 2, E - EGP
       i - IS-IS, L1 - IS-IS level-1, L2 - IS-IS level-2, * - candidate default
       U - per-user static route, o - ODR

Gateway of last resort is not set

C    192.168.4.0/24 is directly connected, Ethernet0
R    192.168.5.0/24 [120/2] via 192.168.34.1, 00:00:17, Serial0
C    192.168.34.0/24 is directly connected, Serial0
R    192.168.35.0/24 [120/1] via 192.168.34.1, 00:00:17, Serial0
R    192.168.1.0/24 [120/2] via 192.168.34.1, 00:00:17, Serial0
R    192.168.2.0/24 [120/1] via 192.168.34.1, 00:00:17, Serial0
```

The route to 192.168.1.0/24 shows up as any other RIP route. For more information on redistribution, please see Chapter 8.

To be able to reach the rest of the network, R1 also needs one or more static routes. Rather than entering each remote network as a static route on R1, this example uses a static default route that points back to R2. Because R1 only has one way to send data, this configuration suffices. The configuration of R1 is as follows:

```
username R2 password 0 isdn
!
interface BRI0
 no ip address
 encapsulation ppp
 dialer pool-member 6
 ppp authentication chap
!
interface Dialer0
 ip address 192.168.254.1 255.255.255.0
 encapsulation ppp
 dialer remote-name R2
 dialer string 5552000
 dialer load-threshold 1 either
 dialer pool 6
 dialer-group 1
 ppp authentication chap
 ppp multilink
!
ip route 0.0.0.0 0.0.0.0 192.168.254.2
!
dialer-list 1 protocol ip permit
```

Caution

Using a default route pointing across the DDR link causes the router to forward all traffic to unknown destinations across the DDR link. Traffic to nonexistent destinations also crosses the link. If this causes problems with utilization of the ISDN line, replace the default route with individual static routes to all networks across the DDR link.

Static routes can be used with other routing protocols in addition to RIP. The key is to redistribute the static routes, so all other routers in the network learn how to reach the remote sites.

Implementing DDR with Snapshot Routing

In a large network, such as that shown in Figure 9-3, the ISDN connection separates two sizable portions of the network. In this case, RIP (or another protocol) could be run on each side of the ISDN connection to propagate the routes manually, and static routes could be configured and redistributed on R1 and R2 to reach the networks across the DDR link. The drawback to this solution is that the static routes on each side of the DDR connection would have to include every network on the other side of the connection. Although the initial configuration may not be too difficult, the static routes must stay updated with changes in the network. Failure to keep the static routes current can lead to significant routing problems.

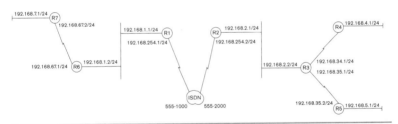

Figure 9-3 *A network with a DDR connection separating two large parts of the network*

Unfortunately, the nature of routing protocols makes them unsuitable to use over demand connections in their native form. Most protocols require periodic traffic, either routing table advertisements or Hello packets, to be sent from all of the active interfaces. If the periodic traffic is considered interesting, it continues to keep the demand circuit up indefinitely, thus defeating the purpose of using a demand circuit and significantly increasing the cost of that circuit.

If the routing protocol traffic is defined as uninteresting, it cannot keep the DDR connection up all the time. The routing protocol traffic can traverse the link when it is up, but when the demand circuit goes down, the router is no longer able to send or receive routing protocol traffic. When no packets arrive from the remote router, it is considered down. The routes that point toward that router eventually timeout and are removed from the routing table. Then, when legitimate traffic destined for a remote network is received, none of the local routers has a route for those networks, and the packets are dropped.

Snapshot routing alleviates this problem by modifying the behavior of distance vector protocols, such as RIP and IGRP. The purpose of snapshot routing is to inform the routing protocol that the dialer interface is a demand interface, so it is subject to a different set of rules than usual. In particular, the router does not attempt to send periodic updates across the demand circuit, nor does it allow the routes from the remote router to timeout from the routing table in the normal fashion. The routes remain in the routing tables of all routers even after the connection is torn down.

Snapshot routing details

Snapshot routing requires one router to function as the snapshot server and the other as a snapshot client. The *snapshot client* is the router that places the call to the *snapshot server*, which awaits the connection from the snapshot client(s). When one site acts as a hub site, usually that router is configured as the snapshot server. This way, each snapshot client needs to be configured for only one snapshot server. The selection of the client and server does not significantly impact the performance of snapshot routing.

Snapshot routing uses a quiet period and an active period. The names are fairly intuitive — the active period is the time during which routing updates are exchanged between the snapshot client and snapshot server, and the quiet period is the time during which the routers "freeze" their routing table entries from the snapshot interface. The client and server must agree on a snapshot active interval, but the client alone specifies the quiet interval. In the example network shown in Figure 9-3, R1 is the snapshot client and R2 the snapshot server.

Configuring the snapshot server

Configuring the snapshot server is the simpler of the two, requiring only one additional interface configuration command. This command can be used with dialer profile configuration, so it is easily inserted into the DDR configuration that you have been using. The following command must be entered in interface configuration mode:

```
R2(config-if)# snapshot server 5 dialer
```

The `snapshot server` command takes two parameters. The first is the active period, which should match the active period configured on the snapshot client. The second is the optional use of the `dialer` keyword. If used, the client is allowed to bring up the DDR connection if it is down when the quiet period expires. (The same keyword is specified in the configuration of the snapshot client.) With this change, the configuration of R2 is as follows:

```
username R1 password 0 isdn
!
interface BRI0
 no ip address
 encapsulation ppp
 dialer pool-member 6
 ppp authentication chap
!
interface Dialer0
 ip address 192.168.254.2 255.255.255.0
 encapsulation ppp
 dialer remote-name R1
 dialer string 5551000
 dialer load-threshold 1 outbound
 dialer pool 6
 dialer-group 1
 snapshot server 5 dialer
 ppp authentication chap
 ppp multilink
!
router rip
 network 192.168.2.0
 network 192.168.254.0
!
dialer-list 1 protocol ip permit
```

Note that the network 192.168.254.0/24 is included in the RIP configuration, but Dialer0 is not a passive interface. If not for the `snapshot server` configuration command, this would keep Dialer0 connected as a result of RIP updates. However, the snapshot configuration prevents that traffic on the dialer interface.

Configuring the snapshot client

Snapshot configuration for the client requires two commands. These commands must be entered in interface configuration mode as follows:

```
R1(config-if)#snapshot client 5 30 suppress-statechange-update dialer
R1(config-if)#dialer map snapshot 80 5552000
```

The `snapshot client` command has four parameters, the first two of which are the active period and the quiet period (in minutes). The third parameter is the optional `supress-statechange-update` keyword. This keyword tells the router to suppress updates during the quiet period when the DDR connection comes up due to interesting traffic. Finally, the `dialer` keyword tells the router to dial a DDR connection to the snapshot server if a connection does not already exist when the quiet period expires.

The `dialer map snapshot` command tells the router what number to dial in order to exchange snapshot updates. Before the dial string, the integer parameter (80 in this case) is a unique ID for this particular snapshot session, which appears in show command output and debugging messages.

Unfortunately, the `dialer map snapshot` command poses a special problem for dialer profile configurations. Because it uses a form of the `dialer map` command, snapshot routing is not compatible with dialer profile configuration. You can still use a logical dialer interface, but the dialer profile commands must be eliminated. With the appropriate changes, the configuration of R1 appears as follows:

```
username R2 password 0 isdn
!
interface BRI0
 no ip address
 encapsulation ppp
 dialer rotary-group 0
!
interface Dialer0
 ip address 192.168.254.1 255.255.255.0
 encapsulation ppp
```

```
dialer in-band

dialer map snapshot 80 5552000

dialer map ip 192.168.254.2 name R2 broadcast 5552000

dialer load-threshold 1 either

dialer-group 1

snapshot client 5 30 suppress-statechange-update dialer

ppp authentication chap

ppp multilink

!

router rip

 network 192.168.1.0

 network 192.168.254.0

!

dialer-list 1 protocol ip permit
```

In addition to the two snapshot routing commands, you can see the return of legacy configuration commands on Dialer0. Because you cannot use dialer profiles, R1 has a dialer map statement, and the dialer pool has been replaced by a rotary group. The `dialer rotary-group 0` command ties the physical interface to Dialer0, rather than using the dialer pool. When using snapshot routing, these changes are required.

Snapshot routing in action

With snapshot routing configured and operational, the routing table of every router holds all of the routes for both sides of the network. On the snapshot routers, you can see one important difference — the ages of the snapshot routes continue to increase beyond the normal maximum. The routing table of R1, shown here, illustrates this:

```
R1#show ip route
Codes: C - connected, S - static, I - IGRP, R - RIP, M - mobile, B - BGP
       D - EIGRP, EX - EIGRP external, O - OSPF, IA - OSPF inter area
       N1 - OSPF NSSA external type 1, N2 - OSPF NSSA external type 2
       E1 - OSPF external type 1, E2 - OSPF external type 2, E - EGP
       i - IS-IS, L1 - IS-IS level-1, L2 - IS-IS level-2, * - candidate default
       U - per-user static route, o - ODR
```

```
Gateway of last resort is not set

R    192.168.4.0/24 [120/3] via 192.168.254.2, 00:29:46, Dialer0

R    192.168.5.0/24 [120/3] via 192.168.254.2, 00:29:47, Dialer0

R    192.168.67.0/24 [120/1] via 192.168.1.2, 00:00:15, Ethernet0

R    192.168.7.0/24 [120/2] via 192.168.1.2, 00:00:15, Ethernet0

R    192.168.34.0/24 [120/2] via 192.168.254.2, 00:29:47, Dialer0

C    192.168.254.0/24 is directly connected, Dialer0

R    192.168.35.0/24 [120/2] via 192.168.254.2, 00:29:47, Dialer0

C    192.168.1.0/24 is directly connected, Ethernet0

R    192.168.2.0/24 [120/1] via 192.168.254.2, 00:29:47, Dialer0
```

Note that all RIP routes received across the Dialer0 interface are more than 29 minutes old. Normal RIP routes are never more than 30 seconds old if they are still active. Under normal conditions, if a RIP route reaches 180 seconds in age, it goes into hold down. However, the snapshot routes are retained, enabling the DDR connection to stay down for longer periods. The other routers on the network receive the snapshot routes in the periodic RIP updates, so their routes never age beyond the normal limits.

Implementing DDR with OSPF Demand Circuit

Because OSPF is a link state protocol, it is not compatible with snapshot routing. All OSPF routers in an area must have identical link state databases, so all topology changes must be communicated immediately. Preventing the updates from crossing the DDR connection hampers the ability of OSPF to route effectively. Fortunately, OSPF sends routing updates when topology changes occur, rather than at periodic intervals.

OSPF has built-in functionality to support demand circuits, called OSPF demand circuit. This configuration option prevents all Hello packets from traversing the DDR connection, but it allows topology changes to bring up the connection. Therefore, the frequency of topology changes on the network should be considered when evaluating OSPF demand circuit because the changes bring up a dial connection if one is not already established. Because the link state databases must be identical, this behavior cannot be changed.

OSPF demand circuit support must be configured on one of the two routers with the DDR connection. By configuring one of the routers to recognize the demand circuit, both routers treat Link State Advertisements (LSAs) from across the connection as remote LSAs. No other routers on the network need any configuration changes, but all of the routers in the OSPF area must be able to support demand circuits. One of the option bits in the Hello packet and in LSAs is the DC bit, which indicates that the router is capable of supporting OSPF demand circuit. If any router in the area is incapable of supporting OSPF demand circuit, the other routers will not recognize the demand circuit. OSPF demand circuit is supported in Cisco routers as of IOS 11.2.

We will continue to use the example network in Figure 9-3 to illustrate OSPF demand circuit. To create a demand circuit, only the following interface configuration command is required:

```
R1(config-if)#ip ospf demand-circuit
```

This command must be entered on the OSPF-enabled interface that communicates with the remote end of the connection. It could be a BRI interface or a dialer interface. In this example, a dialer interface is used. When this command is issued on R1, its configuration is the following:

```
username R2 password 0 isdn
!
interface Loopback10
 ip address 10.0.0.1 255.255.255.255
!
interface BRI0
 no ip address
 encapsulation ppp
 dialer pool-member 6
 ppp authentication chap
!
interface Dialer0
 ip address 192.168.254.1 255.255.255.0
 encapsulation ppp
 ip ospf demand-circuit
```

```
dialer remote-name R2

dialer string 5552000

dialer load-threshold 1 either

dialer pool 6

dialer-group 1

ppp authentication chap

ppp multilink

!

router ospf 1

 network 192.168.0.0 0.0.255.255 area 0

!

dialer-list 1 protocol ip permit
```

Remember that R2 is *not* configured with the demand-circuit command — only one of the two routers needs it. Therefore, R2 has a standard OSPF configuration with basically the same commands as R1, minus the `ip ospf demand-circuit` command.

With the demand circuit configured, R1 and R2 connect to establish their neighbor relationship. They exchange Hello packets and then exchange LSAs across the link. When this is completed, they will not communicate again until there is a topology change. After the LSAs have been exchanged and the link brought back down, the routing table of R1 contains the following:

```
R1#show ip route
Codes: C - connected, S - static, I - IGRP, R - RIP, M - mobile, B - BGP
       D - EIGRP, EX - EIGRP external, O - OSPF, IA - OSPF inter area
       N1 - OSPF NSSA external type 1, N2 - OSPF NSSA external type 2
       E1 - OSPF external type 1, E2 - OSPF external type 2, E - EGP
       i - IS-IS, L1 - IS-IS level-1, L2 - IS-IS level-2, * - candidate default
       U - per-user static route, o - ODR


Gateway of last resort is not set


O    192.168.4.0/24 [110/1869] via 192.168.254.2, 15:03:32, Dialer0
O    192.168.5.0/24 [110/1884] via 192.168.254.2, 15:03:33, Dialer0
     10.0.0.0/32 is subnetted, 1 subnets
```

```
C       10.0.0.1 is directly connected, Loopback10

O       192.168.67.0/24 [110/74] via 192.168.1.2, 15:03:33, Ethernet0

O       192.168.7.0/24 [110/99] via 192.168.1.2, 15:03:33, Ethernet0

O       192.168.34.0/24 [110/1859] via 192.168.254.2, 15:03:33, Dialer0

C       192.168.254.0/24 is directly connected, Dialer0

O       192.168.35.0/24 [110/1859] via 192.168.254.2, 15:03:33, Dialer0

C       192.168.1.0/24 is directly connected, Ethernet0

O       192.168.2.0/24 [110/1795] via 192.168.254.2, 15:03:33, Dialer0
```

Notice that all of the routes to networks across the DDR connection list Dialer0 as their outgoing interface, as if the line were still up. In fact, the routes appear just as they would without demand circuit enabled, except that they can be much older. Another significant difference can be seen in the link state database of R1, shown here:

```
R1#show ip ospf database

        OSPF Router with ID (10.0.0.1) (Process ID 1)


            Router Link States (Area 0)


Link ID        ADV Router        Age        Seq#        Checksum Link count
10.0.0.1       10.0.0.1          1039            0x8000001F 0x71B0 3
10.0.0.2       10.0.0.2          1     (DNA) 0x80000004 0xB187 3
10.0.0.3       10.0.0.3          6     (DNA) 0x80000028 0x740D 5
10.0.0.4       10.0.0.4          84    (DNA) 0x80000002 0x6D3  3
10.0.0.5       10.0.0.5          8     (DNA) 0x80000026 0x841D 3
10.0.0.6       10.0.0.6          1652           0x80000025 0x5DA5 3
10.0.0.7       10.0.0.7          1610           0x80000022 0x854  3


            Net Link States (Area 0)


Link ID        ADV Router        Age        Seq#        Checksum
192.168.1.2    10.0.0.6          1653           0x80000020 0x1172
192.168.2.2    10.0.0.3          52    (DNA) 0x80000001 0x4660
```

Notice that all LSAs received from across the DDR connection are flagged as DNA (Do Not Age). The age column lists the age of each LSA when it reached R1, but it does not change, whereas the ages of the other LSAs increase. This is how OSPF prevents the demand circuit LSAs from reaching MaxAge and being removed from the database, while avoiding the periodic LSA refreshes. All routers on the same side of the demand circuit list the same routes as DNA. For example, the link state database for R7 reflects the same DNA entries as that for R1, as shown here:

```
R7#show ip ospf database

        OSPF Router with ID (10.0.0.7) (Process ID 1)


            Router Link States (Area 0)


Link ID        ADV Router      Age           Seq#       Checksum Link count
10.0.0.1       10.0.0.1        1056          0x8000001F 0x71B0   3
10.0.0.2       10.0.0.2        3     (DNA) 0x80000004 0xB187   3
10.0.0.3       10.0.0.3        8     (DNA) 0x80000028 0x740D   5
10.0.0.4       10.0.0.4        86    (DNA) 0x80000002 0x6D3    3
10.0.0.5       10.0.0.5        10    (DNA) 0x80000026 0x841D   3
10.0.0.6       10.0.0.6        1667          0x80000025 0x5DA5  3
10.0.0.7       10.0.0.7        1623          0x80000022 0x854   3


            Net Link States (Area 0)


Link ID        ADV Router      Age           Seq#       Checksum
192.168.1.2    10.0.0.6        1668          0x80000020 0x1172
192.168.2.2    10.0.0.3        54    (DNA) 0x80000001 0x4660
```

At R7, the DNA entries are two seconds older than at R1 because the LSAs are aged one second (by default) at each hop as they are flooded. But after entering them into its link state database, R7 does not age them any further.

The link state databases for all of the routers on the other side of the demand circuit would list the opposite LSAs as DNA. Even though the `ip ospf demand-circuit` command is issued on only one side of the link, its effects are felt throughout the area on both sides of the link.

R1 also treats its neighbor R2 in a special way when it is configured with a demand circuit, as seen here in the neighbor table:

```
R1#show ip ospf neighbor
```

Neighbor ID	Pri	State	Dead Time	Address	Interface
10.0.0.2	1	**FULL/** -	-	**192.168.254.2**	**Dialer0**
10.0.0.6	1	FULL/DR	00:00:30	192.168.1.2	Ethernet0

Notice that the entry for R2 has a blank dead time. As you can see from the entry for R6, usually this column has a value, which is the number of seconds until that neighbor is considered dead. The dead time is ordinarily reset by the Hello packets. The absence of the dead time allows the routers to stop exchanging Hello packets without losing the neighbor relationship.

Tip

Remember that OSPF demand circuit brings up the DDR connection when topology changes require LSAs to be flooded across the link. One way to minimize the impact of topology changes is through the use of stub areas, especially totally stubby areas. Inter-area routes are not advertised into a totally stubby area, so topology changes outside the area do not bring up the DDR connection. In addition, if you make the area smaller, topology changes within the area are less likely.

Using DDR as a Backup Link

In many environments, a dedicated connection between sites is not just desirable; it may be necessary. In fact, many organizations rely heavily on their WAN links to conduct business, and they are dependent upon the reliability of those links. In order to reduce the dependency on individual links, they may implement redundancy in parts of the network. Fully redundant dedicated WAN links can be expensive, so many organizations choose ISDN as their backup medium. With ISDN, an organization pays for the amount of time the connections are actually established, making it ideal for backup use.

Implementing Dial Backup

Cisco routers have a built-in feature that enables them to treat one interface as a backup of another interface. When the primary interface is active, the backup interface is in standby mode and is unusable. When the primary interface fails, the backup interface takes over the properties of the primary.

Because it must be in standby mode when the primary interface is up, configuring a physical BRI interface as a backup prevents its use for other purposes. However, if you configure a logical dialer interface as a backup, it is put into standby mode, leaving the BRI interface available for other uses. For this reason, dialer profiles are recommended when configuring dial backup.

In Figure 9-4, R1 and R2 are connected by a serial link. In addition, they both have BRI interfaces, which provide backup for the serial link. To implement dial backup, the first step is simply to make sure the primary interface is operating correctly. The second step is to configure the DDR connection without the backup commands and to make sure it is operating correctly. Finally, put the interface into backup mode and test it again.

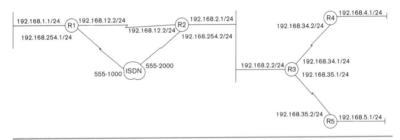

Figure 9-4 *A network with a DDR connection as backup for a serial connection*

Assuming that the serial link and the DDR connection both function correctly, it is simple to put an interface into backup mode. Simply enter interface configuration mode for the primary interface, which is Serial0 in the example. Then enter the backup configuration commands, as shown here:

```
R1(config)#interface serial 0
R1(config-if)#backup interface dialer 0
R1(config-if)#backup delay 5 30
```

The `backup interface` command configures the roles of primary and backup interface. The `backup delay` command specifies the timers for the backup interface. In the example, Serial0 is the primary interface, and Dialer0 is the backup interface. The backup interface in this example waits five seconds after the failure of the primary interface before coming up. When the primary interface returns to an operational state, the backup interface stays active for 30 seconds before returning to standby mode. The timers can prevent unnecessary cycling of the backup interface when the primary interface is flaky. The appropriate values depend on each individual environment, and some of the factors to consider are the frequency of link outages, the frequency of short (< 1 minute) outages, the usage rate of the ISDN, and any connect charges for the ISDN. If certain timer values are tried and found to be unsuitable, they can always be changed.

The dial backup feature also enables you to bring up the backup interface for bandwidth-on-demand. This is specified with the `backup load` command, as seen here:

```
R1(config-if)#backup load 75 25
```

This command brings up the backup interface when the load on the primary interface reaches 75 percent of its bandwidth, and it disconnects when the utilization is 25 percent. You can use the `backup delay` and `backup load` commands together on the same interface, so the backup interface could be used for both purposes at the same time.

When configured for dial backup, the configuration of R1 is as follows:

```
username R2 password 0 isdn
!
interface Serial0
 backup delay 5 30
 backup interface Dialer0
 ip address 192.168.12.1 255.255.255.0
!
interface BRI0
 no ip address
 dialer pool-member 6
```

```
!
interface Dialer0
 ip address 192.168.254.1 255.255.255.0
 encapsulation ppp
 dialer remote-name R2
 dialer string 5552000
 dialer load-threshold 1 either
 dialer pool 6
 dialer-group 1
 ppp authentication chap
 ppp multilink
!
router rip
 redistribute static
 network 192.168.1.0
 network 192.168.12.0
 network 192.168.254.0
!
dialer-list 1 protocol ip permit
```

The configuration for R2 closely matches that of R1, using the same
backup interface commands. Notice that the Dialer0 interface is not listed
as a passive interface under the configuration for RIP. If it were, then dial
backup would not work as desired. Although it is not configured as passive,
Dialer0 does not broadcast RIP updates when it is in standby mode—
standby mode keeps the interface down until needed. Note that Dialer0
broadcasts RIP updates when it comes up to backup Serial0. This keeps
the DDR connection up as long as Serial0 is down. The properties of
Dialer0 are as follows when the primary interface is functioning:

```
R1#show interface dialer 0
Dialer0 is standby mode, line protocol is down
  Hardware is Unknown
  Internet address is 192.168.254.1/24
  MTU 1500 bytes, BW 56 Kbit, DLY 20000 usec, rely 255/255, load 1/255
  Encapsulation PPP, loopback not set
  DTR is pulsed for 1 seconds on reset
```

```
Last input never, output never, output hang never

Last clearing of "show interface" counters never

Input queue: 0/75/0 (size/max/drops); Total output drops: 0

Queueing strategy: weighted fair

Output queue: 0/1000/64/0 (size/max total/threshold/drops)

    Conversations  0/0/256 (active/max active/max total)

    Reserved Conversations 0/0 (allocated/max allocated)

5 minute input rate 0 bits/sec, 0 packets/sec

5 minute output rate 0 bits/sec, 0 packets/sec

    2457 packets input, 358836 bytes, 0 no buffer

    Received 0 broadcasts, 0 runts, 0 giants, 0 throttles

    0 input errors, 0 CRC, 0 frame, 0 overrun, 0 ignored, 0 abort

    2387 packets output, 337920 bytes, 0 underruns

    0 output errors, 0 collisions, 0 interface resets

    0 output buffer failures, 0 output buffers swapped out

    0 carrier transitions
```

Notice that Dialer0 is in standby mode. This does not change as long as Serial0 is active. The properties of Serial0 list the backup interface and properties:

```
R1#show interface serial 0

Serial0 is up, line protocol is up

  Hardware is HD64570

  Internet address is 192.168.12.1/24

  Backup interface Dialer0, failure delay 5 sec, secondary disable delay 30 sec,

  kickin load not set, kickout load not set

  MTU 1500 bytes, BW 1544 Kbit, DLY 20000 usec, rely 255/255, load 1/255

  Encapsulation HDLC, loopback not set, keepalive set (10 sec)

  Last input 00:00:05, output 00:00:04, output hang never

  Last clearing of "show interface" counters never

  Queueing strategy: fifo

  Output queue 0/40, 0 drops; input queue 0/75, 0 drops

  5 minute input rate 0 bits/sec, 0 packets/sec

  5 minute output rate 0 bits/sec, 0 packets/sec

    4551 packets input, 349338 bytes, 0 no buffer
```

```
Received 4498 broadcasts, 0 runts, 0 giants, 0 throttles

0 input errors, 0 CRC, 0 frame, 0 overrun, 0 ignored, 0 abort

4563 packets output, 294570 bytes, 0 underruns

0 output errors, 0 collisions, 2311 interface resets

0 output buffer failures, 0 output buffers swapped out

19 carrier transitions

DCD=up  DSR=up  DTR=up  RTS=up  CTS=up
```

Notice also that the properties of Serial0 list not only the failure delay timers but also the load thresholds for bandwidth-on-demand, even though they are not set. The routing table for R1 shows that it is receiving RIP routes from R2 over the serial link, as shown here:

```
R1#show ip route
Codes: C - connected, S - static, I - IGRP, R - RIP, M - mobile, B - BGP
       D - EIGRP, EX - EIGRP external, O - OSPF, IA - OSPF inter area
       N1 - OSPF NSSA external type 1, N2 - OSPF NSSA external type 2
       E1 - OSPF external type 1, E2 - OSPF external type 2, E - EGP
       i - IS-IS, L1 - IS-IS level-1, L2 - IS-IS level-2, * - candidate default
       U - per-user static route, o - ODR


Gateway of last resort is not set


C    192.168.12.0/24 is directly connected, Serial0
R    192.168.4.0/24 [120/3] via 192.168.12.2, 00:00:02, Serial0
R    192.168.5.0/24 [120/3] via 192.168.12.2, 00:00:02, Serial0
R    192.168.34.0/24 [120/2] via 192.168.12.2, 00:00:02, Serial0
R    192.168.35.0/24 [120/2] via 192.168.12.2, 00:00:02, Serial0
C    192.168.1.0/24 is directly connected, Ethernet0
R    192.168.2.0/24 [120/1] via 192.168.12.2, 00:00:02, Serial0
```

Notice that all of the routes list Serial0 as the outbound interface. However, when the serial link between R1 and R2 goes down, Dialer0 waits the configured backup delay (five seconds in this case), and then it becomes active. When Dialer0 comes up, its properties show the following new state:

```
R1#show interface dialer 0
Dialer0 is up (spoofing), line protocol is up (spoofing)
```

```
Hardware is Unknown

Internet address is 192.168.254.1/24

MTU 1500 bytes, BW 56 Kbit, DLY 20000 usec, rely 255/255, load 1/255

Encapsulation PPP, loopback not set

DTR is pulsed for 1 seconds on reset

Last input never, output never, output hang never

Last clearing of "show interface" counters never

Input queue: 0/75/0 (size/max/drops); Total output drops: 0

Queueing strategy: weighted fair

Output queue: 0/1000/64/0 (size/max total/threshold/drops)

    Conversations  0/0/256 (active/max active/max total)

    Reserved Conversations 0/0 (allocated/max allocated)

5 minute input rate 0 bits/sec, 0 packets/sec

5 minute output rate 0 bits/sec, 0 packets/sec

    2467 packets input, 359816 bytes, 0 no buffer

    Received 0 broadcasts, 0 runts, 0 giants, 0 throttles

    0 input errors, 0 CRC, 0 frame, 0 overrun, 0 ignored, 0 abort

    2397 packets output, 338501 bytes, 0 underruns

    0 output errors, 0 collisions, 0 interface resets

    0 output buffer failures, 0 output buffers swapped out

    0 carrier transitions
```

Dialer0 says that its state is "up (spoofing)". The spoofing of the interface indicates that it is considered up even when the ISDN connection is not dialed. A look at the routing table of R1, shown here, indicates that it is still learning the same RIP routes from R2, but now the source is the Dialer0 interface:

```
R1#show ip route
Codes: C - connected, S - static, I - IGRP, R - RIP, M - mobile, B - BGP
       D - EIGRP, EX - EIGRP external, O - OSPF, IA - OSPF inter area
       N1 - OSPF NSSA external type 1, N2 - OSPF NSSA external type 2
       E1 - OSPF external type 1, E2 - OSPF external type 2, E - EGP
       i - IS-IS, L1 - IS-IS level-1, L2 - IS-IS level-2, * - candidate default
       U - per-user static route, o - ODR
```

```
Gateway of last resort is not set

R    192.168.4.0/24 [120/3] via 192.168.254.2, 00:00:10, Dialer0

R    192.168.5.0/24 [120/3] via 192.168.254.2, 00:00:11, Dialer0

R    192.168.34.0/24 [120/2] via 192.168.254.2, 00:00:11, Dialer0

C    192.168.254.0/24 is directly connected, Dialer0

R    192.168.35.0/24 [120/2] via 192.168.254.2, 00:00:11, Dialer0

C    192.168.1.0/24 is directly connected, Ethernet0

R    192.168.2.0/24 [120/1] via 192.168.254.2, 00:00:11, Dialer0
```

This is exactly the desired result. Traffic destined for the rest of the network continues to reach its destination, as long as the ISDN connection can support the volume of traffic. When the serial connection becomes active again, Dialer0 waits the configured time (30 seconds in this example) before returning to standby mode.

Implementing Backup Using Floating Static Routes

Floating static routes are an alternative to interface backup commands for DDR backup. A floating static route has a high administrative distance, so dynamic routes can replace it. One advantage of this method of configuration is that the backup interface never participates in the routing protocol. Therefore, even when the primary interface is down, the backup interface does not keep the DDR connection up with routing updates. Of course, as with ordinary static routes, floating static routes require extra effort to configure, not only upon implementation, but also when the network topology changes.

Normally, when a static route and a dynamic route exist for the same network, the static route takes precedence and is entered into the routing table. This is because the default administrative distance of a static route is 1, which is lower than all other routes, except directly connected networks. When using static routes to configure a back path to a destination, you want the dynamic routes to supercede the static routes. To do this, the administrative distance of static routes can be increased, as shown here:

```
R2(config)#ip route 192.168.1.0 255.255.255.0 192.168.254.1 250
```

The last parameter on the line is the administrative distance. At 250, this static route has a greater administrative distance than all routing protocols. Therefore, it never supercedes a dynamic route. This makes that route a floating static route. If a RIP route were received for 192.168.1.0/24 (administrative distance of 120), it would replace the above static route in the routing table. If the source of the RIP route becomes unreachable (for example, the WAN link is down), the RIP route is removed from the routing table, and the static route is added to the routing table.

With floating static routes, the configuration for R1 in Figure 9-4 is as follows:

```
username R2 password 0 isdn
!
interface Serial0
 ip address 192.168.12.1 255.255.255.0
!
interface BRI0
 no ip address
 encapsulation ppp
 dialer pool-member 6
 ppp authentication chap
!
interface Dialer0
 ip address 192.168.254.1 255.255.255.0
 encapsulation ppp
 dialer remote-name R2
 dialer string 5552000
 dialer load-threshold 1 either
 dialer pool 6
 dialer-group 1
 ppp authentication chap
 ppp multilink
!
router rip
 redistribute static
```

```
 passive-interface Dialer0
 network 192.168.1.0
 network 192.168.12.0
 network 192.168.254.0
!
ip route 192.168.2.0 255.255.255.0 192.168.254.2 250
ip route 192.168.4.0 255.255.255.0 192.168.254.2 250
ip route 192.168.5.0 255.255.255.0 192.168.254.2 250
ip route 192.168.34.0 255.255.255.0 192.168.254.2 250
ip route 192.168.35.0 255.255.255.0 192.168.254.2 250
!
dialer-list 1 protocol ip permit
```

The configuration for R2 is the following:

```
username R1 password 0 isdn
!
interface Serial0
 ip address 192.168.12.2 255.255.255.0
!
interface BRI0
 no ip address
 encapsulation ppp
 dialer pool-member 6
 ppp authentication chap
!
interface Dialer0
 ip address 192.168.254.2 255.255.255.0
 encapsulation ppp
 dialer remote-name R1
 dialer string 5551000
 dialer load-threshold 1 either
 dialer pool 6
 dialer-group 1
 ppp authentication chap
```

```
ppp multilink
!
router rip
 redistribute static
 passive-interface Dialer0
 network 192.168.254.0
 network 192.168.2.0
 network 192.168.12.0
!
ip route 192.168.1.0 255.255.255.0 192.168.254.1 250
!
dialer-list 1 protocol ip permit
```

With this configuration and the primary interface up, the routing table for R2 has a route to 192.168.1.0/24 from RIP through Serial0, as seen here in its routing table:

```
R2#show ip route
Codes: C - connected, S - static, I - IGRP, R - RIP, M - mobile, B - BGP
       D - EIGRP, EX - EIGRP external, O - OSPF, IA - OSPF inter area
       N1 - OSPF NSSA external type 1, N2 - OSPF NSSA external type 2
       E1 - OSPF external type 1, E2 - OSPF external type 2, E - EGP
       i - IS-IS, L1 - IS-IS level-1, L2 - IS-IS level-2, * - candidate default
       U - per-user static route, o - ODR

Gateway of last resort is not set

R    192.168.34.0/24 [120/1] via 192.168.2.2, 00:00:05, Ethernet0
R    192.168.35.0/24 [120/1] via 192.168.2.2, 00:00:05, Ethernet0
C    192.168.12.0/24 is directly connected, Serial0
R    192.168.1.0/24 [120/1] via 192.168.12.1, 00:00:25, Serial0
C    192.168.2.0/24 is directly connected, Ethernet0
R    192.168.4.0/24 [120/2] via 192.168.2.2, 00:00:05, Ethernet0
R    192.168.5.0/24 [120/2] via 192.168.2.2, 00:00:05, Ethernet0
C    192.168.254.0/24 is directly connected, Dialer0
```

However, when the link between R1 and R2 goes down, the floating static route becomes the active route to 192.168.1.0/24. It appears in the routing table, as follows:

```
R2#show ip route
Codes: C - connected, S - static, I - IGRP, R - RIP, M - mobile, B - BGP
       D - EIGRP, EX - EIGRP external, O - OSPF, IA - OSPF inter area
       N1 - OSPF NSSA external type 1, N2 - OSPF NSSA external type 2
       E1 - OSPF external type 1, E2 - OSPF external type 2, E - EGP
       i - IS-IS, L1 - IS-IS level-1, L2 - IS-IS level-2, * - candidate default
       U - per-user static route, o - ODR


Gateway of last resort is not set


R    192.168.34.0/24 [120/1] via 192.168.2.2, 00:00:14, Ethernet0
R    192.168.35.0/24 [120/1] via 192.168.2.2, 00:00:14, Ethernet0
S    192.168.1.0/24 [250/0] via 192.168.254.1
C    192.168.2.0/24 is directly connected, Ethernet0
R    192.168.4.0/24 [120/2] via 192.168.2.2, 00:00:14, Ethernet0
R    192.168.5.0/24 [120/2] via 192.168.2.2, 00:00:14, Ethernet0
C    192.168.254.0/24 is directly connected, Dialer0
```

Notice that the administrative distance for 192.168.1.0/24 is 250, as entered in the configuration. Because the RIP route is no longer present, this is now the lowest administrative distance available for this route, so it is entered in the routing table.

Note that the RIP route to 192.168.1.0/24 is not removed until after the flush timer expires. Therefore, the fail-over to the DDR connection is not immediate. Remember that with floating static routes, a link failure that should result in DDR backup behaves as any other link failure. Therefore, the characteristics of the routing protocol in use must be considered when implementing floating static routes.

R1 has several floating static routes—one for each network on the other side of the DDR link. This configuration does require extra effort to maintain as the network grows. For a larger network, even the initial configuration could be difficult. However, this is the most efficient configuration from a traffic standpoint.

The static routes on R1 could be replaced by a static route to 192.168.0.0/16 or even to 0.0.0.0/0. If there is a default route on the network, these solutions may be required. However, bear in mind that in the network shown, R1 will never receive a RIP route for 192.168.0.0/16 or 0.0.0.0/0. Therefore, these will never be removed from the routing table, even when Serial0 is up. This means that traffic destined to an unknown network will be routed over Dialer0 because the static route points there. This can result in the DDR connection (intended for backup) being dialed even when the primary link is up. Although this configuration is easier to implement and maintain, it has some undesireable side effects. Careful consideration must be given when deciding how to configure floating static routes, especially on the remote end.

Troubleshooting DDR

Troubleshooting DDR can be somewhat difficult, as there are many interrelated aspects of DDR that could cause problems. For example, if you try to implement OSPF demand circuit, but no routes are exchanged, the problem could be the dial string, the password, the IP address, the interesting traffic specification, or a router in the area that does not support demand circuit. A careful and methodical approach must be taken to configure and troubleshoot DDR effectively.

This section starts with a method for configuring DDR in such a way that troubleshooting is much easier. Then it covers troubleshooting various aspects of DDR, including Cisco IOS commands that help with troubleshooting.

Tip

When troubleshooting a problem with DDR, try to remember this fundamental tenet of troubleshooting: Change only one thing at a time, and change it back if it does not fix the problem. This is especially important when troubleshooting something that had been working correctly and then started to malfunction. In addition, remember to turn off all debugging (with the undebug all command) after you finish troubleshooting. This saves CPU cycles on the router.

Recommended Configuration Steps

If you configure DDR following a carefully thought-out approach, troubleshooting is much easier. By configuring DDR in a certain order and testing along the way, problems are limited in scope. Of course, any router configuration should be done methodically, but this section provides one suggestion for a methodical approach to DDR implementation.

1. Enter the minimal amount of configuration required to test the ISDN line. This includes the ISDN switch type, IP address, dial string, and dialer list. The dialer list should permit all traffic and not use dialer profiles. Because no routes to other networks exist yet, ping the address of the DDR interface of the remote router to bring up the DDR connection. When the routers are capable of pinging each other, you can be sure that not only are your configuration statements correct, but the information provided by your ISDN carrier is correct, as well.

2. Now update the configuration to use dialer profiles, but leave everything else the same. Even if you do not need dialer profiles now, you should still use them because of their flexibility. Move the appropriate configuration commands from the BRI interface to the dialer interface, and create a dialer pool. Then test the link using the same procedure as in step 1.

3. If you wish to implement authentication or use both B-channels together, change the encapsulation to PPP on both the physical BRI interface and the logical dialer interface. Test the connection again.

4. If you need authentication, enter a common password on both routers with the `username` configuration command. Enter `ppp authentication chap` on both the BRI and dialer interfaces. Test the connection and make sure it works. It might also be a good idea to temporarily change the password on one router to ensure that the connection is refused when the passwords do not match.

5. To bind both B-channels together for more bandwidth, enter the `ppp multilink` command. Use the `dialer load-threshold` command to specify the amount of traffic that should bring up the second B-channel. Test that both channels are used.

6. If the DDR link is going to serve as a backup, make sure that the primary interface is already configured and tested. Then enter the `backup` interface configuration commands on the primary interface, or configure floating static routes in the global configuration. Bring down the primary link to make sure that the backup operates as desired. (Do not bring down the primary link in a production environment unless you are prepared for downtime.)

7. If the DDR link is going to be a primary connection, enter the static routes for the link or configure the routing protocol. For snapshot routing, configure RIP/IGRP without the snapshot commands first and make sure it operates correctly. Then configure snapshot routing. If using OSPF demand circuit, configure OSPF without demand circuit enabled and make sure it works. Then enter the `ip ospf demand-circuit` interface configuration command on only one of the routers. Whatever method you are using to route across the DDR link, test it thoroughly.

8. If you wish to limit interesting traffic, change the dialer list to allow only the desired traffic. Make sure to fully test the DDR connection again after changing the dialer list. Test various kinds of traffic, and make sure that the link behaves as desired.

After the DDR connection is completely configured, be sure to follow a similar methodical approach when making changes to the configuration.

Tip

Whenever making changes, it is a good idea to save a copy of the configuration after each step. If there is a question about something that was changed, you can review the changes later.

Viewing Interface Information

The `show interfaces` command can help troubleshoot many problems, including but not limited to DDR. This command lists a great deal of information about the interfaces, including status, addressing, input and output statistics, queue statistics, and error information. With DDR, the information for both the BRI interface and the dialer interface is of interest. If DDR is used as a backup, the information about the primary interface is also of interest.

The following output is an example of the information displayed for the physical BRI0 interface:

```
R1#show interfaces bri 0
BRI0 is up, line protocol is up (spoofing)
  Hardware is BRI
  MTU 1500 bytes, BW 64 Kbit, DLY 20000 usec, rely 255/255, load 1/255
  Encapsulation HDLC, loopback not set
  Last input 00:00:00, output 00:00:00, output hang never
  Last clearing of "show interface" counters never
  Input queue: 0/75/0 (size/max/drops); Total output drops: 0
  Queueing strategy: weighted fair
  Output queue: 0/1000/64/0 (size/max total/threshold/drops)
     Conversations  0/1/256 (active/max active/max total)
     Reserved Conversations 0/0 (allocated/max allocated)
  5 minute input rate 0 bits/sec, 0 packets/sec
  5 minute output rate 0 bits/sec, 0 packets/sec
     2355 packets input, 10382 bytes, 0 no buffer
     Received 5 broadcasts, 0 runts, 0 giants, 0 throttles
     0 input errors, 0 CRC, 0 frame, 0 overrun, 0 ignored, 0 abort
     2402 packets output, 10626 bytes, 0 underruns
     0 output errors, 0 collisions, 5 interface resets
     0 output buffer failures, 0 output buffers swapped out
     3 carrier transitions
```

Because the interface statistics can accumulate over long periods of time, they may not indicate whether a problem is occurring now. To aide in troubleshooting, you can clear the counters on the interface with the following command:

```
R1#clear counters bri 0
```

If you suspect a hardware problem, the show interfaces command can help determine if that is a possibility. In addition, you can use the show controllers command to get information about the interface hardware. The output of the show controllers command is lengthy and includes much low-level information. It is most useful when working with technical support, but it may give some indication of errors.

Troubleshooting the Dialer

When experiencing problems with DDR, it is usually helpful to find out what is happening with the dialer. The show dialer command displays the interfaces configured for DDR, along with their timers and current states. In addition, there is a summary of the number of dial successes and failures for each dial string.

When a connection is up, the show dialer command includes additional information about the current connection(s). It shows the connect time, the amount of time until disconnect, and the dial reason, which is a particularly useful piece of information. The following output shows that both B-channels are currently connected:

```
R1#show dialer


BRI0 - dialer type = ISDN


Dial String      Successes   Failures    Last called   Last status
0 incoming call(s) have been screened.
0 incoming call(s) rejected for callback.


BRI0:1 - dialer type = ISDN
Idle timer (120 secs), Fast idle timer (20 secs)
Wait for carrier (30 secs), Re-enable (15 secs)
Dialer state is data link layer up
Dial reason: ip (s=192.168.254.1, d=192.168.5.1)
Interface bound to profile Dialer0
Time until disconnect 61 secs
Current call connected 00:00:14
Connected to 5552000


BRI0:2 - dialer type = ISDN
Idle timer (120 secs), Fast idle timer (20 secs)
Wait for carrier (30 secs), Re-enable (15 secs)
```

```
Dialer state is data link layer up

Dial reason: Dialing on overload

Interface bound to profile Dialer0

Time until disconnect 105 secs

Current call connected 00:00:16

Connected to 5552000


Dialer0 - dialer type = DIALER PROFILE

Load threshold for dialing additional calls is 1

Idle timer (120 secs), Fast idle timer (20 secs)

Wait for carrier (30 secs), Re-enable (15 secs)

Dialer state is data link layer up


Dial String      Successes   Failures    Last called   Last status
5552000                  6          0     00:00:16      successful   Default
```

Notice that the first B-channel connected due to an IP packet destined for the IP address 192.168.5.1. The second B-channel was dialed due to an overload condition, which can be configured with the dialer load-threshold command. If the dial reason indicates a particular packet, that packet meets the definition of interesting traffic. If the packet should not be considered interesting, there may be a problem with the dialer list. Of course, the dial reason only provides the source and destination addresses, so it is of limited help when attempting to filter based on more detailed information, such as port numbers.

The show dialer command displays the interesting traffic that brings up a link, but it never indicates what traffic is uninteresting. To view information about all dialer traffic, use the debug dialer packets command. It provides information about traffic that is being both allowed and filtered by the dialer list. Issue this command in privileged EXEC mode:

```
R1#debug dialer packets

Dial on demand packets debugging is on
```

When the router receives interesting traffic, it generates a message giving the reason (ip PERMIT in this case), as shown here:

```
Dialer0 DDR: ip (s=192.168.254.1, d=192.168.254.2), 100 bytes, outgoing interest
ing (ip PERMIT)
```

If it receives uninteresting traffic, the reason it is considered uninteresting is identified (access list 101 in this case), as shown here:

```
Dialer0 DDR: ip (s=192.168.254.1, d=192.168.2.100), 100 bytes, outgoing unintere
sting (list 101)
```

Bear in mind that the traffic listed as uninteresting by the debugging output is still forwarded over the link if the DDR connection is already established. However, it does not reset the idle timer or bring up an idle link.

Caution

Use care when issuing the debug `dialer` `packets` command, as it can generate a lot of logging output. It is particularly dangerous when you are logged onto the router remotely.

The debug `dialer` events command provides some other useful information regarding the dialer. Enter the following command in privileged EXEC mode:

```
R1#debug dialer events
Dial on demand events debugging is on
```

The most useful information this command displays is an indication of the dial string and the cause of the event. The following output indicates that the router is dialing 555-2000 because it received a packet from 192.168.254.1 to 192.68.254.2:

```
BRI0 DDR: rotor dialout [priority]
BRI0 DDR: Dialing cause ip (s=192.168.254.1, d=192.168.254.2)
BRI0 DDR: Attempting to dial 5552000
```

The debug `dialer` events command can provide some additional information, such as error output. This can help determine if a problem is caused locally or on the remote end.

Troubleshooting ISDN

If a problem appears to be with the ISDN configuration, use the show isdn commands to view details specific to ISDN interfaces. The show isdn status command identifies the switch type configured and whether or not the interface is communicating with the ISDN switch. The output below shows the information displayed when one call is active:

```
R1#show isdn status
Global ISDN Switchtype = basic-5ess
ISDN BRI0 interface
        dsl 0, interface ISDN Switchtype = basic-5ess
    Layer 1 Status:
        ACTIVE
    Layer 2 Status:
        TEI = 112, Ces = 1, SAPI = 0, State = MULTIPLE_FRAME_ESTABLISHED
    Layer 3 Status:
        1 Active Layer 3 Call(s)
    Activated dsl 0 CCBs = 1
        CCB:callid=0x8037, sapi=0x0, ces=0x1, B-chan=1
    The Free Channel Mask:  0x80000002
    Total Allocated ISDN CCBs = 1
```

The layer three status indicates the number of currently active calls. If it indicates 0, then the ISDN interfaces are not connected to a remote node. However, the layer one status indicates whether or not the router is communicating with the ISDN switch. If layer one is not active, then there is either a problem with the configuration (such as the wrong switch type) or with the carrier's switch.

The show isdn active command displays all currently active calls. This is especially useful for routers that can have several ISDN calls concurrently active. The information is shown in the following columnar format:

```
R1#show isdn active
--------------------------------------------------------------------------------
                            ISDN ACTIVE CALLS
--------------------------------------------------------------------------------
History table has a maximum of 100 entries.
History table data is retained for a maximum of 15 Minutes.
--------------------------------------------------------------------------------
Call    Calling    Called     Remote  Seconds Seconds Seconds Charges
Type    Number     Number     Name    Used    Left    Idle    Units/Currency
```

```
-------------------------------------------------------------------------------
Out                  5552000                    45     76     44     0
-------------------------------------------------------------------------------
```

This output gives the direction of the call (in or out), the called/calling number, and the status of the timers for that call. This only shows calls that are currently active, but you can view information about all calls in the last 15 minutes with the show isdn history command, as shown here:

```
R1#show isdn history
-------------------------------------------------------------------------------
                             ISDN CALL HISTORY
-------------------------------------------------------------------------------
History table has a maximum of 100 entries.
History table data is retained for a maximum of 15 Minutes.

-------------------------------------------------------------------------------
Call    Calling     Called       Remote  Seconds Seconds Seconds Charges
Type    Number      Number       Name    Used    Left    Idle    Units/Currency
-------------------------------------------------------------------------------
Out                 5552000              168                     0
Out                 5552000              120                     0
Out                 5552000              120                     0
Out                 5552000              120                     0
Out                 5552000              120                     0
In      5552000     5551000              120
In      5552000     5551000              120
-------------------------------------------------------------------------------
```

Note that the only timer displayed for disconnected calls is the seconds used. The other timers do not apply to inactive calls. Unlike show isdn active, this output also shows calls that failed, although it does not provide information about why they failed.

To view information about ISDN as problems happen, you can use the debug isdn commands to see events on the ISDN interfaces. The debug isdn q921 and debug isdn q931 commands provide a high amount of low-level technical detail and are most useful to someone who understands low-level ISDN packets. Without this low-level understanding of ISDN, you can still use the debug isdn events command.

Before viewing the output of the debug isdn events command, take a look at the nondebug output generated by the router when ISDN calls are placed. With debugging disabled, the following messages are logged when an ISDN connection is established:

```
%LINK-3-UPDOWN: Interface BRI0:1, changed state to up

%DIALER-6-BIND: Interface BRI0:1 bound to profile Dialer0

%LINEPROTO-5-UPDOWN: Line protocol on Interface BRI0:1, changed state to up

%ISDN-6-CONNECT: Interface BRI0:1 is now connected to 5551000 R1
```

From the messages above, you can see the physical interface and line protocol changing state to up, and you can see the physical interface bound to the dialer interface. In addition, the dial string (5551000) and name (R1) are displayed with a connect message. In order to see more detailed information, issue the following command in privileged EXEC mode:

```
R2#debug isdn events

ISDN events debugging is on
```

With event debugging enabled, additional messages are output when a router connects or disconnects an ISDN connection. The following output is the result of an ISDN connection being successfully established:

```
ISDN BR0: Outgoing call id = 0x808C

ISDN BR0: Event: Call to 5551000 at 64 Kb/s

ISDN BR0: received HOST_PROCEEDING

ISDN BR0: received HOST_CONNECT

%LINK-3-UPDOWN: Interface BRI0:1, changed state to up

%DIALER-6-BIND: Interface BRI0:1 bound to profile Dialer0

ISDN BR0: Event: Connected to 5551000 on B1 at 64 Kb/s

%LINEPROTO-5-UPDOWN: Line protocol on Interface BRI0:1, changed state to up

%ISDN-6-CONNECT: Interface BRI0:1 is now connected to 5551000 R1
```

As you can see, the router displayed several additional messages. Although the debugging messages do not provide much new information, this output is particularly helpful when the interface fails to connect. If the connection fails, the interface never comes up, so normal logging messages are not generated. The debugging output is the only output displayed, as shown here:

```
ISDN BR0: Outgoing call id = 0x8089

ISDN BR0: Event: Call to 5551000 at 64 Kb/s

ISDN BR0: received HOST_PROCEEDING

ISDN BR0: received HOST_INFORMATION

ISDN BR0: received HOST_INFORMATION

ISDN BR0: Event: Hangup call to call id 0x8089

ISDN BR0: received HOST_DISCONNECT_ACK
```

Even though the call fails, you can still see the number that is being called. Notice that the sequence of events starts the same as a successful connection, but then after the HOST_PROCEEDING event, there is no HOST_CONNECT event, so the interface stays down. This is the reason that no normal logging messages were generated. After waiting for the wait-for-carrier time to expire, the router closes the attempted connection.

Troubleshooting Dial Backup

If using dial backup, the show backup command displays a list of primary and secondary interfaces, along with the status of the backup. For example, the following is displayed when the primary interface is operational:

```
R1#show backup

Primary Interface   Secondary Interface   Status

----------------    ------------------    ------

Serial0             Dialer0               normal operation
```

The status field can be one of the following four values:

- *normal operation*: The primary interface is up and operational. The secondary interface is in standby mode.

- *waiting to backup*: The primary interface is down, but the secondary interface is still in standby mode, waiting for the timer to expire before coming up.

- *backup mode*: The primary interface is down, and the secondary interface is up and routing traffic.
- *waiting to revert*: The primary interface is up, and the secondary interface is up as well. The secondary interface is waiting for the timer to expire before returning to standby.

The waiting-to-backup and waiting-to-revert states also display the amount of time left before transitioning to the next state. If either of the timers (specified in the `backup delay` command) is set to zero, the corresponding waiting state is skipped.

The `debug backup` command generates messages about backup events and state changes as they take place. The `debugging messages` contain most of the same information as the output of the `show backup` command. To generate the debugging output, simply enter the following in privileged EXEC mode:

```
R1#debug backup
Backup events debugging is on
```

In all of the example output below, the primary link is Serial0, and the secondary link is Dialer0. When Serial0 goes down, the following two messages are displayed:

```
BACKUP(Serial0): event = primary went down
BACKUP(Serial0): changed state to "waiting to backup"
```

These messages indicate the event that took place and the resulting change of state. At this point, the activation timer is started, and when it expires, the secondary interface is activated and the backup state changes, as shown here:

```
BACKUP(Serial0): event = timer expired
BACKUP(Serial0): secondary interface (Dialer0) made active
BACKUP(Serial0): changed state to "backup mode"
```

When the primary link returns to normal operation, another event is generated, and the state changes, as shown here:

```
BACKUP(Serial0): event = primary came up
BACKUP(Serial0): changed state to "waiting to revert"
```

In addition, the deactivation timer is started. When it expires, the backup interface returns to standby mode and the state changes once again, as shown here:

```
BACKUP(Serial0): event = timer expired

BACKUP(Serial0): secondary interface (Dialer0) moved to standby

BACKUP(Serial0): changed state to "normal operation"
```

Troubleshooting Snapshot Routing

When using snapshot routing, the debug snapshot and show snapshot commands display information about the current status of the snapshot client or snapshot server. The snapshot server information is less interesting than the client information because the client controls the snapshot sessions and keeps the timers. All of the sample output shown in this section is from the snapshot client.

The show snapshot command lists information about the snapshot configuration, including the timers and the current state of the snapshot process. In addition, it lists the amount of time remaining in the current state. To view the snapshot events as they take place, enter the debug snapshot command, as shown here:

```
R1#debug snapshot

Snapshot support debugging is on
```

During the quiet time, the output of the show snapshot command is as follows:

```
R1#show snapshot

Dialer0 is up, line protocol is upSnapshot client

  Options: dialer support, stay asleep on carrier up

  Length of active period:        5 minutes

  Length of quiet period:         30 minutes

  Length of retry period:         8 minutes

   For dialer address 80

    Current state: quiet, remaining: 23 minutes
```

When the quiet timer expires, the client moves to active state. At this time, the client dials the server, if a connection is not already established. As this takes place, the client generates the following debugging output:

```
SNAPSHOT: Dialer0[80]: Move to active queue (Quiet timer expired)
SNAPSHOT: Dialer0[80]: moving to active queue
SNAPSHOT: Dialer0[80]: Starting aging of ip protocol
```

The last message displayed here indicates that IP routing updates have been successfully exchanged. After the routing information has been exchanged, the output of the show snapshot command appears as follows:

```
R1#show snapshot
Dialer0 is up, line protocol is upSnapshot client
  Options: dialer support, stay asleep on carrier up
  Length of active period:        5 minutes
  Length of quiet period:         30 minutes
  Length of retry period:         8 minutes
  For dialer address 80
   Current state: active, remaining/exchange time: 5/1 minutes
   Connected dialer interface:
     BRI0:1 , BRI0:2
  Updates received this cycle: ip
```

Notice that the last line of the output lists the routing updates received, only IP in this case. Before the routing protocol updates are exchanged, the last line is omitted. After the active timer expires, the router enters a post-active state. This is signaled by the following debug message:

```
SNAPSHOT: Dialer0[80]: moving to client post active->quiet queue
```

The following information given by show snapshot indicates the same:

```
R1#show snapshot
Dialer0 is up, line protocol is upSnapshot client
  Options: dialer support, stay asleep on carrier up
  Length of active period:        5 minutes
  Length of quiet period:         30 minutes
  Length of retry period:         8 minutes
```

```
For dialer address 80

  Current state: client post active->quiet, remaining time: 2 minutes

  Updates received this cycle: ip
```

If the router experiences a problem during the active state and cannot exchange routing updates, the last line (indicating the update success) does not appear. In this case, the expiration of the post-active state results in a quiet state lasting only as long as the retry period. Only if the updates were successful would the quiet state last the entire quiet interval. When the routing updates cannot be exchanged, the following debug messages are seen:

```
SNAPSHOT: Dialer0[80]: retrying; no updates exchanged

SNAPSHOT: Dialer0[80]: moving to quiet queue
```

If there were no errors, only the second message would appear, and the quiet state would last the entire quiet interval.

Troubleshooting Authentication

If DDR problems could be related to the authentication process, use the debug ppp authentication command to view information about authentication as it takes place. This debug command enables you to determine whether or not the router is getting to the point of authentication and, if so, what the problem may be. To view authentication events, enter the command in privileged EXEC mode as follows:

```
R2#debug ppp authentication

PPP authentication debugging is on
```

When a connection is successfully established, debugging output similar to the following is generated:

```
BR0:1 PPP: Treating connection as a callout

BR0:1 PPP: Phase is AUTHENTICATING, by both

BR0:1 CHAP: O CHALLENGE id 21 len 23 from "R2"

BR0:1 CHAP: I CHALLENGE id 21 len 23 from "R1"

BR0:1 CHAP: O RESPONSE id 21 len 23 from "R2"

BR0:1 CHAP: I SUCCESS id 21 len 4

BR0:1 CHAP: I RESPONSE id 21 len 23 from "R1"

BR0:1 CHAP: O SUCCESS id 21 len 4
```

From this output, you can see the sequence of the CHAP authentication procedure. The lines that start with "I" indicate input, and the lines that start with "O" indicate output. Each router issues a challenge to its peer and responds to the challenge from its peer. Upon successful authentication, each router sends its peer a success message. However, if the authentication fails, debugging messages similar to the following appear:

```
BR0:1 PPP: Treating connection as a callout

BR0:1 PPP: Phase is AUTHENTICATING, by both

BR0:1 CHAP: O CHALLENGE id 25 len 23 from "R2"

BR0:1 CHAP: I CHALLENGE id 25 len 23 from "R1"

BR0:1 CHAP: O RESPONSE id 25 len 23 from "R2"

BR0:1 CHAP: I FAILURE id 25 len 25 msg is "MD/DES compare failed"
```

In this example, R2 sends its challenge and receives a challenge from R1. Because R2 has a different password than R1, when R2 sends its response, R1 sends back a failure message. From this output, it is easy to see that the passwords are out of sync.

Wrap-Up

As you can see from its various uses, DDR is a desirable alternative to dedicated connections for sites with limited budgets and/or long periods of idle time. In addition, DDR is a cost-effective backup solution for dedicated connections that are critical to an organization. DDR must be configured carefully — misconfiguration can result in a loss of functionality or extremely high usage costs. Several strategies for configuring DDR are available, and the appropriate one to use depends on the network environment. As always, whether using DDR as a backup solution or as a primary network link, it is advisable to test the configuration to ensure that it performs as expected. It is also a good idea to track the usage, perhaps with a monitoring tool, so that usage costs are never a surprise.

Appendix A

Configuring Access Lists

Controlling traffic on a network, in any form, be it user data or network overhead such as routing protocol update traffic, is a must. In addition, the ability to be very granular in specifying what is being controlled or filtered is paramount. In today's networking environments, the responsibilities of filtering traffic usually fall under the auspices of network security, although you will see in this appendix that security is not the only reason. The actual process of configuring traffic filtering is accomplished through the use of access control lists, or simply ACLs, a feature available in the Cisco Internetwork Operating System (IOS).

Understanding an Access Control List

An ACL is used to filter packets coming into or out of a router's interface. Based upon what you have configured, the router determines whether to drop or forward the packet. How an ACL is implemented is based upon a number of considerations.

Once the decision has been made to institute a traffic filtering policy, one or more router interfaces must be chosen for the ACL. An ACL can be applied to a variety of network interfaces, including serial, Ethernet, and Token Ring interfaces. The ACL must also be applied in a direction; either inbound or outbound. Finally, the network protocol being filtered, for example, Internet Protocol (IP), Internetwork Packet Exchange (IPX), or Apple Talk, must be identified. Almost, every network protocol can be filtered using ACLs; however, because this is an IP-focused book, the examples used here reflect only IP ACLs. Other protocols you may want to filter are configured using the same mechanics as IP, but with slightly different syntax.

Tip

Cisco IOS permits only one ACL per protocol, per interface, and per direction.

Figure A-1 presents a typical scenario for using ACLs. In this example, an ACL is configured and applied to interface Serial 0 in an inbound direction. You'll construct your ACL to filter certain types of traffic coming from the Internet into the router, and subsequently, into the network.

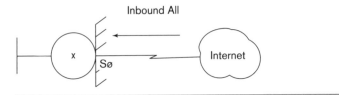

Figure A-1 *A router configured with an inbound ACL to filter Internet traffic*

The Cisco IOS can filter based upon many different criteria. An IP packet can be filtered based upon any combination of the source IP address, the destination IP address, the destination port, the source port, and the source protocol. Source protocols include IP, Transmission Control Protocol (TCP), User Datagram Protocol (UDP), Internet Control Message Protocol (ICMP), and others. The granularity you wish to achieve when filtering indicates which type of ACL should be used. ACLs come in two flavors: standard and extended; extended ACLs have more options for controlling filtering granularity. When deciding which ACL to use for your particular situation, take into account the performance impact the ACL will have on the router. The instant you apply an ACL to an interface, every single packet for the protocol you specified must be checked against the ACL. As a result, the more you check or filter, the more of an impact the ACL will have on the router's performance. The general rule of thumb is to use a standard ACL if it can fulfill your filtering policy, and to only go to the extended ACL when necessary.

Constructing Standard Access Lists

When filtering traffic with a standard IP access list, the router uses only the source IP address of the data packet to determine if the packet is matched. If a match is made, the packet is then permitted or denied based on the key word configured for that line of the ACL. . A standard IP access list permits or denies the entire IP protocol. The syntax for a standard IP access list is entered from global configuration mode as follows:

```
access-list access-list-number {permit | deny} source [wildcard-mask]
```

The permitted *access-list-number* range for a standard IP access list is 1 through 99. This number defines the access list as a standard IP access list.

Once the global access list statements have been created, they must then be bound to an interface using a command entered from interface configuration mode. If the global statements are not bound to an interface, they perform no function. In other words, all traffic continues to flow. The syntax for binding an ACL to an interface is as follows:

```
ip access-group access-list-number [in | out]
```

The following example would permit all IP traffic originating from subnet 10.1.1.0 inbound on Ethernet 0. All other IP traffic would be denied.

```
Router(config)#access-list 1 permit 10.1.1.0 0.0.0.255
Router(config)#access-list 1 deny any
Router(config)#interface ethernet 0
Router(config-if)#ip access-group 101 in
```

Notice that the ACL statements themselves were constructed one line at a time, in global configuration mode and subsequently tied to Ethernet 0 in interface configuration mode. In the following two sections, you will see that the order of the statements is important as is the mask that is used. Finally, be aware that the ACL statements all share the same ACL number; in the preceding case, it's the number 1.

Understanding the Wildcard Mask

The wildcard mask defines the criteria for an ACL statement. A wildcard mask is a 32-bit string that is compared to the 32 bit address that is used in the same ACL statement. Within the 32-bit wildcard mask, a 0 (zero) means "must match exactly" and a 1 (one) means "don't care." Examine the following statement:

```
access-list 1 permit 10.1.1.0 0.0.0.255
```

The wildcard of 0.0.0.255 is compared to the IP address 10.1.1.0. They are both 32-bit strings, so

0.0.0.255	is equal to	00000000 00000000 00000000 11111111
10.1.1.0	is equal to	00001010 00000001 00000001 00000000

When these two 32-bit strings are compared, you can see that the first three octets (10.1.1) must be matched exactly, and the final octet can be any valid number. Therefore, in this example, any packet starting with an IP address of 10.1.1 will be matched. Using this combination of "0" and "1" to create a wildcard mask, any IP address, subnet, network, etc., can be defined.

Understanding the Order of the Access List Statements

When creating an access list, the order of the global `access-list` statements is very important, because the router processes the statements from the top of the list to the bottom. The first statement of the access list is always considered by the router first. The second statement is next, the third follows the second, and so on.

Tip

More specific access list statements should appear before more general access list statements.

However, as each packet is checked against the statements in the ACL, once a match is made against an ACL line, the action — either *permit* or *deny* — is executed and the router ceases to process the remainder of the statements in the ACL for that packet. Therefore, it makes good sense to put your most-used statements near the top of the list, if possible, because the sooner a match is made for a given packet, the sooner the packet is filtered, and the less processing that needs to take place. However, you must be careful not to alter your intended filtering policy in order to make the router process fewer statements, as the following example shows:

```
Router(config)#access-list 1 permit any

Router(config)#access-list 1 deny 10.1.1.0 0.0.0.255

Router(config)#interface ethernet 0

Router(config-if)#ip access-group 101 in
```

The intention in this example was to deny IP traffic from subnet 10.1.1.0 and permit all other IP traffic. However, if you installed this ACL, *all* IP traffic, including subnet 10.1.1.0, would be permitted. This is because subnet 10.1.1.0 would be matched against the first line of the ACL, which permits all IP traffic, and no packets would ever be denied. In this case, even though the majority of traffic will match the permit statement, it must go below the more granular deny statement to achieve the desired effect.

Understanding the concept of 'implicit deny all'

Whenever an IP access list is created on a Cisco router, the IOS appends an unwritten `implicit deny all` command to the ACL. This is true whether your access list consists of one line or many lines. To make matters more complicated, the implicit deny all will *not* show up in the router output; you just have to assume that it is there. Because of the implicit deny all, unless your intent is to deny all traffic, at least one permit statement must be in your access list. If not, you will be denying all IP traffic.

The following text shows an example of using the implicit deny all to your advantage:

```
Router(config)#access-list 1 permit 10.1.1.0 0.0.0.255

Router(config)#interface ethernet 0

Router(config-if)#ip access-group 101 in
```

In this example, the filtering policy is to permit network 10.1.1.0 in on Ethernet 0, and to deny everything else. Because every ACL has an unwritten `implicit deny all` command built in after the last statement, this policy can be instituted using only one line in the ACL. Network 10.1.1.0 will be permitted and all remaining IP traffic will be denied.

Constructing Extended Access Lists

An extended access list follows all the same rules and conditions as a standard access list, except that more criteria can be matched. In addition to the source IP address, the destination IP address can be matched, as can higher layer protocols such as TCP and UDP. Even source and destination port numbers of applications can be specified. The permitted access-list-number range for an extended access list is 100 through 199. It is this number that defines the access list as an extended IP access list.

The syntax for an extended access list is as follows:

```
access-list access-list-number {permit | deny} protocol source wildcard-mask
[operator] [operand] destination wildcard-mask [operator] [operand]
```

The next example would permit telnet (TCP port 23) coming only from host 10.1.1.1 and going to the network 11.0.0.0 inbound on serial 1.

```
Router(config)#access-list 101 permit tcp 10.1.1.1 0.0.0.0 11.0.0.0
0.255.255.255 eq 23
Router(config)#interface serial 1
Router(config-if)#ip access-group 101 in
```

In this example, notice that the source and destination IP address are being checked, as is the layer 4 protocol TCP, as is the destination port, in this case 23. As packets are checked against this line in the ACL, every single part of the ACL statement must be matched before the statement action — in this case, permit — would be applied. For example, if a TFTP packet coming from 10.1.1.1 and destined for 11.0.0.0 came inbound on Serial 1, the packet would not match the first line, and would be dropped due to a match of the implicit deny all after the last statement of every ACL.

Using Access Lists with Routing Protocols

Because IP routing is the focus of this book, it is important to know that an ACL can be used to filter and control routing update information. An ACL can be used in combination with routing protocols through what are known as *distribute lists*. A distribute list links a routing protocol to an ACL to filter and control routing-update information. In this manner, instead of filtering traffic on a given interface, filtering of specific networks can be done within the routing protocol environment.

Figure A-2 shows an example of route filtering through the use of distribute lists

10.1.1.0   **10.1.2.0**   **10.1.3.0**

RA   RB

E1   E0   E0   E1

Figure A-2 *A simple network utilizing outbound distribute lists under the RIP routing process*

```
RA(config)#access-list 5 deny 10.1.1.0

RA(config)#access-list 5 permit any

RA(config)#router rip

RA(config-router)#network 10.0.0.0

RA(config-router)#distribute-list 5 out E0
```

In the preceding example an ACL that denies network 10.1.1.0 and permits all other networks has been created on RA. That ACL is tied to router RA's RIP routing process via the `distribute-list` command, which references the ACL number, in this case 5. The keywords `out E0` specifies that when sending RIP routing updates from E0, do not include network 10.1.1.0 in the update. Under this specification, RB will not receive network 10.1.1.0 in the RIP update from RA.

Notice in this example the `permit any` statement is the last statement of ACL 5. The unwritten `implicit deny all` statement is appended to this ACL by the IOS, but because of the `permit any` statement, there are no packets to deny. They have all been permitted, so the `implicit deny all` statement cannot be exercised.

Distribute lists can also be used to affect routing updates being sent to a router, as shown in Figure A-3.

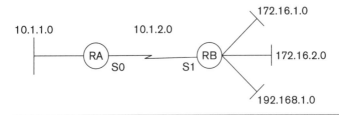

Figure A-3 *A simple network utilizing inbound distribute lists under the IGRP routing process*

```
RA(config)#access-list 6 permit 172.16.0.0 0.0.255.255

RA(config)#router igrp 200

RA(config-router)#network 10.0.0.0

RA(config-router)#distribute-list 6 in S0
```

In this last example, an ACL has been created on RA. This ACL will permit any network that is part of the major network 172.16.0.0. The distribute-list statement is used to tie the ACL to the IGRP routing process. The keywords in S0 control which IGRP routing update information will be accepted into S0. In this case networks 172.16.1.0 and 172.16.2.0 will be accepted into the routing table of RA, but network 192.168.1.0 will not be allowed.

Appendix B

Virtual Local Area Network Routing

Virtual local area networks (VLANs) are becoming more and more prevalent in networks today. VLANs provide an efficient means for splitting a network across logical boundaries while eliminating the need for extra equipment. Although a single switch that will support two VLANs may cost more than two workgroup hubs, VLANs let you extend the reach of the higher-speed switch to more users. As switching becomes more commonplace, many organizations will find that VLANs are an option for them.

Conceptually, VLAN routing is no different from routing between local area networks (LANs) that are physically separated. However, because of the unique structure of networks using VLANs, traffic can be routed between VLANs in some unique ways. Several methods for VLAN routing are presented in this appendix.

VLAN Basics

VLANs are fairly simple in concept, even though they can initially be confusing. An important thing to remember is that VLANs in a switch separate the traffic just as two separate hubs would.

This section explains the concept of VLANs and how they are used. Because the focus of this text is IP routing, the focus of this appendix is the configuration of VLAN routing for IP. Therefore, it does not cover the configuration of VLANs on switches, because different vendors offer different methods of configuration. (Even various families of Cisco switches are configured differently.)

Using VLANs

Traditionally, all ports in a hub have been in a single collision domain and broadcast domain. As the demands on networks grew, switching became a popular solution to breaking up collision domains. However, switches did not change the layout of broadcast domains; broadcast domains were still troublesome for organizations that experienced a lot of broadcast traffic. Unfortunately, separating users into separate LANs used to require physically separate network equipment. At this time, subnets were designed based on the physical location of the users, rather than their logical location within the network topology. This was a severe limitation of network architecture within an organization.

Today, VLANs solve this problem by separating a network into separate subnets within one switch. An administrator usually numbers VLANs in a switch. For example, if both engineering and marketing users are connected to the same switch, the ports to which the engineering users are connected could be VLAN 1, and the other ports could be VLAN 20. Any non-routed traffic, including broadcasts, sent by a PC in VLAN 1 stays in VLAN 1. Figure B-1 shows an example of the layout of VLANs in a switch.

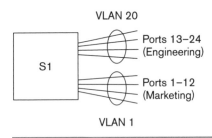

Figure B-1 *A switch with two VLANs*

It is important to note that ports in a VLAN do not necessarily have to be contiguous; Figure B-1 shows them as such for simplicity. In fact, the reason VLANs are so flexible is that they allow an administrator to change the VLAN membership of any switch port. Therefore, moving a user to a new office no longer requires moving cables to the correct ports on the switch.

Although the benefits of VLANs should be obvious already, the scenario described above still requires all users on those two VLANs to be physically close to the switch configured for those VLANs. The use of *trunking,* described in the next section, eliminates this requirement and dramatically increases the flexibility of VLANs.

Trunking

In addition to being able to separate groups of users that share a common switch, VLANs enable you to extend your network segments across multiple switches. This is probably the most useful feature of VLANs — they do away with the limitation of physical location when designing logical networks. By configuring trunking, switches throughout a network can share a common set of VLANs, which perform the same as a VLAN within a switch (see Figure B-2).

Trunking allows switches to communicate VLAN information when they send traffic between one another. In addition, trunking is not limited to switches — servers and routers can also support trunking. Servers may support trunking in order to serve several subnets using local addresses. This can be especially helpful when using a non-routable network protocol. The combination of routers and trunking is discussed in "Routing on a Stick," later in this appendix.

In Figure B-2, each switch is on a separate floor of a building. The network needs to be broken down into three subnets, based on department. Without trunking, the most likely solution to this problem would be to put three hubs or switches on each floor, and run three connections, rather than one, between the floors. In addition to saving on the cabling and equipment requirements, trunking is much more flexible, because the VLANs can be moved around as needed, or another VLAN can be added to any floor at any time.

When switches transmit a frame over a trunk, they tag it with information identifying the VLAN of the frame. When they receive a frame over a trunk, switches forward that frame only to ports in the same VLAN. Several different trunking protocols can be used on a trunk, depending on what the equipment on each end supports. Inter-Switch Link (ISL) is a Cisco-proprietary protocol for trunking across Fast and Gigabit Ethernet. The Institute of Electrical and Electronic Engineers (IEEE) specification 802.1q also supports these media and allows for inter-vendor operability. IEEE specification 802.10 supports trunking over Fiber Distributed Data Interface (FDDI). LAN emulation (LANE) allows for trunking over Asynchronous Transfer Mode, or ATM. Whatever the medium, both ends of the trunk must use the same trunking protocol.

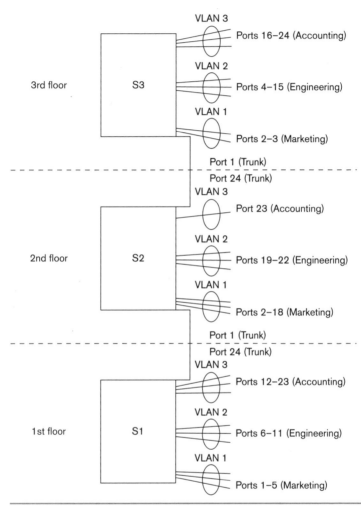

Figure B-2 *These switches are trunking to preserve VLAN information as they pass frames between floors. This enables users of every subnet to be located on each floor.*

Tip

Unlike normal ports, which reside in only one VLAN, trunk ports typically belong to all VLANs. This allows switches to pass traffic from any VLAN to neighboring switches.

Under most circumstances, you need to manually configure a switch to use certain ports as trunks. Some switches support auto-negotiation of trunking. When creating a trunk, make sure that both switches are configured for trunking on the ports over which they are connected.

Routing between VLANs

To set up routing between VLANs, you have several options. You can use multiple router interfaces, route over a single interface (using trunking), or install a multi-layer switch. Each of these options achieves the same end result. The primary trade-offs among them are equipment cost, ease of configuration, and VLAN routing speed. Each option is explained in the following sections, and configuration examples are provided.

Using Multiple Router Interfaces

Because VLANs are separate broadcast domains, they are conceptually identical to physically separate LANs. To route between two separate LANs, we would normally connect each LAN to a separate interface of a router. Using the same model, one router with multiple LAN interfaces can be used to route between VLANs on a single switch. Each router interface must be connected to a port on the switch in a different VLAN from the other interfaces. Figure B-3 shows an example of this setup.

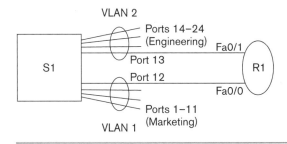

Figure B-3 *Router R1 can be used to route between VLANs 1 and 2 by connecting each LAN interface on R1 to a separate port on the switch S1.*

In Figure B3, R1 has two Fast Ethernet interfaces, and S1 is configured with two VLANs—1 and 2. The interfaces on R1 are each connected to ports on S1 in separate VLANs. FastEthernet0/0 is connected to VLAN 1; FastEthernet0/1 is connected to VLAN 2. Each interface is configured to be on a separate IP subnet. The relevant parts of the R1 configuration are as follows:

```
interface FastEthernet 0/0
  ip address 192.168.1.1 255.255.255.0
!
interface FastEthernet 0/1
  ip address 192.168.2.1 255.255.255.0
```

As you can see from this configuration, nothing special has been done to inform R1 that these two networks are VLANs in the same switch. R1 is configured just as it would be for two physically separate LANs. R1 considers each VLAN to be a separate LAN, which is logically correct.

Tip

When using VLANS, be sure to configure other nodes on the network as you would in physically separate LANs. For example, to communicate across the subnets, all end nodes need to be configured with a default gateway, which may be the router that is routing between the VLANs.

After configuring the interfaces as shown, you can also configure routing protocols on R1 as needed. For information on configuring a particular routing protocol, please see the corresponding chapter in this book. R1 did not need to be configured specially for VLAN routing in this scenario, and routing protocols also require no special configuration in this case.

Routing on a Stick

Routing between VLANs with multiple router interfaces is simple, but it makes inefficient use of the interfaces and switch ports. Although prices for both switches and routers continue to shrink, this is not a desirable situation. For this reason, it is wise to use a router that supports trunking; this type of router enables you to use only one connection between the router and the switch.

Normally, a router with only one network connection is useless, because it needs at least two networks to route between. There are times, such as during a network migration, when it may be necessary to use only one interface on a router, but these situations are usually temporary, and they are less than optimal. However, with trunking, a router can route between two networks by using only one physical interface.

Many Cisco routers support trunking, as long as they have Fast Ethernet interfaces (trunking is not supported on Ethernet). With trunking, the router and switch communicate VLAN information between each other, thereby giving the router a connection to every VLAN carried on that trunk. Because only one router interface is connected with one switch port, a nickname for this kind of routing is *routing on a stick* (see Figure B-4).

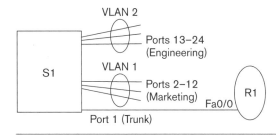

Figure B-4 *Routing on a stick*

To configure a switch for routing on a stick, configure the port that is connected to the router as a trunk port. On the router, each VLAN on the trunk requires a separate subinterface of the physical Fast Ethernet interface. The following configuration for R1 would enable it for routing on a stick:

```
interface FastEthernet0/0

 no ip address

!

interface FastEthernet0/0.11

 encapsulation isl 1
```

```
ip address 192.168.1.1 255.255.255.0
!
interface FastEthernet0/0.12
encapsulation isl 2
ip address 192.168.2.1 255.255.255.0
```

First of all, note that no IP address is assigned to the physical interface; instead, each of the subinterfaces is assigned an IP address. Each subinterface also has an `encapsulation` configuration command (shown in bold), which specifies not only the trunking protocol (ISL, in this case), but also the VLAN number. Make sure to configure the router to use the trunking protocol that matches your switch configuration. For example, if S1 were to be reconfigured to use 802.1q, R1 would be configured as follows:

```
interface FastEthernet0/0
 no ip address
!
interface FastEthernet0/0.11
encapsulation dot1Q 1
 ip address 192.168.1.1 255.255.255.0
!
interface FastEthernet0/0.12
encapsulation dot1Q 2
 ip address 192.168.2.1 255.255.255.0
```

Note also that the only difference between these two configurations is the `encapsulation` configuration command — all other information stays the same.

Each LAN subinterface is treated independently, much like serial subinterfaces configured for Frame Relay. Therefore, other processes on the router can be configured as they would on physical interfaces, such as routing protocols and Hot Standby Router Protocol (HSRP).

Using Multi-Layer Switches

Thus far, we have described VLAN routing with a separate device — a router. While the use of a physically separate router accomplishes the end goal of VLAN routing, this solution sacrifices speed. Each time a packet needs to be routed between VLANs, it must leave the switch, enter the router, leave the router, and reenter the switch. In high demand situations, this process can be prohibitively slow. Even though a trunking port must minimally support Fast Ethernet, most switch ports also operate at this speed, meaning more traffic may be entering the switch than can be sent to the router. Even if the switch is not overwhelmed, this can cause delays.

The solution to this problem is to merge the switch and router into one physical device. Multi-layer switches, such as the Cisco Catalyst 5000 and 6000 family of switches, combine the functionality of routing and switching. To achieve this combination in one box, the Catalyst chassis is modular and supports several types of *line cards* (or *blades*), three of which are of interest here. The first type of blade is a *line card module*, which typically has a high port density; it usually acts as the end node connection point for the switch. The second type of blade is a *supervisor engine module,* which serves as the switching engine. And finally, a *router switch module* (RSM) can be inserted into the device to provide the routing functionality. When a Catalyst switch is configured with an RSM, the device can route between VLANs across the high-speed backplane of the switch. Routing between VLANs no longer requires frames to leave and reenter the switch; instead, the VLAN routing happens within the switch, yielding much better performance.

Configuring the RSM of a Catalyst is actually quite simple, because it behaves similarly to an actual router. The major difference is that instead of configuring physical interfaces, you are configuring VLAN interfaces. The RSM does not have physical port interfaces; instead, it has a logical interface for each VLAN. For each VLAN you configure on the switch that you want to route, you need to configure a corresponding VLAN interface on the RSM. Each interface is given an IP address within the appropriate network assigned to each VLAN, and end nodes are commonly configured with their default gateways pointing towards the RSM VLAN IP address. This configuration code from an RSM shows an example of routing between two VLANs:

```
interface Vlan20

 ip address 20.0.0.1 255.0.0.0

!

interface Vlan30

 ip address 30.0.0.1 255.0.0.0
```

With the VLAN interfaces configured on the RSM as shown here, the RSM builds a routing table, just like any other router. The following routing table is from the RSM of a Catalyst 6509 with the above configuration:

```
6509#sh ip route
Codes: C - connected, S - static, I - IGRP, R - RIP, M - mobile, B - BGP

       D - EIGRP, EX - EIGRP external, O - OSPF, IA - OSPF inter area

       N1 - OSPF NSSA external type 1, N2 - OSPF NSSA external type 2

       E1 - OSPF external type 1, E2 - OSPF external type 2, E - EGP

       i - IS-IS, L1 - IS-IS level-1, L2 - IS-IS level-2, ia - IS-IS inter area

       * - candidate default, U - per-user static route, o - ODR

       P - periodic downloaded static route


Gateway of last resort is not set


C    20.0.0.0/8 is directly connected, Vlan20

C    30.0.0.0/8 is directly connected, Vlan30
```

From this output, you can see that routing is possible between the VLANs without physically leaving the Catalyst switch. In addition, the RSM can be configured in the same way as any other router, including the addition of routing protocols or HSRP.

Wrap-Up

As networking technology progresses and devices become more powerful and feature-rich, the lines between routing and switching blur. VLAN routing can be thought of as one of the first examples of how these two previously distinct worlds are colliding and morphing into one. The Cisco Catalyst 6500 product is sold under the switching line of products; however, it is a box that can be as much a router as it is a switch. As is the case with the Catalyst 6500, we will soon see a day when all ports of a network device can be either switched or routed ports. As these changes take place, the need for VLAN routing will continue to grow. As network devices become more multi-functional, we will see VLAN routing, especially with multi-layer switches, become the de facto standard method of routing between user segments.

Appendix C

Network Address Translation

Network address translation (NAT) is a mechanism that enables one IP address to be translated to an address on a different IP network. Though it's not an IP routing protocol, NAT is included here because it is becoming an increasingly important part of building IP networks.

NAT acts as a boundary between networks. It is used mostly for separating them into public and private networks. Public networks are those that are not under the control of the local administrator, such as the Internet. Private networks are managed by the local administrator. Public addresses are assigned to an organization from the owner of the addresses; private addresses are chosen for use inside the organization. NAT translates between public and private addresses.

Network Address Translation Overview

The impending exhaustion of the registered IP addresses on the Internet is one of the major reasons that NAT was created. NAT permits IP address reuse, thereby reducing the demand for publicly registered IP addresses. Because the majority of networked devices that access the Internet are clients, rather than servers, they do not necessarily need unique IP addresses. It is possible to multiplex all of these client connections from multiple private addresses to a smaller number of public addresses.

Making use of private addresses also gives network administrators much more flexibility in the way they design their IP addressing schemes. There are many more private addresses available than there are globally unique addresses that one would be able to register with an Internet registry. In addition, registering fewer IP addresses on the Internet reduces costs.

The guidelines for implementing private address spaces are explained in the Request for Comments (RFC) 1918: "Address Allocation for Private Internets." The Internet Assigned Numbers Authority (IANA) www.iana. com has set aside three IP address spaces for private use. These are

- 10.0.0.0 – 10.255.255.255, or 10/8 in CIDR notation, one Class A network

- 172.16.0.0 – 172.31.255.255 (172.16/12), 16 Class B networks

- 192.168.0.0 – 192.168.255.255 (192.168/16), 256 Class C networks.

Normally, hosts with addresses in the private ranges above would never be able to communicate on the Internet because the RFC forbids those addresses from being routed. NAT provides a way to translate the private, or illegal, addresses if one of the reserved blocks is not used, so that hosts in the private network can communicate with hosts in the public Internet.

Many types of devices perform NAT, including Application Layer Gateways (proxies), firewalls, and routers. Cisco's Internetwork Operating System (IOS) 11.2 and later versions offer this functionality. In this appendix, we cover the configuration of a Cisco router for NAT.

NAT is useful in several situations, including the following:

- You are using one of the private address spaces from RFC 1918 and need to access resources on the Internet.

- An unregistered IP address space was randomly chosen for your network before connecting to the Internet, and would conflict with another organization once your network is connected to the Internet.

- You are joining two networks that use the same IP address space and need to share resources.

NAT works by maintaining a table of all the connections that it is currently handling. This table contains the original source and destination IP address, the translated source and destination IP address, the original source and destination port number, the translated source and destination port number, as well as Transmission Control Protocol (TCP) and Internet Control Message Protocol (ICMP) sequence numbers.

Understanding the Language of NAT

There are several NAT related terms that you should be familiar with before we continue.

- **Global.** A global address is from an address space that has been assigned by an Internet Registry, a service provider, or another company that the local network uses for its external addresses.

- **Local.** A local address is one that exists in the enterprise network; it's most likely not an externally routable address.

- **Inside.** Inside networks are those that are under the administration of the enterprise. The local administrator assigns addresses.

- **Outside.** Outside networks are usually not under the control of the enterprise; Their administrators assign the addresses.

These terms are combined to define four types of addresses that are associated with NAT.

- **Inside local.** This is the actual address of a host that exists in the internal, private network.

- **Inside global.** This is the external address to which an inside local address is translated. The Inside global address is used for communication with external hosts.

- **Outside local.** This address is an outside host with a global address translated into a local address. An outside-local address, in effect, translates the destination address from a global address to a local address, so local hosts are able to communicate with an external host with an inside address.

- **Outside global.** This is actual address of an external host on the outside network.

Advantages of NAT

NAT gives a network much more portability than it would normally have. In the event that you change service providers, it is very likely that you will be allocated a new block of globally routable addresses from your new provider. NAT gives you the capability to change providers easily, without having to renumber your network internally. Most changes will only happen on the device performing the translation, to reflect the address range that was allocated by the new provider.

Using the reserved addresses from RFC 1918 also gives you a much larger range of addresses than would be possible if you requested addresses from an Internet registry. This allows you to more effectively design your networks by using various address-assignment techniques on whichever private address space you choose to implement.

Disadvantages of NAT

Many protocols do not function when addresses are translated, often because the source, the destination address, or both, are located somewhere in the data that the gateway is either not aware of, or has no possible way to modify. The IP Security (IPSEC) standard is one of those protocols that are affected by NAT. In order to authenticate and identify the endpoints, the source and destination addresses are embedded in the encrypted data of the transmission. Because the NAT device has no way of reading the encrypted transmission, data in the IP header will not match that in the encrypted data. IPSEC will not work correctly in this situation. Some vendors have provided mechanisms to work around this behavior, but a common solution has not yet been standardized.

FTP is another protocol that contains the address of the host in the payload. However, because this is a clear-text and popular protocol, most NAT implementations are able to account for this by changing the source address that is transmitted in the data. By doing so, it is possible that the actual size of the data will be changed, causing more packets to be transmitted. The NAT device must then modify the sequence numbers of these packets as they pass through.

The NAT device cannot perform these modifications for protocols of which it is unaware; consequently, these protocols will not behave properly. Without specific proxies or gateways written for these protocols, the applications that rely on them will no longer function when addresses are translated.

Configuring NAT

There are three different ways in which NAT can operate on a Cisco router: static translation, a fixed one-to-one address mapping; dynamic translation, an as-needed one-to-one address mapping; and address overloading, an as-needed many-to-one address mapping. In this section, we will cover the steps and commands used to configure these methods on a Cisco router.

When configuring NAT, there are few steps that are common among the different methods of translations. In order to indicate to the router which interface is considered the inside interface, and which is considered the outside, we must explicitly configure the interfaces in question.

We do this by going into interface configuration mode and entering the `ip nat inside` or `ip nat outside` command, whichever is applicable to that interface.

The sample network diagrammed in Figure C-1 demonstrates this . In this sample network, we will be using BorderRouter as the router that performs the NAT functions. InternalRouter will be acting as our private host, and ISPRouter, will be configured to act as an external host. In this case, the external host is the next hop router.

Tip

Both of the address spaces used in our example were taken from the reserved private pool of addresses, but the 172.20.80.2 address looks foreign enough that it could easily be mistaken for a publicly routable address. The use of this address should help to keep the local and global addresses clearly delineated.

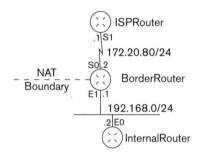

Figure C-1 *This sample network will be used as a template for NAT configurations.*

```
BorderRouter(config)#int s0
BorderRouter(config-if)#ip nat outside


BorderRouter(config)#int e0
BorderRouter(config-if)#ip nat inside
```

The previous code excerpt indicates that we have applied these commands to the appropriate interfaces. We can verify our configuration by looking at the new interface configuration:

```
interface Ethernet0
 ip address 192.168.0.1 255.255.255.0
 no ip directed-broadcast
 ip nat inside
!
interface Serial0
 ip address 172.20.80.2 255.255.255.0
 no ip directed-broadcast
 ip nat outside
```

The Ethernet interface with the IP address of 192.168.0.1 is now designated as the inside interface, because that is the interface that will be connected to our stub enterprise network. The Serial interface addressed as 172.20.80.2 is designated as the interface connected to the public, or foreign, network — the outside interface.

Now that the interfaces have been configured, we need to decide which method of translation we want to use. We have two choices: We can choose to use static translations, which permanently associate an inside-local address with an inside-global address. Alternatively, we can make use of dynamic translations that will enable us to dynamically associate inside-local addresses with inside-global addresses on an as-needed basis.

Configuring Static Translations

A static translation is a permanent association between an inside-local address of a host on our private network and an inside-global address managed by our NAT device. Any traffic going to or from that particular host will always appear to be originating from the same global address. This function is most useful for hosts that provide resources that are accessible from the Internet, and for servers that provide things such as File Transfer Protocol (FTP) and Hypertext Transfer Protocol (HTTP). Generally, you do not want these addresses to change because users expect those servers to be available at certain addresses.

To configure a translation as static, you would enter the following command in global configuration mode:

```
ip nat inside source static inside-local-address inside-global-address
```

This command tells the router to create a translation, originating from the inside where the source address will be modified, and to create a static translation associating the inside-local address to the inside-global address. See Figure C-2.

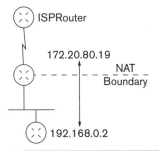

Figure C-2 *Our network configuration after static translation has been applied*

Because the inside host we have configured has an IP address of 192.168.0.2, we will set up the translation with that address as the inside-local address. For the inside-global address, we can choose any address we like that is not already used on the outside subnet, so let's arbitrarily choose 172.20.80.19.

Our configuration will look like this:

```
BorderRouter(config)#ip nat inside source static 192.168.0.2 172.20.80.19
```

Once that command is entered, all traffic generated from host 192.168.0.2 that passes through the NAT router will appear to have originated from 172.20.80.19.

There are a couple things we can check to make sure this configuration works.

First, we can try to verify that traffic is actually going through the router from our internal host to an external host. From Figure C-2, we can see that a host exists on the outside network with an IP address of 172.20.80.1. If we can ping from 192.168.0.2 to 172.20.80.1, we can verify that the translation is working.

```
InternalRouter#ping 172.20.80.1

Type escape sequence to abort.
Sending 5, 100-byte ICMP Echos to 172.20.80.1, timeout is 2 seconds:
!!!!!
Success rate is 100 percent (5/5), round-trip min/avg/max = 8/8/8 ms
```

The successful pings show that our translation is working from the inside out. Note that InternalRouter has a default route set for the inside interface of BorderRouter. This means that InternalRouter can access the 172.20.80.x network by following its default route. However, ISPRouter does not have a route to 192.168.0.x, so the only way it could have responded to the pings from InternalRouter was by responding to the translated address on BorderRouter's serial interface.

Second, because the translation is static, we should also be able to show that it works from the outside in.

```
ISPRouter#ping 172.20.80.19
```

```
Type escape sequence to abort.

Sending 5, 100-byte ICMP Echos to 172.20.80.19, timeout is 2 seconds:

!!!!!

Success rate is 100 percent (5/5), round-trip min/avg/max = 4/4/8 ms
```

Again, our pings are successful. Another way to demonstrate that our NAT configuration is successful is by using the following command:

```
sho ip nat translations
```

This command displays the current translation table. On our NAT router, the output of the command looks like this:

```
BorderRouter#sho ip nat translations
Pro Inside global     Inside local     Outside local     Outside global
--- 172.20.80.19      192.168.0.2      ---               ---
```

We can get a more definite picture of NAT operating properly by viewing the packets that are being transmitted by InternalRouter from the perspective of ISPRouter.

On ISPRouter, we have enabled the `debug ip packet` command to display the packets that it has received. Also, an access list has been built and used with the debug command to display only the source addresses in which we are interested:

```
ISPRouter(config)#access-list 100 permit ip host 172.20.80.19 any

ISPRouter(config)#access-list 100 permit ip host 192.168.0.2 any

ISPRouter(config)#exit

ISPRouter#debug ip packet 100

IP packet debugging is on for access list 100
```

The `debug ip packet` command is a very useful tool when troubleshooting IP connectivity problems.

Caution

Be sure to specify access lists with `debug ip packet`. The command can generate a lot of debug messages and cause performance problems if all IP traffic is being debugged.

The preceding access list shows traffic from both the original source address and the translated source address; we will see the traffic even if the translation did not occur. By generating traffic from InternalRouter, we can watch the debug output on ISPRouter to verify the source address:

```
1w0d: IP: s=172.20.80.19 (Serial0), d=172.20.80.1 (Serial0), len 100, rcvd 3
1w0d: IP: s=172.20.80.19 (Serial0), d=172.20.80.1 (Serial0), len 100, rcvd 3
1w0d: IP: s=172.20.80.19 (Serial0), d=172.20.80.1 (Serial0), len 100, rcvd 3
```

Because the only address displayed is that of the translated address, we are now confident that our NAT configuration is working, and we can move on to different NAT configurations.

NAT and Address Resolution Protocol

On a multi-access medium such as Ethernet, the router is able to respond to requests for addresses that are not explicitly assigned to any of its interfaces because it sends traffic using the translated IP address and the Media Access Control (MAC) address of its own physical interface. This way, when another device attached to that network attempts to deliver a packet to an address that does not exist on any of the interfaces attached to the network, that device will know where to deliver. The device will send an Address Resolution Protocol (ARP) request for the destination address in question, and the router performing NAT will respond with its own MAC address. If the router is performing NAT for many addresses, all of these addresses will exist in the ARP table with the same MAC address, which is that of the router's physical interface. This is a by-product of NAT that is often overlooked, and you should be aware of its implications. If you are having difficulty getting NAT to work, make sure there are entries in the ARP tables of neighboring devices. Without the layer-2-to-layer-3 associations, traffic destined for a translated address will never reach its destination.

An example of this follows. The interface we configured on Border-Router is going to be servicing the physical address we assigned to it, 172.20.80.2, as well as the virtual address that is assigned to it via NAT, 172.20.80.19. In the table below, you can see that both of these addresses are associated with the same MAC address. Once an interface is configured for NAT, it will respond to ARP requests for these virtual addresses with its own MAC address.

```
ISPRouter#sho arp
Protocol  Address      Age (min)  Hardware Addr   Type   Interface
Internet  172.20.80.1        -    0000.0c5d.6f99  ARPA   Ethernet0
Internet  172.20.80.2        0    0030.9468.d900  ARPA   Ethernet0
Internet  172.20.80.19       0    0030.9468.d900  ARPA   Ethernet0
```

On point-to point-interfaces, this issue does not occur. Because only two devices exist on the network, any address that does not exist on the local router must have originated from the remote router.

Configuring Dynamic Translations

More often than not, the number of addresses used on the private network will far exceed the number of addresses assigned to you for the public address space. This limitation can be overcome, however, because practice has shown that the number of hosts communicating outside of the local domain at any given time is only a small percentage of the total number of hosts in the inside network. This is why dynamic translations work.

When a host needs to access a resource outside of the local network, the traffic passes through the NAT device on its way out of the network. At this time, if an IP address has not already been assigned to this internal host via static or dynamic means, the next available address in the outside address pool will be associated with that address. So now, any traffic that our host sends out of the network will appear to come from the same IP address. If our host stops sending information, the address originally assigned to it will then be put back into the pool for assignment to the next host, after a predetermined period. After this, if our host wishes to transmit data outside the network, it could be assigned a different address than the one it had originally.

In order to configure dynamic translation, we first define the inside and outside interfaces as we did previously. Next, because the configuration varies a bit from the static translation, we have to perform a couple of extra steps. We need to define a pool of global addresses for the router to use for new connections, and then create a standard access list that filters the addresses allowed to use this NAT pool. We then associate the NAT pool with the access list and configure it to translate the source address of the transmissions:

```
ip nat pool pool-name first-address last-address netmask netmask prefix-length
prefix-length
access-list access-list-number permit source-ip source-wildcard
ip nat inside source list access-list-number pool pool-name
```

Caution

Remember, access lists permit only those addresses that are explicitly defined. There is an implicit deny all at the end of the list that will prevent other hosts from being accepted.

For our example, shown in Figure C-3, we will need to allow only the 192.168.0/24network to be translated dynamically. If we had other networks that were not directly connected, we would need to take that into account when we created the access-list.

```
BorderRouter(config)#ip nat pool dynamic-pool 172.20.80.20 172.20.80.23 prefix-
length 24
BorderRouter(config)#access-list 10 permit 192.168.0.0 0.0.0.255
BorderRouter(config)#ip nat inside source list 10 pool dynamic-pool
BorderRouter(config)#exit
BorderRouter#
```

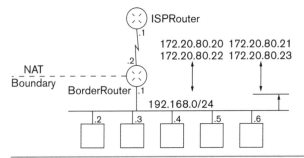

Figure C-3 *To reflect the configuration, our network diagram now looks like this.*

If we executethe `show ip nat translations` command now, we won't actually see any translations in the table:

```
BorderRouter#sho ip nat translations
Pro Inside global     Inside local     Outside local     Outside global
BorderRouter#
```

This is because the translations are not associated until a host sends traffic through the router. Let's attempt our ping test again from InternalRouter to ISPRouter, and then see what information the translation table gives us:

```
BorderRouter#sho ip nat translations
Pro Inside global     Inside local     Outside local     Outside global
--- 172.20.80.20      192.168.0.2      ---               ---
```

Now, if we use another internal IP address to make a connection outside of the NAT device, we should see another entry appear in the translation table:

```
BorderRouter#sho ip nat translations
Pro Inside global     Inside local     Outside local     Outside global
--- 172.20.80.20      192.168.0.2      ---               ---
--- 172.20.80.21      192.168.0.3      ---               ---
```

Because our pool of dynamically allocated addresses contains four addresses, four internal hosts can access the outside network at the same time:

```
BorderRouter#sho ip nat translations
Pro Inside global     Inside local     Outside local     Outside global
--- 172.20.80.20      192.168.0.2      ---               ---
--- 172.20.80.21      192.168.0.3      ---               ---
--- 172.20.80.22      192.168.0.4      ---               ---
--- 172.20.80.23      192.168.0.5      ---               ---
```

However, if a fifth host attempts to access the outside network, it will not be able to do so. Instead, the router will return a destination unreachable ICMP packet. This is evident from the ping output from a device that we assigned the address 192.168.0.6, which follows:

```
InternalRouter6#ping 172.20.80.1

Type escape sequence to abort.
```

```
Sending 5, 100-byte ICMP Echos to 172.20.80.1, timeout is 2 seconds:
U.U.U
Success rate is 0 percent (0/5)
```

In certain implementations, this is viewed as a disadvantage of dynamic address translation, but the next topic we cover remedies the shortcoming of one-to-one dynamic-address translations.

Overloading

When dynamically creating NAT associations, it is also possible to multiplex many inside IP addresses to a single outside address. This helps to remedy the problem of having more internal addresses than external (global) addresses. This is called overloading, network address port translation (NAPT), or port address translation (PAT).

To accomplish this, the NAT device changes the port numbers of the packets as they are passing through it. When functioning this way, the NAT device must not only keep track of the IP address associations, but it also must keep track of the TCP/User Datagram Protocol (UDP) port changes that it has made. For instance, if our host makes an HTTP connection from 192.168.0.2 to 172.20.80.1, the destination port will be the HTTP port, port 80, and the source port, will be some number between 1024 and 65535; we will use port 1100 in our example. When using static translations, or classic dynamic translations, the source and destination port will remain unchanged. The transmission can be displayed as such: 192.168.0.2:1100 ⇨ 172.20.80.1:80, which would then be translated to 172.20.80.19: 1100 ⇨ 172.20.80.1:80. This behavior changes in overloading. It is very likely that the translated source port number will not be the same as the original source port number. The transmission might look something similar to this: 192.168.0.2:1100 ⇨ 172.20.80.1:80, which is then translated to 172.20.80.5:2432 ⇨ 172.20.80.1:80, assuming that we are using 172.20.80.5 as our overload address.

The configuration of overloading is similar to that of dynamic translations, with the exception of the overload option being appended to the ip nat inside command.

```
ip nat inside source list access-list-number pool pool-name overload
```

As in Figure C-3, we will use 172.20.80.5 as our translated address (See Figure C-4):

```
BorderRouter(config)#ip nat pool dynamic-overload 172.20.80.5 172.20.80.5
prefix-length 24
BorderRouter(config)#ip nat inside source list 10 pool dynamic-overload overload
BorderRouter(config)#end
```

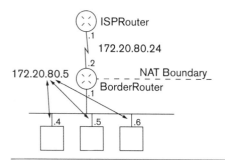

Figure C-4 *All local addresses are translated to the same global address when performing NAT overloading.*

Tip

Only one address is used for overloading. Translating ports allows for approximately 64,000 sessions to exist at the same time.

By sending pings from three different internal addresses to ISPRouter, we have built new associations in our translation table:

```
BorderRouter#sho ip nat translations
Pro Inside global      Inside local       Outside local       Outside global
icmp 172.20.80.5:2220  192.168.0.4:2220   172.20.80.1:2220    172.20.80.1:2220
icmp 172.20.80.5:2221  192.168.0.4:2221   172.20.80.1:2221    172.20.80.1:2221
icmp 172.20.80.5:2222  192.168.0.4:2222   172.20.80.1:2222    172.20.80.1:2222
icmp 172.20.80.5:2223  192.168.0.4:2223   172.20.80.1:2223    172.20.80.1:2223
icmp 172.20.80.5:2224  192.168.0.4:2224   172.20.80.1:2224    172.20.80.1:2224
icmp 172.20.80.5:5439  192.168.0.6:5439   172.20.80.1:5439    172.20.80.1:5439
icmp 172.20.80.5:5440  192.168.0.6:5440   172.20.80.1:5440    172.20.80.1:5440
icmp 172.20.80.5:5441  192.168.0.6:5441   172.20.80.1:5441    172.20.80.1:5441
```

```
icmp 172.20.80.5:5442  192.168.0.6:5442  172.20.80.1:5442  172.20.80.1:5442

icmp 172.20.80.5:5443  192.168.0.6:5443  172.20.80.1:5443  172.20.80.1:5443

icmp 172.20.80.5:8641  192.168.0.5:8641  172.20.80.1:8641  172.20.80.1:8641

icmp 172.20.80.5:8642  192.168.0.5:8642  172.20.80.1:8642  172.20.80.1:8642

icmp 172.20.80.5:8643  192.168.0.5:8643  172.20.80.1:8643  172.20.80.1:8643

icmp 172.20.80.5:8644  192.168.0.5:8644  172.20.80.1:8644  172.20.80.1:8644

icmp 172.20.80.5:8645  192.168.0.5:8645  172.20.80.1:8645  172.20.80.1:8645
```

Because ICMP was used in this example, NAT behaves a little differently than it would for TCP and UDP. When translating TCP or UDP packets, the number shown next to the IP address in the NAT table is the source and destination port numbers being used by that particular protocol. However, ICMP does not make use of port numbers; instead, the NAT table keeps track of the sequence number in the ICMP packets.

Note also the extra information displayed in the translation table when NAT performs overloading. We see much more information about the address association than we did before, when we were using only static translations. The table now shows the protocol that was used, the original and translated addresses, and the original and translated sequence numbers.

Each packet transmitted through our NAT router was assigned a different sequence number. Note that although the inside global addresses differ from the inside local addresses due to the translation, the sequence number does not. The router will try to retain the same source port or sequence numbers to aid in identification and troubleshooting. This is not always possible however, if you have multiple devices transmitting from the same source port. This is evident in the output of `show ip nat translations`:

```
InternalRouter#sho ip nat translations
Pro Inside global       Inside local       Outside local     Outside global
tcp 172.20.80.5:11000  192.168.0.6:11000  172.20.80.1:23    172.20.80.1:23
tcp 172.20.80.5:11001  192.168.0.5:11001  172.20.80.1:23    172.20.80.1:23
tcp 172.20.80.5:11002  192.168.0.5:11002  172.20.80.1:23    172.20.80.1:23
tcp 172.20.80.5:11003  192.168.0.5:11003  172.20.80.1:23    172.20.80.1:23
tcp 172.20.80.5:1024   192.168.0.6:11002  172.20.80.1:23    172.20.80.1:23
tcp 172.20.80.5:1025   192.168.0.6:11003  172.20.80.1:23    172.20.80.1:23
BorderRouter#
```

Two devices were used to open telnet sessions to 172.20.80.1. When the TCP port numbers were unique, the router reused the same port number with the inside global address. However, when a duplicate source port number was used, the router then began allocating port numbers starting with 1024.

Troubleshooting NAT

For whatever reason, NAT may not be operating in the way that you would expect it to. For this reason, the Cisco IOS offers several NAT-specific commands that aid in troubleshooting and debugging any problems that you may be experiencing.

Modifying Translation Timeouts

When using dynamic and overloaded NAT, many devices are trying to use the same addresses; therefore, unused addresses need to be reused for other connections. NAT accomplishes this by setting timeout values for the translations. When a timeout has been reached, the port or address will be put back into the available pool for other hosts to use.

The router output shown below lists the types of timeouts that can be configured:

```
BorderRouter(config)#ip nat translation ?
  dns-timeout      Specify timeout for NAT DNS flows
  finrst-timeout   Specify timeout for NAT TCP flows after a FIN or RST
  icmp-timeout     Specify timeout for NAT ICMP flows
  port-timeout     Specify timeout for NAT TCP/UDP port specific flows
  syn-timeout      Specify timeout for NAT TCP flows after a SYN and no further
                   data
  tcp-timeout      Specify timeout for NAT TCP flows
  timeout          Specify timeout for dynamic NAT translations
  udp-timeout      Specify timeout for NAT UDP flows
```

Caution

It is not a good idea to set NAT timeouts to zero. This prevents addresses and ports from being released, and eventually no new hosts will be able to communicate through the NAT router.

The `ip nat translation timeout` command is for dynamically allocated addresses that do not use overloading. The rest of the commands are used only when overloading NAT. Because overloading keeps track of layer four information, such as TCP, UDP, and ICMP, mechanisms are provided for more granular control over the timeouts. For instance, UDP is a connectionless protocol, so the timeouts for it don't need to be as large as they are for TCP.

The timeout defaults are as follows:

- `timeout` — 86400 seconds (24 hours)
- `udp-timeout` — 300 seconds (5 minutes)
- `dns-timeout` — 60 seconds (1 minute)
- `tcp-timeout` — 86400 seconds (24 hours)
- `finrst-timeout` — 60 seconds (1 minute)
- `icmp-timeout` — 60 seconds (1 minute)
- `syn-timeout` — 60 seconds (1 minute)
- `port-timeout` — 0 (never)

Displaying NAT Information

The first step in troubleshooting a problem is to display as much information about the current state of NAT as possible. The `show` commands provide information about the accumulated NAT statistics, and about the current translations that exist in the NAT state table.

```
BorderRouter#sho ip nat ?

  statistics    Translation statistics

  translations  Translation entries


BorderRouter#show ip nat statistics
```

```
Total active translations: 1 (1 static, 0 dynamic; 0 extended)
Outside interfaces:
  Serial0
Inside interfaces:
  Ethernet0
Hits: 132  Misses: 0
Expired translations: 0
Dynamic mappings:
```

The preceding output shows the statistics for a simple NAT translation. Several instances of the show ip nat translations command appear earlier in this appendix and provide good examples of the format and output of the command.

Debugging NAT

Debug commands are provided by the Cisco IOS to aid in debugging NAT issues. A ping was initiated from 192.168.0.2 to 172.20.80.1. In order to do this, a static translation was configured to translate 192.168.0.2 into 172.20.80.19. The debug command displays the translation that occurred, first showing the translation of the inside-local source address to the inside-global address, and then showing the translation from the inside-global destination address to the inside-local address. A sample output of the debug ip nat command follows:

```
BorderRouter#debug ip nat
1w2d: NAT*: s=192.168.0.2->172.20.80.19, d=172.20.80.1 [40]
1w2d: NAT*: s=172.20.80.1, d=172.20.80.19->192.168.0.2 [40]
1w2d: NAT*: s=192.168.0.2->172.20.80.19, d=172.20.80.1 [41]
1w2d: NAT*: s=172.20.80.1, d=172.20.80.19->192.168.0.2 [41]
1w2d: NAT*: s=192.168.0.2->172.20.80.19, d=172.20.80.1 [42]
1w2d: NAT*: s=172.20.80.1, d=172.20.80.19->192.168.0.2 [42]
1w2d: NAT*: s=192.168.0.2->172.20.80.19, d=172.20.80.1 [43]
1w2d: NAT*: s=172.20.80.1, d=172.20.80.19->192.168.0.2 [43]
1w2d: NAT*: s=192.168.0.2->172.20.80.19, d=172.20.80.1 [44]
1w2d: NAT*: s=172.20.80.1, d=172.20.80.19->192.168.0.2 [44]
```

The debug ip nat command also has a detailed option that provides a little more information about the translations that are occurring. Below is a sample of the same ping used above, but you can see the additional information added, such as protocol, port number, and if the packet was received on the inside (i) or outside (o) interface.

```
1w2d: NAT*: i: icmp (192.168.0.2, 5594) -> (172.20.80.1, 5594) [35]

1w2d: NAT*: o: icmp (172.20.80.1, 5594) -> (172.20.80.19, 5594) [35]

1w2d: NAT*: i: icmp (192.168.0.2, 5595) -> (172.20.80.1, 5595) [36]

1w2d: NAT*: o: icmp (172.20.80.1, 5595) -> (172.20.80.19, 5595) [36]

1w2d: NAT*: i: icmp (192.168.0.2, 5596) -> (172.20.80.1, 5596) [37]

1w2d: NAT*: o: icmp (172.20.80.1, 5596) -> (172.20.80.19, 5596) [37]

1w2d: NAT*: i: icmp (192.168.0.2, 5597) -> (172.20.80.1, 5597) [38]

1w2d: NAT*: o: icmp (172.20.80.1, 5597) -> (172.20.80.19, 5597) [38]

1w2d: NAT*: i: icmp (192.168.0.2, 5598) -> (172.20.80.1, 5598) [39]

1w2d: NAT*: o: icmp (172.20.80.1, 5598) -> (172.20.80.19, 5598) [39]
```

The debug ip nat command can also be used in conjunction with a standard access list to limit the amount of information output. This is helpful when trying to view debug outputs for specific addresses and protocols.

```
BorderRouter#debug ip nat ?
 <1-99>    Access list
 detailed  NAT detailed events
 <cr>
```

Similarly, the debug ip packet command is very helpful when debugging NAT, as you saw from the example earlier in the chapter. When coupled with an access list, the information output can be trimmed down to only the information that we find helpful for a particular problem.

Clearing NAT Information

Clearing information related to NAT is pretty much self-explanatory. Use the clear ip nat statistics command to reset all of the NAT statistics to zero. This aids in debugging when you want to view the operation of NAT from the time you clear the statistics. When NAT has been operating for some time, many statistics will accumulate, possibly disguising a problem that has only surfaced recently.

The `clear ip nat translation` command gives you the ability to remove NAT translations from the NAT state table.

Caution

When using dynamic NAT, clearing the translations will break any sessions that are currently active through the NAT device. TCP transmissions will also be affected if the command changes the port numbers or sequence numbers.

The syntax for the `clear ip nat` commands is:

```
BorderRouter#clear ip nat ?
  statistics   Clear translation statistics
  translation  Clear dynamic translation


BorderRouter#clear ip nat translation ?
  *        Delete all dynamic translations
  inside   Inside addresses (and ports)
  outside  Outside addresses (and ports)
  tcp      Transmission Control Protocol
  udp      User Datagram Protocol
```

The options available with the `clear ip nat translation` command give you granular control over which entries you may delete. When entered with the asterisk, all dynamic NAT entries will be deleted, and any new connections will be built with a fresh state table. The `inside` and `outside` options enable you to clear a translation based on a particular address, and the protocol options, `tcp` and `udp`, give you even finer control, allowing you to only delete entries for a specified address, and for a particular protocol.

Wrap-Up

Network Address Translation has proven to be effective in slowing the depletion of public addresses that the Internet began to experience a few years ago, and it has given the Internet standards bodies more time to develop the next generation of protocols.

It is a helpful technique that gives the network administrator much more flexibility when designing the network's addressing scheme, and it offers some security by distancing important hosts from the chaos of the Internet.

Appendix D

Using Cisco's Hot Standby Router Protocol

Hot Standby Router Protocol (HSRP) is a router function developed by Cisco that enables hosts to overcome the limitation of having only one default gateway. The majority of Internet Protocol (IP) hosts have the capability of using only a single router as their default gateway. All traffic not destined for the local network will go through the specified router. This shortcoming will hamper connectivity if that router becomes unavailable.

HSRP solves this problem by enabling multiple routers to service requests for a single IP address, which is completely transparent to the end system. No matter which router is being used to deliver Internetwork traffic, the process will look the same to the end system, requiring no additional configuration on the network hosts.

In this appendix, we cover the general operation of HSRP, as well as how to configure and deploy it in your enterprise network.

HSRP Overview

Anyone who has ever had their default gateway fail knows what a bother it is to lose connectivity to the rest of their network. This is especially frustrating when more than one router is on the network, but only one can be specified as the default gateway. This situation is illustrated in Figure D-1:

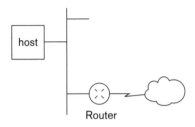

Figure D-1 *A typical network with only one default gateway*

The presence of only one router on a network leaves that network open to isolation should that router fail. Unfortunately, the solution isn't as easy as just placing another router on the network. Most hosts only allow for one default gateway to be configured; and no matter how many routers exist on the network, the host can only use the configured default gateway for traffic destined to other networks.

This problem leads to the development of HSRP. A simple illustration of HSRP is shown in Figure D-2:

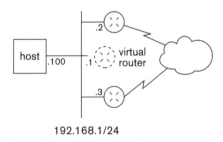

Figure D-2 *A Local Area Network (LAN) designed with multiple routers running HSRP*

In Figure D-2, two routers, each with a unique IP address, are present on the network. Normally, the user would have to choose one of the two routers to use as the default gateway. However, when HSRP is enabled on the two routers, a third virtual router is created and assigned its own IP address. This address is then used as the default gateway of the host. At any given time, one HSRP router is the active router, and one HSRP router is the standby router. The active router is responsible for servicing traffic that goes through the virtual IP address. If the active router becomes unavailable, the standby router will take over operation. Any traffic destined for the virtual IP address actually goes through the active router.

Alternatives to HSRP

Besides HSRP, several other techniques have been developed to allow for a backup default gateway. Some systems run a routing protocol, such as Routing Information Protocol (RIP), to listen for router advertisements. The routers on a particular subnetwork would advertise their presence via RIP broadcasts, and the hosts would be able to choose the default gateway based on the routing protocol. However, it may not always be desirable to have every router or every host on a network running RIP.

Some hosts are also capable of running routing daemons that support other routing protocols such as OSPF. Another alternative, which enables a host to discover a router using Internet Control Message Protocol (ICMP), is a protocol called *ICMP Router Discovery Protocol* (IRDP). This protocol is documented in Request for Comments (RFC) 1256. Hosts find routers on their network by either listening for a special ICMP packet advertising their presence, or by querying the network for routers running IRDP.

The problem with these methods is that the host must be able to support these different protocols, and the installation and configuration of such support can be an administrative burden. HSRP allows the burden of discovering an alternate gateway to be kept off the end host; instead, this becomes the responsibility of the gateways on the network. Now, every IP host can have router redundancy without having to support extra protocols.

HSRP is documented in the informational RFC 2281. Although this document explains the function of HSRP, HSRP is a proprietary Cisco protocol. The Internet Engineering Task Force, or IETF, is working on a similar protocol *called Virtual Router Redundancy Protocol* (VRRP). This protocol, documented in RFC 2338, is an open protocol, and is not bound by the usage restrictions that exist with HSRP.

Understanding the Operation of HSRP

What makes HSRP work is that a virtual IP address and a Media Access Control (MAC) address are created; thus, a virtual router is added to the network. The hosts on the network communicate with the virtual router, without having any knowledge of the physical routers on the network. One HSRP router is designated as the active router, and the other physical-router acts as a standby in case the active router fails. The active router responds to its own IP and MAC addresses, and also to the virtual IP and MAC addresses.

When a host sends a packet outside the network, the host's configuration tells the packet that the next hop is the default gateway. The IP address of the default gateway is configured, but in order to actually send the Ethernet frame to the router, the hostneeds to learn the router's MAC address. The host sends out an *Address Resolution Protocol* (ARP) request to the network, asking for the MAC address of the default gateway. Because no actual host on the network has the IP address of the virtual router, the active router responds to the ARP request by sending the virtual MAC address that corresponds to the virtual IP. The active router also listens for any traffic bound for the virtual MAC address, and services that traffic as if it were addressed to the active router.

The HSRP-configured routers announce their presence with multicast User Datagram Protocol (UDP) *hello* messages. These announcements are used to detect the failure of a router, to negotiate parameters such as the virtual IP addresses, and for the router elections. At any time, only one active and one standby router exist on the network. All of the other routers configured in the same standby group are in the *listen* state until the next router election, which happens when the active or standby router becomes unavailable.

On Token Ring networks, HSRP uses functional addresses, and thus is limited to only three concurrent standby groups. On Ethernet and *Fiber Distributed Data Interface* (FDDI) media, HSRP can have up to 256 concurrent standby groups. This is called Multigroup HSRP, and is explained in the section "Creating Multiple HSRP Groups."

Three types of packets are defined in HSRP. The first is the hello packet, which is sent by the active and standby routers to notify the members of the group of their presence. The hello packet also contains configuration parameters, such as IP address and timer values. A router that has not had these values explicitly defined can learn the values of the parameters from the hello packets.

The second type of packet is called a *resign* packet, which is sent from the active router when it withdraws from the HSRP group because of a configuration change, or because the router is being shut down.

The third type is the *coup* packet. This is sent when a router is overriding the active router due to the `preempt` configuration command. If that router is the highest priority standby router, it will become the active router. We discuss router priority in more detail later on.

The HSRP process will be in one of six states while it is running:

1. The *Initial* state is the starting state. The router is in this state when there has been a configuration change, or when the interface first comes up.

2. Next is the *Learn* state. At this point, the router is waiting to hear a hello message, which contains the virtual IP address and other parameters, from the active router.

3. After the Learn state is the *Listen* state. If an active and standby router already exists in this group, the router stays in this state. At this point, router does not participate in hello messages, it only listens to those broadcast from the active and standby routers.

4. Once out of the Listen state, the router enters what is called the *Speak* state. At this point, the router is sending hello messages, and is participating in the election process.

5. When in the Standby state, the router will send HSRP hello messages, but will not forward any packets that are destined for the virtual address.

6. In the Active state, the router will send periodic hello messages, and will be servicing forwarding requests to the virtual IP address.

Tip

If elected, a router will either be in either the *Standby* state or *Active* state.

In order to make network devices, such as learning bridges, aware of the virtual MAC address, the active router uses that address when it transmits hello messages. The remaining routers transmit hello messages by using the MAC address of their physical interface. This ensures that a bridge or switch knows where to send packets destined for the virtual MAC address. The active router is the only device that transmits anything using the virtual MAC address; otherwise, a learning bridge would be confused, and wouldn't know on what port that MAC address resided.

Configuring HSRP

Now that you have a basic understanding on how HSRP works, let's configure it using a few different examples.

To get HSRP up and running on a router requires only a few steps. First, HSRP must be enabled on the router, and then any additional options can be added to the configuration. All commands are entered in interface configuration mode, because HSRP configuration applies to specific interfaces, and not to the whole router.

For the purpose of this configuration, we will be using Figure D-3 as our guide. We want to get Router A and Router B configured so that HSRP is operating in the way shown in the diagram:

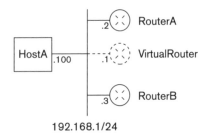

192.168.1/24

Figure D-3 *A basic HSRP configuration, with Router A and Router B configured to form VirtualRouter*

We begin by configuring Router A:

```
RouterA#conf t
Enter configuration commands, one per line.  End with CNTL/Z.
RouterA(config)#int fa 0/0
RouterA(config-if)#standby ip 192.168.1.1
```

Once this has been entered, HSRP will be operational on the router. We can verify this by using the show standby command in privileged mode:

```
RouterA#show standby
FastEthernet0/0 - Group 0
  Local state is Active, priority 100
  Hellotime 3 holdtime 10
```

```
Next hello sent in 00:00:00.484

Hot standby IP address is 192.168.1.1 configured

Active router is local

Standby router is unknown expired

Standby virtual mac address is 0000.0c07.ac00
```

From the output, we can gather a lot of information about the HSRP process. It shows the group number, which is 0 by default, the state of the router, which will be Active, Standby, or Listen, once everything settled down, and finally, the priority of the router in this group.

To complete the configuration of Figure D-3, we need to configure the standby group on Router B:

```
RouterB#conf t

Enter configuration commands, one per line.  End with CNTL/Z.

RouterB(config)#int fa 0/0

RouterB(config-if)#standby ip
```

Note that the IP address of the virtual router was not needed on Router B. Router B learns the address from Router A through HSRP Hello messages, as illustrated by the following show standby output on Router B:

```
RouterB#sho standby

FastEthernet0/0 - Group 0

  Local state is Standby, priority 100

  Hellotime 3 holdtime 10

  Next hello sent in 00:00:02.136

  Hot standby IP address is 192.168.1.1

  Active router is 192.168.1.2 expires in 00:00:08

  Standby router is local

  Standby virtual mac address is 0000.0c07.ac00
```

The HSRP specification dictates that configuration messages contain all of the information associated with a standby group, so that additional routers that join the standby group do not need to have the information explicitly configured on them. They can learn this information from the contents of the hello messages from the active router.

You might wonder what happens to the HSRP configuration should this router become the active router. It will actually keep its configuration, because it has been learned already from another HSRP participant. We can prove this by making Router A unavailable, and then examining what happens to Router B:

```
RouterB#
04:18:39: %STANDBY-6-STATECHANGE: Standby: 0: FastEthernet0/0 state Standby
-> Active
RouterB#show standby
FastEthernet0/0 - Group 0
  Local state is Active, priority 100
  Hellotime 3 holdtime 10
  Next hello sent in 00:00:01.584
  Hot standby IP address is 192.168.1.1
  Active router is local
  Standby router is unknown expired
  Standby virtual mac address is 0000.0c07.ac00
RouterB#
```

We were also notified of the HSRP state change on the console of the router. From the output we can see that although none of this configuration information actually exists in Router B, the information remained when Router B transitioned to the active state. We can experiment more by removing the standby IP information from Router A, and then watching what happens when neither router is explicitly configured with the standby IP information:

```
RouterA#conf t
Enter configuration commands, one per line.  End with CNTL/Z.
RouterA(config)#int fa 0/0
RouterA(config-if)#no standby ip 192.168.1.1
RouterA(config-if)#standby ip

RouterA#sho standby
FastEthernet0/0 - Group 0
  Local state is Standby, priority 100
```

```
Hellotime 3 holdtime 10

Next hello sent in 00:00:01.914

Hot standby IP address is 192.168.1.1

Active router is 192.168.1.3 expires in 00:00:08

Standby router is local

Standby virtual mac address is 0000.0c07.ac00
```

Now, although neither router is configured with the standby IP address, as long as one of them stays up and doesn't lose the configuration, the standby IP address will stay valid.

This information is also reflected in the ARP table of Host A:

```
HostA#sho arp

Protocol  Address        Age (min)  Hardware Addr   Type   Interface

Internet  192.168.1.100      -       0000.0c5d.6f99  ARPA   Ethernet0

Internet  192.168.1.1        0       0000.0c07.ac00  ARPA   Ethernet0

Internet  192.168.1.3        0       0030.9468.d900  ARPA   Ethernet0

Internet  192.168.1.2        0       0030.9468.d9a0  ARPA   Ethernet0
```

The standby priority can be changed so that certain routers are favored over others in a standby group. The router with the highest priority value wins the election, and becomes the active router. The next highest priority becomes the standby router; the remaining routers sit dormant in the listen state until the next election.

 Tip

Only the HSRP process of the remaining routers is dormant. The routers themselves can still perform other tasks, such as participating in routing protocols.

The following router output shows the options that are available with the standby command, which can further customize an HSRP standby group.

```
Router(config-if)#standby ?
  <0-255>          group number
  authentication   Authentication string
  ip               Enable hot standby protocol for IP
  mac-address      Specify virtual MAC address for the virtual router
  mac-refresh      Refresh MAC cache on switch by periodically sending packet
```

```
                    from virtual mac address

preempt             Overthrow lower priority designated routers

priority            Priority level

timers              Hot standby timers

track               Priority tracks this interface state

use-bia             Hot standby uses interface's burned in address
```

The defaults for the HSRP parameters are shown in Table D.1:

Table D.1 *Defaults for HSRP Parameters*

Parameter	Default
Group number	0
Authentication string	cisco
MAC address	0000.0c07.ac??
	with ?? being the group number
MAC refresh	10 seconds
Priority	100
Preempt delay	0 seconds
Hello timer	3 seconds
Hold timer	10 seconds
Track interface priority decrement	10

To change the priority of a router, enter the following command in interface configuration mode for the interface in question:

```
standby [group-number] priority value
```

If the group number is not specified, the default group of zero will be used.

The higher the value, the more likely a router is to become the active router. This value can also be combined with the standby preempt command to force a higher priority router to become the active router as soon as it joins the group. It does this by issuing a coup command to the other routers, telling them that it intends to become the active router. Without the standby preempt command, a higher priority router will not become the active router until the next election takes place.

When the `preempt` parameter is used, you can also configure a delay that instructs the router to wait a certain amount of time before issuing the `coup` command. The parameters of the delay option are as follows:

```
RouterA(config-if)#standby preempt delay ?
  <0-3600>  Number of seconds to delay
  minimum   Delay at least this long
  sync      Wait before sync to complete
```

Another priority-related option is the `standby track` configuration command. This command allows certain interfaces to be monitored, and it penalizes the HSRP interface priority each time the interface goes down. By default, the priority is decremented by a value of 10, but the administrator can also choose this value manually. The format for this command is as follows:

```
standby track interface-type interface-number (value-to-decrement)
```

If we wanted to implement this functionality on Router A, the command would look like this:

```
RouterA(config-if)#standby track Serial 0/0 20
```

This command tells Router A to decrement the priority of Group 0 by a value of 20 if interface Serial 0/0 becomes unavailable. If another standby group member now has higher priority than Router A, and it is configured to preempt those with a lower priority, the standby group member will now become the active router for this group.

Once the tracked interface comes back up, the priority returns to what it was before the interface went down. To illustrate this behavior, consider the following example:

Router A has been configured to track interface FastEthernet 0/1. Entering `show standby` will show any interfaces we are tracking.

```
RouterA#sho standby
FastEthernet0/0 - Group 0
  Local state is Active, priority 100, may preempt
  Hellotime 3 holdtime 10
  Next hello sent in 00:00:01.542
  Hot standby IP address is 192.168.1.1 configured
```

```
Active router is local

Standby router is 192.168.1.4 expires in 00:00:09

Standby virtual mac address is 0000.0c07.ac00

Tracking interface states for 1 interface, 1 up:

   Up   FastEthernet0/1
```

Notice that the Fast Ethernet 0/1 is up, and the priority of Router A in Group 0 is 100. If Fast Ethernet 0/1 goes down, it will have an effect on the priority of Router A:

```
RouterA#sho standby

FastEthernet0/0 - Group 0

   Local state is Active, priority 90, may preempt

   Hellotime 3 holdtime 10

   Next hello sent in 00:00:00.908

   Hot standby IP address is 192.168.1.1 configured

   Active router is local

   Standby router is 192.168.1.4 expires in 00:00:08

   Standby virtual mac address is 0000.0c07.ac00

   Tracking interface states for 1 interface, 0 up:

     Down FastEthernet0/1
```

You can see in this output that Fast Ethernet 0/1 has become unavailable, and is marked down in the standby group configuration. This has detrimentally affected the priority of the interface; it is now 90 instead of 100. Once the interface comes back up, the priority is returned to its previous value of 100.

It is recommended that all of the HSRP routers be configured to preempt when tracking is being used. If an interface is being tracked, there's probably a particular reason; if that interface goes down, you will want the traffic to go to a router with a higher priority.

Handling MAC Addresses

The only thing missing from the configuration messages of HSRP is the MAC address associated with the standby IP address. These are chosen by the router, or statically configured by the administrator. When not explicitly configured, the MAC addresses are automatically chosen in the format of 0000.0c07.ac??. The last two hex digits of the MAC address correspond to the group number when the router chooses the MAC address. Because the routers have to be explicitly told the group number they are to use, when it is anything other than zero, they automatically know what MAC address to use.

However, this can cause a problem with explicitly configured MAC addresses. If a MAC address is explicitly configured on one member of the standby group, then it needs to be configured on all members of the standby group. Otherwise, connectivity may be affected if a failure occurs, because the MAC address associated with the standby IP address has changed, and this change may not be reflected in the ARP cache of hosts on the network.

Creating Multiple HSRP Groups

It is also possible for an interface on a router to be a participant in more than one HSRP group. This is called *Multigroup HSRP* (MHSRP). An advantage to having multiple groups is the ability to split the network load between two or more routers. The configurations shown in previous examples waste the resources of the routers that are not active, because only the active routers areservicing traffic. The remaining routers sit idle, waiting for the active router to fail.

For this example, we will configure Router A, Router B, and Router C to reflect the HSRP implementation shown in Figure D-4:

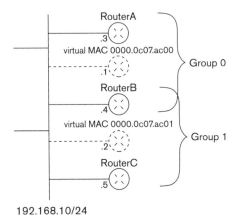

Figure D-4 *A network implementing Multigroup HSRP*

On Router A, the configuration would look like this:

```
RouterA#conf t
RouterA(config)#int fastEthernet 0/0
RouterA(config-if)#standby 0 ip 192.168.1.1
```

For Router B:

```
RouterB#conf t
RouterB(config)#int fa 0/0
RouterB(config-if)#standby 0 ip 192.168.1.1
RouterB(config-if)#standby 1 ip 192.168.1.2
```

And for Router C, the configuration looks like this:

```
RouterC#conf t
RouterC(config)#int fa 0/0
RouterC(config-if)#standby 1 ip 192.168.1.2
```

Executing the show standby brief command on Router B shows that it has two standby groups enabled:

```
RouterB#show standby brief
                   P indicates configured to preempt.
                   |
Interface  Grp Prio P State    Active addr    Standby addr   Group addr
Fa0/0      0   100    Standby  192.168.1.3    local          192.168.1.1
Fa0/0      1   100    Active   local          192.168.1.5    192.168.1.2
```

The only thing that one must do differently when implementing MHSRP is to explicitly define a unique group number for each new group created. Otherwise, the configuration is basically the same.

There is a caveat to MHSRP, however. Hardware limitations of some older routers prevent the routers from participating in multiple HSRP groups. In order to participate in MHSRP, the router's network interface must be able to listen to the MAC address that has been chosen as the virtual MAC address. If multiple HSRP groups exist, then the router needs to be able to listen for multiple virtual MAC addresses. Older Cisco routers are unable to do this.

The routers affected are the Cisco 1000, 2500, 3000, and 4000 series routers that make use of the Lance Ethernet network controller. To view what kind of Ethernet hardware is being used by a particular router, use the `show interface` command.

This output shows the Ethernet hardware type that exists in a 2500 series router with a 10 megabit-only interface:

```
Router#show interface ethernet 0
Ethernet0 is administratively down, line protocol is down
  Hardware is Lance, address is 0000.0c8d.cb5b (bia 0000.0c8d.cb5b)
  MTU 1500 bytes, BW 10000 Kbit, DLY 1000 usec, rely 252/255, load 1/255
```

The second line of the output displays the type of hardware that is used in the Ethernet controller. We can see that indeed this 2500 series router is using the Lance Ethernet hardware, which precludes it from participating in multiple HSRP groups.

In fact, the Cisco IOS will inform us that the router does not have the hardware to support multiple HSRP groups by giving us the following error message when we try to configure it:

```
Standby: Interface hardware cannot support multiple groups.
```

Because the Lance Ethernet hardware can only accept traffic for a single MAC address, the IOS will actually change the MAC address of the interface to that of the virtual MAC address when the interface becomes the HSRP active router:

```
Router#sho int e0
Ethernet0 is up, line protocol is up
  Hardware is Lance, address is 0000.0c07.ac00 (bia 0000.0c8d.cb5b)
```

You can see that the address the Ethernet interface is using is no longer *its burned-in address* (BIA).

Following is the `show interface` output of the 10 megabit-only interface of a 2600 series router:

```
Router#show interface ethernet 0/0
Ethernet0/0 is administratively down, line protocol is down
  Hardware is AmdP2, address is 0050.737b.e560 (bia 0050.737b.e560)
  MTU 1500 bytes, BW 10000 Kbit, DLY 1000 usec, rely 252/255, load 1/255
```

This output is the Ethernet hardware type from the 10/100 interface of a 2600 series router:

```
Router#show interface fa 0/0
FastEthernet0/0 is administratively down, line protocol is down
  Hardware is AmdFE, address is 0030.9468.d900 (bia 0030.9468.d900)
  MTU 1500 bytes, BW 100000 Kbit, DLY 100 usec,
```

We used routers with the AMD Ethernet controllers for the preceding MHSRP example, so we did not experience this limitation.

Troubleshooting HSRP

The show standby command will help you get through most HSRP configuration problems. It is important to make sure that all HSRP participating routers have the same parameter configurations for the same standby groups. If things such as the hello timer or hold timer are inconsistent within the group, then HSRP will not function properly. So we want to check these parameters when we are troubleshooting any HSRP issues:

```
Router#show standby ?
  FastEthernet  FastEthernet IEEE 802.3
  TokenRing     IEEE 802.5
  Ethernet      IEEE 802.3
  brief         Brief output
  <cr>
```

Following is a sample output of the show standby command:

```
RouterA#show standby
FastEthernet0/0 - Group 0
  Local state is Active, priority 100, may preempt
  Hellotime 3 holdtime 10
  Next hello sent in 00:00:01.576
  Hot standby IP address is 192.168.1.1 configured
  Active router is local
  Standby router is 192.168.1.4 expires in 00:00:08
  Standby virtual mac address is 0000.0c07.ac00
```

By looking at this output, we can get all of the information we need to determine the configuration of this standby group. All of the timer values are shown, as are the priority, IP address, and MAC address. The output also shows that this router is configured to preempt the other group members.

All of this information is not always needed. You may just want to see a short list of the groups configured on a router. An example of show standby brief is shown here:

```
RouterA#show standby brief
                     P indicates configured to preempt.
                     |
Interface  Grp Prio P State   Active addr    Standby addr   Group addr
Fa0/0       0   100   Active   local          192.168.1.4    192.168.1.1
```

This command is not as verbose as show standby, but it provides the basic information we need to examine the operation of the protocol.

The command can further be used to display the HSRP groups that exist on a particular interface by giving the interface type and number as arguments to the show standby command.

The IOS also offers a debug command for HSRP that will aid in troubleshooting problems:

```
Router#debug standby
```

When enabled, the router will display the contents of hello message on the console. This lets you see what it is the router is sending or receiving in the hello messages. By looking at these, you will be able to see any parameter mismatchs on any of the group members that may be causing problems with HSRP. Following is a debug standby output from Router B, which we configured earlier:

```
01:47:44: SB0:FastEthernet0/0 Hello out 192.168.1.3 Standby pri 100 hel 3 hol 10
ip 192.168.1.1
01:47:47: SB0:FastEthernet0/0 Hello in 192.168.1.2 Active pri 100 hel 3 hol 10
ip 192.168.1.1
01:47:47: SB0:FastEthernet0/0 Hello out 192.168.1.3 Standby pri 100 hel 3 hol 10
ip 192.168.1.1
01:47:50: SB0:FastEthernet0/0 Hello out 192.168.1.3 Standby pri 100 hel 3 hol 10
ip 192.168.1.1
```

```
01:47:52: SB0:FastEthernet0/0 Hello out 192.168.1.3 Standby pri 100 hel 3 hol 10
ip 192.168.1.1
01:47:55: SB0:FastEthernet0/0 Hello out 192.168.1.3 Standby pri 100 hel 3 hol 10
ip 192.168.1.1
01:47:57: %STANDBY-6-STATECHANGE: Standby: 0: FastEthernet0/0 state Standby
-> Active
01:47:57: SB0:FastEthernet0/0 Hello out 192.168.1.3 Active pri 100 hel 3 hol 10
ip 192.168.1.1
01:47:57: SB: FastEthernet0/0 Adding 0000.0c07.ac00 to address filter
01:48:00: SB0:FastEthernet0/0 Hello out 192.168.1.3 Active pri 100 hel 3 hol 10
ip 192.168.1.1
```

The output shows the group that the message refers to, the interface it was sent and received on, and various parameters that correspond to that group. During debugging, Router A became unavailable, and Router B took over as the active router. Note the line referring to the address filter. This means that the IOS is programming the Ethernet hardware to listen for a MAC address other than its permanent, or burned-in, address. Note also the transition in the hello packets being transmitted by Router B. At first it was identifying itself as the standby router, but once the hold timer expired, it began to identify itself as the active router.

Wrap-Up

The merits of HSRP are quite obvious once it has been implemented on a network. No longer will the failure of a single router on a network prevent the hosts on that network from having outside connectivity. Also, by placing the processing burden on the gateways instead of the end hosts, much time is saved by not having to add the support to the hosts, and then configure them properly.

The ease with which HSRP can be configured and implemented makes it a very attractive tool for building stable networks.

Index

Continued

Continued

Continued

my2cents.idgbooks.com

Register This Book — And Win!

Visit **http://my2cents.idgbooks.com** to register this book and we'll automatically enter you in our fantastic monthly prize giveaway. It's also your opportunity to give us feedback: let us know what you thought of this book and how you would like to see other topics covered.

Discover IDG Books Online!

The IDG Books Online Web site is your online resource for tackling technology — at home and at the office. Frequently updated, the IDG Books Online Web site features exclusive software, insider information, online books, and live events!

10 Productive & Career-Enhancing Things You Can Do at www.idgbooks.com

1. Nab source code for your own programming projects.

2. Download software.

3. Read Web exclusives: special articles and book excerpts by IDG Books Worldwide authors.

4. Take advantage of resources to help you advance your career as a Novell or Microsoft professional.

5. Buy IDG Books Worldwide titles or find a convenient bookstore that carries them.

6. Register your book and win a prize.

7. Chat live online with authors.

8. Sign up for regular e-mail updates about our latest books.

9. Suggest a book you'd like to read or write.

10. Give us your 2¢ about our books and about our Web site.

You say you're not on the Web yet? It's easy to get started with IDG Books' *Discover the Internet*, available at local retailers everywhere.